TRUDEAUMANIA

Trudeaumania

PAUL LITT

UBCPress

VANCOUVER & TORONTO

25 24 23 22 21 20 19 18 17 16   5 4 3 2 1

Printed in Canada on paper that is processed chlorine- and acid-free, with vegetable-based inks.

Library and Archives Canada Cataloguing in Publication

Litt, Paul, author
Trudeaumania / Paul Litt.

Includes bibliographical references and index.
Issued in print and electronic formats.
ISBN 978-0-7748-3404-9 (hardback). – ISBN 978-0-7748-3406-3 (pdf).
ISBN 978-0-7748-3407-0 (epub). – ISBN 978-0-7748-3408-7 (mobi)

1. Trudeau, Pierre Elliott, 1919-2000 – Public opinion. 2. Canada – Social life and customs – 20th century. 3. Canada – Social conditions – 1945-1971. 4. Canada – Politics and government – 1968-1979. 5. Nationalism – Canada. I. Title.

FC625.L58 2016   971.064'4   C2016-905341-5
                                            C2016-905342-3

Canadä

UBC Press gratefully acknowledges the financial support for our publishing program of the Government of Canada (through the Canada Book Fund), the Canada Council for the Arts, and the British Columbia Arts Council.

This book has been published with the help of a grant from the Canadian Federation for the Humanities and Social Sciences, through the Awards to Scholarly Publications Program, using funds provided by the Social Sciences and Humanities Research Council of Canada.

Printed and bound in Canada by Friesens
Set in Futura, Novel, and Steiner by Artegraphica Design Co. Ltd.
Text design: Jessica Sullivan
Copy editor: Sarah Wight
Proofreader: Frank Chow
Indexer: Cheryl Lemmens

UBC Press
The University of British Columbia
2029 West Mall
Vancouver, BC V6T 1Z2
www.ubcpress.ca

FOR JANE AND RAY LITT

In reading the history of nations, we find that,
like individuals, they have their whims and their peculiarities,
their seasons of excitement and recklessness,
when they care not what they do. We find that whole
communities suddenly fix their minds upon one object,
and go mad in its pursuit; that millions of people
become simultaneously impressed with one delusion,
and run after it, till their attention is caught by some
new folly more captivating than the first.

CHARLES MACKAY, *Extraordinary Popular*
Delusions and the Madness of Crowds, **1841**

What a great show the guy had put on … living in his
Canada felt like participating in one big performance.

GEOFF PEVERE, **"Requiem for a Northern Dream:**
On Canada, Pop Culture and a Gunslinger's Sunset"

Contents

ACKNOWLEDGMENTS

A **TALENTED AND GENEROUS** group of friends, colleagues, and family helped me with this book. When I first started this project in 2003, Paul McIntyre, CBC's intellectual archivist and a storied touch-football player, provided a surprise gift: television clips of Trudeaumania that have entertained and edified me and my students ever since. Later he provided helpful advice on how to find further television and radio sources. It's always nice to have a friend in the archives.

Michelle Seville read the manuscript and provided feminist perspectives on the meaning of the kissing campaign, gender issues more generally, and how age modulated women's responses to Trudeau. I drew upon former Black Pelican legend Michael Zeitlin's expertise in literature to explore ways in which life imitated art in Trudeaumania. Christopher Pengwerne Matthews, known for his blazing speed and soft hands on the touch-football field, and Adil Sayeed, a nonplayer who talks a good game, read an early draft of this book and provided valuable critiques, especially in relation to US political history.

Years ago, when he was working on his book on Canada in the 1960s, Bryan Palmer and I discussed Trudeaumania. He subsequently read a draft of an article I was writing on the subject and offered helpful comments. I benefited too from Paul Rutherford's response to that draft article. His insistence on the importance of sex to this story was a welcome slap to the side of the head. "Established historian" and erstwhile sixties folk singer David

MacKenzie and public history/public administration impresario Patrice Dutil read an early draft of the book, commented on it thoughtfully and at length, then together sat me down and gave me a gentle talking-to. They have provided leads, advice, and salutary skepticism throughout the long development period. I am indebted too to Claire Litt, who offered some subtle insights into the behaviour of Trudeau's female fans that enriched my interpretation of the phenomenon.

As a university professor I am privileged to have time for research and writing, and to also have an employer with some tolerance for the multiyear timelines required to write books. I have benefited greatly from the intellectual community at Carleton University, where teaching and discussions with students and colleagues constantly provide new ideas and insights. Way back when, my colleague down the hall in what was then the School of Canadian Studies, Allan J. Ryan, told me about his hit single of yesteryear, "PM Pierre," and gave me a copy. I dusted off my turntable, located my 45 rpm adapter, and have savoured it ever since. I often discussed this project with another kid in the hall, the irrepressibly interdisciplinary Peter Hodgins. He read the manuscript with his honorary historian's hat on, sent me his thoughts in writing, and more than once steered me along valuable new lines of inquiry. I have also profited over the years from discussions with my friend Susan Haight, whose knowledge of the history of consumerism influenced my thinking on its role in Trudeaumania. Emily Litt read sections of the manuscript dealing with the sexism of contemporary portrayals of women and made constructive suggestions that I also incorporated into my thinking.

After playing the first Monkees album for me on his turntable and performing parts of it on his guitar (this was prior to his zz Top/gypsy jazz phase), Bruce Hildebrand read the draft manuscript, offering comments and queries that drew my attention to various oversights and muddles. He served as a sounding board for my ideas throughout the project. One-time officemate and LaFontaine imposter Louis-Georges Harvey, who has twentieth-century

Quebec political history in his bones (and knows still more about early-nineteenth-century French Canada), generously took time in the middle of a teaching term to read a later draft of the manuscript and send me a thoughtful critique. Subsequently we had fruitful discussions and email exchanges that strengthened my interpretation greatly. My colleague Joanna Dean in the Department of History at Carleton helped me out by reading sections of the manuscript on gender issues and critiquing my interpretation, prompting me to rethink and refine it. I'd also like to thank the two anonymous readers commissioned to review the manuscript by UBC Press. They offered both encouragement and sensible queries that forced me to reconsider or clarify my positions on a number of points. While I'm deeply obliged to everyone who advised me, they should not be held responsible for my final judgments or lack of judgment.

Rosemary Shipton dispensed sound advice about publishing prospects. Richard Stanbury kindly permitted me to consult his papers at Library and Archives Canada. Forgetting, or at least pretending to forget, noisy tribal rites of yesteryear, Derek Allen supplied a lead that addressed a question I was pondering. Charles Pachter saved me from embarking on a wild goose chase. Lakru Vidya voluntarily conducted research and mapped out collections full of promising material, while Mike LaDeudle assiduously retrieved materials. At York University's Clara Thomas Archives, Julia Holland, Brittany Nolan, and Alyssa Miranda provided excellent service, while Michael Moir steered me towards valuable materials I otherwise would have overlooked and bargained fairly over the cost of permissions. Andrea Gordon at Canadian Press was extraordinarily helpful with my search for old photos of Trudeaumania. Along the way archivists too numerous to name at many different repositories guided me to and through relevant textual, photography, video, and sound sources. Without their efforts this book could not have been written.

I would like to thank Melissa Pitts of UBC Press for throwing her support behind this project from the beginning. UBC Press editor Darcy Cullen led me expertly through all the stages required to get the book into production. Holly Keller, the production editor, cheerfully and resourcefully tackled the additional challenges involved with a book that has enhanced illustrations and design elements. She completed a lot of finicky work under the pressure of tight timelines with superb results. The final product also reflects the care and creativity of copy editor Sarah Wight, designer Jessica Sullivan, and typesetter Irma Rodriguez. I am grateful to the Faculty of Arts and Social Sciences and the School of Indigenous and Canadian Studies at Carleton University for underwriting costs related to securing illustrations for this publication. The visual culture of Trudeaumania is a big part of its story, and this support has allowed it to be presented here in a richer, more illuminating fashion than would have been possible otherwise.

Despite all this help my failings are numerous and persistent, and I take full responsibility for any errors – factual, interpretive, or moral – in this work.

TRUDEAUMANIA

Trudeau is kissed by an admirer at a campaign stop in
St. Catharines, Ontario, June 14, 1968. Scenes such as this were repeated
across the country and became emblematic images of Trudeaumania.

Kiss Power!

He's really hunky! …
It's like all time stops …
I touched him on the back …
I'd die for him …
I didn't want to live anyway.

**CBC TV coverage of teenage girls
commenting on Pierre Trudeau upon his
arrival at a campaign event, 1968**[1]

IN THE SPRING OF 1968, Canada was in the throes of passion. The new prime minister, Pierre Elliott Trudeau, fresh from a dramatic Liberal Party leadership convention victory in Ottawa, was on an election tour of the country, attracting adoring crowds wherever he went. He came into town like a pop star on a concert tour, arriving from the airport in a motorcade, waving from a convertible en route to a rally where people jockeyed to get his autograph, take a snapshot, or just touch him. As Trudeau mingled with the crowd, teenyboppers pogoed to catch a glimpse, fathers hoisted toddlers onto their shoulders, and camera shutters clicked all around. When he took the stage, hands stretched out from below to make contact. Then the crowd settled down to listen to his message of national unity and destiny.[2]

Another conquest behind him, the hero would jet to his next campaign stop while television crews rushed their footage off for broadcast. Those in attendance could go home and watch themselves on TV. The news would feature shots of Trudeau glad-handing through surging, effervescent crowds and kissing young women, then an obligatory line or two from his speech before the reporter signed off with details of his next appearance.

In the concert tours of pop singers, the tunes were sung by the star; in this case they were sung about him. Montreal folk singer

Allan J. Ryan wrote a song about the phenomenon, "PM Pierre," that nicely captured the mod vibe Trudeau was generating:

There's a new infatuation that's been sweeping the nation
Shakin' the roots in the ground
Of an old generation, a new inspiration
Takin' a new look around
But he's quickly disarming and utterly charming
Quite enough to make you let down your hair
In a Society Just, a society must
Check out PM Pierre
Pierre, with the ladies, racin' a Mercedes
Pierre, in the money, find him with a bunny
Pierre, a little brighter than the northern lights
He oughta add a lotta colour to the Ottawa nights.
Charismatic and dynamic with a trans-Atlantic flare
Regardez PM Pierre.[3]

Ryan wasn't alone in his musical tribute. A long-haired, bell-bottomed Quebec pop group called The Sinners recorded "Go Go Trudeau" (English on one side of the 45 rpm single; French on the other), and sold ten thousand copies in the first week following its release. "You've got the nation right behind," called one. "Go ahead and blow their mind," responded another.[4]

The fun had begun when a race for the leadership of the Liberal Party had gotten under way the previous December. Beguiled by Trudeau's style, journalists had already pegged the minister of justice as an up-and-comer. When the Liberal leadership came open, they thought "what if?" and floated the idea of Trudeau as a candidate. As Trudeau himself later explained it, they dared the Canadian public to take a chance on a new kind of politician.

The response was more than they could ever have expected. A meeting of Quebec Liberals in Montreal in January was a "love-in" as Trudeau sauntered down the escalators to the ballroom, followed by a crowd of pubescent youth, "Oohing" and "Aahin" every word. "I think this guy's the greatest," said one shocking-stockinged micro-bopper to her similarly decorated companion, as they happily trailed the jaunty figure along the corridor. They gambolled around him like puppies, laughing too hard at his jokes, asking cheeky questions and loving the firm put-downs they got.[5]

Trudeau was acquiring film-star glamour. By midwinter he was trailed by a gaggle of reporters and recording equipment that created a buzz of excitement and attracted crowds whenever he appeared in public.

1968 was a year of political and social tumult around the world, but in the imagined Peaceable Kingdom, love was all around. The day after Trudeau declared his candidacy for the Liberal leadership in mid-February, the front page of the *Toronto Telegram* pictured him with two bunnies from the Montreal Playboy Club in the "psychedelically-decorated" ballroom of the Château Laurier. The "swinger," it reported, was always surrounded by women.[6]

Pictures of Trudeau being kissed by female fans became a staple feature of the news. "If it puckers, he's there," wrote George Bain of the *Globe and Mail*.[7] Trudeau liked being seen as a ladies' man. When asked whether he would have a hostess at 24 Sussex if he became prime minister, he responded saucily, "Could I change hostesses from time to time?"[8] Since the public had a right to know, a reporter in Edmonton asked, "As an eligible bachelor, which do you prefer, blondes or brunettes?" "Any exciting party should have both," Trudeau replied.[9] "Perhaps 24 Sussex will become known as Pierre's Pad," speculated another journalist.[10] When Trudeau called a federal election for June 25, the love-in went national, with regular television coverage of rapturous receptions for him across the country.

Love, Love, Love. "LUV THAT MAN TRUDEAU" declared a placard on his convertible in one motorcade.[11] Was it a confession or a command? Either way, the "luv" was physical, a contact sport driven by a compulsion to get some sort of proof he was real. Crowds

This May 4, 1968, *Toronto Telegram* cartoon by John Yardley-Jones depicts a mod Trudeau transforming 24 Sussex Drive into a swinging bachelor pad.

pursued Trudeau for an autograph or a kiss. One enterprising souvenir hunter managed to get his wristwatch. Others settled for
swiping hairs from his head.[12] At a campaign stop in North York,
Ontario, a zealous fan made a grab for Trudeau's lapel flower and
nearly ripped the collar off his suit. "Perhaps I could have break-
away lapels," he mused.[13] A young woman whose attempt to corner
him for a private chat was thwarted told a television reporter,

> He's probably way above my head. His brain level is probably so far
> above me. This is it, he just passes right over me like a wave, you see.
> What I want to do is talk to him, and I don't see that I can have the
> chance, he's so busy. Oh. And yet I'd do anything for the chance.[14]

On one occasion, girls who couldn't get close to him settled for
kissing the hubcaps of his car.[15]

"Like a cavalier among Puritans," Trudeau played along.[16] When
a television interviewer challenged him about all the frivolity, he
downplayed it. "When some young kid pecks you on the cheek I
think it's kind of sweet," he said. He regarded a kiss merely as
a form of greeting, one somewhat warmer than a handshake. If
people wanted to express their enthusiasm in that way, he was not
going to rebuff them.[17] Since he was an eligible bachelor and the
kisses came from young women, others interpreted it differently.
"Everybody was having orgasms every time he opened his mouth,"
exclaimed an unnerved Tory strategist.[18]

Sex injected excitement into the formerly staid proceedings of
federal politics. "When young girls with long hair and short skirts
elbow one another to get close enough to the Canadian Prime
Minister to touch him and, preferably, to kiss him, that is a phenomenon," wrote a seasoned observer. "There is no tradition in
Canadian politics even of baby kissing, and the suggestion that
nubile maidens could take to hurling themselves at the neck of the
Prime Minister – any Prime Minister that ever was or was likely
to be – would have been considered laughable a short time ago."[19]

The Conservatives countered on behalf of their leader, Robert Stanfield, with the slogan "Kiss me Pierre, but run my country Bob!" yet could not dispel the association between sexual and political potency.[20]

While cases of a charismatic figure generating a devoted following can be found throughout history, in modern times rapid improvements in communications technologies allowed such phenomena to develop faster and spread further. In nineteenth-century North America, populist politicians inspired political rallies as passionate as evangelical revivals. William Jennings Bryan, a three-time Democratic candidate for the US presidency renowned as a spellbinding speaker, pioneered the national political tour in the 1890s. Those who'd never seen him in person knew of him ahead of time through newspapers, magazines, and partisan pamphlets. In the days before his arrival, circulars trumpeted his imminent appearance. Everyone from loyal followers to the merely curious would turn out and thrill to his rousing oratory and the excitement of the crowd.

Another American political legend, Louisiana governor Huey Long, used similar techniques to amplify his personality cult. Rising to prominence in the 1920s, he was an early adopter of radio to cultivate a following and sent sound trucks ahead to announce his arrival in a community. In Canada, both William Aberhart in 1930s Alberta and Joey Smallwood in 1940s Newfoundland used radio for political ends with great success. Then, just a decade prior to Trudeaumania, Progressive Conservative leader John Diefenbaker employed the new mass medium of television to advantage. In 1957 he projected the image of a caring, populist leader who offered a positive alternative to an arrogant, out-of-touch Liberal government. Canadian nationalism was burgeoning in the postwar period, and when Diefenbaker went to the polls again in 1958 he tapped into it, inspiring voters with his vision of equal citizenship for all and an independent destiny for Canada as a northern power. Greeted by wildly enthusiastic crowds on his leader's tour, he ended up winning the largest parliamentary majority in Canadian history.

A parallel history exists of performing artists generating a more sexualized version of celebrity worship. When the virtuoso pianist Franz Liszt toured Europe in the 1840s, women threw their garters at him and swooned. In the 1920s, film actor Rudolph Valentino inspired a similar adoration from female fans, and in the 1940s Frank Sinatra became a teen idol, moving hordes of adolescent girls to displays of infatuation. Public demonstrations of sexually charged adulation became a fixture of popular culture in the postwar West. The Elvis craze of the late 1950s again featured a male pop star rocketing to fame and being greeted by lustily enthusiastic female fans at his public appearances.[21]

In all these cases crowds were excited by the appearance, live in the flesh, of a celebrity whom they otherwise knew only through the media. An exalted being who had formerly been imagined now materialized, however briefly, in their everyday world. Fans were thrilled to be connected to something bigger than themselves, a more glamorous realm inhabited and personified by their idol.

In the 1960s, Beatlemania was the most spectacular example of this phenomenon. In 1964 the Beatles crossed the Atlantic to play *The Ed Sullivan Show* and a twenty-three-city North American tour. Fans were primed by saturation marketing that distributed millions of posters and stickers proclaiming "The Beatles Are Coming." Disc jockeys were provided with reams of promotional materials, including prerecorded Beatle answers to their yet-to-be-asked questions. Fans began counting the days until the Fab Four arrived. Reports of near riots in England gave them a primer on how to behave – or misbehave – in the presence of their idols. Hysteria was part of the fun. Each concert was a mob scene, with girls' screams drowning out the music.

By the late 1960s, this strain of popular culture was infecting politics. Bobby Kennedy's campaign for the Democratic nomination for the United States presidency in 1968 generated wild crowd scenes much like those that attended Trudeau's appearances. Midway through that winter, the media began using the term "Trudeaumania," adapted from "Beatlemania," to describe the enthusiasm Trudeau was generating.[22] The term had all kinds of suggestive connotations. Was there really a mania, in the sense of an irrational enthusiasm that infected the populace? If so, was it a flash in the pan, an example of the superficial combustibility of popular culture now colonizing politics? Was this just a case of a successful political campaign being enhanced by an evocative label? Or was something more profound afoot? What exactly was going on in Canadian politics in the winter and spring of 1968, and did it matter?

Trudeau supporter at an election rally in Toronto, June 19, 1968.
The outfit was meant to attract attention, and it worked – this woman
became a favoured object of the media gaze that day.

INTRODUCTION

Sex and the Body Politic

"The whole country needs a cold shower."

LETTER TO THE EDITOR, *Maclean's*, **July 1968**

THE SEXUAL SIZZLE BETWEEN Pierre Trudeau and his adoring female fans in 1968 signalled a deeper impulse to revitalize the nation. For those caught up in the mania, 1968 was a historic turning point in which Canada left its dowdy colonial past behind and assumed a new autonomous identity as a model modern liberal democracy. They may have been deluding themselves, but since nations are fictions with real-world effects, Trudeaumania had lasting influence.

In Canada, as in many other Western countries, the sixties were marked by wide-ranging assaults on the consensus culture of the 1950s. Cold War technocracy, militarism, and paranoia gave rise to ban-the-bomb protests that morphed into the anti–Vietnam War movement. A new human rights consciousness, inspired by the Holocaust and invigorated by decolonization around the world and the civil rights movement in the United States, assailed the bigotry of Western societies, inspiring liberation movements for marginalized groups. Meanwhile, modern rationalist certainties were challenged by a new humanism. The latter half of the decade saw the emergence of lifestyle liberations that celebrated free love, drugs, and the animal spirits of rock 'n' roll, all widely publicized by a sympathetic media.

In Canada the feisty sixties spirit was further complicated and energized by a rising, expectant nationalism. Over the course of the decade, Canadians retheorized their national identity, updated official symbols, and participated in a series of grand nation-building exercises. Canada, nationalists proclaimed, was coming of age, its escape from colonial status in tune with the liberation ethos of the sixties. They sought to distance the country from both its British heritage and the influence of its superpower neighbour, while beating back the grave threat to national unity presented by the rise of separatism in Quebec.

Developments in the United States profoundly shaped this nationalist project. The glamorous Kennedy presidency had impressed Canadians deeply in the early 1960s, and they longed to see Canada updated in similar style. By the midpoint of the decade, however, the image of the US was tarnished by Cold War jingoism, nuclear brinksmanship, Vietnam, political violence, a radicalizing politics of race, and ghetto riots. America was showing its ugly side. Canada was not without its own problems, but for many nationalists the trials besetting their southern neighbour engendered a smug sense of superiority.

The radical challenges of the sixties caused a rift in the American political mainstream, splitting public opinion between a reactionary impulse to re-establish social order and a moderate openness to accommodating demands for change through incremental reform. As the forces of reaction and reform came to a fractious stalemate south of the border, nationalism skewed Canadian political culture towards a reformist response to the challenges of the decade.[1] The federal government was then putting in place social programs that would be the last major components of the Canadian welfare state. The political centre in Canada was further left than it had ever been (or would ever again be), raising expectations that Canada would over time become still more social democratic. In response to the spirit of the times and the nationalist imperative for a distinctive identity, Canada steered left of the United States. Sixties critiques of the US "establishment" pointed towards how Canada might be constructed as a comparatively humane society. Peaking nationalism at the height of the sixties forged the myth of a Peaceable Kingdom in the northern half of North America.

Celebrations of Canada's centennial in 1967 and the international acclaim garnered by Expo 67 generated collective energy, enthusiasm, and pride, but as the year wound down and the excitement faded, nationalists feared that the nation's potential had been glimpsed but not fulfilled. The opportunity for more substantial, permanent change came late that year with leadership turnover in the major federal political parties.

Pierre Trudeau came into focus as a potential leader that fall. One of the initial attractions of a Trudeau candidacy was that he had a refreshing no-nonsense approach to national unity that unapologetically defended federalism on the basis of high-minded principle. In addition, nationalists saw in Trudeau a cosmopolitan intellectual who could garner for Canada the type of international attention and status it had achieved with Expo 67. Better still, he was single, youthful, athletic, and fashionable, with a liberated lifestyle seemingly right in step with the times. His style exemplified nationalists' ambitions for Canada. Trudeau's image would be embroidered and enhanced through fashion, posters, pop songs, and other forms of contemporary popular culture that interacted in the mass media, amplifying the message and stimulating a mania. It was all rendered in a contemporary "mod" style that branded Trudeau as the man who would make Canada's Great Leap Forward a safe step to a stable new order – the status quo updated in the latest style. Trudeaumania would be characterized by a mod nationalism, with "mod" short for both modern and moderate.

The fusion of contemporary popular culture and Canadian nationalism that gave Trudeaumania its oomph was a transitory formation whose moment would soon pass. There was never a genus of "mod nationalist" Canadians who would have defined themselves as such. There was, however, an active network of communications about Canadian issues through which the compelling contemporary logic of mod nationalism exerted influence long enough to affect the course of Canadian political history.

The kiss was the perfect mod sign. Its power derived from the sexual revolution that both led and symbolized the myriad cultural liberations of the decade. As that revolution unfolded, it transformed sex from a topic that was largely off-limits in polite public discourse into a central obsession of a popular culture that exploited its power to titillate and sensationalize. Trudeaumania derived much of its sizzle from the sex-obsessiveness and sexism of the times.

Sexual liberation was all the rage by 1968. Progressive men found the conflation of their sexual pleasure with righteous politics profoundly seductive. Yet the sexual revolution was a double-edged sword for women, increasing their freedom to express and enjoy their sexuality but leaving them bearing the brunt of responsibility for its reproductive consequences. Double standards about promiscuity persisted as well.[2] In 1968, second-wave feminists were holding consciousness-raising sessions about these issues, but the mainstream press was not paying much attention to them or giving their critiques serious consideration.[3] The women's liberation movement had yet to get its message out widely enough and with sufficient force to start changing the prevailing sexism.

Meanwhile, when a camera focused in on Trudeau seemingly besieged by crazed females, it was a male gaze that guided the shot. The editorial cartoonists who lampooned Trudeau's female admirers were all men. The producers and managers who directed the collection of news and also edited and interpreted it for consumption were also predominantly male. The masculine media's focus on female fans and its presentation of them as witless ciphers overwhelmed by the celebrity's charms were typical of the gender discrimination of the times. Male journalists felt free to portray women as airheads driven by their passions and trade on this stereotype as a reliable source of amusement. By infantilizing women they rationalized and perpetuated women's exclusion from power in the male-dominated public sphere.

In doing so, ironically, they displayed the same emotionalism and herd mentality that they ascribed to Trudeau's female fans. A

"As convenor of this meeting of the 'West Toronto Housewives for Trudeau,'
I say let's cut out all this nonsense and get down to business ...
girls ... GIRLS!"

Pierre Trudeau's status as a sex symbol
was well enough known to provide the basis
for this editorial cartoon.

strange passion swept the media ranks, precipitating an idolization of Trudeau akin to that of an ancient religious sect worshipping a fertility god. The factors driving this phenomenon can only be guessed at – excitement about taboos being breached by the sexual revolution; a vicarious enjoyment of the power they claimed Trudeau exercised over women – but whatever the motives, the male-dominated media exemplified the very irrationalism that they ascribed to women's role in the affair.

Male journalists' amusement with women's public displays of emotion was boundless when women ventured from their proper sphere to kiss a politician. As they ridiculed this feminine incursion, they failed to appreciate that its girlishness was seditious. Women were exploiting one of the few entrées into the masculine political game available to them. Once in, they made fun of the pompous stolidity of male politics. Humour was an equal-opportunity weapon in the battle of the sexes.[4] Accompanying all the fun was an assertion of power. Conventional gender roles assigned to middle-class women a special responsibility for cultural affairs. As domestic managers and "purchasing agents" in a consumer society, they were assumed to be particularly conversant in the current trends of popular culture that determined fashionable choices.[5] When a woman kissed a pop star she was deploying her gendered agency to endow him with cultural currency.

On one level, women's gender performance in Trudeaumania was new, part of the larger invasion of politics by popular culture. Yet it had venerable antecedents. The "rational male, emotive female" stereotype traditionally assigned to women the emotional labour of keeping the community together. Their contemporary political role could also be traced back to the nineteenth-century belief that women's reproductive capability gave them responsibility for the biological continuity of the race and a special function in nation building.[6] Though racial nationalism lost currency after the Second World War, the work of nation building continued to be gendered.

Underneath all the blithe sexism of Trudeaumania ran an undercurrent of meaning in which women's role in the mania was equated with renewal. In earlier eras, modernization was male, the product of masculine-coded fields such as technology, business competition, and affairs of state. But in the sixties that form of modernity was on trial. The forces of liberation were attacking the establishment, and challenging conventional masculinity was one of their tactics. Defenders of the establishment reflected the same gender assumptions by demonizing deviations from the norm as effeminate. It followed that those of a reformist bent, female or male, would generally welcome, even celebrate, the symbolic import of women's influence in the public sphere and the challenge to gender roles that attended it. All the frothy fun of fandom superficially associated with women's role in Trudeaumania disguised its substance. Through public displays of approval women anointed Trudeau as the leader who would update the nation.

Canadian nationalism was central to Trudeaumania, making an appreciation of the nature of nations and nationalism critical to an understanding of the phenomenon. A nation is not quite the same thing as a state or a country. Rather, the idea of nation invests such entities with romantic notions of collective identity, cultural solidarity, and shared destiny. Nationalism is an ideology that celebrates the nation and assigns it primacy in political affairs. Recent decades have seen a vigorous and illuminating scholarly debate about the origins and nature of nations and nationalism. It includes three schools of thought: primordialists, constructionists, and perennialists.[7]

Primordialists believe nations are the natural way in which humanity is organized into its largest sovereign political units. For primordialists, nations have always existed. They are sociological facts from which political consequences logically follow. In a sense, primordialists do not think about the nation at all. For them, the nation and its corollary, the international community of nations, are givens – integral, taken-for-granted parts of the way the world functions. Primordialists tend to further naturalize nations by endowing each with a unique personality, life trajectory, and rights analogous to those of individual human beings.

Constructionists offer varying genealogies of the nation, but in general share the belief that it is a cultural construct arising out of modernization, the profound changes that began with the decline of feudalism and the rise of liberal capitalist democracies in the West. "Modernity" is a general term that encompasses the shared characteristics of Western societies in the wake of this great transformation. Modernization was driven by the mutually reinforcing interaction of capitalism with a scientism born of the Enlightenment that produced a deep-seated faith in progress through rational mastery of the world. It led to profound social changes such as industrialization, urbanization, state formation, and bureaucratization, as well as a democratization advocated by a rising capitalist class to wrest power from feudal elites. With the decline of absolute monarchies, the legitimate basis of sovereignty was no longer the crown but the people, which created the need for a counterweight to the anarchic potential of individualized loci of power. Nationalism was just such a communal principle. Since the bourgeoisie advocated liberal democracy with one-man-one-vote for its class but fretted about its extension to the masses, Marxist constructionists see nationalism as a form of social control, an ideological feint deployed to win mass acquiescence to elite leadership.

Perennialists acknowledge that the modern nation is a powerful new force, but do not think it unprecedented in history. While also a varied group, they generally trace the ways in which different ethnic groups have understood their collective identities over time, noting continuities and fluctuations. An important strain of nationalism theory that is common to both constructionism and perennialism holds that while biological notions of kinship or race underpin definitions of ethnicity, such beliefs are sustained not by blood but by culture, and that a complex of myths, symbols, and other such communicative devices evokes memories of an ancient core ethnic group as the basis for collective identity.[8]

The social control·interpretation of constructionists has been challenged by scholars who see nationalism as having bottom-up as well as top-down dynamics. With modernization, the constituent elements and internal relationships of relatively small, geographically compact, and personally mediated premodern communities were reconstituted on a mass scale. These changes came quickly – indeed, constant, bewildering change became a distinguishing feature of modernity. In the process, the face-to-face interpersonal relations that distinguished premodern communities were transcended, leaving the individual vulnerable to the modern malaise of alienation, the product of anonymity amid the masses, of social, geographical, and employment mobility, and of the perceived artificiality of a mass-mediated apprehension of the world.[9] The nation can be seen as a symptom of its members' desire for meaningful community amid all these dislocations. In other words, the nation helped humanize modern mass society.

The constructionist and the perennialist approaches to the nation share an emphasis on its discursive character. The nation is a cultural construct, dependent on the circulation of ideas sufficient to instill shared understandings. When Benedict Anderson famously defined the nation as an "imagined community," the term quickly became a catchphrase because it so aptly captured the notion of the nation as a consensual belief sustained by ongoing communication within a collective. This communication can range from grand spectacles, staged rituals, or invented traditions down to quotidian signs and symbols.[10] The intangible character of a nation does not make it any less real; on the contrary, a nation is a product of that most human of powers, the ability to manipulate symbols to create a shared understanding of the world.

The shared beliefs that underpin the nation include particular formulations of space and time. According to nationalist ideology, a people have a claim to a land based on their historical occupation of it. Over time a way of life has arisen out of the people's engagement with the unique geography and climate of their homeland,

and this is the wellspring of their distinctive national identity.[11] The nineteenth-century French political philosopher Ernest Renan famously declared that a nation is a group of people who have done great things together in the past and have a will to continue doing so.[12] Invoking the nation's past experience lends it immanence in the present and a temporal momentum that projects it into the future.

The importance of temporal momentum to the sense of nation, and to its discursive construction, led Homi Bhabha to describe nations as narrations.[13] Narrating the nation's past is indeed necessary to sustain its existence, but it is not sufficient. To be useful, the narrative must change along with shifting present-day conditions. The flux of past, present, and future requires continual negotiation of the national destiny. This negotiation takes place through communication within the public sphere aimed at building a consensus, a process in which different voices interact to form public opinion.[14] A nation is thus an ongoing conversation that renegotiates communal identity and goals in accord with constantly changing circumstances.[15]

The coherence of modernity's emergent large-scale communities was attributable to mass communications as well as to their elites' modern epistemology. A dawning recognition of these dependencies and their insufficiencies eventually generated critical perspectives on modernity that would be grouped under the term "postmodernism." For some the term implies a shift to a new cultural era that supersedes modernity. Others regard postmodernism as a set of critiques of the internal contradictions of the modern condition, some of which were starting to come into focus by the mid-twentieth century. Modernity endures, but since the 1960s postmodernism has accompanied it like an annoying younger sibling, asking embarrassing questions.[16]

Postmodernism has convoluted origins and has been defined in multiple, sometimes contradictory ways. There are, however, three postmodern perspectives that are useful in understanding

Trudeaumania. The first is encapsulated in Jean-François Lyotard's description of postmodernism as "incredulity towards meta-narratives."[17] The point of questioning metanarratives was not to expose them as patently false, but rather to suggest that they had become modes of thinking that shaped consciousness to an extent unwarranted by their basis in reality. One of the most fundamental modern metanarratives was the belief in progress. It was under-written by bountiful evidence of the power of technique, informed by science and driven by capitalism, to generate wealth. As the na-tion-state became the primary guarantor of the emergent liberal democracies of the West, a powerful metanarrative of national progress developed, consisting of the nation-state according its cit-izens ever-greater liberty and democracy. In Canadian nationalist thought of the 1960s, this narrative was embedded in the story of Canada's progress from colony to nation.

Another postmodern insight is exemplified by Jean Baudrillard's concept of the simulacrum. In contrast to the conceit of modern epistemology that it built with technocratic expertise to precise specifications on a solid grounding in reality, Baudrillard pointed out that modernity was, in its most distinctive characteristics, any-thing but. As mass print was supplemented by electronic media, the mobilizations of modernity were enabled by abstractions circulated in the ether. It was a cliché that the West had by the late twentieth century entered an information age. Ephemeral images shimmered on screens, projecting symbols to be decoded by audiences initiated into the arbitrary rules of interpretation that governed their mean-ing. Knowledge of modern mass society depended as much on pixellated representations as direct experience of reality.

Think of Times Square, in which pulsing neon promotes brands with characters concocted on Madison Avenue, and you already have multiple layers of simulation. The circulation of meaning in modern mass-mediated society involves reproducing such rep-resentations multiple times in different contexts to the point that any connection with an underlying reality is beyond recovery. To drive home his point, Baudrillard wrote of the simulacrum, the "perfect reproduction of a non-existent original," an example of simulation taken to its logical extreme. Beneath the seductive surface there lies no substance, yet consensual acceptance of the illusion allows everyone to work with it, producing an operative virtual reality that substitutes for a reality based on direct experience of the tangible world.[18]

A third useful postmodern critique questioned the Enlightenment view of the individual as a rational creature with a fixed character. In the nineteenth century, respectable character was idealized, and men of solid moral values were accorded great public esteem. Yet in modern mass society, success was increasingly dependent upon negotiating with strangers and adapting to constant change in urban geography, social hierarchy, bureaucratic organization, and other discrete contexts. In this new world, the successful individual was the shape-shifter who could adapt easily to different milieus. The modern belief in a whole, stable self, knowable both to oneself and to others, was at odds with modern conditions that encouraged a contingent, situational self, always adapting to circumstances, always performing in accord with anticipated expectations. Success meant standing out in a crowd, so character gave way to personality, a simulacrum of the individual that was mutable according to circumstances. Whereas character had been described by terms such as "self-sacrifice," "honour," "duty," and "integrity," personality was linked with adjectives like "fascinating," "charismatic," "dynamic," and "masterful."[19] Accordingly, the burgeoning celebrity culture of the twentieth century privileged seductive personality over reliable character.

Trudeaumania occurred at a particular stage in the emergence of these postmodern perspectives. Whereas from today's point of view the nation appears to be a metanarrative worthy of skepticism, Canadian critical discourse at the time included no such insight. In terms of nationalism theory, all the players in 1968 were good primordialists. Although some had in mind a different project, the Québécois nation, the same nationalist ideology prevailed. When it came to notions of simulation and the self, however, there were glimmers of a postmodern consciousness in the making. People wanted to have leaders of character, but the politics of image was too obvious to ignore. People believed in the nation, yet knew it primarily through its representation in the mass media. Indeed, the media were a critical constituent part of modern mass society.[20] In a country such as Canada, with a relatively small population dispersed across a large territory and a history coincident with the rise of the mass media, their role was all the greater.

Tracing the development over time of the relationship among politics, nationalism, and the mass media in Canada suggests how tightly they are intertwined. At its outset, Canada was heir to a parliamentary system of government whose antecedents stretched back through centuries of English history. Transplanted to North America and eventually adapted into a federal system at the time of Confederation in 1867, the system was supposed to work by having different districts elect members to Parliament to represent their local interests at the centre of power. The Member of Parliament was nominally the primary medium of political communication between the people and the centre, and Parliament was the forum in which political issues were debated and leaders emerged. The system originally assumed a restricted franchise, limiting the vote to upper-class men with a stake in the system and denying it to the unwashed masses, who were presumed to be too witless or self-interested to play an enlightened, constructive role. Thus a responsible minority of the population would elect to the House of Commons an exemplary representative who would contribute to its decision making – including the selection of a prime minister – based on his informed judgment of the best way to reconcile his constituency's interests with those of the larger political community.

Party politics and partisan newspapers were an entrenched feature of Canadian politics by the time the federation was established, so from the start Canadian representative government did not function according to the theoretical ideal. And the context in which it operated was transformed radically in the ensuing century. The same democratic logic that the bourgeoisie had used to wrest power from feudal elites worked inexorably to extend the vote to formerly excluded groups, making politics more populist.

The price of mass democracy is an electorate in which the majority of voters are only sporadically engaged. It is unrealistic to ask them to pass rational judgment on complex matters of public policy – doing so only makes them feel guilty about their inability to exercise their vote responsibly. Besides, even the idealized citizen of earlier eras – the educated, propertied, presumably politically engaged burgher to whom the franchise was limited – had been expected only to send to Parliament a man of character to make such judgments. The expanding modern electorate gradually grew less concerned with the character of the local representative and more attentive to the personality of the national party leader. The prime minister's power rested decreasingly on his effectiveness in Parliament and increasingly on the support he could win in a general election.

The politics of image was boosted further by developments in culture and communications. With the rise of public schooling, literacy, and mass print, newspapers became less partisan, more popular, and far more widely circulated. Film, which first appeared at the end of the nineteenth century, simulated reality in moving pictures that were eventually accompanied by a soundtrack. The subsequent development of radio permitted simultaneous shared experience for the national citizenry from coast to coast. The arrival of television made the audiovisual attribute of film available in a broadcast medium, delivering it to a wide audience with an enhanced immediacy that suggested simultaneity. In modern Canada, the mass media gradually eclipsed Parliament as the main forum within which issues were debated and leaders selected. As the leader's personality became critical to the party's electoral success, leadership conventions were transformed into popularity contests staged as media-friendly spectacles.[21]

These developments also had significant consequences for Canadian nationalism. In positing shared cultural characteristics as constituent of a "people" whose popular will legitimized the sovereignty of the state, nationalism invariably encountered contradictory demographic realities and accompanying resistance. This was true even in the Western European context in which nationalism flourished from the late eighteenth century on, but in Canada the disparity between conditions on the ground and the ideology's quest for a shared homegrown essence was greater still. Canada came to the game relatively late and was trying to transplant an ideology of European origin to North America. The persistence of its Indigenous peoples, French Canadian *survivance,* the distinctive colonial histories of its constituent provinces, the contrasting ways of life of its disparate regions, and the influence of its not-so-different southern neighbour were all incommensurate with the nationalist drive for bounded homogeneity. For generations Canadian nationalists tried to apply nationalist ideology to a recalcitrant Canadian reality. But the modern nation-building project was at odds with the modern epistemology of building empirically from the facts on the ground.

By the late 1960s, simulation facilitated the former by transcending the latter. In a print and electronically mass-mediated community, the nation was much easier to imagine in real time than it had been at the time of Confederation. The modern Canadian nation was a national simulation – a "simunation" – the only kind of nation possible under the circumstances.[22] Trudeaumania was a symptom of this condition, an exercise of the national simulation required to foster community under conditions of modernity.

In imagining community to compensate for the alienation of modernity, nationalism and celebrity fandom have a lot in common.[23] The celebrity community transcends mundane existence, hovering above the everyday world like Jonathan Swift's Laputa. In the sixties, media outlets were relatively few in number and sought broad audiences, big-tent, national parties were still the ideal, and the leader's personality provided a human interest angle through which to present politics. For the average Canadian, federal politics were conducted by a group of politicians who, if not quite celebrities, were at least well-known across the nation. Party leaders were luminaries of the Canadian public sphere.

Yet those who identified with celebrities, political or otherwise, were troubled that the mediated community with which they identified was somehow artificial. Even as it unfolded, Trudeaumania was distinguished by a self-consciousness about the very process that enabled it. Contemporary commentators fretted terribly, regularly, and publicly about whether the media were subverting the democratic process. Modern mass media allowed direct communication between leaders and voters, bypassing the traditional constituent-MP relationship and patron-client networks. People watched politicians on television and came away with the impression of knowing them personally. Were they right? Could television's flickering images be trusted? Did the politics of image pervert the democratic process by eclipsing substantial issues? The national conversation was attended by an anxiety about its mediation that brought its legitimacy into question.

Pierre Trudeau was particularly well-suited to the needs of the sixties simunation. It was said that he had an inner reserve and was hard to get to know, and, indeed, his personality fascinated Canadians then as it has ever since. Competitive and disciplined, he tested his mettle in various prized realms of modern life – politics, travel, sport, the arts and letters, romance – exhibiting his prowess in each. Even though he was in his late forties, his hip lifestyle projected youthfulness in a popular culture that celebrated youth. Raised in the big band era, he had no problem "frugging" to sixties rock 'n' roll. His adaptable personality showed in the way he could be both a cosmopolitan and a backwoodsman, an intellectual and an athlete, proving himself in terms of different sets of expectations in diverse settings. He performed for television superbly, speaking articulately with a screen actor's mastery of expression and gesture, and providing plenty of the action shots demanded by the medium. His unique genius as a political campaigner, however, lay in his propensity to take a detached perspective on the media

Trudeau performs an athletic stunt for the cameras at a stop in Saskatoon during the spring 1968 federal election campaign. It would be hard to imagine Robert Stanfield or Tommy Douglas (let alone John Diefenbaker or Lester Pearson) doing anything similar. Visual representations of Trudeau, whether in television footage or still photography, played an important role in the construction of his image.

that acknowledged the emergent postmodern anxiety about them. In expressing his awareness of voters' concerns about mass mediation, he signalled his own authenticity and won their confidence.

The similarities between showbiz celebrities' cross-country tours and political campaigning helped as well. Canadians' expectations of Trudeau were primed by months of media coverage of his emergence from relative obscurity to vie for the country's highest political office. The dictates of an election campaign made it likely that he would at some point appear in a nearby locale live in the flesh. Trudeau would step out of the screen and into their world. Knowing that they were in the media spotlight, the crowd acted accordingly. Then Trudeau quickly disappeared, resuming his place among the simunation's screen celebrities. This mediated/unmediated two-step, which might be called a reel-to-real synthesis, soothed anxieties about the artificiality of the simunation, making its representations all the more potent.[24] The excitement of Trudeau rallies generated intense emotions that imbued crowd members with a lively sense of group solidarity that could easily be conflated with belonging to the nation.[25] The reel-to-real synthesis made the national community whole, authentic, and meaningful.

While the above discussion provides some concepts and context with which to make sense of Trudeaumania, this study is historical in sensibility and methodology. It interprets Trudeaumania in terms of the unique time and place in which it arose, explains this context as the product of the interaction of a variety of causal factors over time, provides documentation from extant sources from the period, and contextualizes its discussion within relevant historical scholarship.

There is already an extensive secondary literature on Trudeau that includes coverage of his rise to power. While it provides much useful information and analysis, its emphases are different from those of this study. Much of the existing literature focuses on Trudeau the person: his life and times, his character, and his thought. Another stream emphasizes the behind-the-scenes machinations that brought Trudeau to power. This study is not as concerned with who Trudeau was as with his public image in 1968 and its relationship to the context of the times. And while Trudeau's "backroom boys" astutely played the politics of image, this study eschews revelations of conspiratorial manipulations and concentrates instead on how Trudeaumania exploited and gratified a Canadian nationalism shaped by the tumultuous sixties.

Cultural history that grapples with nebulous objects of inquiry such as nationalism and the "spirit of the times" is rife with methodological challenges. It is difficult to know what people were thinking, either individually or collectively, in times past. It is impossible to prove that ideas have agency, let alone the extent of their influence. To generalize about such matters requires connecting the dots between scattered fragments of proof. These challenges, however, do not constitute an excuse for abandoning the field. An interpretation based on limited direct evidence, contextual knowledge, and informed speculation is better than nothing at all.

This account relies heavily on primary sources from the 1960s, many of which were produced by the media, including newspaper articles, cartoons, photographs, advertisements, and television and radio shows. Media sources provide information not just on events themselves but also on the style in which they were presented and how they were interpreted at the time. Trudeaumania was considered so remarkable as it unfolded that it generated significant critical commentary in the form of opinion columns and feature articles in newspapers and magazines, public affairs show punditry, instant books by journalists, and even scholarly studies. The last two types of sources in particular provided background information and context, tried to weave events into a coherent narrative, and interpreted the meaning of the phenomenon, giving them more depth than the media's quotidian reporting and commentary.

While substantial media sources about Trudeaumania are accessible today, documentation of other expressions of contemporary public opinion is harder to come by. Traces can be found in the views expressed in letters to the editor, man-in-the-street interviews, and media reports on audience responses to Trudeau's appearances. At times snapshots of general patterns are revealed by political polling or election results. Yet most of this information still comes to us through surviving media sources. We remain highly dependent on the media for clues to the content of the national conversation. The constraints of the available evidence dictate that one must see through these sources, however limited the view beyond. This method is not perfect, only the best available. The upside of this predicament is that the media were deeply involved in the national conversation and left sources rich in description, opinion, and analysis. The downside is that the bias of the archive can easily exaggerate their significance. The historian cannot presume that the media represent Canadian society accurately or fully.

This predicament makes the nature and extent of the media's influence a critical methodological question. After much debate, media scholars have come to two main conclusions on this issue. First, media messages are interpreted variously depending on the receiver's biases. Often they are simply ignored, and at other times they are radically reinterpreted to conform to the recipient's prejudices. People tend to accept uncritically only those messages that confirm their existing views. The second insight is that the media's main power lies in agenda setting. Agenda setting may seem a weak form of agency, but it can be very effective. These two main forms of media power combined suggest that the media can exercise considerable influence by putting an item on the public agenda and presenting it in a way they anticipate will prompt a particular response. In the case of Trudeaumania, for instance, they put Pierre Trudeau on the agenda in a manner that resonated with an influential segment of the public.

Yet this formulation does not fully encompass the extent of media influence in Trudeaumania. The conclusions noted above apply to single instances of one-way, media-to-audience messaging that have been isolated for the purposes of study. Communications scholars have extended this analysis by conceptualizing a circuit of communication that includes audience feedback to the media, yet even this remains a relatively simplistic model that fails to capture the complexity of information flows through networks. To represent a conversation such as that through which the media helps constitute the simunation would require a model that captures multiple participants of varying influence at innumerable locations within a web of connections. In practice such an approach is frustrated both by its complexity and by the paucity of evidence from sources beyond the media.

The resulting heavy dependence on media sources makes it all the more important to be alert to their biases. Some of these are easy to identify. To begin with, those who worked in the Canadian media in 1967-68 generally were more educated, urban, and prosperous than the population as a whole. They were also overwhelmingly white, middle-class, Euro-Canadian males educated in the Western humanist tradition. More specifically, a substantial percentage of the media figures who promoted Trudeau were modern in sensibility and nationalist in outlook.

Yet another media bias was metropolitan. Though a far-flung network, Canada's national media were concentrated in Toronto, home to its biggest and most influential newspapers, headquarters of the national radio and TV networks, and the centre of Canadian book and magazine publishing. The professoriat, a significant portion of which was headquartered at the University of Toronto's downtown campus, provided the media with big ideas, while news of the latest trends came from Canada's fashion, advertising, and public relations industries, most of which huddled together for warmth and comfort in Toronto as well. Inputs from these sources were mashed together in the Toronto media, processed, packaged, and marketed nationwide.

Exceptions to this Toronto-centricity included the national press gallery in Ottawa, an outpost necessary to extract information about national political affairs at the source of the raw material. Another exception was Montreal, a metropole with considerable cultural heft in its own right. Its contribution to Canadian nationalism was less than Toronto's, however, because its cultural producers were divided between an English Canadian minority and a French Canadian majority, with a significant portion of the latter prioritizing Quebec nationalism over Canadian nationalism.

In the discussion that follows I will be using the term "Canadian nationalism" to denote the nationalism that energized Trudeaumania. While its original impetus came from English Canada, it was not an exclusively English Canadian phenomenon. True, contemporaneous Quebec nationalism had goals that were often in direct contradiction to Canadian nationalism. Yet identities and allegiances, like the self, are not fixed. A French Canadian nationalist could be torn between Quebec nationalism and Canadian nationalism and support both in different degrees, either simultaneously or under different circumstances. A French Canadian nationalist who prioritized cultural survival over political sovereignty might feel at home with Trudeau's promise to accommodate French Canadians with bilingualism and a charter of rights and freedoms. Given the choice between an ethnic Quebec nationalism and a Canadian nationalism that, however ethnocentric it had been historically, now espoused a modern pluralistic Canada, she might opt for the latter.

It was also possible for Quebec nationalists who were not avowed separatists to admire Trudeau as an exemplary representative of French Canada. Since nationalism seeks the status of external recognition as well as internal unity and identity, Trudeau's success on the Canadian and international stages greatly gratified French Canadian nationalists. On the other hand, some French Canadians, like Trudeau himself, opposed nationalism generally and the rise of neonationalism in Quebec in the wake of the Quiet Revolution in particular. Those who saw the true legacy of the Quiet Revolution to be modernization rather than nationalism took great pride in the fact that Trudeau, one of their own, now exemplified the cutting edge of modernity in the wider Western world. His promise to protect the rights of French Canadians and give them a greater stake in the larger Canadian national modernization project was attractive. For French Canadians outside of Quebec this option was far preferable to the province becoming a nation-state that would exclude them.

The journalists, anglophone or francophone, who mattered most in Trudeaumania were those who covered the federal political scene.[26] It was their job to follow, analyze, and opine on the federal government. In that role they liked to style themselves as representatives of the people, dedicated to ensuring that power operated in the public interest. Far from being stand-ins for ordinary Canadians, however, they knew more and cared more about this politics than most of their compatriots. This bias was reinforced by their sources of information. As facilitators of debate in the public sphere, journalists voiced, either directly or indirectly, the opinions of officials, politicians, academics, pundits, and other authorities. When national media reached out to sources across the country, they were frequently dealing with local elites – the grasstops rather than the grassroots – who had national connections and interests. Since these sources were also invested in federal politics, their contributions reinforced the media's national bias. Even if these voices numbered in the thousands, they would still be a relatively small proportion of Canada's 1968 population of 20.6 million people.

The media were susceptible to thinking nationally for other reasons as well. By manipulating the cultural symbols that discursively constructed communities – local, regional, and national – journalists addressed and trained their audiences as markets to be sold to advertisers, thereby creating economic value for their employers. For those who worked for the Canadian Broadcasting Corporation, the national interest was an explicit part of their mandate. Yet private broadcasters also worked within a national framework. Licensed by the state, private radio and television stations belonged to networks that had markets congruent with Canada's territory.[27] A similar complicity with the nation was evident in other media as well. Though not state-regulated, newspapers sold national news. Domestic magazines, like the electronic media networks, also served the national market. The media complex of print, radio, and television thus naturalized and popularized the nation, continuously reinforcing it by providing the populace with simultaneous shared experiences that sustained a sense of belonging to a national community. Though Canada was also inundated with American media, Canadian media supported a separate political culture, chronicling the imagined life of the very simunation they constructed discursively on an ongoing basis through their own cultural work.

The idea of a mania was very seductive for such nationalist cultural producers. The notion that Canadians could collectively experience the same psychological state and act on it with a singular purpose suggested the existence in the populace of the type of shared characteristics that were the *sine qua non* of nationhood. It also played to their weakness for novelty. Having something like a mania to report on was in their interests – it was news. Being in step with the times was something of a professional imperative for media workers, even more so given recent developments within their field. The intellectual formation of most media practitioners had been in print culture, and now a screen medium, television, was rising to ascendancy. Fears that they would be caught out as obsolescent made it all the more important for journalists to identify with the latest thing. The media were biased towards the modern.

While media workers played a leading role in the national conversation, they were by no means the only participants. The discourse of nation circulated within a complex ecology of cultural producers and consumers. As Pierre Bourdieu has noted, many occupations outside the media proper involve manipulating symbols to create and communicate meaning.[28] This observation is particularly pertinent to Trudeaumania because it was powered not just by the circulation of information among different media, but by the interaction of text and image. Producers of the latter, such as photographers, artists, and fashion designers, generated a rich visual culture of Trudeaumania.

Even so, their efforts would have had limited impact had they not been picked up by the media and disseminated widely across the land. Artists and photographers knew what would sell. Particular images were selected from among other possible representations by editors before being disseminated through the media. With Trudeau the media bias was to show him being adored by fans, performing physical feats, modelling fashionable clothes, or striking other admirable poses. During the Progressive Conservative leadership convention in September 1967, a photograph of leadership candidate Robert Stanfield eating a banana in the stands circulated widely in the media. With Trudeau, in contrast, the mundane, the goofy, or the embarrassing did not make it into mass circulation.[29]

Cultural producers exercised more influence than mere consumers, yet in the context of an election, members of the politics-consuming media audience were producers too insofar as they voiced their opinions, participated in election events, and voted. At a minimum it is safe to say that media literacy and consumption were prerequisites to full participation in Trudeaumania.[30] Trudeaumania found its strongest support among the professional managerial class, an occupational group that had arisen over the previous century to provide efficient administration of a complex modern capitalist society. Its métier was mastery of ideas and information, knowledges that could then be deployed in the name of progress in the economic, social, and cultural spheres.

Over the course of the twentieth century, many occupations of the educated middle class had professionalized with degrees of success that varied according to their capacity to demonstrate quantitatively their contribution to material production, monopolize knowledge in their fields, or otherwise exert economic leverage.[31] Cultural producers tended to be less successful in finding such professional security because their labours had less direct demonstrable economic benefit.[32] Many found a place in the modern economy as teachers, professors, journalists, television and radio personalities or producers, artists, filmmakers, designers, or public relations and advertising creators. Some made a living by arbitrating taste, an alchemists' trade in which they managed transubstantiations between cultural, financial, and political capital. Others lacked a regular paycheque and a feeling of useful engagement in contemporary society. Even those who enjoyed provisional job security nevertheless could harbour the imposter's fear that they didn't deserve it and could easily lose it at any time. Their economic marginality stood in stark contrast to the technicians of their class, who rarely lacked employment, earned more, and enjoyed upward mobility through the ranks of corporate management. The artsy precariat was particularly susceptible to the lure of nationalism because it had the potential to connect their expertise in culture and communications with the interests and power of the state. Their knowledge and skills could be useful in nation building, and in return they stood to gain a reliable patron and public prestige. More articulate in pronouncing their altruism than comparable demographic cohorts, they were the natural apologists of nationalism.

The Second World War had brought big government to Canada, and after the war the public sector grew rapidly with the expansion of the welfare state and a boom in education. The numbers and influence of this professional managerial class, and its identification with the state, grew apace. These new members of the middle class were disproportionately engaged and influential in the national conversation that facilitated Trudeaumania. They owed their existence to modernization and they lived in a modern world of high labour and social mobility, large-scale productive and communications systems, and fast-paced social change. The more modern one's way of life, the more traditional, local, or ethnic allegiances were attenuated, and the more likely one was to identify with the community of nation. The most influential voices in the national conversation were those of these educated, middle-class urban denizens of modernity. The cultural producers within this group were particularly vocal because communicating was their forte and they had a vested interest in promoting nationalism. Catered to and given voice by the media, a powerful estate that they dominated, they carried the conversation that propelled Trudeaumania.

The modern and modernizing Canadians who favoured Trudeau wanted change, but they were not radicals. They faced the classic political dilemma of how to expedite desirable reforms while preserving social order. Amid the welter of experimentation in sixties popular culture, they gravitated towards a stylistic mode that suited their purposes. Mainstream cultural industries had already channelled the rebellious spirit of the decade into profitable enterprises. One of the hallmarks of this process was a strain of contemporary popular culture defined loosely as the "mod" style. The term had originated as the name of a subculture of fashion-conscious British youth, but by the midpoint of the decade had developed into a general term covering a prominent form of presentation in the advertising, fashion, and media industries.

Mod was exuberant and fun. It invited indulgence. It mocked the buttoned-down, sober rationality of the establishment, signalling its solidarity with the sixties spirit of liberation by promoting a risqué hedonism and destabilizing established ways of knowing with disorienting sensory inputs – vibrant colours, bold graphics, futuristic fabrics, and discordant sounds. Yet mod emphasized the aesthetics and titillation of rebellion without concern for any of its messy political implications. Ultimately its credo of freedom and experimentation was simplistic, shallow, and incoherent. Its transgressive thrills came at the expense of residual and expendable cultural values rather than any underpinnings of the political or economic status quo. Indeed, mod's valorization of change for the sake of change accelerated stylistic obsolescence in the service of consumer capitalism.

Mod's lack of political content did not mean that it was without political utility. The style offered an effective means by which to promote a candidate like Trudeau as a risk-free way to update the nation. Mod could distinguish Canada as more "with it" than the United States by emphasizing soft values rather than tampering with fundamental institutions. Trudeau supporters would use a mod vocabulary to communicate and coordinate their political activism because it was the contemporary pop culture idiom best suited to their project. Trudeaumania applied the mod sell of popular culture to politics.

The media, cultural, and political literacy of Trudeau's supporters also facilitated Trudeaumania. Media literacy allowed them access to the same information at the same time and enabled them to provide feedback in the public sphere, giving them an inordinate influence on public opinion. Cultural literacy meant that they were attuned to the fashion cycle of modern popular culture – how trends emerged, grew, and faded in a wave pattern. They were adept at picking up the lingo of the latest fad and using it to define a group identity for themselves. Political literacy was important because political events had a definite structure. Leadership campaigns and general elections were established rituals with predictable stages, clear timelines, and dramatic climaxes through which specific issues were resolved. Those in the know could easily anticipate how things would unfold.[33] These three competencies interacted in a mutually reinforcing fashion. Elites did not need to conspire behind the scenes – they had what it took to get their way through open democratic process.

Trudeaumaniacs shared a belief in a Canadian nation, a regard for its fate, and a rough consensus about its current condition and immediate needs. The nation was a common object of concern around which their opinion coalesced, giving its imagined existence a discursive reality.[34] Theirs was a decolonization project through which a virtuous young nation would shed its past subordination to Britain, parry the contemporary threat of us hegemony, transcend sectionalism, find itself, and assert its autonomy in the international community. They worked together to make this happen by exploiting a happy conjunction of opportunities. Political events triggered predictable electoral processes through which they could see a way to effect the change they desired. They discovered an appropriately protean personality, Pierre Trudeau, to represent their project. Drawing on the media's agenda-setting power, they presented him to the public, using a mod vocabulary drawn from sixties popular culture to identify him with the spirit of the times in a way that would appeal to like-minded Canadians. They made his candidacy for the leadership of the Liberal Party possible, helped him win and become prime minister, and then backed him in the spring 1968 federal election.

Trudeaumania consisted less of a widespread contagion than it did of a depth of devotion among those infected by it accompanied by a compulsion to operationalize it publicly. Trudeau's supporters were consolidating their modern group identity and projecting it onto the nation as a whole. More urban, prosperous, educated, and young than the broad Canadian population, more modern in sensibility, and more plugged into the national discourse of 1968, they dared their fellow Canadians to take a chance on a novel candidate.

While the trendy image of the Great Leader papered over major fracture lines in the body politic, it profoundly divided Canadians by setting traditionalists against progressives.[35] For the former, Trudeau's trendiness made his character suspect. He was a risk not worth taking. The latter, however, were willing to leave the old Canada behind to otherwise unite and modernize the nation. They created an image of Trudeau calculated to consolidate support along these lines, pushed it hard, and ended up getting their way. Their gamble paid off, securing a majority mandate for national modernization.

Trudeaumania had more lasting effects than most election campaigns. Trudeau would be prime minister for close to sixteen years, and his approach to national unity, identity, and the constitution shaped late-twentieth-century Canada. His attempts to define Canada along these lines were helped by the fact that he came to power at a formative historical moment when nationalism fused the sixties zeitgeist with Canadian identity in an enduring fashion. It was a moment when nationalists intoxicated by the transformation rhapsodized about the nation coming of age. Young baby boomers were imprinted like baby ducklings with ideas about Canada that would still be reflected in public opinion surveys in the twenty-first century. The neoliberal counterdiscourse of subsequent decades inexorably eroded this consensus but never enjoyed the opportunity of a similar transformative conjuncture through which to successfully reformulate national identity. In this sense, Trudeaumania was the birth of a nation. The kiss of the mod man would linger.

This mod outfit was so avant-garde that even its model seemed a bit shocked. Made of vinyl, it was part of a Montreal designer's "National Collection." The backdrop is the Australian Pavilion at Expo 67.

The Sixties, Modified

What the mod image did was merge
the fashion-consciousness
and respectability of the middle class
with a distinctive youth style.

DOUGLAS OWRAM, *Born at the Right Time*

AN OBJECTIVE RECONSTRUCTION of the past is always difficult, but the sixties are a particularly treacherous minefield of memory. For baby boomers, the very act of recollection lights up pleasure centres in the brain as they look back through a nostalgic purple haze to a presellout era in which adolescent idealism and hedonism conjoin in memories of feeling good both morally and sensually. The retrospective gaze of the progressive-minded wistfully regards the rebellious spirit of the decade as an opportunity missed, a last best chance to make a better world that somehow slipped away. Conservatives, in contrast, excite their base by portraying the sixties as a disaster narrowly averted, imagining a moment when wild-eyed anarchists rocked the pillars of civilization and almost succeeded in bringing the entire edifice crashing down.[1]

As usual, the truth lies somewhere in between and is hard to pin down precisely. Certainly it was a decade in which powerful protest movements captured the headlines. Their targets included technocratic arrogance, a Cold War paranoia that simplistically divided the world into good freedom fighters versus evil commies, and rigid social norms that saw any variation from white middle-class suburban family life as unhealthy if not morally deviant.[2] There were the civil rights crusade in the United States, protest campaigns against the Bomb, mass demonstrations against the Vietnam War, labour unrest, student rebellions against paternalistic universities, and grassroots mobilizations to fight industrial pollution. The late sixties saw the beginnings of liberation movements for women, gay people, Indigenous people, and other subordinated groups. And that was just the political side of things. The cultural radicalism of the sixties combined the sensual trifecta of sex 'n' drugs 'n' rock 'n' roll with spiritual questing to produce radically alternative lifestyles. The second half of the decade ushered into the limelight the hippie, the long-haired freaky embodiment of an emergent counterculture.[3]

Trudeaumania occurred at a climactic moment of the sixties. In the middle of the decade, political and cultural streams of dissent had merged to form a broader challenge to the establishment. The counterculture blossomed, hippies proliferated, young workers staged wildcat strikes, university students marched, protested, and invaded establishment strongholds, and Quebec nationalism took a radical turn. In the early months of 1968, international events were ominous. Events in Vietnam shook Americans' confidence in their military superiority and inevitable triumph in Vietnam, boosting antiwar protests to new heights. Two of America's most prominent leaders, Martin Luther King Jr. and Robert Kennedy, were gunned down in public, snuffing out their lives and the hope they represented. Inner-city ghettoes erupted in racial riots, and a Black Power movement arose that advocated violent means to win social justice. Overseas a series of protests beset European capitals. In May, student demonstrations in Paris led to clashes with police that cascaded into a nationwide strike that paralyzed the nation. The forces of chaos were at the gates. "Call out the instigators," sang Thunderclap Newman, "because the revolution's here."[4]

Except it wasn't. Protest movements and the counterculture defined the sixties because they ably exposed systemic injustice and establishment hypocrisy, were highly publicized by the media, and reflected the adolescent alienation of the rising baby boom generation. But only a small minority, even among the young, seriously challenged authority or lived the counterculture. Radical youth were newsworthy but far from representative of their demographic cohort as a whole. The vast majority of youth went about their lives and more or less conformed to conventional mores, or at least resisted in less colourful or confrontational ways.[5]

Nevertheless, the forces of protest won sympathizers beyond their ranks and stirred debate. The radical challenges of 1968 polarized public opinion in the United States.[6] Some responded to the threat to order by advocating a reassertion of authority, while others supported accommodation of protesters' demands through moderate reform. Neither group seriously questioned the fundamentals of the political and economic systems, but the reformers were in favour of a response to the radical challenge that would bring society more in line with the liberal democratic ideals of freedom and equality.

The liberation crusades of the sixties can be traced back to the human rights movement that emerged in the postwar period as the horrors of the Holocaust began to register. The victorious Allies recognized that their own prewar cultures had been steeped in racist notions akin to those that inspired Nazi anti-Semitism, and began, if begrudgingly, to integrate the lessons learned into their civic ideologies. Meanwhile, decolonization movements around the globe were rolling back Western imperialism and discrediting its racist rationales. Former colonies drew on nationalism, a Western ideology conducive to their cause, to legitimate their declarations of independence. An early sign of the times was the Universal Declaration of Human Rights, proclaimed in December 1948 by the United Nations. Decrying "contempt for human rights [that has] resulted in barbarous acts which have outraged the conscience of mankind," it condemned discrimination on the basis of "race, colour, sex, language, religion, political or other opinion, national or social origin, property, birth or other status."[7]

The full implications of this powerful statement are still being worked through, but the process had begun. In the 1950s, activists in the United States challenged the racist laws underpinning the "separate but equal" Jim Crow system that had segregated blacks in the South since the late nineteenth century. The civil rights movement pursued its cause through the courts and by staging public demonstrations that, disseminated by the media, brought the bigotry and brutality of systematic racism into middle-class living rooms. Peaceful marches, freedom rides, sit-ins, and rallies in support of voter registration or desegregation in the South received widespread media coverage, provided they were the right sort of protests – ones that, for instance, featured respectable, middle-class blacks accompanied by white supporters – and didn't threaten northern white audiences.[8] The result was wide circulation in the public sphere of a collection of potent images – peaceful protesters being attacked by police dogs, clubbed by nightsticks, or blasted by firehoses – that suggested something was terribly wrong with America. The world was watching, and Americans were all too aware that other nations would conclude that their much ballyhooed constitutional proposition that all men were created equal was but a sham. Sympathy, logic, and embarrassment combined to set in train legal and attitudinal changes that began to address entrenched racism. English Canadians followed the civil rights drama with a combination of horror and schadenfreude based on the unjustified assumption that they weren't racist like the Americans. French Canadians, among others, begged to differ.

A second notable protest cause of the era, the crusade against nuclear proliferation, translated more directly into the sixties protest ethos in Canada. As the bleak Cold War strategy of deterrence consolidated in the late 1950s, opposition to the Bomb coalesced. Critics questioned the logic of an arms race overbuilding the capacity to annihilate humanity. The notion of mutually assured destruction provided sixties radicals with a prime example of the moral bankruptcy and warped reasoning of the establishment. There was, it seemed, far too little sense in the consensus.

The antinuke movement provided an institutional structure around which the New Left would develop in Canada. The Combined Universities' Campaign for Nuclear Disarmament was formed in the late 1950s as an umbrella group for coordinating the movement's activities on campuses across the country. It was reinvented

In the early 1960s, Ban the Bomb protests were a harbinger of organized public demonstrations of dissent that would dominate the news later in the decade. The toddler with the sign was part of an Easter protest in Toronto in 1962. In the photo above, demonstrators march en masse down Yonge Street, the city's main thoroughfare.

and renamed in 1964 as the Student Union for Peace Action to allow its activist membership to tackle a broader range of issues. SUPA became the gravitational centre of an English Canadian New Left. In 1962, the vanguard of the New Left in the United States, Students for a Democratic Society, held its first annual conference and released a manifesto, called the Port Huron Statement after the meeting's location, decrying racism and the nuclear arms race and calling for participatory democracy and civil disobedience.[9]

Meanwhile, the United States was getting ever more deeply involved in fighting communism in Vietnam. Few Americans noticed as state paranoia about communism morphed into mindless militarism. Before they quite realized what they were getting into, they found themselves fighting a full-scale war against an elusive foe in an obscure former French colony halfway around the world.

As these issues roiled the public sphere, the baby boomers were coming of age. The postwar West had only recently discovered the teenager, a creature metamorphosing from childhood into adulthood that exhibited distinctive cultural characteristics during this transitory stage of life. Rock 'n' roll had been on the rise on both sides of the Atlantic since the mid-fifties. It provided the boomer generation with its own exclusive musical genre. A nexus of fashion, celebrity, consumption, and deeply felt experience, it became a major focus of youth culture. Radio stations fed a constant stream of sound to new consumer electronics such as transistor radios and stereo systems.[10] The airwaves hit home with far-reaching effects. The music was exciting, the rituals associated with it highly social. As maturing boomers swelled the teenager cohort, its peculiar culture and market impact became more noticeable.[11] Teens listened to rock 'n' roll on the radio, checked hit-parade rankings, bought 45s and LPs, and danced to the music. Pop concerts attracted crowds eager to see their idols in a live performance.

Most early rock music was about romance and dance, with sex as subtext. As they matured and became sexually active, the baby boomers had to fight their way through the tangle of temptation, impulse, emotion, and taboo associated with sexual pleasure. Sex was supposed to be contained within matrimony, which in turn supported the nuclear family, one of the pillars of the postwar consensus. Marriage came at a relatively young age, sex came after marriage, and men and women were supposed to have distinctly different sexual appetites, gender roles, and family responsibilities. It was the teenage girls' duty to curb the boys' animal passions to preserve the premarital female chastity upon which the nuclear family, social order, and the moral integrity of the nation depended. Boys were expected to take as much as they could get. Echoing the Beatles' earlier "Please Please Me," the 1910 Fruitgum Company had a hit in 1968 with the song "1, 2, 3, Red Light," in which the male singer complained that his girlfriend "wasn't right" to stop him when he "tried to prove" he loved her.[12] Everyone knew the deal.

In the sexual realm, the hypocrisy of conformity affected everyone personally, often with tragic consequences. Enforcement of a prudish, outmoded morality led to guilt, unwanted pregnancies, ill-considered marriages, and dangerous abortions, all the result of a natural human appetite that was not amenable to repression. A decade earlier the Kinsey Reports on human sexuality had shown that, behind the scenes, people were having lots of sex that was neither postmarital nor monogamous. Half the marriages in America in the 1950s were between teenagers, and half of them resulted from a pregnancy.[13] The traditional moral guidelines that purported to govern sexual behaviour were out of whack with reality.

Meanwhile, modern science had eliminated some of the unpleasant side effects of sex. Sexually transmitted diseases had been beaten into retreat by antibiotics. The Pill became available in 1961. In Canada, however, it was illegal to advertise or sell birth control, and at first doctors would give the pill only to married women. Yet the gap between stricture and practice yawned ever wider. Defenders of the old morality found themselves fighting a rearguard action. A sexual revolution was under way.

Suddenly sex was everywhere – not just in kids' rock 'n' roll, but all over the media. Advertisers used the sexual sell indiscriminately, while entrepreneurs like Hugh Hefner turned sex into a commodity.[14] Sex was portrayed more explicitly than ever before in literature and movies, and censors were cutting less of it. Governments responded, slowly, by easing moral regulation. Britain decriminalized long-entrenched laws against homosexuality and abortion in 1967, and there were discussions in Canada about doing the same.

With the rise of television, the media seemed increasingly pervasive in the sixties. By 1967 there was a television in 95 percent of Canadian homes.[15] The media were essential not just to the workings of mass democracy but also to the consumer economy. The relentless "sell" mode of capitalism, the intrusiveness of advertising, and, above all, its reductionist interpellation of people as consumers fed mediation anxiety. The relationship between the signified and the signifier, between what was ostensibly being depicted and the representation of it, was attenuated to the point that audiences could not help but be anxious about signal slippage.

Concerns about the media articulated by the intelligentsia earlier in the century were emerging in middlebrow culture. A 1957 bestseller, Vance Packard's *The Hidden Persuaders*, suggested that corporations manipulated consumer behaviour through advertising in the mass media. Betty Friedan's 1963 *The Feminine Mystique* attributed women's subjugation to media-circulated stereotypes. At the start of the sixties, American sociologist Daniel Boorstin published *The Image*, a critique of a culture in which visual imagery had eclipsed text, undermining rationality and realism. "There are no 'originals,'" he lamented, "only the shadows we make of other shadows."[16] Frenchman Guy Debord echoed Boorstin in *The Society of the Spectacle*, a manifesto published in 1967: "Everything that was directly lived has receded into a representation."[17] The late 1960s were arguably the high-water mark of mediation anxiety, with subsequent critics taking more care to contextualize the effects of the media within traditional cultural forms and sociopolitical contexts.[18]

A Canadian academic was then rising to fame because he had profound things to say about the effects of modern communications.

Snagging public attention with the catchphrase "the medium is the message," Marshall McLuhan argued that each medium of communication extended a particular sense, distorting the natural balance of the human sensorium and biasing society towards a particular way of knowing. Print, for instance, was a visual medium that privileged the eye and rationality. It had reigned supreme for the previous four centuries, during which logical, linear Enlightenment thinking had held sway. In contrast, electronic media had resurrected many features of premodern oral societies, and were thus "retribalizing" humanity, albeit on a mass scale, given their ability to conquer space.[19] McLuhan described the resulting paradoxical sociological phenomenon with the oxymoron "the global village."

At a Progressive Conservative "Thinkers' Conference" held in Fredericton, New Brunswick, in September 1964, McLuhan advised the assembled politicians "to study the Beatle phenomenon and translate their image techniques into political persuasion."[20] In 1967 he was interviewed or profiled by dozens of network television shows in Canada and the United States. The continent's most successful mass-market magazines pestered him for an interview or an article, and he usually obliged. His hastily compiled The Medium is the Massage, published that year, would sell more than a million copies worldwide. He was enjoying his fifteen minutes of fame as his ideas on media transformed him, ironically, into a media celebrity. "Every well informed citizen," notes a student of McLuhan, "knew his name and had heard his catch phrases, and knew that he stood for the cultural revolution of the electric/electronic age."[21] Few understood McLuhan perfectly, but he was lionized all the same, for his thinking, though obscure, reassured those anxious about systemic simulation that someone was looking into it.

Canadians had recently had an instructive experience in the hazards of mass-mediated politics. John Diefenbaker's rise to power, including, eventually, the largest parliamentary majority in Canadian history in 1958, had been the first demonstration of the potency of television in Canadian politics. Canadian novelist Hugh

This October 15, 1966, *New Yorker* cartoon shows how Marshall McLuhan came to symbolize the mediation anxiety of the era.

MacLennan had encountered Diefenbaker at the 1948 Republican convention in Philadelphia. It was the first American convention to be televised, and MacLennan observed that the politicians there would "stare at the box and then it was discovered that on that little screen they were more real and impressive than they could ever be in their all-too-palpable flesh."[22] Within a decade, most Canadians were getting most of their political information from television. Diefenbaker's campaigns exploited the latest public relations techniques, including a politics of image calculated to work on TV. Diefenbaker's experience as a courtroom lawyer "had taught him that the greatest speeches were stories designed in the manner of dramas that involved an introduction, a problem and conflict, periods of rising and falling action, a climax, and a resolution. Nearly all dramas require a hero or villain whose activities push forward the action."[23] Diefenbaker played the hero. On top of this, he offered a "northern vision" of the future greatness of Canada. A sincere, engaging personality with a noble quest was hard to beat. He was duly elected, only to fall from grace, painfully, protractedly, and melodramatically, over the first three years of the 1960s.

Dief's coming and going was a cautionary tale at the back of Canadian minds when they considered the role of the media in public affairs generally and electoral politics in particular. In 1962, the topic for the Couchiching Conference, an annual public affairs talkfest for the chattering classes, was "The Press and the Public." By 1967 it had circled back to this theme, challenging its participants with the question "The Image or the Issue?"[24]

Over the course of the decade, the question of whether the media could be trusted became a favourite topic for the media itself, which must have prompted some to wonder whether the media could be trusted about whether the media could be trusted. *Rowan and Martin's Laugh-In*, a mod comedy-variety television show that became a hit in early 1968, prefaced every episode with a scene that referenced mediation anxiety. It framed its antics by showing an old-style announcer at a microphone in front of a television sound stage, proclaiming that they were now "on air" while pandemonium reigned in the background. Comedian Goldie Hawn would randomly ask, "Whatcha doin', Marshall McLuhan?" – making it a cool phrase across North America.

There were signs in the late 1950s of dissident cultural voices that would grow more influential in the 1960s. The Beats, a subculture of romantic misfits immortalized by Jack Kerouac's bestselling *On the Road*, shunned the work ethic, refused to dissemble about indulging their animal appetites, did drugs, and embraced avant-garde literature and jazz music. The media, titillated by deviance, publicized the "beatnik" lifestyle. The critique of conformity it embodied showed the disaffected that an alternative way of life was possible. Meanwhile, many North American cities developed a folk music scene centred on downtown coffehouses where progressive audiences gathered to listen to songs of political protest and other fine sentiments.

By 1966 the protest and countercultural movements of the sixties, once clearly distinct, were merging, in the process mutating into a more formidable challenge to the mainstream.[25] Student radicals who made the news in the early 1960s marching for civil rights dressed in suits and ties now grew their hair long and lost the corporate uniform. The alienation of the Beats, the disaffection of the folkies, the protest movements of the New Left, and the rock 'n' roll youth culture synthesized into a full-colour psychedelic spectacle of alternative lifestyles, free love, acid rock, drug tripping, and other rituals of liberation. The Beatles moved from cranking out top-forty hits to concept albums like *Sgt. Pepper's Lonely Hearts Club Band* and *Magical Mystery Tour*, and other rock acts quickly followed suit. Boy bands that had once worn matching outfits and aspired to drive Cadillacs now dressed idiosyncratically and found other means of taking trips.

The counterculture was not a disciplined movement inspired by logic, a single cause, or any systematic ideology, but rather a loosely affiliated community of disaffected youth united by an oppositional attitude that regarded constituted authority as stupid, hypocritical, and autocratic. Its emblematic figure was the hippie, a neo-Romantic turned off by the materialism, technocracy, and status games of liberal capitalist modernity. Hippies costumed themselves in buckskin, denim, and love beads to symbolize the folk humanism that alienated them from the mainstream, and formed alternative communities in the downtown neighbour-hoods of major North American cities. Small businesses sprang up to serve their needs: head shops that sold drug paraphernalia and psychedelic posters, underground newspapers that documented "the scene," FM radio stations that played rock albums and an-nounced spontaneous "happenings."[26] Towards the end of the dec-ade hippies and hippie-wannabes began to gather by the tens of thousands at outdoor music festivals, spectacular happenings that fixated the media gaze.

The slogan "free love" didn't necessarily mean more sex – by all accounts there had been lots of that going on behind the scenes already – but rather liberating it from the hang-ups imposed by traditional morality. Hippie styles of dress gleefully transgressed conventional concepts of masculinity and femininity with an an-drogynous look that simultaneously challenged rigid distinctions between heterosexual and homosexual. Sexual liberation also in-spired political activism on issues such as the availability of birth control for unmarried women. The old morality by no means col-lapsed and disappeared, but there was now an alternative way of thinking about sex that had a bright future. As the sexual revolu-tion gathered steam, sexual repression became emblematic of all that was wrong with the establishment.[27]

Prior to the 1960s, illegal drugs had been a relatively minor pres-ence in Canada, one associated with deviant criminal elements or relatively harmless occupational groups, like musicians, who had been quietly smoking pot for decades. By 1963, police were report-ing a noticeable uptick in drug use, particularly among the beat-niks, but also among some middle-class kids. In the next three to five years the number of drug charges skyrocketed.[28] It wasn't just pot – there was speed, amphetamines, acid, and heroin. As the rock scene blossomed, the drugs that had been a hidden part of the music scene flowered with it, trumpeted as a creative elixir and flaunted as a symbol of the counterculture's contempt for authority.

With a typical sixties youth blend of scorn and pity for the older generation, Jefferson Airplane's "White Rabbit," which hit the airwaves in 1967, noted that the old folks' drugs "didn't do anything at all." The older generation's ignorance of nonprescription drugs other than alcohol and nicotine was demonstrated by its inability to distinguish between pot, speed, LSD, and heroin in its panicked efforts at enforcement. Police began arresting kids merely for possessing a joint, and harsh treatment and penalties often followed, further discrediting the establishment in the eyes of the young.

The counterculture picked up on the era's mediation anxiety and turned it against the establishment. Slogans invoking authenticity – "get real" or "making it real" – became vague but potent rallying cries of the disaffected. By addling perception, drugs played to the era's anxiety about the contingency of representations of reality. Bob Dylan's "Mr. Tambourine Man" featured spacey lyrics that celebrated sensory distortion. The Byrds, a band that epitomized the genre of folk rock – a musical expression of the late sixties fusion of the decade's political and cultural streams of dissent – had a number one hit with their cover of it in 1965. The psychedelic aesthetic grew fashionable as a way to represent drug use and the problem of perception in the modern, mediated world.

On the January 25, 1968, edition of the CBC television show *The Way It Is*, host John Saywell appeared in front of a psychedelic backdrop to introduce a segment on the drug culture. His initial remarks were followed by footage of brightly coloured pills of varying hues pouring through the air, rapidly intercut with shots of pulsing neon lights, all backed up by a discordant soundtrack. Next came a performance by the Toronto band the City Muffin Boys Ltd. What they were playing was "acid rock," Saywell explained, the "litany of the drug culture," inviting listeners to "come blow your mind." After they had finished, he asked, with a smirk, "Can anybody make any sense out of any of that?"[29]

Through free association, perception was linked to spirituality as well as drugs. One of the expert panellists on the same show, Mark MacGuigan, a legal scholar from the University of Windsor, referred to "the Timothy Leary phenomenon in which the use of a drug has been exalted into a religion." Leslie Fiedler, a prominent American literary critic on the same panel, commented that "if you believe that a legitimate end in life might be vision, instead of action, or vision in addition to action, then you would have a different kind of attitude. In some theological quarters today there are big discussions these days about whether an LSD experience is a genuine or only a pseudo [vision]."[30] Psychedelia, drugs, and spiritual questing were all interrelated parts of the countercultural search for meaning.[31]

Following these paths, the flower children of the late sixties were as likely to retreat inward as they were to identify with the New Left and rush selflessly to the barricades. A prime directive was the self: finding it, loving it, fulfilling it, indulging it. Despite its general opposition to modernity, the counterculture held fast to the modern belief that there was a stable essential self to be found. Those so inspired may not have realized it, but privileging the self also placed them squarely within the church of liberalism.[32] Except, of course, when they were forming communes or conforming to countercultural norms. In terms of political philosophy, which the counterculture didn't much worry about, one of its fundamental contradictions was its simultaneous celebration of communalism and individualism.

The counterculture was encouraged in its experiments by the endless media attention it attracted. Writing about San Francisco's famed "Summer of Love," Joan Didion remarked that "there were so many observers on Haight Street from *Life* and *Look* and CBS that they were largely observing one another."[33] "What we do not need is another television program on hippies," complained a Canadian TV critic. "We've had programs on: hippies are funny, hippies are crazy, hippies are rebels, hippies are dangerous, hippies are people too, etc., etc., etc."[34]

A crowd listens to the music of Country Joe and the Fish in Vancouver. About a thousand hippies gathered for the first "Human Be-In" in Stanley Park in March 1967.

While the counterculture blossomed, more disturbing portents of change loomed. The forces of protest became more radical as the sixties progressed. Black activists in the United States grew impatient with the glacial pace of reform resulting from nonviolent protest. The confrontational style of Malcolm X was the most prominent early manifestation of a more aggressive approach to change. By mid-decade the slogan "Black Power" was ubiquitous. Beginning with the Watts riots in Los Angeles in 1965, every summer brought to the black ghettoes of major cities new outbreaks of rioting, arson, and looting that left dozens dead, hundreds injured, and inner-city neighbourhoods in ruins. In 1967 the Black Panthers captured the media spotlight with threats of race insurrection that heightened racial tensions and fuelled media sensationalism.

By mid-decade Americans were also becoming more aware of, and concerned about, the Vietnam War, the challenges it presented, and their government's reluctance to tell the truth about it. Defending democracy in South Vietnam was one thing, but was the saturation bombing of North Vietnam really necessary? Most still believed that their government was doing the right thing, but not all. Again the media played a role in sowing seeds of doubt. The ugly brutality of war began to show up regularly on the nightly news: corpses of peasants machine-gunned in their villages, a suspected Viet Cong being shot in the head, a little girl running naked, badly burned, and screaming from a napalm attack.

The US government's policies in Vietnam became the focus of an antiwar movement that featured many of the same protesters and tactics as the civil rights movement and was publicized on the same scale. The merging of the politically and culturally disaffected produced colourful new forms of protest – outrageous, visual, often comic – which attracted even more media attention. As part of Stop the Draft Week in October 1967, fifty thousand marched on the US Department of Defense headquarters. Their objective, they said, was to levitate the Pentagon. Upon arrival they deployed flower power by sticking blossoms in the rifle barrels of the troops blocking their way. Canadian youth, reinforced by a small army of us draft dodgers who sought refuge north of the border, staged demonstrations that accused their government of complicity in the conflict through armament production and diplomatic support.

In Quebec, where the Quiet Revolution inspired a new sense of freedom and possibility, sixties radicalism had different implications. Encouraged by colonial liberation movements around the globe and their provincial government's new activism, French Canadian nationalists dreamed of a Quebec nation-state and began to agitate for the province's secession from Canada.[35] Political groups advocating a combination of Quebec independence with some variant of socialism amalgamated, splintered, and reformed in various configurations throughout the decade. The most prominent was the Rassemblement pour l'Indépendance Nationale. It proselytized, staged demonstrations, and eventually ran candidates in the 1966 provincial election, winning 8.8 percent of the popular vote. A parallel, connected underground group, the Front de Libération du Québec, pursued roughly similar goals through revolutionary violence. Beginning in 1963, it attacked sites of Anglo authority such as army facilities, financial institutions, and Westmount mailboxes with Molotov cocktails and bombs, sometimes killing or maiming those unfortunate enough to be in range.

Grassroots separatist activists regularly organized supporters from working-class French Canadian neighbourhoods to march and challenge authority. When Queen Elizabeth and Prince Philip visited Quebec City in October 1964, separatists joined monarchists, the merely curious, and hooligans on the streets and jeered or turned their backs on the royals as they passed. Altercations between demonstrators and police escalated until an overly zealous riot squad waded into a crowd of demonstrators, swinging truncheons, beating and arresting monarchists and separatists indiscriminately. The Quebec media immortalized the affair as "le samedi de la matraque." The brutality of the police served only to prove the protesters' point that they were exploited by a repressive regime. In Montreal, Victoria Day became an occasion to protest the British connection, with demonstrators clashing violently with police in 1964, 1965, and 1966.[36]

"Don't trust anyone over thirty," a famous sixties slogan, underlined the generational dimension of the sixties challenge to the establishment. Thanks to the baby boom, almost half the population in both Canada and the United States was under the age of twenty-five. The baby boomer self turned out to be energetic, fun-loving, and horny, with a considerable appetite for sex 'n' drugs 'n' rock 'n' roll. When youth had acted out in the past, adults had been confident that it was just a phase and that they would soon get a job and be incorporated into the system. This time the demographic weight of the boomers, their distinct generational experience, the vitality of the counterculture, and the sensationalistic press it generated called this resolution into doubt.

The "generation gap" had roots in the disparate experiences of the baby boomers and their parents.[37] The older generation, traumatized by Depression and war, looked at the security and prosperity of the postwar era as a blissful state, long elusive and gratifyingly fulfilled. Their children took it for granted, and asked, "Is this all there is?" At the same time they had the security they needed to worry about social justice, self-fulfillment, and scoring the latest Fugs album rather than getting a job. The power of numbers, idealism, affluence, and the inevitability of their ascent to power made the younger generation unusually cocky.

Although the legions of boomers watching the sixties unfold on the tube did not all drop out and migrate to the nearest urban hippie enclave, they could still dress the part and smoke a joint with their friends. Even nice kids who were good students grew their hair long and wore jeans.[38] The older generation suddenly found itself with pseudo-hippies in its midst. On a CBC public affairs show, the host warned that disaffected youth who looked like hippies were merely "an advance guard of tens of thousands just like them who'll be adrift in the land this summer. They're a new lost generation, the casualties of the baby boom of the 1950s."[39] For most youth, dressing and adopting the lingo and attitude of the counterculture was a low-risk position, never requiring the commitment of putting one's skull in range of a police baton. The position was nevertheless deeply felt, reinforced by peers, and amped-up by the hormones, angst, and alienation of adolescence. In expanding in this way the counterculture lost ideological purity and hard-core commitment but gained a widespread empathy that could, under the right conditions, inspire mass mobilization.

As the baby boomers began to attend university, campuses became political flashpoints. Many campus rules, like social morality generally, were designed to suppress premarital sex. Universities became hotbeds of the information and resources required to free love. For baby boomers, the fraught personal questions that usually attend sexual maturation were simultaneously political issues in the public sphere. Students saw the same knee-jerk repression of the civil rights movement and antiwar protests in play in their universities' control over their lives on campus. Between January and June of 1968, there were 221 major protest demonstrations on 101 US campuses, involving some forty thousand students. In this way the boomers' coming-of-age experience differed radically from that of their parents, adding another unique component to their generational identity. Student activists saw their campaigns against moral regulation as part of a wider array of liberation movements around the world and felt themselves to be in solidarity with the New Left's protests against capitalism, racism, imperialism, and war.[40]

The "old left" that had preceded the sixties New Left had thought in terms of replacing capitalism with a communist or socialist system. Following the Marxist playbook, it had focused on the working class as the agent of revolutionary change. Lacking institutional memory of the oppressive regimes that its ideological forebears had contested, the New Left targeted the regime it knew: the contemporary liberal establishment. It condemned liberalism for having given rise to a technocratic state that was remote, impersonal, and complicit with the abuses of capitalism and the military-industrial complex, disregarding any credit it may have deserved for its social welfare programs. It condemned the liberal system as paternalistic and adept at co-opting dissent in order to reproduce itself and the privilege it sustained. While the New Left shared the broader contemporary critique of modern mass society as inherently dehumanizing, it trained its sights on race, gender, age, and other identity oppressions naturalized in everyday North American culture. It eschewed formal schemes for a substitute system, seeing in any organization the very type of power that animated establishment abuses. It favoured instead direct action through grassroots activism, community work, and quotidian micro-rebellions in pursuit of a "humanistic emancipated society."[41] Veterans of earlier leftist formations criticized the New Left for attacking symptoms rather than prioritizing political economy as the root problem, but the young leftists dominated the contemporary progressive scene. Their diagnosis of society's ills and the means they chose to address them made it easy for them to find common cause with the counterculture.

The Student Union for Peace Action and its radical fellow-travellers in Canada argued vociferously about how to effect change and, less urgently, the nature of the new society they wanted to replace the old. Many doubted that the working class could be truly radical, because in the postwar era unions had been accepted and incorporated into the economic system, their leaders becoming just another establishment elite. SUPA nominally turned its sights on working with marginalized and dispossessed groups as an alternative, only to find its work duplicated, and leaders hired away, by the Company of Young Canadians, an organization created by the federal government in 1966 to employ youth in community work for social justice. At the same time young workers proved SUPA was wrong about them, staging a wave of wildcat strikes across the country in which they showed themselves able to effect change on the shop floor. In Quebec, where French Canadians' historical position as an ethnic proletariat meant social justice questions were fused with nationalism, a powerful provincial union movement was radicalizing in the second half of the decade, offering the left more institutional clout than it enjoyed in English Canada.[42]

The incoherence of inclusive open debate in left-wing circles contrasted with mainstream culture's opportunistic response to the sixties. In the spirit of Mickey Rooney, we can imagine some Broadway producer, inspired by the spirit of the times, declaring "Hey gang! I've got an idea, let's put on a show!" The hippies appeared onstage with the 1967 rock musical *Hair*, celebrating the advent of an "Age of Aquarius" in which psychedelic "mystic crystal revelation" would bring the mental liberation required to attain the communal, humanitarian utopia of their dreams. The school bus that notorious drugmeisters Ken Kesey and the Merry Pranksters took on their psychedelic trips would be retooled on primetime TV as a touring vehicle for the sit-com Partridge Family, a wholesome pop act led by a single (yet wholesome) mother. Another prime example of such commercialization was the Monkees, a rock band put together by Hollywood producers to offer a television show for youth based on a homegrown version of the Fab Four. Their zany stunts were entertaining but no threat to the social order. In 1967, the Monkees sold more records than the Beatles and the Rolling Stones combined.

The producers of pop culture knew what they were doing. Rock 'n' roll may have affected a radical, belligerent tone, but it was less about politics and protest than it was about romantic love, sex, rejection of parental authority, drugs, and other forms of youthful self-indulgence.[43] It was also a lucrative business. If a song was antiestablishment, antiwar, even anticapitalist, it mattered little, as long as it was a profitable commodity. Writing in 1969 about the "rock revolution," Germaine Greer noted that "the capitalist system ... has power to absorb and exploit all tendencies, including the tendencies towards its own overthrow."[44] Moreover, despite all the publicity it generated, the counterculture was just one strain of a North American popular culture that could still lean far to the right. In 1966, when the US public still thought the Vietnam War was winnable, the bellicose "Ballad of the Green

Berets" sold 7 million copies, making it the most popular war-related song ever.[45]

"It is easy to forget," notes Gerard DeGroot, "that while Dylan, Joan Baez, and Phil Ochs alerted listeners to injustice, militarism, and hypocrisy, the Ohio Express made a great deal of money singing 'Yummy, yummy, yummy, I got love in my tummy.'"[46] Rather than making an ideological statement, the safest path to pop success was to adopt a jazzy ambiguity that loosely knit together the old and new, security and daring. The title of one of the biggest pop songs of 1968, Mason Williams's "Classical Gas," encapsulated this approach. Williams used the platform of The Smothers Brothers Comedy Hour, where he was a writer, to launch his song, then worked with an experimental filmmaker to create a video that consisted of classical art works appearing in a rapid-fire sequence timed with the music. Bombarding the viewer with a montage of images was another expression of the psychedelic aesthetic of late-sixties pop culture. "The formal techniques of producing visual trauma in the 1960s," Charles Acland explains, "consisted of changing angles, jumping from close-up to medium shot to extreme close-up, and interposing jarring elements. The sequences ... are noticeably invested in images of images ... The flood of images, especially grave and violent ones, must add up to profundity, right? Perhaps not."[47] It was at one and the same time a symptom and an exacerbation of mediation anxiety.

In The Conquest of Cool, Thomas Frank argues that the process by which the counterculture went mainstream was not straight-forward co-optation. Focusing on advertising, the creative industry at the nexus of pop culture, media, and commerce, he documents a rejection of 1950s conformity that predated the counterculture and made admen, capitalism's creative directors, the pioneers of a new hedonism. Frank points out the powerful synergies between the counterculture and consumer capitalism. Hedonism and consumerism were entirely complementary. If the prime directive was to find yourself, the advertising industry was happy to help you do so. Its genius was to infuse products with meaning, allowing you to buy your unique identity off the rack. Rapid obsolescence, a by-product of the sixties' insistence on change, was a spur to continued consumer spending. Capitalism thrived in the 1960s context because sex, youth, indulgence, and rejection of the old-fashioned were entirely compatible with consumerism.[48]

The fashion industry played a key role in developing a style that could translate the spirit of the age into profit. "Modernity privileged the new and the fashionable," notes one student of the times, "in a reciprocal process that claimed the modern as fashionable and the fashionable as modern."[49] The mod style was the hallmark of this relationship. It fit the bill because its pioneers had used fashion to signal that they were on the cutting edge of modernity. In early 1960s Britain, the mods were a teenage subculture of fashion-conscious youths who wore imported suits, sported shaggy hair, and flocked together to admire and be admired by the like-styled. "The Mods," writes a historian of the style, "believed they were truly modern – that they alone personified 'the future' and 'change.'"[50] Mod was translated into mass culture by British rock bands like the Beatles, the Rolling Stones, and the Who, becoming a commercially successful "look" inspired by the sixties youth culture.

In time the subculture withered away, but the term "mod" lived on in the fashion world to denote the latest "with it" style. Mod celebrated freedom by encouraging its disciples to reject traditional styles and publicly express their individuality in the way they dressed. By the mid-1960s, the term was being used in the mainstream media to describe the latest fashions. One Canadian magazine referred to the "revolution in fashion brought about by youth" against the "tyrannies" of conventional styles. *Maclean's* ran articles such as "How Carnaby Street Invented the Look and How It's Hitting Main Street" and Mordecai Richler's "'Has the Swing Lost Its Zing?' The Bright Young Things Who Triggered London's Mod Revolution."[51]

Mod, like the counterculture, messed with traditional gender roles and heteronormativity. "The Modish Male," a photo spread in the *Canadian/Star Weekly*, presented a "new concept of masculinity."

"Now a man can have as much variety and colour and fantasy in his clothes as a woman," it proclaimed.[52] One of the comforts of mod for Canadians was that it came from Britain (the "Land of Mod," as this article put it), and thus perpetuated the British connection as an offset to American cultural imperialism.[53]

"Throughout 1967," Frank notes, "the year in which the counter-culture's colorful doings became a media obsession, the descendants of Mod began to filter into the mainstream."[54] Mod was in tune with the sixties ethos in its rejection of the past and its embrace of sexual titillation and a psychedelic aesthetic. Advertisers and television producers swirled vivid pastel colours around in vibrant patterns to show their products were in step with the times. Film editors cut from one segment to the next in a jarring fashion that mimicked modernity's disorienting pace of change. Even public affairs programs had sets dressed with futuristic moulded plastic chairs and psychedelic graphics, and played background soundtracks of popular music. For segues the camera would track slowly across pop art posters.[55]

The language of hegemony, sixties style, was mod. Mod put the consumer on the spot by asking, "Are you with it?" Anyone hailed in this manner would have to be firmly grounded in contradictory values to reject the assumptions that underpinned this style of address. Those who were young and less sure of themselves would be likely to respond by identifying with the values projected. Many who weren't so young found an opportunity to be youthful by embracing the mod style.

When, years later, the spirit of the sixties had played out, it became clear in retrospect that the most significant long-term changes set in train by the decade were those that attacked the narrow definition of normalcy by which a conformist postwar society justified its many forms of discrimination. The human rights movement challenged hypocritical liberal democracies to live up to their promises, and they responded with measures to eliminate discrimination and promote individual rights. In the 1960s, Canada, which had until recently had discriminatory laws on its books and enforced them, underwent a "rights revolution."[56] The federal government passed a Bill of Rights, and the provinces began to introduce human rights legislation and human rights commissions to investigate rights abuses. White heteronormative patriarchal biases were assailed and destabilized by civil and human rights organizations that had an increasing weight of public opinion behind them. Racism was the initial focus, but by late in the decade, women's rights and gay rights movements were under way. Aboriginal rights activism developed around the same time. These projects would grow in strength, be joined by similar causes, and delegitimize bigotry in Western societies over subsequent decades.[57]

The lifestyle liberations of the sixties – the new hedonism – also proved enduring.[58] The antinuke and anti–Vietnam War movements enjoyed some success, but in the long term neither the arms race nor America's proclivity towards military adventures abroad were substantially diminished. To the dismay of the left, new and old, the power of the capitalist system continued to grow and the political system retained its legitimacy.

In 1968, however, no one knew how it would all turn out. The sixties were in full swing, a carnival of indulgence, defiance, and iconoclasm besieging the bastions of convention. As protest movements and the counterculture merged into a mad torrent, the threat of radicalism loomed large. A wave of campus protests, antiwar demonstrations, wildcat strikes, and ghetto riots, overlaid with the antics of the counterculture, assailed the mainstream consensus. Fears of incipient anarchy produced a reactionary response as conservatives instinctively retreated into a hard-line defence of social order. Liberals, on the other hand, contemplated reforms to accommodate the legitimate grievances of the protesters and blunt any radical systemic change. For the latter, the mod style was appealing because it signalled change without risk. Mod was trendy without being threatening. Since it incorporated and exploited sixties sentiments for the ends of consumer capitalism, it was even good for business. The challenge of the Port Huron Statement would be answered with a fashion statement.

Members of Parliament show their support for the new Canadian
flag during the flag debate, December 1964.

Constructing the Peaceable Kingdom
Nationalism and Canadian Identity

And as the elders of our time choose to remain blind
Let us rejoice and let us sing
And dance and ring in the new.

DONOVAN, "Atlantis"

IN THE MID-1960S many Canadian nationalists felt that Canada was being held back and that things had to change, and quickly, if the country was to take its rightful place in the world. While slowly but surely Canada had been moving out of the British orbit in the postwar era, that only left it more susceptible to the gravitational pull of a new imperial power, the United States. Concerns about US economic and cultural domination loomed ever larger on the public agenda as the decade wore on. For Canadian nationalists, contemporary American issues like the civil rights movement, the nuclear arms race, pollution, ghetto riots, and Vietnam showed Canada to be the morally superior North American liberal democracy, making it all the more urgent to define their nation's uniqueness, chart for it an autonomous future, and launch it on its way. They believed Canada was at a critical moment in its life trajectory, verging on some significant development, about to be transformed. A hope as much as a hunch, the notion was repeated over and over until it took on a life of its own, with nationalists eventually convincing themselves the transformation had to happen.

By the late sixties, nationalist issues had been agitating the Canadian public sphere for the better part of a decade. The autonomous bent of postwar Canadian nationalism was demonstrated most dramatically by official modifications to the national symbolic order. Out went the Red Ensign, in came the Maple Leaf, a mod marker bereft of any imperialist regalia. The royal coat of arms disappeared from federal property and letterhead. Traditionalist anglophiles protested noisily, but the nation as a whole accepted the symbolic decolonization and moved on. "Our new Maple Leaf flag," wrote historian Frank Underhill in 1966, "will, one hopes, be taken by future generations as the epoch-making symbol marking the end of the era of the Wasp domination of Canadian society."[1]

In the late 1950s, Walter Gordon, scion of an establishment accounting firm in Toronto, emerged as the unlikely pioneer of an economic nationalist movement. As chair of the Royal Commission on Canada's Economic Prospects, he became alarmed at the extent of foreign ownership in the Canadian economy. His commission's 1957 final report warned that Canada's sovereignty was compromised by high levels of American investment. Canadian business elites resisted the message. Though they had in earlier times sought state protection from US competition, now they found profit in serving the American empire. In 1963, as finance minister in Lester Pearson's Liberal government, Gordon introduced a budget that included a tax on foreign investment. Business opposition was overwhelming, forcing him to back down and, eventually, resign. But the number of Canadians who were concerned about foreign ownership was on the rise, and, according to polls, heading into majority territory by mid-decade. The issue united establishment nationalists like Gordon with left-wingers who took a dim view of capital regardless of its origin. The governing Liberals, divided between business-friendly and left-nationalist wings, played for time by appointing economist Mel Watkins to head up an inquiry, the Task Force on Foreign Ownership and the Structure of Canadian Investment, in 1967.[2]

The second great nationalist issue of the era was linked to pacifist organizations' campaign for nuclear disarmament. Canada was a member of the North Atlantic Treaty Organization, and, as the Cold War intensified, allied with the United States in continental air defence through the North American Air Defense Command. In the early sixties the nuclear question became a major federal political issue as John Diefenbaker's Conservative government struggled to decide whether to equip Bomarc missiles purchased to defend North America from a USSR nuclear attack with the nuclear warheads they needed to be effective. This decision was, in part, a question of national identity: Canada's nuclear-free moral purity was at stake. It also became a national sovereignty issue as Diefenbaker accused the Americans of meddling in Canadian politics to get the Liberals elected and the warheads installed. His government's prevarication on the issue contributed to its fall from power in 1963.

American cultural influence also worried nationalists. The rise of the mass media over the previous century greatly facilitated distribution of cultural products continent-wide. Economies of scale enabled US cultural producers to recoup their investment within their domestic market and then sell their lavishly made goods cheaply in Canada. Canadian producers who aspired to serve their own domestic market were limited to an audience one-tenth the size of the United States that was more expensive to reach because it was spread thinly over a sprawling territory. Investments in cultural products had to be relatively modest because there was proportionately less money to be made from them. As a result Canadian works appeared ill-made, when they appeared at all. Often they were shut out of distribution systems set up to move American product. Canadians, especially English Canadians, consumed far more mass culture and entertainment of American than Canadian origin. The worry was that doing so would eventually turn them into Americans.

The Royal Commission on National Development in the Arts, Letters and Sciences had examined the issue in the late 1940s and warned, in its 1951 report,

> We are now spending millions to maintain a national independence which would be nothing but an empty shell without a vigorous and distinctive cultural life. We have seen that we have its elements in

our traditions and in our history; we have made important progress, often aided by American generosity. We must not be blind, however, to the very present danger of permanent dependence.[3]

A decade later the government was experimenting with Canadian content rules for television and with legislation designed to help Canadian magazines compete against American imports. As universities expanded rapidly in the postwar period they hired many Americans as faculty, prompting nationalist Canadian professors to campaign for a Canadian hiring preference to ward off intellectual colonization.[4] This defence of Canadian culture naturally raised the question of what that culture was, and to answer it a Canadian studies movement aimed at getting more Canadian content into schools and universities gathered momentum throughout the decade.

Cultural nationalism was inspired by the primordial nationalist belief that nations were organic societies that had developed naturally from origins obscured in the distant mists of time. The intelligentsia's role was to weave the yarns of quotidian existence into the fine raiment of national identity. This was a seductive proposition for intellectuals, especially those involved in impractical pursuits such as the arts and letters. Nationalist ideology gave them a legitimate place in the power structure as mediators between the *realpolitik* of state and the romance of nation. The federal government's expansion of cultural institutions and programs in the 1960s gave Canadian cultural producers a status and security they had previously lacked. Without state intervention, they would have remained hostage to the inexorable logic of continental cultural economics and deprived of the prestige and income they felt entitled to in their own homeland.

Cultural nationalists knew that Canada did not measure up to the expectations of primordial nationalism. While it boasted a huge territory, its very vastness meant it encompassed varied regions that constituted distinctly different homelands. As a New World country in which Indigenous peoples had been swamped by colonizers from France and Britain, supplemented by immigrants from various parts of the world, Canada was challenged to present the least semblance of cultural homogeneity. Previous generations of English Canadians may have believed that processes of assimilation would eventually make Canada a British North American nation, but French Canadians had proven unassimilable. In fact, Québécois were currently displaying a feisty nationalism that put paid to dreams of Anglo-conformity. The idea of two founding nations was floated as an alternative, only to be assailed by other ethnic formations, most notably western Ukrainians, for failing to include them. Accordingly, by the mid-sixties, nationalists increasingly deployed terms like "unity in diversity," "ethnic mosaic," and other such pluralistic formulations of national identity.[5] "Canada is not a logical construction," wrote Hugh MacLennan in 1967:

> Therefore I believe that the perennial Canadian "racial" problem is our greatest single asset. Again and again it has prevented us from opting for the kind of unity which turns a government into a huge abstraction. In our own muddled way ... we are at least trying to provide in Canada a political home for diversity ... Is it more than wishful-thinking to believe that if Canada succeeds, she will be a pilot-plant for a broader human liberty in this frightened world?[6]

The state of Canadian identity theorizing in the mid-sixties was nothing if not complex. The novel and paradoxical "unity in diversity" formulation was gaining traction among nationalists even as the "two nations" idea was winning acceptance as the basis for constitutional reforms that would accommodate Quebec neonationalism in the wake of the Quiet Revolution. At the same time, the country's new autonomy energized a yearning for a unifying Canadian character of some kind. Despite its obvious unsuitability in the Canadian context, primordial nationalism was so culturally embedded that nationalists continued to venture generalizations about how, despite everything, Canadians still exhibited certain commonalities. Climate, political culture, and history were invoked as substitutes for the now pernicious identity marker of race.

In the postwar era, Canadian intellectuals applied themselves assiduously to the cultural work of nation building.[7] The main difficulty lay in defining for Canada a character that would naturalize its existence as a nation distinct from both its mother country and its powerful southern neighbour. The latter task required much fine hair-splitting. After all, at first blush any comparison of Canada and the United States would find them more remarkable for their similarities than their differences. Both were North American liberal democracies with British founding fragments and government institutions shaped by the British parliamentary tradition. Unlike Britain, Canada had a federal system of government – but so did the United States. Both were heirs to the same Christian traditions; both were countries of immigrants with similar histories of European settlement. Both had free-market capitalist economies. For good reason, the kind of identity theorizing that distinguishes Canada from the United States has been described as "the narcissism of small differences."[8]

Prominent among the identity theorists influential in the postwar period were a clutch of scholars at the University of Toronto: political economist Harold Innis, historian Donald Creighton, and literary critic Northrop Frye. They were assisted mightily by Hugh MacLennan, who taught at McGill University, the University of Manitoba historian W.L. Morton, and McMaster University philosopher George Grant.[9] These intellectuals were at the top of the ideational chain of Canadian being. They contributed key notions about distinguishing national characteristics that percolated through the ranks of cultural producers, winning general acceptance and consolidating into a new conventional wisdom. Whatever the merits of the ideas they formulated, the intensity of identity theorizing activity at the time and the wide acceptance of its results reflected a will to difference among Canadian nationalists.

Narcissism in the snowmelt:
Duncan Macpherson's Canadian Everyman
contemplates his identity and has
his worst fears realized.

This circulation of ideas was an example of how discourse made the simunation – a communicative community constituted by the conversations conducted about it.

Innis had started the ball rolling in the interwar period with his influential economic histories of Canadian staple products. His research revealed the systems of finance, transportation, and communication that spanned the Atlantic Ocean and the northern half of the continent to support the extraction of resources from Canada by European metropoles. He argued that Canada had arisen along east-west lines because that was the axis of the St. Lawrence and Great Lakes waterways that provided access to the staple resources – furs, timber, minerals – of the Laurentian Shield. His development of this point pleased nationalists because it countered a long-standing economic determinist viewpoint that saw Canada as an accident of political history whose continentalist orientation would lead inevitably towards eventual absorption into the United States. According to Innis, Canada developed the way it did because of geography, not despite it. Canada's claim to its territory had a historical pedigree that went back to the fur trade.[10]

In the 1930s Creighton made Innis's interpretation a central theme of Canadian historical development. He described how merchant interests in Canada had assumed the mantle of European metropoles in directing Canada's economic development, in the process greatly influencing Canadian politics. The merchants secured state support for implementing successive new transportation and communications technologies – first canals, then telegraph and railway – and profited from updating the east-west infrastructure that had originated with the fur trade.[11] For 1960s nationalists, the Laurentian thesis, as it was called – by then further evident in broadcasting, airlines, and the recently completed Trans-Canada Highway – was a widely accepted, common-sense explanation of national development and difference. Not the least of its attractions was its distinctiveness from the frontier thesis that historian Frederick Jackson Turner had posited to explain American identity. Whereas the American frontier was a wild west characterized by rugged individualism, the development of the Canadian frontier showed the visible hand of the state and other forms of authority. In contrast with the Hollywood western caricature of a west over-run by gunslingers, north of the forty-ninth parallel the North-West Mounted Police had come first, followed soon after by bank branches.[12]

In the late 1940s, Hugh MacLennan ventured another defining national characteristic. Canada was, he averred, made up of history's losers. Loyalists fleeing persecution after the American Revolution had joined French Canadians conquered in the Seven Years' War, and were later joined by a third defeated population, Highland Scots displaced by the clearances. The result was a ghetto of phlegmatic peoples chastened by experience, happy just to live and let live, resistant to visions of imperial grandeur, and reluctant to take chances. They had come together to form Canada, MacLennan believed, not out of a wish to be united together, but out of a shared desire not to be absorbed by a homogenizing United States.[13]

After Lester Pearson won the Nobel Peace Prize in 1957 for finessing a resolution of the Suez Crisis of the previous year, Canadians increasingly took pride in their military's service as UN peacekeepers, fashioning a self-image as the do-gooders of an international scene otherwise dominated by imperialistic powers. In his 1960 bestseller *Peacemaker or Powder-Monkey: Canada's Role in a Revolutionary World*, James Minifie argued that Canada should withdraw from military alliances like NATO and NORAD in favour of a neutrality that would give it more moral sway in global affairs. Nuclear war, after all, was an unwinnable proposition. Peacekeeping was a way in which Canada could make a positive contribution to world affairs and exhibit its distinctive national character.

In 1961, historian W.L. Morton published *The Canadian Identity*, a historically based argument for Canadian exceptionalism. Like others before him, he made much of the significance of Canada's path to independence through constitutional evolution rather than violent revolution.[14] "Canadian history is not a parody of American," he declared. "Canada is not a second-rate United States, still less a

United States that failed. Canadian history is rather an important chapter in a distinct and even a unique human endeavour, the civilization of the northern and arctic lands."[15] Morton saw Canadians as a northern people with a political culture distinguished by the tradition of British liberty in contrast to the principle of freedom that lay at the heart of the US constitution. Counterintuitively, the greater authority inherent in the British tradition offered better protection for the freedom of individuals, especially those of minority groups. The tradition of liberty that Canada had inherited was more tolerant of diversity than American republicanism, he contended, for citizens need only pledge allegiance to the Crown to win its protection and be accepted, whereas in the United States they had to subscribe to the polity's core principles and thus were sucked into a majoritarian centrifuge. The difference, he cleverly noted, was captured in each country's defining slogans, with the British North America Act being guided by the dictum of "Peace, Order, and Good Government" in contrast to the invocation of "Life, Liberty and the Pursuit of Happiness" that animated the US Declaration of Independence.[16]

One of the projects of the postwar Canadian studies movement was construction of a canon of great works that would establish Canadian literature as a legitimate field of scholarly study. This project featured a vogue for thematic criticism that sought to discover Canadian identity in the nation's literature. In his 1965 conclusion to A Literary History of Canada, a pioneering canon-formation enterprise, Northrop Frye added some fecund identity propositions to those of the historians. He described, evocatively, the experience of entering Canada on an immigrant ship as it proceeded up the Gulf of St. Lawrence into the St. Lawrence River as akin to Jonah being swallowed by the whale, in contrast to arrival in the United States, where the immigrant simply bumped up against the eastern seaboard. He added that the question for settlers shaped by European civilization who found themselves swallowed into the Canadian wilderness was not so much "Who am I?" – their cultural identity was secure enough – but rather "Where is here?" the disoriented response of those displaced into a wholly foreign environment. As settlers began to adapt to their new land, Frye believed their imagination was profoundly affected by what he called the "garrison mentality," a defensive psyche instilled by imagining oneself encircled by a malevolent unknown. Frye concluded his analysis by invoking the image of "the Peaceable Kingdom" – a vision of harmonious coexistence within humanity and between humans and nature. Once a powerful theme in North American literature, it had faded south of the border, he maintained, but continued to animate the Canadian literary imagination.[17]

On the surface Frye's generalizations, derived as they were from Canadian literary tradition, were not readily congruent with those of the historians. Yet he had international recognition as a literary critic, so his pronouncements could hardly be ignored. Fortunately, his concepts were not irreconcilable with those of the other identity theorists. His observations about the immigrant experience of arriving along the St. Lawrence River dovetailed nicely with the Laurentian thesis. His garrison mentality notion had communal and conservative connotations commensurate with Morton's differentiation of the American and Canadian political cultures. Morton's emphasis on the north neatly answered Frye's "Where is here?" Finally, the Peaceable Kingdom's moral of harmonious coexistence was in synch with the pluralism stressed by MacLennan and Morton, which in turn informed the emergent unity in diversity theme.

In 1965, as these ideas were gelling, George Grant published his influential *Lament for a Nation*. It deplored the continentalizing policies of the Liberals over the previous half-century and despaired about the possibility of Canada's continuation as a separate and distinct society. Grant reiterated Morton's idea that in Canada the Crown had been a better guarantor of freedom than the Americans' majoritarian adherence to a charter. Sympathizing with critiques of modern mass society that Western intellectuals had developed in the interwar period, Grant demonized the United States as the source of modernity and all its ills. In his view, America's misguided worship of liberty had given rise to immoral capitalism and amoral technocracy. In the good society, freedom had to be constrained by moral principles embedded in communal values. He mourned the disappearance of Canada for the loss of the comparatively humane ethic he thought it had represented. In death by Grant there was, however, resurrection. His polemic prompted every Canadian pundit worth his or her salt to weigh in on the issues he raised, intensifying the national conversation. Left nationalists adopted Grant's argument, while rejecting his pessimism in favour of a renewed effort to save the nation whose raison d'être he had so nobly defined.[18]

Academics were remarkably active and influential public intellectuals in this period. In 1965, William Kilbourn, a historian at York University, summed up much of the emergent Canadian identity theory in his epilogue to *The Making of the Nation*, an illustrated popular history that was his contribution to the Canadian Centennial Library. In a few pages Kilbourn synthesized and reconciled the main points made by the identity theorists who had directly preceded him. Echoing Grant, he equated the United States with modernity, noting that "everywhere in the twentieth century man is becoming American." Morton's British liberty and "peace, order and good government," MacLennan's exiles, and Frye's Laurentian Jonah and "garrison mentality" constituted a national experience in which "survival itself is a virtue and a triumph." Kilbourn even worked in a little Marshall McLuhan, noting how Canada's marginality gave it a unique outlook, "detached and ironic, always multiple, and useful for living in the electronic age's global village." A peaceful colony-to-nation narrative was also part of the mix, as was the notion of a nonideological and, thereby, tolerant and pluralistic political culture. The latter notion inspired Kilbourn's epilogue title. Borrowing from Frye, he called it "The Quest for the Peaceable Kingdom."[19]

Kilbourn's piece linked Frye's notion of the Peaceable Kingdom to Morton's emphasis on the importance of "peace, order and good government," but the significance of peace in national identity theorizing did not end there. Both tied in nicely with peacekeeping, creating a three-ply firewall of tolerant, pacifistic humanism that insulated Canada from the United States.[20] Since "peace" was a key word of the contemporary protest ethos, this version of Canadian identity made common cause with the radical spirit of the sixties, sharing with it a desire to transcend the bewildering maelstrom of modernity to find firm footing on a moral high ground.[21]

Cultural producers other than scholars also laboured in the identity theory cottage industry. The artsy precariat was then launching small presses to gain a voice in a publishing marketplace otherwise dominated by multinationals and mass products, and there nationalist and countercultural ideas flourished symbiotically. In 1967 the poet Al Purdy collected short pieces of poetry and prose on Canadian-American relations from big names in the arts and letters: Farley Mowat, Peter C. Newman, Margaret Atwood, Mordecai Richler, George Grant, Margaret Laurence, Irving Layton, Laurier LaPierre, Louis Dudek, Hugh Garner, Robert Fulford, Earle Birney, and many others. The resulting collection of anti-American diatribes, *The New Romans*, was a bestseller.[22]

Sometimes the theorists themselves wrote for a popular audience, but more commonly their ideas were popularized by newspaper columnists, editorialists, writers in national magazines, and public affairs shows on radio and TV. What these middlebrow nationalists lacked in originality they made up for with the power to popularize. Since the different media and the cultural producers who worked in them were interconnected in various ways, they also functioned, in the aggregate, as an echo chamber in which identity theory bounced back and forth, gaining credibility with each hearing.

The Canadian media complex was highly centralized and small enough at the centre that most of its major players knew or at least knew of one another. Each of the different media had its strengths and weaknesses, its particular role, and unique relationships with the other media in the complex. Television, the new kid on the block, was recognized as hugely influential, but its visual grammar was so much at odds with that of traditional print culture that it was suspected of terminal superficiality. Newspapers and magazines, and, in particular, journalists with established reputations writing in them, retained status as respected sources of substance even as they lost eyeballs to the tube. Radio, just a couple of decades earlier a technological marvel and a focus of family entertainment, was now a background companion for those whose eyes were occupied. Cultural producers in any one medium were as impressed by a story's telling in another medium as they were by the underlying reality that gave rise to it. They took their cues from the complex as much as from the country, with the result that a story was rarely just one representation removed from reality.

The most esteemed journalists of the day became influential by exploiting the reverberative quality of the media complex. They operated not just in one medium but in the system as a whole and developed their profiles through its self-reinforcing interplay. They paid their dues by writing magazine articles and cranking out newspaper columns, acquiring, in the process, journalistic credibility, but it was their appearances in the electronic media that made them celebrities. Print journalists like Pierre Berton, Charles Lynch, and Peter Newman became household names in Canada because people came to know them through television and radio. Print lent them gravitas; the airwaves gave them exposure.

Once established as Canadian media celebrities, they were able to sell well in yet another medium, the book – and what is more, the nonfiction book – where prospects for Canadian authors were otherwise bleak. They became multimedia performers with recognizable personalities as their brand.[23] Stories came and went, but the celebrity journalists remained fixtures. Nationalism endowed their "beat," Canada, with meaning and purpose, and their voices were influential in the national conversation.

The discourse of nation in postwar Canada was highly Toronto-centric. Many of the identity theorists who seeded the process were from the University of Toronto, which enjoyed a prestige unmatched by other Canadian universities of the day. Most of the book publishers, from small presses to big publishers of Canadian content – McClelland and Stewart, Macmillan, and Ryerson – were based in Toronto.[24] Toronto was home to influential dailies like the *Telegram*, the *Globe and Mail*, and the *Star*, which, given the size of their market, were able to devote more resources to the news, especially national coverage, than smaller rivals elsewhere in the country. Canada's national magazines – *Maclean's, Saturday Night*, and *Chatelaine*, not to mention weekend newspaper supplements like *The Canadian* and *Star Weekly* – were all published out of Toronto. The major radio and television networks had headquarters and major production facilities there. Such centralization of production was to be expected in a country that had a small population dispersed across a large territory.

Toronto's dominance was not absolute. French Canada had its own francophone media ecology, largely centred in Montreal. Radio-Canada, the French CBC network, shared relatively little content with the anglophone CBC. Book publishers serving the French Canadian market were likewise based in Montreal. Montreal's *Le Devoir* was the newspaper to read to know what the French Canadian political class was thinking. French-language trade publications, literary magazines, and mass market magazines were also published out of Montreal. The francophone media in Quebec focused more on provincial politics than their anglophone counterparts, but they did take an interest in federal politics, and the interchange of the two groups was greatest in this area. Still, there were only 14 French Canadians in the national press gallery in 1968 compared with 106 English Canadian journalists. In part this was a function of population distribution: there were 102 English dailies and only 13 French dailies in Canada.[25]

For matters of federal politics, Ottawa was, of course, a centre of significance. Its politicians were the celebrity denizens of the national headquarters, and the journalists who covered them could over time acquire a national profile as well. The press gallery had its own specialized knowledge and status within the media system. Of its 135 members, seventy-nine were reporters for daily papers and another fifteen for magazines. Radio and television reporters had been accepted as members of the national press gallery since 1959, and there were now fifteen of the former and eleven of the latter. Fifteen correspondents from other countries rounded out the complement.[26]

Toronto's hegemony was qualified somewhat by its triangular relationship with Ottawa and Montreal. Still, it was overrepresented in the national press gallery, where its dailies had an average of five members each. Canadian Press, which supplied news to newspapers and broadcasting outlets nationwide, was headquartered in Toronto. Smaller newspapers outside of major cities relied on its wire service for more of their news than did their big-city counterparts.[27] Most of the anglophone journalists in the electronic media reported through Toronto facilities. Toronto had the critical mass to function as a world unto itself and was always in danger of assuming its obsessions were those of the country writ large. Sociologist John Porter presumably had this in mind when he wrote, in 1965:

> As well as their historical sources, images can be traced to their contemporary creators, particularly in the world of mass media and popular culture. When a society's writers, journalists, editors, and other image-creators are a relatively small and closely linked group, and have more or less the same social background, the images they produce can, because they are consistent, appear to be much more true to life than if their group were larger, less cohesive, and more heterogeneous in composition.[28]

William Kilbourn's contemporary observation that Canada's leaders were so few in number that they "can know each other personally" held true for the media sector.[29] Leading figures in the Toronto media not only worked with one another in one capacity or another, they socialized extensively. Ideas circulated not just through their workplaces, but at dinner parties, receptions, drinks after work, and even pillow talk.

A constellation of characteristics and values united media workers. They tended, of course, to be urban rather than rural, educated rather than not, prosperous rather than poor, professional versus working class, and comfortable with mass-mediated as well as traditional, visceral, face-to-face communities. The media's leading lights were white, male, and middle class. Female cultural producers who specialized in national politics tended to work behind the scenes. The French associations of Pierre Berton's first name and the Polish antecedents of Peter Gzowski's surname were as exotic as it got, ethnoculturally. Heteronormativity was as naturalized as the discourse of nation. And while there were still journalists who had begun, Jimmy Olsen–like, as mail boys, got their start on the police beat, and moved up the ladder by dint of native ability, gumption, and street smarts, increasingly journalism was the province of graduates of the expanding postsecondary education system. Most of them were of the first generation in their families to go to university, so while they now found themselves part of the white-collar middle class, they were insecure about it and hoped to fit in. They were comfortable with modernity but steeped in a humanism that made them open to the counterculture's critique of establishment technocracy. Many found the lifestyle liberations of the sixties particularly attractive. It was not uncommon for them to drink a lot, sleep around, and even experiment with drugs.[30]

Nationalism has no affinity for any particular political philosophy or position on the political spectrum. Indeed, it is notorious for its ability to mate promiscuously with other dogmas. Often it serves as an ideological turbocharger, boosting partner doctrines with emotional intensity. Late-sixties Canadian nationalism mated most successfully with progressive politics. If one accepted any part of the left's critique of American capitalism, imperialism, and militarism, it was a natural next step to look to the Canadian state as a potential power base from which to build an alternative society. The main issue separating radicals and moderates on the left was the degree to which capitalism should be mitigated by state power in the interests of social justice. Inevitably the national issue was dragged into the debate because capital could be roughly equated with the United States and the Canadian state with the nation. Radicals advocated a nationalization of the economy that would banish the evils of capitalism and Americanization in one fell swoop. Moderate solutions were based on the same view of the problem but offered incremental reforms such as public ownership in certain key sectors, tighter state regulation of corporations, and more state planning of the economy.

Although the majority of nationalists were moderates, they believed in the metanarrative of progress through expanding liberal democracy and saw it in liberalism's shift from a nineteenth-century laissez-faire doctrine to a twentieth-century adherence to the principle of equality of opportunity, as made manifest in the newly emerged Canadian welfare state. Though not willing to go anywhere near as far left as the radicals would have them go, they nevertheless agreed that greater social democracy was the way of the future. Canada could get ahead of the United States by steering left of it. By 1967 the centre of the political spectrum in Canada was further left than ever before. There was talk in the Liberal and Progressive Conservative Parties, not just the New Democratic Party, of expanding social programs still further to include guarantees of decent housing and free university tuition, and even a guaranteed annual income.[31]

The United States was always the elephant in the room. The question, as framed by novelist Mordecai Richler, was "Is it possible to operate a cautious small corner grocery of a country on the same continent as the most astonishing of supermarket nations?"[32] Perceiving their neighbour's contemporary problems as symptomatic of fundamental shortcomings of American society, Canadian nationalists adopted the counterculture's critique of them, associating Canada with virtues that mirrored the vices they perceived in the United States. They had the luxury of observing the civil rights movement, antiwar protests, inner-city race tensions, and rioting in the United States from a safe distance. It was hard not to draw conclusions about the superiority of the Peaceable Kingdom. Did America have a race problem? Was it blindly prosecuting a misguided, nasty war? Were its cities imploding from the violence of a racialized underclass? Canadian nationalists congratulated themselves that their country did not systemically discriminate against blacks, that it was not napalming Southeast Asian peasants, that its cities were not tinderbox ghettoes.[33]

These distinctions were reinforced by other comparisons. The United States had buccaneer capitalists; Canada had Crown corporations. The left of the US political spectrum was truncated, whereas Canada had long had a healthy social democratic tradition. South of the border the social safety net was minimal; to the north had arisen a compassionate welfare state. America demanded assimilation into its great melting pot; Canada was a tolerant ethnocultural mosaic. Americans were pushy, materialistic, chauvinistic; Canadians polite and deferential, with a genius for compromise. Americans swarmed, Canadians queued. Life, liberty, and the pursuit of happiness had brought the United States to the brink of anarchy. Peace, order, and good government was a more modest vision, yet this low but solid ground provided a sounder foundation for a superior form of liberal democracy in the northern half of North America.[34]

The national narrative was recast to emphasize the antecedents of the present-day Peaceable Kingdom. The United States had been forged in violent revolution, whereas Canada had evolved relatively peacefully. Americans were rugged individualists, made so by the frontier, whereas Canadians had a history of state intervention and deferred to authority. The activist state evident in contemporary social programs could be traced historically from fur trade monopolies to canals and railway building, from the National Policy through the Canadian Broadcasting Corporation to Air Canada and numerous other Crown corporations. Never mind that its intervention

"Our policy here is to not use Negroes in our commercials because we don't have a racial problem in Canada."

This Len Norris cartoon, which appeared in the *Vancouver Sun* on October 25, 1968, lampooned Canadians' self-congratulatory response to the race issues that plagued the United States.

may have been pragmatic rather than ideological in origin. Never mind that American social programs had gone further earlier and had only recently been surpassed by Canada's. This narrative was consistent with the contemporary characterization of Canada that differentiated it from the United States. Being more social democratic than the United States became a key marker of national identity.

The term "Peaceable Kingdom" denoted difference from the militaristic republic, but did not quite capture all of the attributes that distinguished Canada from the United States. Twenty years later an apt phrase was coined, ironically, by a Republican President, George H.W. Bush, when he spoke of wanting a "kinder, gentler America" in his acceptance speech for the Republican nomination for president in 1988. Though anachronistic, that phrase nicely captures the way in which nationalists conceived of Canada's identity in the 1960s. Canada could not rival the United States in power or glory, but it could take solace in moral superiority. The Peaceable Kingdom was a kinder, gentler America. Opportunism and the narcissism of small differences determined that it should be so. The United States was stumbling badly; it was time for Canada to come into its own. "The Canadian has a social and cultural opportunity without parallel in modern life," wrote professor and novelist Hugh Hood in 1967. "He can create the first modern state, the country of the moral imagination."[35]

Unfortunately, such identity theorizing contained a glaring inconsistency. How could Canada be a more progressive North American liberal democracy if it was rooted in a conservative British political culture? Surely conservatism, popularly associated with tradition and the establishment, could not be a virtue in the radical sixties? But this was not as problematic as it first appeared. As the leftist embrace of conservative George Grant's *Lament for a Nation* had shown, traditionalists and progressives shared a critique of liberal modernity.[36] Accordingly, identity theorists performed two neat tricks to rehabilitate the Canadian political tradition for the Age of Aquarius.

As we have seen, one of their central propositions was that in the British-Canadian political tradition, authority came first, ensuring that rights were not vulnerable to that republican scourge, the tyranny of the majority.[37] Allegiance to the Crown permitted a diversity unknown in the United States, where the citizen was expected to pledge loyalty to the American Dream. While on the face of it the Tory tradition might seem less democratic, the accumulation of common law precedent over time created a civil society more accommodating to liberty, individuality, and minority rights.

The second neat trick was the invention of the Red Tory. Political scientist Gad Horowitz, another University of Toronto academic, began with Louis Hartz's fragment theory, which posited that settler societies were ideological outgrowths of the particular European cultures that had originally founded them. According to this interpretation, the United States had internalized at its inception a Lockean political philosophy that made it a liberal society intolerant of collectivist notions, whether traditional or utopian. While Hartz, a US political scientist, had seen English Canada in similar terms, Horowitz disagreed, arguing that it was a polity born of the United Empire Loyalists, the most conservative segment of the thirteen colonies. He went on to identify this as the reason why communitarianism was so much heartier in Canada than the United States. Rooted in an organic view of society, Tory tradition sustained a suspicion of the liberal faith in unfettered individualism, nurturing communal values from which socialism could grow. "Socialism has more in common with toryism than with liberalism," Horowitz explained, "for liberalism is possessive individualism, while socialism and toryism are variants of collectivism." Stripped of its overt British associations, now obsolescent, the conservative tradition in Canada could be rehabilitated as a concern for the common good entirely consonant with modern social democracy. As Horowitz concluded,

> English Canada is not worth preserving unless it can be different from the United States. Our British past provides the foundations

for building on the northern half of this continent a social democratic order ... *better* than the liberal society of the United States. A
tory past contains the seeds of a socialist future.[38]

Canada's political culture need not be a source of embarrassing
backwardness; it had now been rehabilitated to fit into the van-
guard of the sixties. The Red Tory formulation brilliantly reconciled the conservatism of nationalists like George Grant and
Donald Creighton with the social democratic bent of sixties
nationalism.

This was mentally taxing stuff, and not all nationalists appreciated the subtleties of Horowitz's argument. Fewer still were concerned with reconciling the present-day needs of their nation with
history and political theory. For most it was simply a matter of getting in step with the times. Canada was drab and boring, a provincial backwater, lacking any profile or glamour in the world of
nations. Its staid, provincial character had to be discarded for a
more up-to-date image. National politics was a significant sector of
Canadian life that was embarrassingly out of step with the times.
As a journalist for a conservative financial publication observed,

> The switch in Canada's population to the cities has brought on
> new attitudes among the voters and is producing some distinct
> changes in the kind of images newcomers to Parliament are culti-
> vating for themselves ... Modern voters ... want parliamentarians
> who reflect their own temperament and attitudes. The result has
> been a search by political parties for a brand new type of man to
> represent sophisticated city constituencies – young, well-educated,
> bright, straightforward.[39]

Diefenbaker had presented himself as the national saviour as he
rose to power in the late 1950s, only to disappoint. When the
glittering Camelot of the Kennedy presidency arrived in Washington, Canadians were dazzled, and Dief suddenly looked old-

fashioned. So deeply did this leave an impression with Canadians that a yearning for a northern version of JFK was sufficiently common to be named the "Kennedy syndrome."[40]

Lester Pearson's Liberals had presented themselves as Kennedy-esque New Frontiersmen, Canadian-style, but they could never quite pull it off. "In the final agonizing months of the Diefenbaker years," wrote journalist Christina Newman at the end of the Pearson era,

> the men around Pearson had managed to convince themselves and most of Canada's opinion-makers that once elected, the Liberals would turn Ottawa into a subarctic version of the New Frontier. People were telling each other (I swear!) that Canada would "Once again be the envy of the world," that Pearson's New Politics would "get the country moving again," and that the Liberal cabinet was "the most impressive array of brains and professional experts ever assembled in Canada."[41]

By introducing medicare and enhancing pensions and other social programs, Pearson put in place key pillars of the Canadian welfare state, providing a basis for Canadian identity theorists to claim that Canada was a more compassionate liberal democracy than the United States. But Pearson was an older gentleman with a bow tie and a lisp, a diplomat skilled in subtle manoeuvre who was professionally averse to striking dramatic poses. His substance was difficult to discern as his government seemed to stumble from crisis to crisis.[42] The acrimony with which he and Diefenbaker battled in Parliament, the scandals that beset them, and the mud they slung at each other left federal politics in disrepute, making progressives desperate for leadership renewal.

The seeming backwardness of the federal political scene was all the more intolerable given the real and pressing dangers facing Canada. The external threat from the American Empire was accompanied by a growing internal threat from Quebec separatism.

Quebec – transforming itself in the wake of the Quiet Revolution – wanted a new deal in Confederation, and federal politicians were toying with the concept of "two nations" as the basis for a settlement that would accord the province special constitutional powers to protect and promote French Canadian culture.[43] The Quebec challenge grew more significant and intransigent as the decade progressed. Diefenbaker's downfall was hastened by his failure to understand Quebec and address its concerns, and when the Liberals regained power, they struggled to keep meaningful French Canadian representation in cabinet. Early in his first term as prime minister, Pearson established the Royal Commission on Bilingualism and Biculturalism to get out ahead of the issue. The commission issued a preliminary report in 1965 to warn Canadians that they faced a grave crisis: partition rather than continued transcontinental dominion might easily be Canada's fate.

These issues generated headlines and further stimulated nationalist discourse about Canada's history, identity, and destiny. The prospect of renewing the constitution to accommodate Quebec contributed to the sense that Canada was being remade. According to the shared national narrative, Canada had evolved from colony to nation under British tutelage, was tempered in the crucible of two world wars, and should now be coming into its own – yet instead it was being blocked from realizing its destiny. "Canada's national political life has degenerated to a condition beyond patience," declared political scientist Denis Smith in the editorial launching the *Journal of Canadian Studies* in May 1966.

> The parliamentary spectacle of factionalism, deadlock and vengeance has been repulsive and profoundly discouraging ... When it is accompanied by the creative explosion of French-Canadian ambition and optimism expressed through a powerful provincial administration, the future of the Canadian union is placed in doubt.

Believing that some kind of "healing act" was necessary, Smith longed for a "regeneration of political life."[44]

When the prime minister and the provincial premiers were discussing an amending formula for the constitution in the fall of 1964, Duncan Macpherson drew this editorial cartoon for the *Toronto Daily Star* (October 21, 1964). While it is specifically the British North America Act that is being ushered into the manhole by Pearson in this depiction, the cartoon nicely illustrates the more general process through which Canada ostensibly sloughed off its British identity in the postwar period.

Smith was an NDP supporter, yet similar sentiments could be found across the political spectrum. The president of the Progressive Conservatives, Dalton Camp, was trying to renew his party. Part of that change involved replacing Diefenbaker, whose acrid partisanship had contributed to Canadians' disillusionment with federal politics. Camp argued that Canada had entered a more democratic era to which politics had to adapt:

> Canadians ... want their political parties renewed, refreshed and revitalized ... the business of politics is nearly bankrupt, run down by obsolescence and overrun by change ... No one can recall when the practice of politics so needed fresh practitioners ... We have never had a political renaissance in this country, but it is vital that we have one now, and that it be launched in the spirit and resolution of true revolution.[45]

Similar sentiments circulated widely. Celebrity journalist Pierre Berton frequently broadcast his belief that Canada had to change and needed new leadership to do so. He was working on a book called *The Smug Minority* that would flesh out this argument. "The surprising fact," Peter Newman would observe a few months later, "is that the exhaustion of ideologies which took place during the Diefenbaker-Pearson decade has left a political legacy comprised not of cynicism and decay, but of accumulated psychic energies."[46]

Meanwhile the baby boomers were knocking on the door. "Nearly half of the country's electorate is under thirty-five. And now they want to take power," intoned the narrator of a CBC television show in 1967. It then showed a clip of a young voter complaining that "men such as Pearson and Diefenbaker who have had their day are clinging to something that is not really theirs."[47] The coming of age of the baby boomers lent demographic substance to nationalists' tendency to personify the nation as an adolescent about to find itself as it matured into adulthood.[48]

In the late sixties, then, there was a sense among nationalists that Canada was in need of deliverance. The spirit of the sixties, whether in radical dissent or its domesticated mod strain, demanded change. Canadian nationalists felt that their country was morally superior to the United States and consolidating its virtuous identity as it matured into adult independence. Yet a backwards federal political scene was restraining national progress even as Quebec sectionalism threatened to break Canada apart. Tension was ratcheting up. Nationalists were on high alert and ready for action. Perhaps they were deluding themselves, but since they were programming the simunation, their anxieties could produce real effects.

These kids in Scarborough, Ontario, held their own centennial parade in early July 1967.

3

Celebrating the Simunation
The Centennial and Expo 67

To celebrate this year of our maturity this Centennial
issue of *Chatelaine* takes a candid glance backward at
what we were – and a heady look forward at what
we might become – and the prospects are fascinating.

CHATELAINE, July 1967

CANADIAN NATIONALISTS' APPREHENSION of transformation was a psychological state in search of some form of worldly manifestation. It found it in the one-hundredth anniversary of Confederation in 1967. The attendant commemorations were heavily freighted with expectations that were not disappointed. The Centennial Commission promoted the idea of nation by reinforcing the national myth-symbol complex, celebrating the land to bind Canadians together spatially, and emphasizing a shared heritage as the basis for building a common future. In many of its initiatives, all these approaches were operative simultaneously, creating complex, multidimensional representations of the nation. The crowning touch was Expo 67, the world's fair hosted by Montreal that year, which won attention and acclaim from other nations, gratifying nationalist yearnings for international status. Since much of the centennial activity was communicated through the mass media, mediation anxiety was a side effect, one recognized and tackled directly by mod cinema at Expo 67.

The centennial celebrations officially began with a ceremony at midnight of December 31, 1966, at which Prime Minister Lester Pearson lit the Centennial Flame on Parliament Hill. This was just the first in a continuous parade of collective experiences that would reinforce identification with the nation in the year to come. Across the country, communities were busy with centennial projects funded by the commission's $25 million local grants program. The commission had considered setting themes for these grants, but, with revealing realism, decided that rather than pushing an explicit agenda it would be better simply to spread the money around like manure and see what sprang up.[1] This approach had the corollary benefit of mobilizing voluntary effort to do the work of nation building at the local level. The locals presumably would regard favourably the source of their funding, the national government. "Massive in scope and daunting in size, the Centennial celebrations were without doubt the most comprehensive, expensive and extravagant nationalist project ever undertaken by the Canadian state," observes historian Gary Miedema.[2]

Nanaimo, British Columbia, in its wisdom, came up with the Great Centennial Bathtub Race. Most community projects were more conventional: beautification programs, parades, pageants, parties, heritage conservation projects, and commemorative sculptures. Provincial and municipal governments were enticed by matching federal funds into joint projects – frequently temples of cultural edification such as museums, galleries, or concert halls.[3]

The new identity marker was "unity in diversity," a big-tent nationalism that rejected the romantic nationalist ideal of a homogeneous people in the larger interest of saving the nation-state. "We are bound together," proclaimed the Centennial Commission's advertising, "by the knowledge – gained from men and women of many races – that harmony need not mean assimilation."[4] John Fisher, the commission's titular chief, was an appropriate figurehead for national festivities in the simunation. In the decade following the war he had risen to public prominence as a roving radio reporter of stories he called "pride builders" from around the country, earning the nickname Mr. Canada. Fisher saw his assignment as a unique opportunity. The centennial was "our never-to-be-seen-again chance to achieve unity-in-diversity," he proclaimed in May 1965, "to reach a collective faith in the greatness and future of this Canada of ours."[5]

After much intrigue the commission came up with a centennial symbol that aptly communicated unity in diversity in terms of the country's federal structure. It was a stylized maple leaf composed of eleven triangles, each representing a province, with one catch-all triangle for the territories. Its clean modern lines resembled the new Maple Leaf flag. Soon it was ubiquitous. Schoolchildren coast to coast busied themselves reproducing it with Crayola and bristol board. It adorned badges awarded to youth for a centennial fitness program, lapel pins, and souvenirs, and was delineated in white on the blue-backgrounded centennial flag. The media adopted the symbol of the special year, legitimizing it through mass dissemination. In the wash of continental popular culture regularly consumed by Canadians, it marked spaces reserved for Canadian content that year.

The commission also sponsored various pan-Canadian initiatives that cohered the national territory. Through a program called Festival Canada, the commission sponsored cross-country tours by artists and performing arts groups. Here too interpretation was off-loaded. The artists got to do their own thing, yet their sponsored movements across the country nevertheless worked to bind the nation together. The work of popular musicians like Gordon Lightfoot and Ian and Sylvia Tyson suggested that there was a Canadian folk identity, while companies like the National Ballet of Canada demonstrated that Canada was as civilized as the senior Western nations it emulated.[6] The commission ran a national advertising campaign to promote the centennial. It also produced short promotional films and, in cooperation with the National Film Board, two lengthier productions, *Centennial Fever* and *Helicopter Canada*. The former showed the townsfolk of St. Paul, Alberta, preparing for the hundredth-anniversary celebrations, while the latter provided stunning aerial shots of the Canadian landscape from coast to coast, delivering the sublime wonders of the national territory to its inhabitants in spectacular fashion.

Bobby Gimby would become famous as the pied piper of the centennial, parading around in an odd costume with a train of kids

Young women contemplate two artworks based
on the centennial symbol: Ralfe Ewing's
Les Saisons de Confederation (left) and Jack
Friend's Confederation mobile (right).

and pretending to play a bejewelled clarinet, singing the upbeat anodyne anthem "Ca-na-da." Gimby had approached Al Scott, executive vice president of the Vickers & Benson ad agency in Toronto, which was handling promotion for the Centennial Commission, with his song. "I really flipped," Scott said. "We needed the bilingual togetherness angle in our marketing campaign."[7] When it was recorded, there was a French version on one side and an English version on the other, each "diplomatically labelled 'side one.'"[8]

Canadian history was promoted in community projects dedicated to museums, archives, historic sites, and heritage conservation. Papers were collected and preserved, old buildings renovated and repurposed, antique carriages and cars restored. Artifacts were rousted out of attics, documented, and displayed. Canadian historians got government funding for the Centennial Series, a multivolume project to chronicle Canada from earliest times, and the private sector joined in with cross-promotions. For kids, Quaker Oats offered reproductions of pen-and-ink drawings of Canada's prime ministers. Magazine readers were encouraged to send a dollar in return for a "magnificent portfolio" of portraits of the Fathers of Confederation. RCA produced a seventeen-record set called *Music and Musicians of Canada* that included Canadian composers and every major orchestra in Canada. *Maclean's* published a *Centennial Guidebook.* Book publishers launched centennial cookbooks stuffed with inventive suggestions for authentic Canadian cuisine. A publishing venture called the Canadian Centennial Library pumped out slight but lavishly illustrated volumes with text supplied by big-name authors.

Disinterring, examining, and promoting the past became a fixation of the centennial, and governments at all levels made substantial investments in institutions and infrastructure that would nourish historical consciousness for decades to come. In part the interest arose from the discovery that, after a hundred years, Canada had a history. Invoking the past was also a nationalist imperative, for a sense of shared experience engenders solidarity in the present and a willingness to face the future together. As the Centennial Commission advertising copy put it, "We are grateful to the past, invigorated by our current progress, and inspired by the challenge of the years that lie ahead."[9] An orientation towards the future could be seen in some of the local centennial projects. The town of St. Paul, Alberta, for example, used its centennial grant not for a museum, but to build a UFO landing pad to accommodate any extraterrestrial visitors who might feel like dropping in. More prosaically, Bowsman, Manitoba – the beneficiary of a new sewage system funded by a centennial grant – burnt thirty-three outhouses in a ceremonial bonfire on New Years' Eve, signalling its passage into modernity.

The Confederation Train, a nationalist vehicle if ever there was one, snaked across the country bearing an exhibition on Canadian history. There had always been a train in Canada's history; now Canada's history was in a train. As the promotional materials put it,

> Canada's early growth and indeed her very existence as a nation following Confederation depended on the construction of rail lines to link the provinces and to span the continent. It is fitting, therefore, that the Confederation Train should traverse the country in 1967 to remind Canadians of this historical fact. But the Confederation Train is no ordinary train. It is a train of adventure; a moving panorama of Canada from pre-historic times through Confederation to the present.

Communities not on a rail line received a visit from the Confederation Caravan, which delivered the same display in buses and tractor trailers. Technology helped spruce up the musty past and project it into the future. "Visitors will see, hear, and 'experience' Canada's history ... ice age to space age ... through unique electronic displays," promised the promotional copy. "Climb aboard and see the century of a nation," it exhorted Canadians. "This way to a story a continent wide. In [its] exhibit coaches, you'll come face

The queue to view the Confederation Train in Vancouver; a similar line-up for the Confederation Caravan in Richmond Hill, Ontario.

to face with the past that shaped your present. Get a glimpse of the future your children will inherit."[10] It was estimated that close to half the population visited either the train or the caravan. Ominously, however, attendance in Quebec was a fraction of that in other provinces.[11]

As the mythic, symbolic, temporal, and spatial dimensions of the Confederation Train suggest, no single commemoration operated solely in one register, whatever its emphasis. Typically each deployed a variety of collective identity tactics in concert. The Voyageur Canoe Pageant was another example. Ten teams representing eight provinces and two territories took part in the race, which left Rocky Mountain House in Alberta on May 24, 1967, with the Expo site in Montreal as its destination. The canoes were symbolic in and of themselves, and each bore a centennial logo on its bow. In retracing fur trade transportation routes, they reenacted the pioneering conquest of space by which Europeans came to know and claim Canada, harkening back to the nation's origins in the distant mists of time – in this case, to the fur trade, a commerce through which Europeans interacted with Aboriginal peoples and became sufficiently indigenous to assert a claim to Canada being their native land. The race was an invocation of the earliest iteration of the Innisian east-west infrastructure, the transcontinental railway's own mythic progenitor. Through this popular performance of the Laurentian thesis, time and space were bound by a magic stroke of the paddle. Throughout the summer of 1967 Canadians could follow the reenactors in the news as they made their way across the land, arriving at Expo on September 4.[12]

Their journey paralleled the pilgrimage of many Canadian families to Expo that summer. The world's fair hosted by Montreal on two islands in the St. Lawrence River became the smash hit of the centennial. Modish, fun, and sophisticated, it signalled that Canada was a vibrant nation perched on the brink of a great future. Anticipating the world's fair's opening, *Maclean's* magazine editorialized that it was really a "coming-of-age party."[13] Sixty-one nations participated, the official opening ceremonies on April 27 were

The Voyageur Canoe Pageant began at Rocky Mountain House, Alberta, on May 24, 1967, and ended at Expo 67 in Montreal on September 4. The map shows the 3,283-mile route.

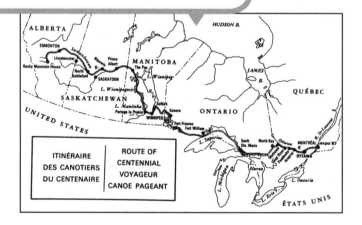

attended by fifty-three heads of state, and fifty million visitors had passed through Expo's gates by the time it closed on October 29.

The fair's visually captivating pavilions were a dramatic departure from the form-follows-function dictum of modern architecture. Unlike the rectangular, steel-framed, glass-curtained modern skyscrapers that were then changing city skylines, Expo buildings experimented wildly with form, texture, and colour. From a bird's-eye view, the fairgrounds resembled a child's play set of three-dimensional geometric forms strewn over a formal garden. Canada's pavilion featured an inverted pyramid that turned the ancient world upside down. A monorail wound its way around the site, gliding high above the crowds and piercing Buckminster Fuller's geodesic dome like a *Jetsons* cartoon come to life. Canadian architect Moshe Safdie won plaudits for stacking prefab concrete cubes like building blocks to create the variegated profile of Habitat, a futuristic housing complex. There were tent-like structures, spheres, pyramids, cubes, and tetrahedrons, cantilevering galore, and everywhere water shimmering in the canals and reflecting ponds that segmented the grounds. One visitor, dazzled, described it as a "futuristic utopian city of buildings, streets, waterways, parks and public squares."[14] An orgy of design whimsy licensed by planned obsolescence, Expo's architecture was an expression of the era's dawning postmodern sensibility.

At the same time it had its prosaic modern side. The site was laid out "more or less as if we were designing a shopping centre," recalled Safdie. "We said the U.S. and Russian Pavilions ought to be at opposite ends of the circulation pattern, like two big department stores, with all the small pavilions in between like small shops."[15] The organizers gave visitors passports that they could get stamped as they visited the various pavilions. Though originally a crowd-control device intended to spread people around, the passports became very popular, reinforcing visitors' illusion that in traversing the grounds they were travelling the world. If not quite a global village, Expo 67 was at least the world in a mall.

The unifying theme was Man and His World or, in French, Terre des Hommes, the title of a 1939 book by Antoine de Saint-Exupéry that celebrated "non-factional and co-operative brotherhood." Such optimistic humanism suggested an establishment in sync with the counterculture, and just as utopian. This dovetailed nicely with the unity in diversity theme, expressed in the Canadian Pavilion by messages about tolerance and peaceful coexistence in Canada.[16]

Expo further contributed to national unity by giving English Canadians an excuse to travel into French Canada, both imaginatively and physically, moving across not just space but cultures to mitigate the sectional crisis threatening the nation. "It was tied with Canada's coming of age," recalled one such visitor. "It seemed like there were convoys of Canadians on the road going to Expo. The highways had just been reworked. We had a feeling of sharing an experience with other travellers on the road."[17] Observers remarked on the surprising number of British Columbians who made the cross-country trek on the Trans-Canada Highway. They would have recognized themselves in the Canadian Pavilion's celebration of how their country had been consolidated by communications and transportation technologies.

English Canadian nationalists made a point of attributing much of the success of Expo to the proverbial Gallic flair of its French Canadian hosts. The flattery was sustained and unstinting; if such blandishments could heal, the national unity crisis would have ended there and then. But hard-core Quebec nationalists were not so easily seduced. The separatist journal *Parti Pris* derided Expo's bilingual and bicultural conceits as the colonizer's new game, baited with gobs of federal money.[18] While Canadians generally regarded Expo 67 as the crowning touch in their centennial celebrations, separatists downplayed the centennial connection and instead saw Expo as part of the post–Quiet Revolution continuum of modernization in their province. In this view, the fair was a coming-out party in which the new Quebec successfully presented to the world its freshly minted identity as a modern society.[19]

Pièce de Résistence

This is editorial cartoonist Duncan Macpherson's take on Quebec's refusal to join in the centennial party. The frustrated chefs are bilingualism and biculturalism co-chairs André Laurendeau (left) and Davidston Dunton (right); the partier getting the bad news is the prime minister, Lester Pearson.

The national unity crisis was acted out dramatically in public when French president Charles de Gaulle came to visit. De Gaulle dreamed of an international Francophonie under his leadership, with Quebec a leading component. Rather than visiting Ottawa first, he deplaned on July 23 in Quebec City, where the premier, Daniel Johnson, provided his official welcome. The provincial government declared a public holiday the next day, and crowds waving French and Quebec flags lined the route of de Gaulle's motorcade to Montreal, where onlookers jammed the sidewalks to cheer his progress through the working-class francophone east end of the city. The centre line on Sherbrooke Street had been painted over with fleurs-de-lys for the occasion. Fifteen thousand people turned out to hear de Gaulle speak at city hall. He told them his arrival there reminded him of his return to a liberated Paris, and, warming to his theme, declared, "Vive Montréal! Vive le Québec! Vive le Québec libre!" The crowd roared its approval.

Here was a delicate diplomatic situation: a foreign head of state supporting separatism, and doing so while he was a guest in the country. The federal cabinet met to deliberate on a response that would rebuke de Gaulle without throwing fuel on the flames of separatism. Prime Minister Pearson appeared on national television to tell Canadians that "the people of Canada are free. Every province in Canada is free. Canadians do not need to be liberated. Indeed, many thousands of Canadians gave their lives in two world wars in the liberation of France and other European countries." Consequently, de Gaulle's statement was "unacceptable to the Canadian people and its government."[20] Pearson's remarks hinted at how many English Canadians saw de Gaulle's remarks as ungrateful behaviour from a leader who had found sanctuary and succour in Britain during the war. The minister of justice, Pierre Trudeau, asked the press how the French would like it if a Canadian prime minister went to Brittany and proclaimed, "Bretagne aux Bretons." He was backed up by Montreal mayor Jean Drapeau, who pointed out that the French had been conspicuous by their absence for the previous three centuries. He told the venerable war hero he had misread his reception, mistaking Québécois pride in the cultural heritage they shared with France for a national liberation movement. Even René Lévesque, a former provincial Liberal cabinet minister then moving into the separatist camp, undercut de Gaulle's imperial pretensions, saying he didn't want imported liberty. De Gaulle visited Expo the next day, but cancelled the remaining Ottawa leg of his visit.[21]

Evidence of other sixties liberations at Expo 67 was mixed. The Indians of Canada Pavilion reflected an emerging Indigenous rights consciousness, both by virtue of its very existence and in the alternative interpretation it presented of Canada's treatment of First Peoples.[22] However, no official awareness of women's liberation was on display. Expo's very slogan, Man and His World, reflected patriarchal assumptions about which feminists would later raise consciousness. Women were much in evidence, but as hostesses and helpmates or as objects of display and desire, in keeping with the sexual revolution's banishment of hang-ups about sex.

As for gay rights, they were nowhere to be seen, although one homophobic visitor denounced Expo's mod design sensibility as a "blatant victory of the homosexual."[23] This was a telling accusation. Cold War–era consensus enforcement commonly equated communism and homosexuality. Like the provocative androgyny of the hippies, Expo's progressive architecture was to some a real threat to social order. Since heteronormativity was an integral part of that social order, there was a certain logic in associating any deviation from that order with sexual deviance. In a similar vein, former prime minister John Diefenbaker dismissed the Expo logo as "weird," while like-minded representatives of an older Canada fretted that it was a beatnik symbol, "creating a troublesome association of the fair's avowed endorsement of world peace with alternative (that is, leftist) youth culture."[24]

Media coverage of the fair was incessant and far-reaching. Over a thousand reporters were at the opening, which was broadcast live via satellite to a worldwide audience of over 700 million viewers and listeners. Thereafter it seemed that not a day went by without a celebrity visitation. The list included Queen Elizabeth II, US president Lyndon Johnson, Princess Grace of Monaco, Jacqueline Kennedy, Hollywood actors, rock stars, ninety-two heads of state, and the federal minister of justice, Pierre Trudeau. Expo 67 was a Laputian touchdown site where figures from the celebrity world materialized on a daily basis. The townsfolk of St. Paul had been right to anticipate otherworldly visitations that year, but their landing pad should have been located on Île Notre-Dame.

Newspapers across Canada constantly promoted the fair, and international coverage was lavish as well. Daily Expo updates were run by radio stations around the world, with one station in Washington, DC, going so far as to provide weather bulletins from Expo at regular intervals during the day.[25] Most of the big national magazines in Canada and abroad ran feature articles on the fair. Interest even percolated down to trade journals, which invariably found some angle by which their sector's vital services supported the great spectacle. With its striking architecture, happy crowds, and nonstop parade of events and celebrities, Expo 67 was ideal for television. It was often on nightly TV news or in network public affairs and talk shows, or was the subject of special documentaries. The CBC scheduled twenty-five weekly half-hour shows called *This Week at Expo*, while CTV had *W5 at Expo* running for an hour at ten o'clock on Sunday evenings. On both May 7 and May 21, *The Ed Sullivan Show* was broadcast from Expo 67. Ed's celebrity guests included Diana Ross and the Supremes, Petula Clark, and the Seekers.

Many nations, Canada included, considered displays of high culture necessary to demonstrate their civility, so Expo featured lots of visual art, symphony, opera, theatre, and ballet. At the Youth Pavilion, a young Leonard Cohen read poetry. Yet there was evidence here too of a postmodern sensibility intent on undermining taste hierarchies by "providing lenses, frames, and perspectives through which to read images in several different ways."[26] Deep seriousness about high art was mixed with celebrations of popular culture, most notably in the American Pavilion, along with crowd-pleasing entertainment, including an extensive amusement park, La Ronde.

A postmodern sensibility was also evident in the rich offerings of experimental film. At Expo, this simulating medium exhibited a fascination with simulation. International expositions had been venues for screening the latest in cinema since the 1900 Paris Exposition, when the medium was in its infancy. By the New York World's Fair of 1964-65, the traditional emphasis on exhibiting objects had given way to exhibiting images. Fifty-five of the sixty-two participating countries at Expo 67 screened a film. "Expo is a many-screened splendour," wrote arts journalist Wendy Michener in *Maclean's*. "Everywhere you look there are movies, movies, movies. The whole site is a mass of reflecting surfaces, flashing lights and refracted images ... There's no avoiding the great visual onslaught ... It might just as well have been an experimental film festival as a world's fair."[27] Filmmakers from around the world took advantage of the artistic licence offered by commissioned works to experiment self-consciously with the form of the medium. *Film Quarterly's* Judith Shatnoff wrote that "at Expo one saw the technological advances in optics, electronics, computer programming, and film production that allow explorations the first experimenters only dreamed of; and, significantly, one saw a huge, ready, and responsive audience."[28]

Expo's films called attention to mediation by destabilizing the conventional relationship of audience and screen. "Somebody said, 'After [the] New York [World's Fair], you've got to use multi-screen,'" explained Graeme Ferguson, one of the Canadian film-makers whose work was featured.[29] In the Cuban Pavilion, projectors hung from the ceiling, presenting scenes of the recent revolution onto moving plastic blocks. Hidden projectors in the Quebec Pavilion shone images of furs, forests, water, and textiles onto cubes and tubes, deliberately problematizing perception. In Ferguson's

Polar Life at the Man the Explorer Pavilion, the audience sat on a turntable rotating around a cube of four screens.

The National Film Board's *In the Labyrinth* was a flick with pretensions. Billed as a "philosophical journey" that equated the Minotaur myth with humanity's continual search for meaning, it even boasted Northrop Frye as an advisor. Visitors took elevators in its stand-alone pavilion to four different levels and were then ushered into eight balconies on either side of a teardrop-shaped theatre. Sound was delivered through 288 speakers, while mirrored corridors and psychedelic patterns further bombarded the senses. The twenty-minute film was presented with multiple simultaneous images on vertical and horizontal screens, forcing the viewer to view outside the box.[30]

This approach was not unique. The Canadian Industries Pavilion's *Kaleidoscope*, which used mirrors to explore the perception of colour, was deemed "the ultimate psychedelic experience."[31] The Ontario Pavilion's *A Place to Stand* packed ninety minutes of footage into seventeen minutes of multiple juxtaposed images. It was a smash hit, winning an Oscar for live action short film. Even films that celebrated the modern metanarrative of nation deployed post-modern techniques. *Canada 67* at the Telephone Pavilion featured a parade of iconic Canadian images on a 360-degree "Circle-Vision" screen. Shot with nine cameras mounted in a circle and projected onto nine screens forming a circle, it besieged the audience of fifteen hundred people with wraparound sights and sounds. All of these productions highlighted and celebrated the artificiality of the film medium rather than hiding it. "What could be more appropriate to express our mixed-up modern times than multi-media and the fragmented image?" asked Michener. "Speed, simultaneity and diversity are basic to the urban way of life. One screen doesn't give enough information fast enough anymore."[32]

Two films explored mass mediation by highlighting the reel-to-real rituals of contemporary popular culture. One was a Czech film, *Laterna Magika*, that had debuted at the Brussels World's Fair a decade earlier and now played at La Ronde. Live actors staged a play in front of a movie screen that showed footage in which parts of their roles had previously been filmed. They walked into and out of the screen, morphing from real to reel and back again. In antici-pation of the postmodern play with narrative later closely associ-ated with video games, the movie *Kinoautomat* offered the audience a choice between two courses of action at key junctures in the plot. The film would freeze at these points. The lead actor in the film then appeared onstage and asked the audience to vote for one of two ways for the plot to proceed. The votes were shown on a series of red and green lights round the screen. The decision points arose several times in a highly amusing story.

New modes of perception affected not just film, but the way exhibits were presented in pavilions. In describing the US Pavilion, Pierre Berton wrote,

This kind of psychedelic walk-through seems to me to point the way to the future of communication. It reaches its peak at Expo in the marvelous Man in the Community Pavilion, a McLuhanesque series of experiences – using sounds, flashing lights, sculptures, music, animated cartoons – everything you can think of that moves, jiggles and goes plonk – to get its message across. The information is conveyed emotionally, through the pores, not the mind, and I'm all for that.[33]

The language used by commentators in their efforts to describe Expo followed suit. It was "a color-splashed display of Carnaby Street's mad mod styles," wrote one; "a psychedelic experience," claimed another. "It's too much, baby; it's something else, total environment, romantic synaesthesia, the way things are," declared Hugh Hood.[34]

Nationalism simultaneously seeks internal unity through iden-tity and external gratification through international status, and all too rarely finds them both simultaneously. Expo 67 was one of those occasions. It projected a shiny new and trendy Canada that won acclaim from visitors from around the world. Expo challenged outsiders' stereotype of Canada as God's country, a wilderness populated sparsely by lumberjacks and Red Indians on the margin of an Arctic wasteland. "What's got into our good, grey neighbors?" asked Look in the United States. Expo was not "just a world fair, it has glitter, sex appeal, and it's given impact and meaning to a word that had neither: Canadian," wrote another journalist south of the border.[35] Canadian commentators were hugely relieved that the country had pulled it off. They had been deeply worried that the fair would be an embarrassment, and here it had materialized into a dream come true, winning international attention and praise.

The coming-of-age metaphor was liberally deployed. "Canada has attained adulthood," proclaimed Le Figaro. "Canada Discovers Itself" was the headline in Time.[36] We should have more confidence in ourselves, Expo commissioner Pierre Dupuy concluded at the closing ceremonies, saying, "Canada has acquired a new stature as a great nation."[37] Deputy commissioner Robert Shaw claimed in another closing speech that Expo was "proof that Canada had reached maturity after 100 vigorous years."[38]

The excitement of the moment generated rhetorical overkill, as when the Montreal Star deemed Expo 67 "the most staggering Canadian achievement since this vast land was finally linked by a transcontinental railway." That lines such as this could be penned was a testament to the impact the fair had at the time. The relationship between such rhetoric and the real, tangible effects of 1967 is, of course, as debatable as the existence of the Canadian identity, or, for that matter, the unicorn. We don't really know how Canadians felt. Some, no doubt, were totally tuned in, grooving to the national vibe. Others may have had yard work to do. Still others may have been paying attention without taking all the hype too seriously.

Clearly, however, nationalists in the media were all a-twitter. "Expo brought us together for the first time in mutual appreciation

US Pavilion and the minirail at Expo 67.

and celebration of our talents. We discovered ourselves," cultural critic Robert Fulford wrote in the months that followed:

> For one beautiful and unforgettable summer, Expo took us into the future that can be ours ... The feeling – not only of an accomplishment in hand, but of even greater accomplishments to come – lasted ... and among some of us it lives yet ... Expo seemed to suggest we were now entering a new and happier period in our history.[39]

"How after sponsoring the World's Fair can we ever be the same again?" concluded Peter Newman. "This is the greatest thing we have ever done as a nation ... if this little sub-arctic, self-obsessed country of twenty million people can put on this kind of a show, then it can do almost anything."[40] "Shall We Ever Be the Same Again?" asked the editors of *Chatelaine*:

> This might just be the year in the history of Canada that will be known forevermore as the year we came of age. We have been burdened down – we've been told for years – with a national inferiority complex. Long before "cool" was commonly used to describe attitudes, we were playing it cool about our country.
>
> We have never been button wearers, singers of national songs, wavers of flags or tub thumpers. But in this year of our Centennial birthday we are wearing buttons, singing Centennial songs, waving our brave red-and-white flag and indulging in some down-right jingoistic talk about our country.
>
> Can we ever go back as we were?
>
> Whatever this Centennial year and its dazzling accompaniment Expo have accomplished, we have proved to the world, but more importantly to ourselves, that we are capable of great achievements. Even more jarring to the Canadian mind is the knowledge that we've pulled off Expo and the Centennial with verve, style and originality.[41]

For journalist Peter Desbarats, everyday prose could not do justice to the experience, so he resorted to the higher diction of poetry:

> Somehow, in this unreal world
> We discovered our first true love
> For ourselves.[42]

In 1967, potent currents of emotion were exciting Canadian nationalists. Pride in their country and ambitions for it coexisted with fears of its breakup, frustrations about its progress, a keen anticipation of change, and a willingness to experiment. At the end of the year they were riding high on the euphoria of the centennial celebrations, goosed even higher by the smash hit of Expo 67. What could they do for an encore?

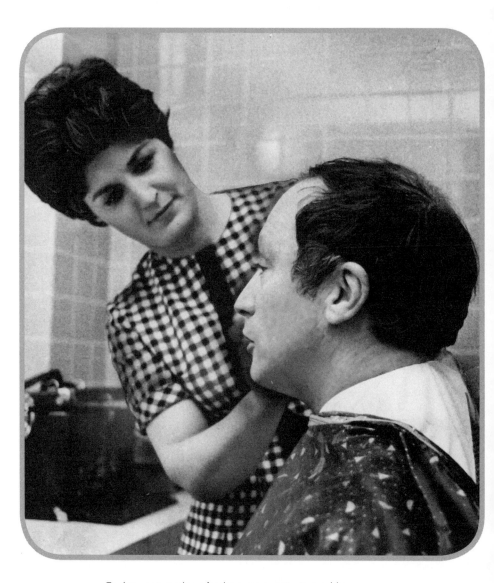

Trudeau gets made up for the cameras prior to a public appearance.

4

"A Liberal to Watch"
Pre-Mania Pierre

If you'd come today
you would have reached the whole nation
Israel in 4 BC had no mass communication.

JESUS CHRIST SUPERSTAR

THE COMING OF the prophet is a meta-myth deeply inscribed in Western lore. According to Joseph Campbell, the famed scholar of mythical patterns across different cultures, such a hero is acknowledged as a person of exceptional gifts that marked him for greatness early in life. Then he is cast out of society and endures trials that test his character. He responds with an asceticism that leads him to develop knowledge that sets him apart and lends him a mystique. The hero returns to society just in time to save it, bringing with him "the means for regeneration."[1]

In the wake of 1967, Canada was fertile ground for this trope. The centennial and Expo 67 had fulfilled, temporarily, nationalists' desire to see Canada transformed – was it only to recede as the *annus mirabilis* came to a close? How to consolidate the gains of 1967 and project them into the future? Fortunately, key features of the federal political scene were in flux, making it a promising forum for the fulfillment of nationalist ambitions. Leading members of the parliamentary press gallery were always scanning the horizon for the next big thing. By 1967, Pierre Trudeau was starting to show up on their radar screens. Not a lot was known about him, but people were struck by his style and found him intriguing.

Before his arrival in Ottawa, Trudeau had been an active commentator on Quebec politics. Throughout the 1950s, *Cité Libre*, a journal he cofounded, opposed the Duplessis regime, accusing it of using a nationalism that defined French Canada in premodern terms to secure French Canadians' acquiescence in their own exploitation. Trudeau saw nationalism as a retrograde ideology that blocked his compatriots from full participation in modern society and full enjoyment of its benefits. He criticized those who, in the wake of the Quiet Revolution, wished to wed modernization and the attendant empowerment of the provincial government with a new nationalism that would make Quebec a quasi- or completely independent nation-state.

Though well known in Quebec political and intellectual circles, Trudeau did not have much public profile in English Canada. In 1952, he made a well-received appearance at the Couchiching public policy conference and established some contacts among English Canadian intellectuals. Thereafter he was recognized in academic circles as an authority on French Canada and federalism. Peter Gzowski interviewed Trudeau for *Maclean's* in 1961 and anticipated – or perhaps influenced – later coverage by presenting Trudeau as an impressive combination of intelligence, erudition, activism, athleticism, and style.[2] A year later, Trudeau gained some public notoriety by attacking Lester Pearson's flip-flop on nuclear warheads during the Bomarc missile affair, deriding the Liberal leader as the "defrocked priest of peace." In March 1964 Trudeau published an article in *Maclean's* arguing for a charter of rights, including language rights.[3] He was onside in the emergent "unity in diversity" project, having advocated in *Cité Libre* that Canada transform itself into "a truly pluralistic state."[4] But he hadn't become a recognizable personality on television, the medium in which celebrity was made.

By the mid-point of the decade, with Quebec separatism on the rise, Canada's Liberal government had lost much of its credible French Canadian representation in cabinet, and Lester Pearson was looking to plug the holes. He wooed the highly regarded Quebec labour leader Jean Marchand, but Marchand made his recruitment conditional on his bringing with him two friends and allies, Trudeau and Gérard Pelletier. Trudeau had decided that the best way to counter the neonationalist direction of Quebec politics would be through developing influence in the party in power at the federal level. The Liberals duly arranged to find the trio constituencies, and in 1965 the "three wise men," as they were called in English Canada, were elected to Parliament. In French Canada they were "les trois colombes" (the three doves), emissaries of peace who would be responsible for finding an honourable settlement of the mounting tensions between the new Quebec and the old federal system. "[Trudeau's] political fate will likely be the political fate of Canada," historian Kenneth McNaught predicted soon after, though at the time few in English Canada would have thought so.[5]

Once in Ottawa, Trudeau quickly rose to positions of influence. The Liberal Party needed competent French Canadians in its highest councils, and there he was – highly intelligent and hard-working, with a deep knowledge of Quebec and well-reasoned, confident opinions on all issues Québécois. Trudeau was named parliamentary secretary to the prime minister on January 9, 1966. Pearson came to trust his counsel, and increasingly incorporated his views into his constitutional stance.[6]

The Quebec Liberals, who had overseen the Quiet Revolution under the leadership of Jean Lesage, lost the provincial election in June 1966 to the Union Nationale. The new premier, Daniel Johnson, had campaigned under the slogan of "Égalité ou indépendance" and was now using the threat of the latter to win from English Canada a new constitutional arrangement that would give Quebec a special status sufficient to satisfy nationalists and halt their drift towards separatism. Since Quebec nationalism was compatible with French president Charles de Gaulle's dream of an international Francophonie under the mother country's leadership, France had been supportive by helping Quebec establish an international diplomatic presence. Marcel Cadieux, Canada's undersecretary of state for external affairs, set up a committee to monitor Quebec's diplomatic manoeuvres. Allan Gotlieb from external affairs was a member, as were Marc Lalonde and Michael Pitfield, two of Pearson's advisors, while Trudeau chaired. Trudeau travelled to Africa in early 1967 to see if Canada's relations with francophone African states, many of which regarded France as their former imperial oppressor, could be leveraged to hinder Quebec's push for international recognition. He took to this kind of political intrigue like a duck to water.[7]

In February 1967, Canadian Press named Trudeau a "Liberal To Watch."[8] Yet he still had no significant national profile. He hadn't made any memorable English-language television appearances since being elected to Parliament, but in early 1967 that began to change.[9] The first exposure came from the CBC public affairs show *Twenty Million Questions*. Its March 16 segment opened with shots of Trudeau striding purposefully through the halls of the Parliament buildings. "Pierre Elliott Trudeau, professor, constitutional lawyer, journalist, and man about Montreal, has been a member of parliament just sixteen months," intoned the narrator, yet he was "already a power in the Liberal Party and the government." Viewers were told that Trudeau had a "restive mind" and had given a speech in Montreal the previous Sunday opposing special status for Quebec.[10]

This was all by way of introduction for an interview with the show's host, Charles Lynch. National affairs columnist for the Southam newspaper chain, Lynch was well-informed, tough-minded, right-wing, and populist. He peppered Trudeau with questions on substantive issues. One line of questioning was, ostensibly, about the welfare state, but after a bit of back and forth it turned out Lynch was probing to see if Trudeau was a socialist. Eventually Lynch just asked flat out. Unfazed, Trudeau said he was consistent in his ideas. He said he'd been called a socialist in reactionary 1950s Quebec, and that while he felt that a socialistic policy like nationalization was fitting in a certain time and place, he didn't think it appropriate for contemporary Canada. Well, did he believe in big government? Lynch asked, trying to pin him down from a different angle. Trudeau, cool as a cucumber, said that was simply a fact of modern life, and government would get still bigger, but this was not necessarily a marker of socialism.

The interview then turned to the constitutional issue. Lynch asked Trudeau about the "two nations" doctrine. Trudeau responded by problematizing the notion of nation, and when he was done had made two nations look doubly preposterous. Two official languages was a more concrete and practical policy goal, he suggested. He could legislate that. Lynch took him up on that by questioning Canadians' tolerance for bilingualism. Paraphrasing nineteenth-century French political philosopher Ernest Renan, Trudeau countered that a nation is a daily plebiscite, and that Canadians would accept bilingualism as a price worth paying to keep Canada intact.

The interview ended with sparring over Vietnam, the legitimacy of France's current interest in Quebec, and whether the monarchy should be abolished. Trudeau continued to be unflappable, lucid, and rational. His replies seemed to come from thoughtful consideration in the moment of the question at hand rather than from scripted lines. Though Lynch was no shrinking violet, Trudeau controlled the interview by refuting the premises of the questions, setting out his own vision of Canada, and referencing erudite authorities. While exhibiting a critical distance, he was nevertheless wholly engaged in the exchange. Indeed, he seemed to thrive on it. It was a remarkable onscreen performance for a relative newcomer to federal politics.

The Lynch interview set out Trudeau's policy positions. Next came the construction of image. Norman DePoe, the chief Ottawa correspondent for CBC TV, began interviewing Trudeau that winter for a profile on the CBC public affairs show *Newsmagazine*. A familiar face on television since CBC TV began broadcasting in 1952, DePoe had a bluff, gruff, everyman manner that belied his smarts and made him a trusted figure in Canadians' living rooms. Trudeau's elevation to cabinet as minister of justice on April 4 became a convenient pretext for the show when it aired in mid-April. Entitled "Minister on the Move," the segment led off with shots of Trudeau zipping around Ottawa in a sporty foreign convertible.[11] The action was set off with mod touches such as an upbeat, jazzy soundtrack and shots of the Peace Tower off-kilter at a rakish forty-five-degree angle. The mod mode of presentation signalled that this fresh face in cabinet was a trendy, "with it" kind of guy, someone to keep an eye on.

Then came footage of Trudeau executing flips off the diving board at the Château Laurier pool. Afterwards Trudeau answered DePoe's questions about his athletic interests while reclining in a deck chair, chin resting on the back of his hand and a towel around his neck, bathhouse style. In the next scene he materialized on Parliament Hill in business suit and trench coat, a transition that fused the worlds of stylish leisure and federal politics. The only thing missing from scenes of Trudeaumania to come was adoring female fans. But sex was in the air. Early on, DePoe made a point of mentioning, admiringly, Trudeau's success with beautiful women. Later he asked why Trudeau wasn't married. "I guess I just haven't found the right girl," he replied demurely.[12]

Footage not used for the *Newsmagazine* episode revealed that DePoe had become a big fan of Trudeau. In setting the scene for an interview with Trudeau in Montreal he gushed that "from the intellectual ferment of which Pierre Trudeau has been a leader since his student days, to the feverish general ferment of the swinging Montreal he helped to create, he comes equipped with formidable qualifications." He then called Trudeau an "astute political philosopher," listed his university degrees and his world travels, and suggested that despite all that he was a saucy guy who'd "thrown snowballs at the statue of Lenin in Moscow, and the one of Sir Wilfrid Laurier in Ottawa."[13]

"Minister on the Move" anticipated Trudeaumania with its action-packed, TV-friendly visuals and its emphasis on image and lifestyle. Its mod mode foregrounded Trudeau's consumer choices and active body and loaded them with political portent, signalling imminent change in federal politics. At its conclusion, DePoe asked Trudeau if he wanted to be prime minister. "Hell no," he replied. "I won't even be justice minister if you don't let me get back to work." Tellingly, however, Trudeau had taken a lot of time out of his schedule to film the show, as he would for many others.

Perhaps Claude Ryan, editor of *Le Devoir*, was watching, for a few days later he editorialized that "this country's English-language press ... has set out once again in search of a messiah from

Quebec."[14] Peter Newman, the young hotshot in the national press gallery, soon provided justification for Ryan's comment. Newman had solid and varied sources in cabinet, among party officials and MPs across partisan lines, and in the junior ranks of the public service, particularly among those who, like him, were intellectual and reform-minded. He had solidified his reputation with the 1963 bestseller *Renegade in Power*, a chronicle of Diefenbaker's fall from grace. In his column of April 25, 1967, he gave the new justice minister a rave review, extolling "the complete contrast he offers to the kind of florid, self-satisfied personages who have governed this country for most of the last 100 years" and approvingly anointing him "an agent of ferment" and a "radical."[15]

Newman's column appeared in twenty newspapers across the country, including dailies in all the big cities and the powerful *Toronto Daily Star*, which had a circulation of over 670,000. "What Newman says this week," one cabinet minister had observed, "becomes the conventional wisdom the next."[16] And so it was. Soon Douglas Fisher, one of the top half-dozen or so most influential press gallery scribes, and his co-columnist, Harry Crowe, featured Trudeau in their syndicated column.[17] The Canadian edition of *Time* carried an article on Trudeau by its parliamentary correspondent Richard Gwyn. As they started tracking this new, intriguing figure, the press got excited. Wouldn't it be something, they thought, if he could he rise from obscurity to become PM?[18] Could it possibly happen? It was an enticing prospect, and what a story it would make!

The fact that Trudeau was getting so much favourable press made this improbability seem possible. Marc Lalonde, a friend of Trudeau's who was an advisor to Pearson, believed Trudeau had a shot at the brass ring, and told him so. Lalonde also began meeting with a group of like-minded political operatives to explore the possibility. Gordon Gibson, then working as executive assistant to Arthur Laing, the minister of Indian affairs and northern development, was a recruit to the cause. A picture of Trudeau in the paper in a yoga pose wearing a turtleneck sweater had caught his attention, and after watching him operate on the Hill, Gibson concluded Trudeau had the right stuff.[19]

Appearances mattered. In the first week of July, an unexpected vote brought Trudeau into the House of Commons clad in a sports jacket, ascot, and sandals.[20] Diefenbaker was outraged, interpreting his casual dress as a breach of decorum that displayed contempt for Parliament. The incident made all the papers and cemented the Trudeau brand as a mod alternative to the outmoded style of Ottawa. With the House adjourning for a summer that would be dominated by Expo 67 and the ongoing centennial celebrations, Trudeau seemed more in step with the times than any other political figure on the Ottawa scene.

Trudeau's rising public profile was accompanied by growing influence behind the scenes. Gaullist support for Quebec's ambitions aggravated the federal government throughout early 1967. External affairs minister Paul Martin counselled a conciliatory response, but Trudeau and Marchand disagreed, successfully convincing Pearson to take a hard line.[21] After de Gaulle's "Vive le Québec libre" declaration on July 24, this split in cabinet became even more pronounced, especially since Martin's stance was seen to be influenced excessively by a desire to keep his Quebec supporters onside in anticipation of his candidacy for the Liberal leadership.

Lalonde's behind-the-scenes planning included careful management of Trudeau's public profile. He arranged for Trudeau to deliver the keynote address to the Canadian Bar Association, the professional group that was most plugged in to the federal political process as party operatives, candidates, and bagmen, at its annual meeting at the Château Frontenac in Quebec City on September 4, 1967. Meanwhile, his friend Gérard Pelletier was working with Éditions HMH of Montreal to publish a collection of Trudeau's political essays under the title *Le fédéralisme et la société canadienne-française*, which would appear that October. They also placed an excerpt from Trudeau's speech to the Canadian Bar Association in *Canadian Forum*, an influential left-leaning public affairs journal, that fall.

When he became minister of justice, Trudeau had decided that the constitutional file merited special attention. He reassigned responsibility for preparing studies for the constitutional conference slated for February 1968 from his departmental bureaucracy to a special task force of hand-picked experts that would report directly to him. The Canadian Bar Association speech was his first major public statement of how he would approach the issue. The de Gaulle affair had brought the simmering issues around Quebec and the constitution to a boil, and Trudeau coolly laid out his solution: a renewed federalism through a fairer Canada that would offer linguistic rights for French and English speakers across the land, along with patriation of the constitution accompanied by a charter of rights. It was all quite rational and rather dry until he held a press conference the next day. When journalists asked about the two nations approach, he dismissed it as an "intellectual hoax," thereby repudiating a wide spectrum of Quebec politicians that included both Premier Daniel Johnson and former Liberal premier Jean Lesage. This annoyed nationalist French Canadian reporters, who prodded him sharply. Trudeau got combative and upped the ante, calling special status "une connerie," a slang term suggesting it was the work of idiots.[22] Once again Trudeau had generated publicity that marked him as unconventional.

Trudeau was taking the Liberals in a different policy direction from the other leading parties. The New Democrats had supported two nations since their founding convention in 1961. At first the implications of this position were vague, but as the Quebec issue heated up in mid-decade, the party endorsed a redistribution of powers that would give Quebec special status within the Canadian federation. At its July 1967 national convention in Toronto, the NDP reiterated and strengthened this position, making it a policy on which it would run in the next election.[23] The leader of its Quebec wing, Robert Cliche, used Trudeau's opposition to special status to differentiate his party from the Liberals in Quebec.[24]

Early fall 1967 was dominated by the Progressive Conservative leadership convention, which ran September 6-9 in Toronto. In the lead-up to the convention, party policy discussions about Quebec and the constitution led to acceptance of the two nations principle. Although convention organizers hesitated to present it to delegates for approval for fear of a reactionary backlash from supporters of the outgoing leader's "One Canada" position, most of the leading leadership candidates supported the idea of two nations in their nomination speeches.[25] Whether this would lead the Conservatives to endorse special constitutional status for Quebec was unclear.

When the convention dumped Diefenbaker, electing Robert Stanfield in his stead, political commentators applauded them for changing with the times. Stanfield, the premier of Nova Scotia, was not tainted by association with the embarrassing Ottawa scene. In the wake of the leadership convention, the Tories rose to 43 percent in the opinion polls, up from their usual 30-35 percent range, and held there for the rest of the year. Had there been an election that fall in which Stanfield faced Pearson, odds were the Conservatives would have won a majority government.

In any case, Pearson's imminent departure was anticipated. His replacement as Liberal leader would also be prime minister, at least until the next election, and pundits were already speculating on the race. Paul Martin had been in the two previous leadership contests, and this would be his last chance. Mitchell Sharp, the finance minister, had substantial support, as did Paul Hellyer, the minister of defence. A young up-and-comer, Registrar General John Turner, was expected to run as the candidate of youth and change. All four had been planning to attend the Alberta Liberal Association convention in Edmonton on November 11-12 until Pearson called them off, telling them he wouldn't stand for an unofficial leadership race while he was still in power and there was government work to be done.[26]

That fall, dramatic new developments on the national unity front followed one another in rapid succession. The first was a poll conducted by the *Toronto Daily Star* and *Le Soleil* of Quebec City showing that 83.3 percent of the members of the Quebec legislature favoured some form of new constitutional arrangement. While slightly less than a third wanted some form of associate state-hood, a third favoured political independence.[27] Only a measly 2.6 percent defended the status quo. These results, published on October 7, were not directly representative of the Quebec elector-ate's sentiments, but were enough to send stabs of fear into feder-alist hearts.

Next came a dramatic conference of the provincial Liberal Party of Quebec, held at the Château Frontenac from October 13 to 15. René Lévesque, a popular and prominent cabinet minister in Jean Lesage's Liberal government before its recent defeat, had a resolu-tion favouring separatism on the agenda and was threatening to leave the party if it was rejected. To outflank Lévesque, Lesage and former provincial cabinet minister Eric Kierans won approval for a counterproposal calling for Quebec to have new powers over media, immigration, employment, social programs, economic and trade policy, and foreign relations.[28] It was more than had been de-manded to date by the Union Nationale government, but not enough for Lévesque. As predicted, he left the provincial Liberal Party to start a separatist party, Le Mouvement Souveraineté-Association. Separatism gained new respectability and a leader with the stature to unite its various splinter groups into a con-certed movement.

Trudeau's book of essays came out on October 16, 1967, the day after the Quebec Liberal convention. The *Globe and Mail* reported its impending release under the headline "Special Status Plans Lack Logic, Trudeau Says," and presented Trudeau's arguments that giving unique powers to Quebec would limit the French fact to the province and that it was illogical to have more power for Quebec and equal power for MPs from the province.[29] As the constitutional issue heated up that fall, it became clear that Pearson's position had stiffened along similar lines. The next week the prime minister gave a speech at a fundraising dinner of the Quebec wing of the Liberal Federation of Canada in Montreal that echoed Trudeau's arguments.[30]

The issue ramped up further when the Saint-Jean-Baptiste Society, with provincial funding, sponsored a meeting of the "Estates General" of French Canada in Montreal from November 24 to 26. Nationalists and separatists debated the merits of sovereignty-association versus outright separation. The meeting passed resolutions favouring the abolition of English as an official language and a workplace language in Quebec, phasing out English schools, nationalization of the media, annexation of Labrador and Baffin Island, and claiming for Quebec parts of Hudson Bay, James Bay, and the Atlantic continental shelf. Annexation of francophone New Brunswick, it was reported, was proposed but not passed.[31]

The Estates General was by no means the most extreme contemporary expression of Quebec nationalism. Since 1963 the Front de Libération du Québec had been targeting Montreal sites of anglophone capitalist power with time bombs. The blast damage was psychological as well as physical. Collective consciousness became haunted by the threat of violent extremists who were prepared to use any means to achieve Quebec independence. Their shadowy underground existence frustrated attempts to comprehend the extent of the threat they presented and made them all the scarier. Three bombs went off that fall, and doubtless there were more to come.

On November 27, the provincial premiers gathered in Toronto for the Confederation of Tomorrow conference, a conclave arranged by Ontario premier John Robarts to address the future of the federation. The federal government thought Robarts's initiative impinged on the federal prerogative and refused to send official representatives. Although Daniel Johnson presented his case, the other premiers were more concerned about the economy and considered ameliorating economic disparities between provinces more important than the constitution. When Johnson backed away from his call for an entirely new constitution and let it be known that he'd accept an amended and patriated British North America Act, most agreed to go along. Premier Ernest Manning of Alberta was the only premier to resist.

Meanwhile, French president Charles de Gaulle reentered the lists, holding a press conference to explain his July visit to Canada. He likened French Canadians to children who had been abandoned by their mother. France had been unavoidably distracted by matters close to home for a few centuries, but now it was time to atone for that oversight. He called for "the elevation of Quebec 'to the level of a sovereign state with mastery of its national existence.'"[32]

On December 5, the first volume of the final report of the Royal Commission on Bilingualism and Biculturalism was tabled in the House of Commons by Prime Minister Pearson. It confirmed the alarming declaration of its 1965 interim report that Canada was passing through the greatest crisis in its history. Pearson declared that the government "fully endorses the principle of linguistic and cultural equality that forms the core of this report."[33] He reminded Canadians that a federal-provincial conference on the constitution was scheduled for the following February to discuss official languages policy.

Given the way that national unity issues dominated the political news that fall, it was not surprising that the cover story of Maclean's that December was "The Day Quebec Quit Canada."[34] It was a sensationalistic title, but not outrageously so – the prospect of Quebec separating was suddenly very real. The crisis the bilingualism and biculturalism commission had warned about two years earlier was now front and centre in the Canadian political scene.

Yet Trudeau came to public prominence that December for an entirely different reason. Following Britain's lead, the Department of Justice had been working on legislation to reform Canada's divorce law as well as on an "omnibus" bill of wide-ranging Criminal Code changes that included, most controversially, provisions decriminalizing abortion and homosexuality. While national unity preoccupied the national media that fall, these legal reforms opened a second front for Trudeau. On the evening of November 22, CBC National News featured a one-minute news clip in which parliamentary reporters questioned Trudeau about the omnibus bill. He

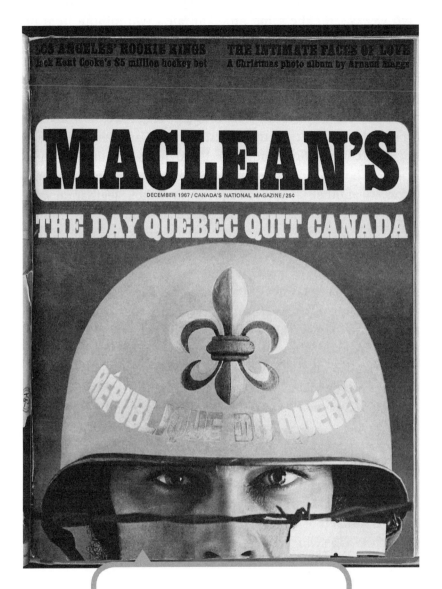

Front cover of *Maclean's* magazine in December 1967.

was composed and urbane, responding with precision and clarity. Two weeks later the same program ran a two-minute item on the same legislation in which he again performed with cool eloquence. Trudeau was becoming a familiar personality on the national scene, one who appeared in different roles in interweaving plot lines, making a favourable impression each time.

When Trudeau had become minister of justice, new divorce legislation was already in the works. Existing Canadian divorce law was a patchwork. Some but not all provinces had divorce legislation, with the grounds for divorce varying widely from one jurisdiction to another. Couples in a province without legislation were bound by the federal law, which recognized only adultery as grounds for divorce, an anachronistic embarrassment that was out of step with public attitudes and social reality. Frequently couples would arrange to have one of them caught in staged compromising circumstances in order to get out of their marriage. The new bill expanded the grounds for divorce to include perversions (bestiality and rape), physical and mental cruelty, and a broad, all-inclusive category, marriage breakdown. Since his appointment to cabinet the previous spring, Trudeau had mastered the file and fine-tuned the legislation. He presented Bill C-187 to the House of Commons on the evening of December 4 and won praise for his erudite explication of his brief.

Key elements of Trudeau's image were coalescing as his public profile rose. From the Quebec issue he had gained a reputation for substance. He was principled, analytical, articulate, and cool in the face of a national crisis. The divorce legislation associated him with the liberation ethos of the sixties. Publicity about his lifestyle portrayed him as a swinger in step with the times. When his ability to perform on television was added to the mix, all the requisites for celebrity were present.

Barbara Amiel, host of CBC TV's public affairs show *The Way It Is* on December 10, introduced Trudeau as "the young, eligible, rich, handsome, and bachelor minister of justice."[35] He was then interviewed about his divorce legislation by Peter Desbarats and

Starr Côté. As usual, Trudeau challenged the premises of questions and didn't let himself get backed into a corner. He also made a point of flirting with Ms. Côté. In both cases it was an issue of power, and he wanted to be in control. The interview ended up being more about Trudeau than it was about the bill. He got a lot of air time given the amount of coverage of the ostensible subject; when he digressed, the footage didn't end up on the floor. Evidently the producer thought he was good TV no matter what the pretext.

At one point Trudeau told the interviewers that he thought he could have made a point more succinctly and asked if they wanted to redo the segment. They agreed, but aired both the exchange and the promised outtake. Mediation anxiety induced them to reveal how the sausages were made. Such self-consciousness about the artificiality of media representations was endemic at the time.[36] Subsequent television coverage of Trudeau would feature shots of him being made up for the cameras, reporters taking notes as he spoke, and reel-to-reel tape machines spinning their tales.

Trudeau's arrival in the limelight raised a question mark, underlined with an "N.B.," for most members of the press gallery. They had the feeling that they should know more about him. He retained some of his earlier outsider and radical associations, manifested in part by talk about his past union work, his anti-Duplessis politics, and his erstwhile affiliation with the Co-operative Commonwealth Federation. Anglophone scribes felt guilty that they weren't familiar with him because he had for so long operated behind the opaque cultural screen that separated them from Quebec. This background heightened their perception of him as an emergent figure. When they did interview him, they learned about his political philosophy and positions on issues, but Trudeau had a detached, rational approach that left them feeling that they still didn't really know him. They were used to politicians trying to use them to raise their profiles or get their message out. With Trudeau, that dynamic was reversed, which whetted their professional appetites. "Almost alone among Canadian politicians, Trudeau does not truckle to us in any way," wrote Blair Fraser, "and most of us like him for it."[37]

Meanwhile Trudeau's backers continued to monitor developments and plan. They rented office space in Ottawa for a Trudeau leadership headquarters – quarters, appropriately enough, newly vacated by the Confederation Train organization. Lalonde convinced Pearson that Trudeau, who as minister of justice was responsible for the constitutional file, should visit each of the premiers in the provincial capitals in the weeks leading up to the February constitutional conference. Ostensibly the reason was to conduct preliminary talks to facilitate the work of the conference. It would not hurt, however, to give Trudeau exposure around the country should he decide to run for Pearson's job.

One issue standing in the way of a Trudeau candidacy was the gap between his constitutional position and the two nations policy stance recently adopted by the Quebec branch of the federal Liberal Party. This disagreement was exacerbated by the fact that many Quebec members of caucus deemed Trudeau to be an aloof and arrogant ivory tower intellectual. A meeting between Trudeau and Quebec MPs about constitutional policy was arranged for late December to see if they could find common ground. When it took place, Trudeau impressed them as approachable, charming, and, more importantly, convincing. By that point, however, they were also factoring in the probability of winning power under his leadership, given his rising profile.[38] They were also being subjected to intense pressure from power brokers in the Quebec wing to swing into line behind a French Canadian candidate.

Gérard Pelletier, who was abroad on external affairs business in early December, returned to discover that the book of Trudeau's essays, which had moved slowly when first published in October, had now sold out its print run of three thousand copies. The buzz about Trudeau had been sufficient to move at least a couple of thousand of his books in less than a month to the restricted market of those who could read French. A paperback edition was now in the works, and obviously an English edition was called for. Toronto historian Ramsay Cook, who had known and admired Trudeau for years, was a neighbour of John Gray, president of Macmillan

Canada, and when Cook pitched him on the idea Gray quickly agreed to publish it. Since "Trudeau was still largely unknown for anything but his often casual dress and his legal reforms," Cook wanted someone high-profile to write the introduction.[39] He recruited his colleague John Saywell, who, as the regular host of the CBC public affairs show *The Way It Is*, was also a media personality. The book would come out in the new year under the title *Federalism and the French Canadians*.

Pearson announced his resignation on December 14.[40] Although a number of English Canadian members of cabinet were expected to run for his job, the Liberals had a tradition of alternating French and English leaders, so the question of a French Canadian candidate quickly arose. Some Liberals were second-guessing the tradition, seeing it as something that emphasized Canada's sectionalism. Others thought that, in the midst of constitutional controversy, an English Canadian would be better positioned to negotiate with Quebec.[41] According to this logic, an English Canadian prime minister could be objective in dealing with Quebec, whereas a French Canadian prime minister would be vulnerable to accusations of favouritism. Perhaps he would bend over backwards to contradict such a perception – if so, that too would compromise his objectivity. In any event, it would be easier for an English Canadian leader to sell a new deal for Quebec to the rest of the country. Still others, especially Quebec Liberal MPs, worried that if a French Canadian ran and ran badly, it would be a snub to French Canada, and there would be a backlash.

A more traditional school of thought maintained that a French Canadian candidate was essential if the federal case was to get a fair hearing from Quebeckers. The Tory convention had not played well in Quebec, it argued, because there had been no candidate from the province in the running. Who, then, would be the French Canadian candidate? Paul Martin had French Canadian ancestry but was not Québécois. Jean Marchand, Pearson's Quebec lieutenant, was the obvious choice. Reporters asked Trudeau his intentions. "There's no question of it," he declared emphatically.[42] Pearson summoned Trudeau and Marchand to 24 Sussex and told them that one of them had to run. He argued, "This is a tradition of the Liberal Party – and he may or may not win. But he must be a good candidate and get a lot of votes, and we must show that although the Tories can't, we can always come up with the alternative from Quebec."[43]

At this point it was possible for otherwise astute observers of the federal scene to not see a Trudeau candidacy coming. Blair Fraser, who wrote on national politics for *Maclean's* magazine, was the éminence grise of the national press gallery. He was wise and well-informed, with highly placed sources in the public service and the Liberal cabinet. His piece on the leadership race in the December 1967 issue of *Maclean's* listed the regular suspects but argued that to counter Stanfield, "the Liberals ... require a fresh face, instead of those tired old images on today's Treasury benches." Instead of thinking of Trudeau, whom he'd known since the 1950s, he mentioned Eric Kierans as a possibility because he was bilingual, progressive, and antiseparatist.[44] *La Presse* was running features on Kierans at the time and showing no awareness that Trudeau could be a contender.[45] When Dalton Camp gave odds on the Liberal leadership contenders in the *Star Weekly* magazine in early January, he at least included Trudeau, but had him a long shot at 75-1, noting that as a "socialist and political dilettante" he was "just too much for the square majority of the Liberal party."[46] The only publication to identify Trudeau as a possible Liberal leader at this early stage was Ottawa's *Le Droit*, which ran an editorial extolling his potential on December 21.[47]

That very day Trudeau was back in the headlines. He introduced into the House Bill C-195, the omnibus bill of Criminal Code reforms that proposed, among other measures, to remove legal sanctions against homosexuality and loosen restrictions on abortion. Afterwards, in the hall of the House of Commons, Trudeau spoke with reporters about the bill. Surrounded by a half-dozen microphones, he was calm and frank. The TV lights accentuated his high cheekbones, and his facial features worked together eloquently as he answered reporters' questions. "It's bringing the laws of the land up to contemporary society," he told the assembled scribes. His eyes narrowed, and he looked down for a moment or two while he was thinking and formulating his answer, but as he delivered the final lines they fixed on the questioner and drilled into him.

> Take this thing on homosexuality. I think the view we take here is that there's no place for the state in the bedrooms of the nation, and I think that, you know, what's done in private between consenting adults doesn't concern the Criminal Code. When it becomes public it's a different matter.[48]

The "state in the bedrooms" line resonated: in the staid forum of the parliament buildings a politician was talking about liberating pleasure, and doing so in a quotable sound bite.[49] Reporters ran with it, and soon it was being repeated nationwide. No matter that Trudeau had cribbed the phrase from a *Globe and Mail* editorial from the previous week: he was the one who uttered it on TV with an air of cerebral detachment.[50]

That afternoon the House adjourned until January 22. But Trudeau's parting remark continued to echo around the press gallery. It got a lot of media play, first on the evening news, then in editorials that dissected it in search of meaning, and then in an afterlife of reruns on public affairs shows. Trudeau had been discovered. He was now identified by the press as a leadership candidate even though he had given no indication of interest in the job. A couple of days after Parliament adjourned, the *Toronto Daily Star*, a reliably Liberal paper, reported that "people are saying" that Trudeau should be the next PM. The "people" in question were, of course, mostly media and political insiders. But then again, they were people too.

In reflecting upon the phenomenon a few months later, Norman DePoe explained the attraction Trudeau held for journalists. Covering federal politics was a grind. Reporters easily fell into the trap of thinking of themselves as experts who could judge what was best for the country. They grew tired of the same old faces long before the public did. At the same time, they were under constant pressure for "news, which is the plural of 'new.'" When someone new and different like Trudeau appeared, DePoe explained, "he's greeted with heartfelt hosannas" not least because "he's copy – or great TV." The scribes wanted to believe that "this man has The Answers."[51] Add to that the herd-like quality of the press gallery, and you had all the ingredients for a stampede.

The opinions of the parliamentary press gallery were widely read and assimilated by colleagues in other locations, circulating throughout the media complex. Journalists in the electronic media followed what the leading national affairs columnists had to say. Yet what the columnists had to say about candidates' viability was in turn influenced by how they came across on TV. The profile Trudeau was gaining on television, heightened by his deft handling of the medium, made him look like a winner to those who worked in print.[52] "TV is replacing print and personal contact as a way of 'knowing' our leaders," explained a CBC TV producer.[53] As the different media began to feed each other positive images of Trudeau, each was as impressed by the impression he made on the other as it was by the man himself.

With Trudeau's name reverberating throughout the media complex, the buzz was not lost on the political establishment. "Your really shrewd and ambitious pol," said a really shrewd and ambitious pol, "reads at least six to eight newspapers a day. He'll probably look at all three Toronto papers, three or four of the dailies published in Ottawa and Montreal, plus his hometown paper and his province's voice."[54] Those who weren't that assiduous had clipping services. The opinion leaders had "set off a chain reaction."[55]

Instead of staying around and milking the situation, Trudeau flew to Tahiti for the Christmas break. It was a brilliant stroke that confirmed his playboy image and signalled indifference to power. In his absence support coalesced. On Parliament Hill, a clutch of young executive assistants to cabinet ministers, wowed by Trudeau, gravitated to his as yet unofficial organization. Prominent figures in television such as producer Roy Faibish and host Patrick Watson were enthusiastic. Reform-minded MPs, including Toronto's Donald Macdonald, approached Marc Lalonde about the justice minister's availability. Lalonde was also in touch with Ramsay Cook, who, along with William Kilbourn, another Toronto-based historian, led pro-Trudeau opinion among a widening circle of academics. At the urging of Toronto artist Mashel Teitelbaum and his wife Edith Teitelbaum, they helped circulate a petition advocating a Trudeau candidacy. Over the holidays it was signed by more than six hundred writers, artists, academics, and journalists across the country.[56] For modern-minded progressives at the centre of the national conversation, Trudeau was the answer to the questions then confronting Canada.

By the end of 1967, then, Pierre Trudeau had suddenly emerged centre stage on the Canadian political scene. He was a leading candidate for the Liberal leadership without having declared his interest in the job. More importantly, he was the favoured candidate of the progressive nationalists in the media, the only one they believed could fulfill all their hopes for the nation. They had found their man. The cause was just. It was now just a simple matter of getting him elected. As *Time* put it, "Trudeau's admirers had barely to strain their wishful imaginations to visualize a script propelling him into the prime ministry."[57]

To that end, it helped that the structure of events in the immediate future was predictable. There would be a leadership campaign in which candidates would criss-cross the country, courting delegates, culminating in early April with the spectacle of a convention featuring the nail-biting drama of a winner-take-all contest on the national stage.[58] "It was not only Trudeau's qualities that made him irresistible, it was his situation," one observer noted. "TV is usually without dramatic form ... There is no beginning, no middle and, most tedious of all, no end. Here was a real-life drama with all three plus a gimmick: the audience was invited to write its own ending."[59]

Bashfulness, or, as Richard Gwyn put it, "a delicious matinée idol bit of teasing"?

5

Coy Wonder
How to Win a Leadership Race without Even Running

What we are witnessing is an attempt by our self-styled
"progressives" to create a Trudeau psychosis that
would irresistibly carry the justice minister to victory.

LUBOR ZINK, *Toronto Telegram* **columnist**

WHILE TRUDEAU WAS in Tahiti, flirting on the beach with a teenager named Margaret, his allies began to worry that, not realizing what was transpiring at home, he would decide not to run. They sent him a telegram, begging him not to speak to the press immediately upon his return. The day after he got back, Trudeau met with Gérard Pelletier and Jean Marchand for dinner. They agreed that there should be a French Canadian candidate for the Liberal leadership, and Marchand said that since he wasn't running, it would have to be Trudeau. The decision was obvious – Trudeau was suddenly the flavour of the month and had a better chance of winning. Trudeau acted surprised and reluctant. It was a part he had to play in order to be a good friend.[1] Moreover, delaying was to his political advantage. The media's continuing excitement about him was beginning to infect the general public in the early months of 1968. "By now the TV drama featuring Pierre Elliott Trudeau was incontestably the nation's number-one show," television producer Richard Nielsen recalled later that year.[2]

According to the law of supply and demand, Trudeau increased his desirability by playing hard to get. He would continue this game until mid-February, creating drama that ensured he got more publicity than any of the declared candidates. Meanwhile, Trudeau could benefit from national exposure on the constitutional file, which he would have had to forfeit had he declared himself a candidate.

Lester Pearson had to be careful not to be seen to play favourites by giving any of the declared candidates any advantage, but so far he was under no such constraint with his justice minister. While the declared candidates were warned to mind the shop and not be out campaigning while there was government business to be done, Trudeau would generate headlines by holding preliminary talks with the premiers in the weeks leading up to the opening of the federal-provincial constitutional conference on February 5.[3]

In the second week of January 1968, the candidacy announcements came in rapid succession: Eric Kierans, the former Quebec Liberal cabinet minister, stepped forward on January 9. John Turner followed on January 10, a week after he had officially become minister of the new Department of Consumer and Corporate Affairs. Paul Hellyer, minister of transport, threw his hat in the ring on January 11, and Allan MacEachen, minister of national health and welfare, announced on January 12. When Trudeau flew in from Tahiti that day, he told reporters that he wasn't going to give the leadership any thought until after the constitutional conference in mid-February. Nevertheless, he was Pierre Berton's choice for Liberal leader:

> Trudeau is the guy who really excites me; Trudeau represents a new look at politics in this country; he is the swinging young man I think the country needs. What we need is a guy with ideas so fresh and so different, that he is going to be able to view the country from a different point of view.[4]

A week later, on Friday, January 19, three more candidates joined the race: External Affairs Minister Paul Martin, Finance Minister Mitchell Sharp, and Agriculture Minister Joe Greene.

On January 18, Trudeau left for the western leg of his tour of the provincial capitals; the following week he went east. For most Canadians he had been until then just some new guy in far-off Ottawa with his name in the paper or his face on the evening news. Now he materialized closer by, becoming more real.

Hardly a day [went] by without front-page pictures of him greeting one premier or saying goodbye to another. And in the evening, on television there was always the wintry figure of the Minister of Justice, striding purposefully through the snow from a steaming jet in frigid January weather, bundled in his father's old coonskin fur or wearing his own ankle-length leather greatcoat, reminiscent of newsreels, old Mercedes-Benzes, and déclassé Wehrmacht generals.[5]

Scenes such as these played well on television. Trudeau's awareness of the performative aspect of his mission inspired a little practical joke he played during the tour. Carl Goldenberg, a leading constitutional lawyer, accompanied him as an advisor, and when they landed at a provincial capital Trudeau would walk behind him, carrying the bags, so that Goldenberg would be greeted as the minister of justice.[6] As his national profile rose, the gag soon stopped working.

Media coverage focused on what the premiers thought of Trudeau as much as what they thought of the constitution. In Victoria, W.A.C. Bennett said they had "very friendly discussions" and that "if he ever decides to move to British Columbia, there's a place for him in my cabinet. He's a great Canadian." At the opposite end of the country, Newfoundland premier Joey Smallwood, not to be outdone, called Trudeau "the perfect Canadian" and "the most brilliant man in the House of Commons of the 260-odd. He is the one great political intellectual in Canada." Smallwood subsequently told anyone who would listen that "the odds are reasonably good that that man will be the next Prime Minister of Canada."[7]

While Trudeau was criss-crossing the country, binding it together, the United States seemed to be falling apart, making Canadians feel comparatively good about themselves. That month the Tet offensive exploded the American public's faith that the Vietnam War could be won. The youth of the nation mobilized in support of Senator Eugene McCarthy's antiwar campaign to defeat incumbent president Lyndon Johnson for the Democratic presidential nomination. Suddenly it was a political season for alternative candidates.

Canadians didn't have to look far to find theirs. The way forward for a Trudeau candidacy was not without obstructions, however. There was still support in the Liberal party for a two nations, special status policy. Trudeau had met with Liberal MPs from Quebec to discuss the issue in December, but the Quebec wing of the federal Liberal Party was still formally on record as favouring a two nations stance. How was that position to be squared with Trudeau's? Lalonde arranged for Trudeau to address a meeting of Quebec Liberal MPs held in Montreal's Hotel Bonaventure in late January. Anticipation ran high as he took to the podium. He began with a joke at the expense of mother France. Constitutions aren't sacrosanct, he pointed out – France had gone through seventeen of them since the revolution. No wonder, he continued, that the French feel so well qualified to advise others on them. This drew a huge laugh.[8]

Then he got serious. Trudeau admitted that outside of Quebec the rights for the French language had been eroded since the time of Confederation. There were unfortunate historical reasons for why this had happened, but the necessity of the moment wasn't to rue the past, but to seize the future. On the one hand, there was special status, handmaiden to separatism, both of which would empower provincial elites "so they can arrive at the Château Frontenac in a large car," he sneered (federalists in sports cars, presumably, were OK). Don't confuse the rights of French Canadians with the desires of a provincial government to build its own little empire, he warned. The choice as he saw it was

> more rights for French-Canadians or more power for the province of Quebec ... Personally, I believe that it is not a particular status in Confederation for the government of Quebec but an equal status for all French-speaking Canadians in all of Canada that will bring enduring unity to our country.[9]

The way forward was to implement the bilingualism and biculturalism commission's recommendations on official languages.

Trudeau sparkled in the question period that followed. A seasoned commentator observed that for "the first time in eight years
... French-Canadian federalists were hearing words that were not
defensive, not apologetic, but aggressively confident."[10] Happy to
have a spirited defence of federalism laid out by a native son who
looked like a winner, the delegates' earlier constitutional position
was quickly forgotten. They cheered Trudeau, singing "Il a gagné
ses épaulettes," and scrapped the two nations policy in favour of
an unrepentant federalism. "Good crowd, good policy discussions
and a good launching pad was built for Trudeau if he decides to
run," Senator Richard Stanbury confided to his diary.[11] "There was
no question in the minds of anyone present that they had been witness to some kind of political phenomenon," wrote a journalist
who'd attended, "no one knew for sure just what; but something
big had happened."[12]

It was indeed remarkable that one speech could change everyone's minds and reverse a high-profile policy. In *Le Devoir*, Claude
Ryan marvelled at the "consecration to a dominant place of Mr.
Trudeau's thinking in the Quebec section of the Liberal Federation
of Canada" and wondered how a man formerly seen as distant and
cold was now being hailed as charismatic and eloquent.[13] No doubt
there had been much orchestration and arm-twisting behind the
scenes. When Walter Gordon, now president of the Privy Council,
worried that Trudeau was unpopular in Quebec, Marchand reputedly replied, "I can fix that. Give me three weeks. If I say he should
be popular in Quebec, you wait. He will be."[14] Complaints about
Marchand's heavy whip hand would emerge from Quebec in the
months to come.

Wherever Trudeau went now he was followed by a retinue of
photographers and television cameras. In *Time* he was described
as "last week's conversational favorite for the leadership."[15] "From
now on," concluded Val Sears in the *Toronto Daily Star*, "the swinger

is the man to beat if he runs and the man to court if he doesn't."[16]
A late-January poll in the Toronto suburb of Scarborough put
Trudeau ahead in the leadership race even though he still wasn't a
candidate.

The next event on the political agenda was the federal-provincial
constitutional conference. The media marketed it as a dramatic
showdown in the national unity crisis. In the lead-up to the conference, CTV aired a public affairs special entitled *One Canada! Two
Nations?* that opened with a map of Canada from which Quebec had
been removed, leaving a gaping hole. The show went on to personify
the issue through the figures of Trudeau and René Lévesque. For a
few minutes it followed Lévesque as he barnstormed the lower St.
Lawrence and Lac St. Jean regions, passionately pitching his fledg-
ling Mouvement Souveraineté-Association. Then it switched to
Trudeau, the soul of reason. There was nothing wrong with debating the constitution, he said: it was a healthy democratic exercise.

> The destructive tensions are those that divide people according to
> religion or according to race or to ethnic origin or colour ... Surely
> we are evolved enough now and civilized enough now to set these
> things above the government to protect them in the constitution
> and then tackle the problem of government from a functional point
> of view – from a technical point of view. This is what we are trying
> to do with the federal-provincial conference, which will try to en-
> trench certain rights, and put them above government, so they will
> not be endangered, and then we can move on to the creative things.

He ended this soliloquy with a winning little smile, as if to say
"don't you agree?" While the pretext of the show was to compare
Lévesque and Trudeau, the latter ended up with most of the air
time and the final word.[17]

Trudeau was also interviewed at length by Ron Collister and
Norman DePoe on CBC's *Newsmagazine*. Predictably, he rejected the
two nations approach.

I don't think it has much to do with the fact that they were founding or not founding races, I think it's just a fact of politics that ¹/₃ of
the people speak French and the other ²/₃ more-or-less speak
English as their mother language and we have to find a constitutional solution to it.

Therefore I think the accommodation we are looking for is not in
the entrenchment of two nations as it were, one of them to be
represented by the Quebec Government and the other by the other
Governments, this is a conception we completely repudiate. We
feel that there are two languages in Canada that they should be entrenched in the Constitution that they should be considered as the
official vehicles of communication, that's all, I mean we don't think
that this leads on to the existence of two nations and we certainly
deny any one Government in Canada any one Provincial Government or any Federal Government for that matter, the right to say
that it speaks for one nation, this is not so ...

I think the essential thing is to ensure that French speaking Canadians are not locked into the Province of Quebec and that therefore no one Provincial Government can say I speak for the French
and you other governments speak for the English. And I think that
after we've solved this language problem and if we manage to make
sure through Constitutional amendment or through Provincial act
and Federal act, if we could ensure that the rights of the French language outside of Quebec are spread across the Country then I think
the so called crisis is finished.[18]

Trudeau said he was willing to discuss redistribution of powers on
the basis of which jurisdiction could do the job better, but any proposal involving asymmetrical federalism was, for him, a nonstarter.
He had defined the issue, and the sooner it was resolved the better.
"It may be that we need a showdown," he declared.[19]

The conference opened in the Confederation Room of the West
Block in Ottawa on Monday, February 5. Broadcast by the CBC on
national television, it would be a three-day reality-TV extravaganza
featuring rising star Pierre Trudeau. The prime minister opened the

proceedings with a solemn declaration about the significance of the task ahead and how posterity would judge their work, and asked for the provinces' agreement to extend French-language rights outside Quebec. As television drama, the conference didn't live up to the hype. The proceedings were boring. The first ministers spoke in elliptical phrases, often flogging their own tired hobby horses rather than advancing the main issues on the table. Trying to make sense of it all would have been impossible for the vast majority of Canadians, if they had been able to stay awake.

Those who caught just a few minutes of the action or saw highlights on the news may not have understood the subtleties of the points being debated, but if they went by visual impressions alone, Trudeau stood out. The conference chamber was full of white men in dark suits. Many of them were smoking. He was not. Most of them had grey hair. His was brown. Many of them had moustaches. He was clean-shaven. Practically all of them were fleshy, with jowls, a grey pallor, and suits tented over sagging bellies. Trudeau was lean, taut, and tanned, an action hero in an old folks' home.[20]

The colour commentary zeroed in on the conflict between Daniel Johnson and Pierre Trudeau. It erupted on Tuesday when Premier Johnson demanded constitutional reform to recognize Quebec's special status as the homeland of French Canadians. "If there is a lesson to be learned from our history, it is that French Canadians in Quebec cannot be expected to entrust direction of their social and cultural life to a government in which their representatives are in a minority," he argued. Trudeau, sitting on the right hand of the prime minister, challenged Johnson's logic. What kind of "extended jurisdiction" was Johnson contemplating? If Quebec were to have special powers, unlike those of other provinces, what would happen to the role of Quebec MPs in Ottawa? Presumably they shouldn't be able to have an equal say in Canadian policy if their province was exempt from those policies. And if their role were circumscribed, would that not propel Quebec down a slippery slope to separation?

This was such a bald-faced repudiation of Johnson's position that Pearson felt obliged to intercede with a call for a coffee break,

At the federal-provincial constitutional conference, February 5-7, 1968, Trudeau looks like he's telling Prime Minister Lester Pearson what to do while Jean Marchand (second from right) looks on. On the far right is Quebec premier Daniel Johnson.

the diplomat's version of a time out. But the dispute continued to unfold in front of the TV cameras in the corridors outside. "If Mr. Trudeau's policies are followed, it will mean the end of Canada," Johnson declared. "If Mr. Johnson's policies are followed, it will mean the end of federalism," Trudeau retorted.[21]

Despite, or perhaps because of, this dust-up, the federal government considered the conference a success. The provinces weren't enthusiastic about a charter of rights, but they agreed in principle to official bilingualism. They would continue to look at the charter and redistribution of powers, striking subcommittees to do so. Depending on how those talks went, substantial constitutional change of some sort in response to Quebec's demands was still possible. But the immediate concrete results of the conference pointed down the path for fulfilling French Canadian rights recommended by Trudeau. Those initially attracted to Trudeau by his opposition to special status were pleased to see that in the full glare of the public spotlight he had stuck to his principles. He had again advanced the federal position unapologetically and there was hope that it might yet carry the day. He had passed a high-profile stress test with flying colours.

The media were pleased – the much-hyped summit had paid off. They sensed a new mood in the country, a willingness to sacrifice in the interest of national unity. The press response to the conference displayed less regionalism than usual, and the charter proposal met with widespread media approval.[22] This general response prevailed among Quebec newspaper editorialists as well. Whereas most had been pessimistic about the conference at its outset, they were encouraged by the other provinces' willingness to accept official bilingualism. This was true even for advocates of special status, although they still held out hope for a redistribution of powers downstream.[23]

Historian Frank Underhill, an inveterate commentator on Canadian political affairs, weighed in with a longer-term view. He accused political and media elites of concocting mass-media spectacles to engage a distracted public. In the recent conference, he wrote, "not an idea was expressed which wasn't drearily familiar to anyone who has been following public affairs; and not a prime minister or premier committed himself to anything to which he hadn't been committed for years, or from which he couldn't withdraw quietly."[24] Evidently Underhill was not comfortable with the modern, mass-mediated public sphere. Political actors gained credibility from being seen by the public as characters in a drama wrestling with formidable obstacles yet fighting their way through to a happy ending. Television, Peter Newman mused, might save Confederation because "no politician can afford to be the villain of the piece before a national audience."[25]

Trudeau continued to sparkle under the television lights throughout the bleak midwinter. He was the subject of an hour-long interview on CTV's *The Pierre Berton Show* and shorter segments on CTV's W5 and CBC TV's *The Way It Is* and *The Public Eye*. "Mr. Trudeau himself is now the beneficiary of a select opinion represented by television and its allies," observed Maurice Western of the *Winnipeg Free Press*. "Our screen personalities had been referring to the minister of justice as the 'acknowledged' front-runner. Who had done the acknowledging they did not explain."[26]

Big city newspapers were equally kind to Trudeau. A Laval University study of the coverage accorded nine Liberal leadership candidates between January 1 and March 20 found that sixteen leading newspapers across the country gave Trudeau 26 percent of the space they devoted to the leadership campaign.[27] This percentage was skewed somewhat by the powerhouse *Toronto Star*, which started pushing Trudeau early and never gave up. On the other hand, some small and mid-sized newspapers tried to ignore the Trudeau candidacy. Their motives, which can only be guessed at, were no doubt mixed. A few were traditionally Progressive Conservative; others perhaps resisted because they were socially conservative or didn't want to alienate conservative readers. Ultimately, however, they were outflanked by the power of the national media. When Trudeau came to town, there would be a fuss, which was news, which they had to cover. The way national political reporters covered Trudeau was also significant. Whereas they would grill most candidates skeptically, they tended to accept Trudeau's answers to their questions uncritically.

From his right-wing perch at the *Toronto Telegram*, columnist Lubor Zink observed these developments and glowered. He thought Trudeau had suspect political views and couldn't believe the herd mentality at work in the media. Yet he conceded that Trudeau's boosters were effective:

> Since these [progressive] elements in our society, though numeric-ally quite small, are very articulate and command ... important pos-itions in the information media, their voice sounds from coast to coast as the consensus of an already crystallized public opinion ... The Trudeau build-up has already reached the stage where every journalist who lives in holy fear of being branded a "reactionary" ... would sooner swallow his typewriter or microphone than write or say anything that could be regarded as disagreement with the tone-setting line.
>
> They are all jumping on the Trudeau bandwagon ... for two obvious reasons. One is that Mr. Trudeau, as a former "socialist" aca-demic, is the only member of their fraternity who could conceivably capture the leadership of the ruling political party right now; the other reason is that in their theorizing about Canada's future as a model welfare and "neutralist" state, the leftists are genuinely convinced that Trudeau is the best available man for the leadership of the country at this critical juncture in our history.[28]

Zink may have had his own colleagues in mind. Hoping not to lose a planned interview with Trudeau, the *Telegram* editorialized that "Trudeau is rapidly emerging as the most exciting, lucid and perhaps fearless of the candidates," edited out some of Zink's more incendiary claims, and printed an editorial alongside his column disassociating the paper from his views.[29]

The response to Trudeau in the Quebec media was different from elsewhere in Canada because of the separate nationalist project under way there, led by similar elements: intellectuals, journalists, artists, and other middle-class cultural producers. Over the course of the decade most of the Quebec political and intellectual elite had convinced themselves that some sort of change in the province's relationship with the federal government was necessary and well-nigh inevitable. Trudeau was already a known quantity in Quebec, so they were not dazzled by his sudden appearance on the scene as the anglophone media had been. On the contrary, they had never thought of him as a potential prime minister, and were consequently slower to register the emergence of his candidacy.

Once the Trudeau boom got going in English Canada, however, Quebec opinion leaders had to figure out how to respond. For those heavily invested in making their province a nation-state for French Canadians through special status or separation, it was simple – Trudeau was a traitor. They had thought he had gone to Ottawa as a representative of Quebec's interests, and now his rejection of the two nations consensus had reversed in one fell swoop all their recently hard-won gains. His staunch defence of federalism was bad enough, but the way he characterized them was worse. They didn't like being portrayed as a manipulative, self-serving elite that used nationalism to exploit French Canadians at the expense of progress towards true democracy and full realization of their rights. They liked being denigrated as perpetrators of a "connerie" even less. Obviously anyone who thought like Trudeau wasn't a real French Canadian, and they branded him an anglicized francophone who pretended to be Québécois but had political opinions that betrayed he really wasn't one. Many newspapers printed his name as "Elliott-Trudeau" to suggest that he was an anglo in disguise.

The nationalist journal L'Action Nationale ran a variety of articles highly critical of Trudeau. Radio-Canada, known as a nationalist hotbed with many separatist sympathizers, was accused of misrepresenting Trudeau as more hard-line on the constitution than he actually was, thus implying that he was an enemy of Quebec.[30] Trudeau's denial of the legitimacy of Quebec nationalism seemed

PIERRE ELLIOTT TRUDEAU

Un homme qui a de l'étoffe

This February 28, 1968, cartoon by *Le Devoir* editorial cartoonist "Berthio" questions Trudeau's French Canadian identity by turning his well-known penchant for fashionable dress against him. The "man cut from the right cloth," as the caption puts it, opens his jacket to reveal his suit is "Made in England."

so preposterous that editorialists often responded to it with sarcasm. In Quebec City's *L'Action*, Laurent Laplante, tongue firmly in cheek, wrote that "at last we'll be able to relax and stop wasting our energies on the struggle against assimilation." Lucien Langlois took a similar line in *Montréal-Matin*, making fun of Trudeau's rationalist conceits.[31]

Trudeau was fortunate that one of the most respected French Canadian advocates of the two nations view, André Laurendeau, was sidelined from the public sphere while serving as one of the co-commissioners of the Royal Commission on Bilingualism and Biculturalism. A leading French Canadian thinker on national unity issues and former editor of the influential *Le Devoir*, Laurendeau had been an ally of Trudeau in opposing Duplessis in the 1950s. In the wake of the Quiet Revolution, however, they had found themselves on divergent paths. Whereas Trudeau rejected nationalism, seeing it as a cause of French Canadian backwardness, Laurendeau believed that a progressive nationalism would help Quebec become a social democracy in which French Canadian rights could be fully realized. He also believed that constitutional change was necessary if French Canada was to be accommodated within Canada. Laurendeau was not able to speak out publicly, given his official duties, and instead was pushing the commission to recommend constitutional reforms even as the federal Liberals were stiffening into a Trudeauvian position on the issue.[32]

With Laurendeau out of the picture, the current editor of *Le Devoir*, Claude Ryan, was the leading advocate for two nations. He professed surprise that suddenly Trudeau had become such a sensation in English Canada. A few months earlier it had seemed that all federal parties might adopt a two nations policy and in time come around to accepting that special status for Quebec followed. Then suddenly the upstart Trudeau had appeared to jeopardize everything. Ryan wrote editorial after editorial refuting Trudeau's constitutional views and questioning English Canadians' motives for supporting him. He reiterated his comment from the previous year that Trudeau's rise was the latest instance of an age-old syndrome in which English Canada sought a "messiah" from Quebec who could deliver the country from bothersome national unity issues.[33] Ryan nevertheless prided himself in running a liberal journal of opinion and opened Le Devoir's pages to pieces by Trudeau supporters.

Other major Quebec dailies were, with occasional ambivalence, favourably disposed towards Trudeau. Montreal's La Presse was at first focused on Eric Kierans's candidacy, and its early articles on the leadership made no mention of Trudeau. It wasn't until mid-January that it recognized that Trudeau had become a force in the race. Guy Cormier, one of its editorialists, responded favourably at first, then reconsidered, but otherwise La Presse's editorial position remained supportive. Eventually the paper endorsed him, with some qualifications, for the leadership. Quebec City's Le Soleil took a similar line, endorsing Trudeau while expressing reservations.

Ottawa-based Le Droit was decidedly unenthusiastic about special status and separatist options. This was understandable, because although it had a wide following in western Quebec, it also had a considerable Franco-Ontarian readership that would be on the outside looking in at a newly empowered Quebec. From where it stood, Trudeau's approach of equal rights across Canada was far preferable. Editorialist Marcel Pépin had been one of the first journalists to promote Trudeau for the leadership. Thereafter Le Droit printed a number of editorials and articles, many by Pépin, supporting his candidacy. Other Le Droit editorialists, however, were far less enthusiastic.

In short, opinion about Trudeau in the Quebec media ranged from approval to disapproval in lockstep with positions on the constitution that ranged from federalist through advocacy of special status to outright separatist. However, the vast majority of Quebec voters were not as fixed in their views on the constitution as the political and intellectual classes who dominated the media. Quebec's elites may have seen Canadian and Quebec nationalism as competitive alternatives, but for most Québécois it was not a zero-sum game. They could support Trudeau federally and his opponents provincially without any concern for logical inconsistency. Their response to Trudeau was governed more by cultural factors than the constitutional issue. As was the case across Canada, rural Québécois were less beguiled by Trudeau than their urban counterparts. Those steeped in the province's residual Catholic culture were suspicious of his mod image and his divorce law and Criminal Code amendments. [34] Yet in the wake of the Quiet Revolution, Québécois society, particularly its educated and urban segments, had secularized rapidly. For them, Trudeau's image and legal reforms were right in step with their positive experience of modernization. The controversy generated by Trudeau's candidacy had one undisputable result: he quickly gained widespread name recognition across the province.

Two days after the constitutional conference, Trudeau travelled to Toronto to test the waters with Liberal delegates at the Ontario Liberal Association's annual meeting at the Royal York Hotel. Now that he had benefited from a full month of national television exposure, the reel-to-real effect blossomed. The organizers had reserved a suite of rooms for the meeting, but when they learned of Trudeau's attendance they rented a convention hall. A news conference was scheduled for 5:45 p.m. with a reception for delegates to follow at 6:00. Hundreds of people arrived for the news conference, and more kept pouring in until more than a thousand jammed the room. During the questioning, Trudeau disingenuously claimed that he thought he was going to be meeting a few friends in a hotel suite, and had no idea the press was going to be there. "I should have known, of course," he said, which got a big laugh. Anything he said at this point was gloriously witty.

Trudeau took special pains to draw attention to the media's presence in the room. He differentiated between them and the people there, telling the audience, "I don't want to be intimidated by the press and I want to once again speak over their heads to tell all of you that if I don't run I hope you won't think I'm letting you down." Afterwards he tried to make his way through the crush of the crowd to meet with his some of his local Liberal backers upstairs. The CBC's Warren Davis waylaid him, asking, "Is this reaction to your presence here surprising to you?" "Well, if it's spontaneous it's surprising; if it's organized it just shows that there are good organizing people with me," Trudeau replied, betraying his awareness of staged authenticity. "Run, that's the point," someone in the crowd yelled at him. He said he'd decide whether he'd run for the leadership within ten days.[35]

It was a dramatic example of how the public, primed by all the media attention Trudeau had received, would turn out to see him live. The consequence was exciting crowd scenes, which made good TV and encouraged viewers at home to do the same should he ever show up in their community. Trudeau was now enjoying the benefits of a virtuous, self-reinforcing, reel-to-real synthesis. The experience helped convince him to run.[36]

Trudeau continued to say things that anglophones interpreted as refreshingly candid and Quebec nationalists thought insulting. On February 13, he appeared on CBC's *Under Attack*, where he was questioned by a panel of francophone students from Carleton University. He argued against giving Quebec new powers on the basis that the province hadn't done a good job with the powers it had. For example, despite its responsibility for education, Québécois spoke "awful French." Quebec had controlled education for generations, he continued, so it couldn't blame the rest of Canada for the fact that "our French is lousy." "I think French-Canadians have been betrayed by their elite for 100 years," he concluded.[37] Trudeau's Quebec nationalist opponents chose to interpret "lousy" literally and told Québécois that Trudeau had such disdain for his own people that he derided them as lice-ridden.

In an assessment of how things stood at the midpoint of the Liberal leadership campaign, the *Globe and Mail*'s Geoffrey Stevens thought Trudeau's potential candidacy overshadowed all else. Trudeau was more popular among the press and the general public than in his own party, yet if he remained so the delegates would have to elect him because winning power was what it was all about. Stevens reported that a young Paul Martin supporter had told him,

"This guy Trudeau frightens the hell out of me ... he could stampede the convention." "This refrain is echoed in the other organizations," Stevens continued. "Mr. Trudeau is dangerous because he is the only man who could sweep the convention and there is little any of the other candidates could do to stop him."[38]

The Trudeau bandwagon was swarmed even though officially it had yet to pull out of the carriage shed. *Le Devoir* printed a petition in support of Trudeau's candidacy signed by over a hundred influential citizens from the Montreal and Quebec City regions, while *La Presse* reported that 80 percent of Quebec Liberal MPs were behind Trudeau.[39] "Is Pierre Elliott Trudeau really real," asked Charles Lynch, "or is he merely an invention of the news media? ... The line between reporting a bandwagon and actually getting aboard it, is a fine line, indeed, and there is no doubt that the massive reporting of Mr. Trudeau's moves in recent weeks has given tremendous momentum to his candidacy."[40]

Still Trudeau had not made any commitment. It was Wednesday, February 14 before he told Marchand and Pelletier that he would run. He called a press conference for that Friday at ten in the morning, and more than a hundred members of the media showed up. Seven TV cameramen and a dozen professional photographers focused in on him. The CBC carried the entire hour-long press conference live on its national radio network. In making his announcement, Trudeau half-jokingly blamed the media for his candidacy:

> If I try to assess what happened in the past two months, perhaps, I have a suspicion that you people had a lot to do with it. If anybody's to blame I suppose it's you collectively ... To be quite frank, if I try to analyze it, well, I think in the subconscious mind of the press I think it started out like a huge practical joke on the Liberal party. I mean that, because, in some sense, the decision that I made this morning and last night is in some ways similar to that I arrived at when I entered the Liberal party. It seemed to me, reading the press in the early stages a couple of months ago, as though many of you

were saying, you know, "we dare the Liberal party to choose a guy like Trudeau."

The press wanted to be able, Trudeau opined, to say after the race was over and won that the Liberals hadn't had the guts to go with someone different, and so now he was calling their bluff. They wouldn't be able to say that any longer – "now you're stuck with me."[41]

The announcement generated a wave of support from delegates across the country that quickly boosted Trudeau into first place in the race. The *Toronto Star* ran a profile under the headline "Trudeau: The Hip Saviour?"[42] "Is Canada ready for Pierre Elliott Trudeau?" Peter Newman asked breathlessly. "Does the grasping influence of the young really outweigh the entrenched power of the old, either in the Liberal party or in the country at large?"[43] Charles Lynch noted that the Liberals had managed in a single stroke to put a new face on their party.

> There they were, wondering how they could put on a convention show with a bunch of guys named Sharp, Hellyer, Martin and so on – solid citizens all, but unpromising character material for a great dramatic production. Then they invent Pierre Elliott Trudeau, and suddenly the prospects are for a campaign rivaling the great Diefenbaker ones of the '50s, and a convention that should out-shine the one the Tories put on last September.[44]

Lubor Zink wasn't taken in by Trudeau's story about a last-minute decision to run. After all, a brochure promoting his candidacy had been all printed up and ready to go at his announcement press conference. None of the assembled scribes had picked up on that. "The Trudeau buildup originated, deliberately and artificially, with certain elements in the mass media," Zink explained. It was as if Trudeau "was the one who would singlehandedly transport [Canada] forward into a brilliant future, from black and white to living colour."[45] This observation was interesting, given that the Ottawa scene was often dismissed as grey and drab, while Expo 67 had been portrayed as a multihued kaleidoscope of visual stimulation. Colour TV had been introduced in 1966, and now Canadians were upgrading to a colour PM.[46] The national dream had always been technologically enabled, and now they were dreaming in Technicolor.

By this point the media were becoming self-conscious about their role in the Trudeau phenomenon. Pierre Berton told his television audience that the press was not responsible for making Trudeau; it had simply recognized that he was "the man of the moment ... He had the smell of success on him."[47] That tautology warrants unpacking. A disproportionately high number of media personnel were relatively highly educated, affluent urbanites with a modern mindset. Intoxicated by the spirit of the sixties, they wanted to be hip and progressive. Circumstances seemed to have been holding Canada back, and national progress was axiomatic. When Pierre Trudeau appeared he seemed to them to be exactly what Canada needed.

The media did not consciously conspire to foist Trudeau on a reluctant electorate. On the contrary, they saw themselves as representing the populace. Yet their interpretation of popular sentiment was coloured by their own biases. When Peter Newman wrote, "We have begun to view the politicians ... as agents of our aspirations," by "we" he meant all Canadians. But his comment revealed a natural tendency of his and of many like-minded colleagues to project their own aspirations onto the nation as a whole.[48] They did so in concert with other estates among the professional-managerial class, but it was they who played a key role in presenting the ideal leader to the people. In doing so they viewed themselves not as powerful shapers of opinion but as outsiders crusading for righteous change against an entrenched, out-of-touch establishment. As long as Trudeau was a long shot, they had no compunction about promoting him and did so through extensive and favourable coverage. They put Trudeau on the public agenda and presented him in a manner calculated to win the support of like-minded Canadians.

The media were not omnipotent, however. They had to have a product that would sell. As it turned out, Trudeau proved to be a talented, media-savvy performer. The editors and producers got good feedback, which meant good audience numbers, which meant advertisers were happy, so they put him on again. Once the ball started rolling, it developed a momentum all its own. "The press became a key link in a self-generating cycle of interest," recalled Donald Peacock.

> The newspapers stimulated the public fascination with Trudeau; this fascination made Trudeau seem still more extraordinary than ever, and the press, in turn were left over-awed by the man reinforced by the myth they had helped create. Then, because a figure so awe-inspiring made such good copy, the press would continue discussing Trudeau more intensely than ever – thereby feeding public interest – and so on the cycle went. And, because Trudeau seemed such an enigma and had such depth as a person, the cycle could continue indefinitely without exhausting itself.[49]

The ultimate outcome would depend on whether there were enough voters who thought like the media to carry the day. "Begone!" Norman DePoe jokingly commanded a pesky print reporter at the Quebec Liberal convention in January 1968, "I have a prime minister to create!"[50] The humour lay in his self-awareness and the truth beneath the hyperbole.

Repeating the same image, Warhol-style, was in vogue in 1968. Though
Trudeau's visage dominates this display at Half-Beat Harold's on Granby Street
in Toronto, it is accompanied by individual posters of Raquel Welch in a bikini
and the Mona Lisa smoking something.

Pop Goes the Image
A Mod Candidate for a Mod Canada

[Pearson's] resignation transferred the leadership
of this country to a new generation of
Canadians, and above all, gave it a new style.

Twenty Million Questions, 1968

IN ITS JANUARY 1968 issue, *Maclean's* commissioned five "top image makers and marketing experts" to evaluate the style of the Liberal politicians vying for the party's leadership. The experts weighed in with their insights on key political assets such as "The Image," "Sex Appeal," "Youth Appeal," "The Face," and "The Clothes." "Dull, dull, dull" was the merciless verdict.[1]

There was one possible candidate, however, whose profile was anything but dull. Trudeau's image was as significant a factor in his rise to power as Trudeau himself, whoever he was. It started with his personality, especially the way he came across on TV, and was supplemented by his fashionable dress and lifestyle. His image was then embroidered by media commentary that invested him with key features of sixties culture and nationalist ambition presented in a mod style.

Though media of all types played a role in creating and disseminating Trudeau's image, his rise was attributable primarily to television. It was, by the late 1960s, the medium through which most Canadians got most of their political information. Television was in its second decade and was becoming less studio-bound and easier to produce and edit. Production values were rising rapidly, close-ups were more sharply defined and intimate, and black and white was blossoming into colour. Elites, political and otherwise, were becoming more adept at incorporating it into the existing mass communications regime of radio, film, and mass print.[2]

As television was adapted to existing institutions, practices, and power structures, it had significant effects within them. For one thing, it boosted the existing trend towards a politics of image focused on the party leaders. Its emphasis on the visual accentuated the journalistic proclivity for playing up the human-interest angle by giving viewers the impression they knew politicians personally. In bringing the world into the living room, television made its personalities familiar, naturalizing the association between the nuclear family and the national community.[3]

It was television that first introduced Trudeau to the public, put him on the leadership radar screen with its coverage of his legal reforms, and made him a national celebrity in the opening weeks of 1968. Television provided him with a huge advantage over his political rivals because he came across far better on it than they did. "Trudeau is the only candidate who consistently manages to reach through the lens, through the little square screen, to get at the viewer," wrote a journalist in a piece typical of the media's increasing self-consciousness about the influence of television in politics.[4] In discussing Trudeau, journalists used terms such as his "presence" or his "aura" that showed how the medium still struck them as somewhat magical and mysterious. At other times they called his special power "charisma," without explaining what exactly that was.[5] What was it about Trudeau that made him so telegenic? On this point there was endless speculation.[6]

Contemporary conventional wisdom had it that since television was an intimate medium, political performers should open up about themselves to enhance viewers' impression of having a direct personal encounter with them. A panel of pundits, convened on Pierre Berton's CTV interview program in early March to assess the performance of the Liberal leadership candidates he'd had on the show in preceding weeks, agreed that those who had done this had made the best impression.[7] They criticized Trudeau for his reserve, concluding that he would never reveal all and, in fact, would find such a display distasteful. Yet clearly they were missing something, because it was Trudeau whom the television producers kept inviting onto their shows. They were confusing opening up about one's personal life with the medium's ability to engage the viewer through an up-close, personal encounter. The Berton pundits underestimated the power of holding back, leaving the audience wanting more. "Your own image is a corporate mask, inclusive, requiring no private nuance whatever," seer-du-jour Marshall McLuhan informed Trudeau. "This is your 'cool' TV power. Iconic, sculptural."[8]

Trying to identify the root cause of the Trudeau boom, journalist Anthony Westell thought that, Berton's pundits to the contrary, Trudeau was somehow able to establish a personal connection with TV viewers.[9] One explanation was that he had a face television loved. Gordon Donaldson, a seasoned journalist working for the CBC who met Trudeau as "Minister on the Move" was being filmed early in 1967, was struck by how well he came across on camera: "I don't know what he said, because I was fascinated by the film possibilities of his face – the oriental serenity as he listened, fingertips together as in prayer; the graven elegance of the high cheekbones and the big nose; the sudden animation, the deprecating smile, and the depth of the huge eyes ... masterfully assembled for the lens."[10] Inevitably, celebrity experts were buttonholed to weigh in on the issue. On February 15, Dr. Desmond Morris, author of the bestselling *The Naked Ape*, paused on his way through Montreal to say that the justice minister had "certain animal leadership properties – as a zoologist, I'm tremendously impressed with Trudeau. He has an intellectual virility which is exceedingly important ... His anatomy, his gestures, his facial expressions are animal qualities that set him apart and bring him to the top of the heap."[11] The search for explanation in some atavistic factor was a common feature of such analysis. It was consistent with McLuhan's argument that the privileging of sight and the linear logic of print culture had transitioned into a more holistic sensorium that put emotion and interpersonal chemistry back into play, retribalizing society.

Television was an audio as well as a visual medium, and Trudeau's speech combined with his appearance to lend complexity and depth to his performances. When interviewed, Trudeau was in the moment, fully engaged in the exchange. He was not a scripted performer, ponderously stringing together memorized phrases. When asked a question, he didn't laboriously bridge to a set-piece speech, but rather seemed to consider the question seriously and then respond with a complex and directly relevant answer. He hinted at ambiguity and complications, while structuring his arguments with either/or logic accompanied by proofs that supported his position. He spoke deliberately in long sentences that required verbal skill to complete correctly. Once he was launched into one, there were successive peaks of dramatic tension as the viewer-as-listener tried to anticipate how he would finish it with syntax intact. The contrast with Robert Stanfield, the most politically significant comparison, was stark. Though he too seemed reserved, Stanfield was a slow talker whose speech patterns suggested the creaking of mental wheels turning ponderously.[12]

Trudeau's claims to rationality and his ability to speak in sentences coherent enough to be published provided a counterweight to the seductive visuality of television, thereby soothing mediation anxiety. Viewers thought him candid. Even seasoned media observers were impressed: "His unspoken slogan could have been the street phrase: 'I kid you not.' No temporizing, no sliding away, no circumlocutions. This is pretty shocking stuff, not to be told what you want to hear ... Trudeau doesn't think the people want to be conned."[13] As another journalist put it, he "can be brutally blunt, bitingly scornful, stingingly witty or casually indifferent. It comes out cool and frank."[14] Journalists were suspicious of the prepared response, the pat phrase, and liked Trudeau for "the total lack of any political rhetoric or the little verbal and vocal tricks that get so tiresome in other candidates."[15] In short, Trudeau performed ably that most highly prized of sixties virtues: authenticity.

He also provided action that kept the television viewer entertained. When he was interviewed, his face, hands, and body supplemented his words. His face was mobile, but in subtle ways, with little expressions that refined his meaning. He chuckled or sometimes grinned in a sly, self-conscious fashion. His almond eyes seemed half-hooded, yet crinkled mischievously. Sometimes his eyebrows shot up to suggest that whatever proposition he was rationally refuting really was preposterous. A soon-to-be-famous shrug, performed with hands flipped palm up, often accentuated his incredulity.[16] Historian Paul Rutherford, noting how television helped Trudeau rocket to power, attributed it to his acting ability. "He was something of a showman," he explained, "who had, as [Trudeau biographer] George Radwanski claimed, an instinctive 'sense of drama and timing that most professional actors would envy.' He knew how to appear charming or firm, how to be witty or sincere, how to seem humble or shy, whatever the occasion might demand."[17] Every Trudeau interview was a live performance by a virtuoso jamming in real time. As any jazz musician knows, successful improvisation requires great discipline and training. Trudeau had been working on his television persona for years. It was yet another of the prized arenas of modern life that he challenged himself to master.[18]

Sometimes – dramatically, improbably – Trudeau became a ham, performing stunts for the camera. On a CBC public affairs show, he sashayed like a hep dude down a staircase at the back of the set as the hosts faced the cameras up front, then suddenly collapsed and tumbled out of sight. After a moment he popped back up and continued on as if nothing had happened. On another set, when a TV clapperboard snapped shut near his face as cameras rolled, he snapped his teeth back at it. Once when he was onstage in front of a live audience, he pretended a hanging mike was a punching bag and gave it a playful smack. During the leadership convention, he slid down a banister while leaving the Château Laurier, then, when seated in his box at the arena, tossed grapes up into the air, catching them in his mouth.[19] These stunts worked on two levels – they provided entertaining visuals for a visual medium and at the same time drew attention to the staged nature of proceedings.

Every television appearance enhanced Trudeau's reputation. Fascinated by the television personality, journalists researched his background, assembling various colourful bits into a pleasing arrangement. The result was an image that grew luxuriantly under the bright television lights. Analyzing the Trudeau image is challenging insofar as it was not a rational construct within which various components locked logically into place. This was in part because he was a complex, contradictory character, and in part because his image was shaped as much by what people wanted as by who he was. Mass-mediated images aren't static cardboard cutouts, but rather multidimensional, constantly evolving constellations of impressions. When Trudeau appeared in the media, he acted in response to his perception of what was expected of him, and viewers filtered the impression he made on them through their preconceptions of him. As a result his image was an unstable, evolving montage of prominent features of sixties culture and nationalist ambition. In an age of teenage boomers, sexual revolution, political protest, passionate nationalism, and a fascination with alternative mental states (both drug and eastern-mysticism induced), Trudeau was portrayed as young, sexy, athletic, a political philosopher, an outdoorsman, and a naturally bicultural Canadian who was also a free-thinking cosmopolitan adventurer.

Since the Trudeau image was a projection of the wish for renewal, one of its basic but essential components was novelty. "He makes no promises," said the *Montreal Star*. "He holds before them the prospect of something new and different ... a new kind of Canada in which familiar old things will be changed into something exciting and new."[20] This impression of novelty was facilitated by his recent status as a relative unknown. "Mr. Trudeau's popularity derives first from the fact that he is a new face in the political world at a time when disillusionment with some of the old ones is general," observed the *Halifax Chronicle Herald*.[21]

Christina Newman thought it worth noting that "Trudeau had been in Ottawa for two and a half years but he'd never been of it."[22] Though this seemed improbable, the sentiment was revealing. Not being guilty by association with the desultory federal scene was a significant qualification for success in the new world aborning, so Trudeau was absolved of any such complicity. In an interview with Patrick Watson broadcast during the leadership convention, Trudeau waited until close to the end and then suggested it was time for "new guys with new ideas," a pithy and resonant line designed to appeal to those wanting change.[23]

A closely related attribute was that Trudeau was an alternative to the status quo. "All the other leadership candidates represent the greyness of orthodoxy," editorialized one paper. "He brings to Canadian politics a different and even radical approach."[24] This kind of characterization allied Trudeau with the sixties antiestablishment ethos. In the opening sentence of his foreword to *Federalism and the French Canadians*, the English version of the collection of his old essays that hit the bookstores at the end of February, Trudeau claimed, "No other constant in my thinking need be sought than opposition to accepted ideas."[25] Allusions to his one-time flirtations with the Co-operative Commonwealth Federation reinforced the notion that the Trudeau difference was that he was progressive. When W.A.C. Bennett, premier of British Columbia, called him a "socialist playboy," it did Trudeau more good than harm.[26] The story about him throwing a snowball at Stalin's statue in Moscow got endless play because it symbolized his independence from orthodoxy while providing reassurance that he resisted communism's authoritarianism – and did so in a symbolically Canadian fashion.

The outsider was an increasingly trendy pop culture type. The man of the hour was no longer the organization man, the suburb-dwelling conformist, and standards of masculine good looks shifted to represent the change. The Arrow-shirt masculinity of JFK and the Man in the Gray Flannel Suit had been superseded by the flawed but interesting antihero. "What was handsome in the early 60s is dead," Charles Lynch would observe a few years later, "supplanted by the shaggier, acne-scarred machismo of the newer male."[27] Trudeau had the acne and the outsider posturing. In keeping with the liberation and self-realization imperatives of the sixties, he was also seen to be radically free, an individual who had wilfully shaken off the dead hand of consensus mediocrity in order to realize his unique innate potential. Who better to transform the nation than a man who had already transformed himself in like manner?

"Cool" was the sixties term for an enviable cultural sensibility that was simultaneously laid-back and cutting-edge. To be cool required being on top of the scene and displaying an easy mastery of it without taking any of it too seriously. It was hard for a politician to be cool because the term usually implied an oppositional attitude to authority. Yet Trudeau was universally acknowledged as cool. Here his seeming reluctance to run and indifference to power helped.[28] Yet this was just one of the many contradictions in his image generated by his adaptable personality. He had the time, resources, and will to compete in various exalted contexts of modern life, proving himself against different criteria in diverse settings. Excelling at everything and not making much of it was cool.

The media emphasized Trudeau's fashion sense as evidence he was "with it." "Style," claimed one observer, "is the basis of his tremendous attraction to people. The young especially, because the young … place more store by style than they do by information."[29] The ascot-and-sandals-in-Parliament incident in the summer of 1967 subsequently popped up in every profile of Trudeau.[30] His self-fashioning through style became part of the argument for his candidacy. When the *Toronto Daily Star* first flagged Trudeau as a potential prime minister, it presented him as a "swinging bachelor who wears zippy … attire and who affects what can best be described as a receding, early-Beatle haircut" rather than discussing his policy stances.[31] "A lot of the excitement about Trudeau, especially among the kids," observed George Bain, "is accountable entirely to style. They like the way he dresses, the way he looks, the way he talks (and it doesn't matter much about what)."[32]

Trudeau was known for sporting a flower in his lapel. This seemingly innocuous affectation obsessed the media, becoming a staple feature of news reports on his appearances. Coverage of voting day at the Liberal convention in early April would begin with a young woman pinning an orange chrysanthemum to Trudeau's lapel. Later that day another young woman threw a red carnation to Trudeau as he sat in his box. He smelled it, put it behind his ear, then held it in his mouth, giving photographers a series of photo ops. A flower also featured when Trudeau sent the nation to the polls on April 23. When he stole away from Parliament Hill to ask Governor General Roland Michener for a dissolution, he avoided journalists by entering Rideau Hall through the greenhouse at its back, where he stopped to pick a rose for his lapel. During the subsequent election campaign the flower would remain central and symbolic. When he arrived at a rally he was usually greeted by a young woman with a floral gift whose thanks would be a kiss.

The flower associated Trudeau with "flower power," a counterculture slogan proclaimed in fragrant violation of the sterility of modern technocratic rationality. It evoked the flower children and their "make love, not war," back-to-nature ideals. At the same time the flower signalled that Trudeau was self-aware about being fashionable. His reflexivity on this point suggested that those who feigned indifference to their appearance, not he, were the ones pretending. The flower also troubled gender categories and heteronormativity, simultaneously suggesting sexual ambiguity and a man masculine enough to pull it off.

Polonius's advice to Laertes, "the apparel oft proclaims the man," extended to Trudeau's choice of wheels as well. Commentators were awed by the fact that Trudeau drove a sports car, a stylish statement in a car-crazed culture. When asked at his press conference in Ottawa before the Liberal leadership convention whether he would give up his Mercedes if elected, he asked, "Do you mean the girl or the car?"[33] This became another of his celebrated aphorisms. Upscale, exotic, and sporty, the Mercedes fit perfectly with the Trudeau image. Its ubiquity in media portrayals of Trudeau was a mutually beneficial product placement that represented an unprecedented intrusion of corporate branding into Canadian politics.

The breathless conjurings of the Trudeau image that filled the columns of newspapers and the scripts of TV personalities in early 1968 could be cited ad nauseam, but the dust jacket blurb for *Federalism and the French Canadians* admirably distills it into one hyperbolic paragraph:

> Pierre Elliott Trudeau is almost incredible: a Prime Minister who swings, who is described by *Maclean's* magazine as "an authoritative judge of wine and women," who drives a Mercedes, throws snowballs at statues of Laurier and Stalin, wears turtleneck sweaters, and says things like "the state has no business in the bedrooms of the nation." He is also known to respectful academics as "one of the best political thinkers this country has ever produced."

This concoction was improbable enough to rival James Bond, and not all that dissimilar from Ian Fleming's creation. Trudeau's stylish clothes (turtlenecks!) and other fashionable consumer choices adorned an active body that flirted with danger zones of the exotic and sexual, giving him the allure of a secret agent-cum-international playboy.

Whereas 007's potency came from his licence to kill, Trudeau's came from his intellectual licence. His elite education and authorship of political tracts were celebrated as evidence that he was a bona fide intellectual. "Mr. Trudeau is no ordinary politician. He is an individualist, his intellectual honesty is enhanced by the crispness of his mind, and he appears to think in terms of ideas and of public goals rather than of political opportunities and risks," claimed the *Calgary Albertan*. The average editorialist had little time to read and reflect on Trudeau's body of work, let alone acquire the competence to critique it, so most went along with the consensus that the philosopher's raiment was resplendent. "He possesses great intellectual capacity, independence of mind and courage," wrote the *Prince Albert Daily Herald*. For the *Brandon Sun*, Trudeau showed that "there is a new politics, a politics of issues rather than partisanship, of intelligence rather than ideology. Pierre Elliott Trudeau personifies, in many minds, this new politics. His intellectual capabilities have been well in evidence for years."[34] Trudeau had a law degree from l'Université de Montréal and an MA in political economy from Harvard, and had been a graduate student at l'Institut d'études politiques in Paris and the London School of Economics. Canada had had political leaders with scholarly credentials in the past, but usually their intellectual attainments had been downplayed due to fears of an egalitarian backlash against highbrow airs. Why had things now changed?

For one thing, a university education was not as rare as it had once been. In the postwar period, universities and enrolments had expanded rapidly because more and more Canadians wanted their children to get a good education and the economic security that came with it. The mastery of knowledge signified by postsecondary credentials upheld the professional-managerial class's place in the world. Trudeau's extended sojourns at some of the world's best universities may have been too much of a good thing, yet his educational achievements were still admirable.

Perhaps there was some connection too, through free association, with the counterculture psycho-centrism that emphasized alternative spirituality, psychedelia, and mind-blowing drugs. "Feed your head," commanded Jefferson Airplane in "White Rabbit," and that April the Amboy Dukes released "Journey to the Center of the Mind," inviting listeners to join in cerebral pleasures. Trudeau's mind set him apart from the conformist herd that had brought the establishment into disrepute. His razor-sharp intellect sliced away encrustations of prejudice and punctured hypocrisy. His intellectualism was yet another way in which he could be seen to be an agent of national modernization. Trudeau told *Canadian* magazine that he would like to be remembered as the first prime minister after the "transitional period, ushering us into the electronic age, the age of reason ... where politics will be a different kind of game, a game shifting, one which, to use McLuhan's approach, will be very adaptable to the electronic age."[35]

Yet Enlightenment man Trudeau was simultaneously associated with the romanticism of the counterculture. "He's not rooted in a crippling, archaic linear existence," gushed an expatriate Canadian member of New York City's "Alien Residents for Trudeau."[36] At a time when the Beatles had just gone off to India to sit at the feet of Maharishi Mahesh Yogi, Trudeau was credited with being a yoga practitioner and photographed acknowledging admirers with a Buddhist greeting.[37] Tuned to the sixties vibe, Trudeau said that the Eastern spiritualities that attracted him were the "religions of love" rather than those of commandments; religion should be "an inner thing which commands you." His spiritual heroes were "the moving ones, those who are trying to spread their particular gospel across linguistic and ethnic barriers."[38] Potted biographies described his classical education at Montreal's Collège Brébeuf in hushed tones that suggested that mysterious premodern rites had formed him spiritually. Although these romantic associations were at odds with the rationality on which Trudeau prided himself, no one tried to explain the apparent contradiction.

Journalists also wrote admiringly of Trudeau the cosmopolitan. He was presented as an international jet-setter apt to nip off for a ski holiday in the Alps or a beach vacation in Tahiti, a transgressor of boundaries who travelled strange foreign lands and even flouted Cold War taboos by penetrating the Iron Curtain. Trudeau's youthful beard-and-backpack globetrotting had anticipated the footloose free-spiritedness of the sixties, and a photo of him in this proto-hippie phase appeared frequently in media summaries of his background. Here again, Trudeau the individualist demonstrated his freedom from conventional restraints.

Trudeau knew the world, and, better still, the world knew him. Canadians had thrilled to the international attention and approval garnered by Expo 67, and Trudeau kept the gratifying recognition of Canada from abroad coming. "The main issue of this, the electronic election, is the image Canadians wish to have of themselves

Trudeau offers a Buddhist salutation during the
Liberal leadership convention.

and show to the world," claimed the Toronto Daily Star's TV critic.[39]
The New York Times ran an article entitled "Trudeau Conjures Up a
'Perpetual Expo 67.'"[40] "He's the type of man who should follow
Expo '67, and be a vital part of the new, identifiable Canada," said
Maureen Sweetman, a twenty-one-year-old teacher from Hornby,
Ontario, who was part of a group of young people assembled to
promote Trudeau at the convention.[41] "Last year we had Expo. This
year we've got Trudeau. With action like that going for us, we can
all stop worrying about Canada getting buried inside the back
pages of the foreign press," crowed Maclean's.[42] Trudeau was a "human expo," suggested Scott Young, "the long happy summer that
can be extended and extended, world without end."[43]

Athleticism was another key marker of the Trudeau image. He
was a skier, a brown belt in judo, a performer of flips and stunts
off diving boards. He scuba dived and played tennis, canoed and
climbed mountains, exhibiting a Kennedy-style "viggah." Editorial
cartoonists were delighted by the visual possibilities of depicting
him in athletic mode. Trudeau enjoyed individual sports for which
he had disciplined his body, bending to his will a domain under his
personal control. A critical observer might have noted that he was
not a team player, but at the time no one made this point.

The self-discipline of athleticism was accompanied by asceticism, for which Trudeau's Jesuit education again provided the background. Journalists wrote reverentially of him disappearing to his
remote and spartan weekend cabin in the Laurentians. Trudeau was
not averse to feeding them such material. "Last week I walked about
three hours in the mountains," he told a television interviewer.[44]
Herein lay other unaddressed contradictions: How could he be an
ascetic when so much of his image was defined by expensive goods
and experiences? How could he be such a radically free individual
if he was defined by fashion?

The unarticulated answer was that Trudeau's consumption was
individualistic because he could afford luxury goods rather than
run-of-the-mill mass products. He was able to construct a unique

self by buying scarce symbols of identity and status because he was rich. Wealth gave him the leisure to become multi-talented in varied fields. He was a swinger not just because he was single and sexy, but because he maintained a jet-set lifestyle. He didn't have to defer to "The Man." It was hard to peg him as a member of the establishment when he'd never held a regular job for long. At the root of all this was the fact that he was a man of property, the basis of freedom in a liberal capitalist political economy.

Some politicians have an image as a man of the people, and are loved for it. Trudeau was seen as a cut above, and admired for it. The fact that he wasn't a working stiff with a wife, 2.5 kids, and a station wagon in the driveway of his suburban side-split worked in his favour as the counterculture successfully discredited the conformity of the fifties. The risk was that he'd be condemned as elitist, but he seemed immune to this critique. Perhaps part of the reason was that people wanted to look up to their leader. "He is the man we would all like to be," observed Anthony Westell, "charming, rich, talented, successful."[45] His economic privilege was not so foreign in a wealthy society that had been enjoying two decades of continuously growing prosperity. Here as elsewhere, Trudeau offered Canadians an aspirational model.

Significant aspects of Trudeau's image corresponded with the archetypal hero myth as described by Joseph Campbell. His educational attainments marked him as gifted, his world travels and labours in obscurity in Duplessis-era Quebec corresponded roughly with a period of banishment, and he had developed a discipline and self-sufficiency that set him apart. Claude Ryan's belief that English Canada instinctively sought a messiah from Quebec was borne out by the way journalists emphasized these points. It was as if they were unwittingly following a script deeply embedded in the collective unconscious.[46]

Mixed in with the sixties stylings and hero mythology were some classic Canadian identity tropes. When not portrayed as a cosmopolitan sophisticate, Trudeau was presented as a northern

This 1949 photo of Trudeau taken in the
Middle East during his youthful world travels appeared
frequently in profiles of him published in 1968 and
worked to link him to the counterculture.

frontiersman, at home in a canoe in the great Canadian outdoors (as any French Canadian descendant of *coureurs de bois* should be). His regular retreats to his cabin in the Laurentians signified this role, as did his wilderness canoe trips. Both were described romantically as sacred pilgrimages to the spiritual heart of the country. Presumably he retreated there to recharge his Canadian identity with northernness, naturalness, and masculinity, like Superman in his Arctic fortress.

Another indigenous touch was Trudeau's bilingualism and biculturalism. He was Pierre (French) Elliott (English) Trudeau (French), with a French Canadian father and an English Canadian mother, fluent in both languages, a player in both Quebec and national politics. Lester Pearson predicted that he would be Canada's last unilingual prime minister, and English Canadians were coming to accept bilingualism as the price of keeping the country together. Trudeau's effortless mastery of Canada's two official languages made him an exemplar of this way forward. He modelled linguistic accommodation by speaking briefly in French to English audiences, and vice versa. Although he disapproved of going beyond bilingualism to implant the two nations concept of Canada in the constitution, he personified biculturalism. Trudeau was the exemplary new Canadian who embodied reconciliation of the two solitudes, thereby assuring the nation's future. Ironically, English Canadians simultaneously associated him with stereotypes of Gallic flair and sophistication that trumped an Anglo stolidity closely linked to the evils of conformity.

In the constellation of signs that constituted the Trudeau image, youth and sex shone brightest. The two were closely linked in the media because of the prurient fascination with the sexual mores of the first generation to come to sexual maturity in the post-Pill, sexual revolution age. Youthfulness was a particularly desirable quality in the late 1960s. Youth were the trend-setting target market for popular cultural products from music to fashion. But youthfulness also had political implications – it was associated with resistance to all the evils, real and imagined, of the establishment. To invoke youthfulness was to make a moral claim. Identifying with youth was also pragmatic, given the inevitability of the baby boomers' ascent to power. As the narrator of a 1967 CBC television documentary put it, "This is the call of contemporary Canada. Give us a new generation of political leaders. The yearning of these young voters is a potent political force."[47]

Youth signalled change: the right to change, the power to effect change, the inevitability of change. In the sixties, youth was associated with vitality and idealism, not naiveté and inexperience. Trudeau had it; his political rivals did not. A journalist reporting from Ottawa for the *London Evening Standard* believed that Trudeau would heal the generation gap:

> I am convinced that we shall see, for the first time since Kennedy perished in Dallas, a national leader so lucid and contemporary, so impatient with the platitudes and deceits of public life and so clear sighted about the future, that he could make politics not only relevant but exciting to a generation alienated from the democratic process.[48]

"He appeals to my generation; to the atmosphere of now," explained twenty-seven-year-old Mary Mitchell.[49]

Trudeau's supposed youthfulness gave rise to a farcical episode. The Parliamentary Guide and Liberal campaign literature gave Trudeau's year of birth as 1921. Trudeau was really two years older, but he said nothing to correct media reports that he was forty-six. Only when an enterprising *Time* reporter went rooting in Quebec court records was his true age revealed as forty-eight. Yet Trudeau pretended that he didn't know how old he was. When his age was questioned during a television interview on March 3 on the Montreal French-language station CFTM's *Face à Face*, he replied, "It's somewhere around there."[50] When reporters confronted him about it, he maintained the pretence. "You tell me how old I am. I'm beginning to wonder now. But I think I'll be a swinger for a while yet."[51] On another occasion he feigned horror, as if his questioner had cornered and exposed him, to trivialize the issue.[52] Journalists let the matter slide, providing yet another example of how in their eyes Trudeau could do no wrong.

On the other hand, Trudeau's calendar age mattered little because he possessed the quality of youthfulness. The spirit of the times inspired older "swingers" to try to appear youthful. Youth was "no longer simply an age category," but rather "a metaphor, an attitude toward life, a state of mind that even adults could access."[53] For the teenyboppers bobbing in his wake, it was enough that he wasn't a fusty old married man like their dads. Trudeau was fit, and he looked and acted young for his age. He came across as younger than his thirty-eight-year-old leadership rival John Turner, who, ironically, was criticized for being too young to aspire to the nation's highest political office. "A professional image maker, of which Trudeau has had none visible, would have had a hard time producing a product more saleable to the kids," wrote George Bain of the *Globe and Mail*.[54]

Since youth was in the vanguard of the sexual revolution, it was a short step from portraying Trudeau as youthful to portraying him as sexy. The sexual revolution was transforming sex from an embarrassing procreative function unfit for discussion in polite company into a site of "pleasure, relationship, and personal expression."[55] By the standards of the swinging sixties, openness about sex was one of the key markers of whether someone had freed themselves from the shackles of Victorian morality and gotten in tune with their authentic, sensual self. Prohibitions against mentioning sex in public had loosened so much by the late 1960s that sex was being used indiscriminately by media owners to sell programs to advertisers and by advertisers to sell products. In sixties parlance, inhibition, whether in sex or consumption, was a sign of a hang-up. In this regard Trudeau's unmarried status was a great political asset. Other candidates appeared with their wives by their sides, while Trudeau appeared the eligible bachelor.[56] His sexiness denoted his radical freedom as an individual. Lacking the constraints of wife and family, he was free to consume sex. The candidate's sexiness was highlighted, repeated, and exaggerated as if to celebrate the transgression inherent in such an innovation in Canadian public life.

At this point in the sixties, sexiness was still sexist. *Chatelaine* editor Doris Anderson was raising awareness of women's issues, but second-wave feminism was just getting off the ground. Its damning readings of the sexism embedded in conventional gender roles and relations were only beginning to trouble consciences in the male-dominated media. One of the connotations of "swinger" was promiscuity. In terms of the gendered double standards of the day, this implication was a mark of approval that affirmed Trudeau's masculinity. The image of Trudeau-as-wealthy-bachelor surrounded by beautiful women was an image of male potency.

The media were always looking for love-struck, fawning females to confirm Trudeau's appeal. In an article on candidate John Turner's visit to Vancouver, Allan Fotheringham devoted a good chunk of his report to describing a teenybopper named Margaret who was unmoved by seeing Turner at the airport but had been crazy for Trudeau the previous week – despite the fact that her father, Jimmy Sinclair, was a Turner supporter.[57] CBC television reporter Larry Zolf's street interviews outside St. Lawrence Hall in Toronto during Trudeau's appearance there in March concentrated on women, whom he addressed as "dear." Despite getting serious, considered responses from them, he invariably chuckled at their answers, as if the whole thing was a joke. He asked one teenage girl, "What is he, some sort of Beatle or Monkee for you or what?" The net effect was to position his female interviewees as ditzes irresistibly drawn to Trudeau's charms, not as discriminating citizens making a rational political choice.[58]

The association of Trudeau with the sexual revolution was strengthened by his role in changing the divorce and Criminal Code legislation. These reforms resonated with the zeitgeist more than any other government initiatives of the era. No longer would the law of the land be based on the moral hypocrisy of Victorian prudery. Trudeau presented these reforms as more radical than they were. "We decided to go for broke on this one," he declared. "It has knocked down a lot of totems and overridden a lot of taboos."[59] Right-wing forces opposed the changes, enhancing the impression that he was battling hard to prevail in a righteous cause.

Conservative leader Robert Stanfield became the foil for the sexualized Trudeau image. In an article entitled "Okay, so he's no swinger. BUT ...," Maclean's proclaimed that its correspondent peered "beneath the austere, Calvinist, patrician image of Robert Stanfield and [found] an austere, Calvinist patrician." Stanfield was a man of integrity and moral scruples, but his character was no match for Trudeau's celebrity personality. Maclean's jokingly offered a mod poster of Stanfield, "the first psychedelic political poster in the history of the Tory party," amusing because it was so patently ridiculous to frame him that way.[60] Exploiting Stanfield's image problems, one Liberal supporter crashed a Stanfield meeting in Prince George, British Columbia, with a sign proclaiming "Stale Stagnant Stanfield Is Too Damn Conservative." Stanfield's response was "I cannot nor would not change my personality or try to act out a role simply to achieve an effect and win votes."[61]

At one point, CBC's Newsmagazine went to the streets of Ottawa looking for people's impressions of Trudeau. "He's young. I think he has good ideas," said a middle-aged man carrying groceries. A woman roughly the same age said, "I think he's a brilliant young intellectual. He appeals to the young people in the country." Two young guys with long hair and hippie dress were all for Trudeau because "He's groovy." "He's the only liberal in the race," said another man. "The others are all conservatives." A much older man said, "I'd like to see Trudeau win. He's a man with modern ideas, I think he'd be good for the country."[62] While there was no way of knowing how these streeters had been selected and edited, their opinions were in line with the media's take on Trudeau.[63]

On another occasion, the CBC interviewed a bunch of high school students to see who they thought would win the Liberal leadership. "Trudeau is the only one who's running who's not left over from Mackenzie King," said one girl, sentiments echoed in her classmates' comments. The public broadaster also did on-the-street interviews in Toronto's Kensington market, an immigrant landing zone of greengrocers, butchers, fishmongers, and discount dry-goods merchants, with strikingly different results. Many shoppers and shop owners were hazy about the Liberal leadership contest. Some confused it with the race for the Democratic nomination in the United States. It was an instructive reminder that not everyone was tuned in to national politics.[64]

Canadians from traditional backgrounds found the Trudeau image a bit shocking. "It's not that I don't like Mr. Trudeau, it's just that he's too fast, too new," said an Albertan woman.[65] Others simply didn't like him. Trudeau could provoke a revulsion as strong as the attraction felt by the Trudeauphiles. His image had characteristics so at odds with traditional values that reactionaries branded him with the two worst epithets they could think of: communist and homosexual. The two naturally went together. You could print the first but not the second, although you could imply it. In private you could denounce Trudeau as a pinko queer, which seems to have been the gist of a whispering campaign that the press mentioned without describing fully its sexual component.

In his relentless one-man crusade to deflate the hype over Trudeau, Lubor Zink published columns in which he presented decontextualized excerpts from Trudeau's writings to suggest he had communist sympathies. In one instance he cited Trudeau's contribution to a 1961 compilation of essays entitled *Social Purpose for Canada* that quoted Mao approvingly on a tactical question of how to foster a movement.[66] He drew from this the conclusion that Trudeau was Maoist. It didn't help matters when Trudeau showed up to the opening of Terre des Hommes in Montreal that May sporting a cap like Chairman Mao's.[67]

Outside the mainstream media, brochures and newletters containing slanderous accusations about Trudeau were distributed by a variety of obscure right-wing organizations, most of them located in Ontario and Quebec.[68] Ontario sources included the Edmund Burke Society of Scarborough, a Toronto suburb; the Church of the Reformed Monks and Priests of Stouffville, a small town near Toronto; the Canadian Council of Evangelical Protestant Churches, whose president, Rev. Harry Slade, was the minister of Toronto's Jarvis Street Baptist Church; and the Canadian Intelligence Service, a pamphleteering outfit run by an ex-soldier, Ron Gostick, out of his rural home near Flesherton, another small Ontario town.[69]

The Canadian Intelligence Service (CIS) was the most prominent of the bunch. Gostick, a fervent anti-communist who had grave concerns about international Jewry and the threat to world security presented by the United Nations, had an established subscriber base for his newsletters. In the past the CIS had linked Pearson with communist spy rings. In Trudeau, who had travelled to the USSR and Communist China as a private citizen and had once tried to canoe to Cuba, the CIS had a far fatter target. Gostick printed 150,000 copies of his March 1968 newsletter denouncing Trudeau as a leftist intellectual with communist sympathies under the headline "Trudeau Spearheading Fabian Takeover." Like Zink, Gostick attributed Trudeau's rise to a media conspiracy: "The Trudeau build-up is a frightening demonstration of the power of today's mass media to create and project images and stimulate blind emotions."[70] Gostick approved of, and reprinted, some of Zink's columns. He also printed and distributed a memorandum by famous Soviet defector Igor Gouzenko entitled "Trudeau, a Potential Canadian Castro."[71]

CIS "revelations" circulated by newsletter subscription or bulk purchase for subsequent distribution by hand. The newsletters were reportedly widespread in Winnipeg. In Lethbridge, Alberta, they were found "cached among groceries in supermarkets, and distributed in hospitals."[72] Gostick himself made sure that every delegate to the Liberal leadership got one.[73] Later, during the general election campaign, there were reports of them being circulated at Liberal rallies. Those that were handed out in person were probably accompanied by still more ominous commentary from whoever passed it along. Ralph Cowan, a right-wing rogue Liberal MP who was kicked out of the party caucus in March, repackaged CIS allegations and distributed them in this manner. Robert Thompson, recently Social Credit Party leader but now running for the Conservatives, echoed them in a circular entitled "Candid Comment."[74] CIS content also surfaced occasionally in other public forums. The *Orillia Packet and Times* printed an editorial based on CIS views. An Anglican priest in Victoria drew on similar material to preach against Trudeau from the pulpit, alienating the Liberals in his flock. A local paper in Nova Scotia that usually had a circulation of a thousand printed fifteen thousand copies when it carried the allegations.[75]

The exotic side of Trudeau's image that constituted part of his charismatic appeal contested constructions of the heterosexual male that were deeply entrenched among conservative Canadians. "Those who will re-elect Trudeau," a mechanic in Magog confided to a reporter, "are women, girls and 'fairies.' That's it."[76] During a public meeting in his riding, a Conservative candidate from the Beauce region south of Quebec City said, "Let's call a spade a spade. This [omnibus] bill [is] for queers and fairies," and then noted that Trudeau was a bachelor. The rumours even filtered into the centre of power. Pearson himself asked a close associate of Trudeau whether the justice minister was a homosexual. Walter Gordon was the only Liberal to raise the issue with Trudeau himself. "Do you know what they're saying about you?" he asked. The accusation infuriated Trudeau, who replied that anyone who made such a charge need only leave him alone with his wife for a couple of hours to test it.[77]

The Beauce candidate's sentiments reflected a strong minority current of opinion in rural Quebec. There were numerous reports of Catholic priests denouncing Trudeau from the pulpit as a traitor to his religion. A particularly virulent strain of this opinion appeared in a journal entitled *Vers Demain*. It was published by Louis Even, a former Ralliement des Créditistes organizer and a founder of Les Pèlerins de Saint-Michel (the Pilgrims of Michael the Archangel, also known as "les bérets blancs" for the white tams they wore), a Catholic religious group located in Rougement, less than an hour's drive east of Montreal. Les Pèlerins were united in a conservative rejection of post–Quiet Revolution secularization and sought to uphold traditional Catholic values in Quebec society.

As one journalist put it, Even "painted Trudeau and his followers 'Commie Red' and then overlay that by tarring them with the brush of perversion."[78] Trudeau was guilty by association with writers in Cité Libre whom Even condemned for their communist or Marxist sympathies, and for having attended Harvard, which Even described unappetizingly as "a gelatin meat-broth for leftist intellectuals who poison the United States." Like Gostick, Even suspected a media conspiracy, noting that Trudeau "was catapulted to its [the Liberal Party's] first rank – due to the favours of the mass media that serve subversion and corruption in their effort to ruin the traditional and Christian values of Canada." What really galled him, however, were Trudeau's revisions to the Criminal Code.

It is with a Sodomic stench that Pierre Elliott-Trudeau courted the federal liberal leadership. To the Chamber indeed he has presented his "omnibus" bill, two points of which should put a shameful mark on Trudeau, and would bring the same disgrace on Canada if they were passed. One legalizes homosexuality. The other widens grounds for abortion, thus legalizing murder of innocent human beings.

This is Trudeau. Trudeau branded with the mark of the Beast.

If Trudeau is branded with the mark of the Beast, the Beast of Sodom, he is also the one the beast of Propaganda elected. And the mass propaganda made by the big newspaper, by radio and television, is in service of Hell itself – to catch in the flood of uncautious listeners and spectators who are snatched, hooked, lured, and thus brain-conditioned. The invisible and yet dominating "something" that you felt in the voting hall, was the spirit of the Beast of Propaganda, the very spirit of Satan.[79]

It's in the book.

Editorial cartoonist Duncan Macpherson's
take on the smear campaign, published in the
Toronto Daily Star on June 18, 1968.

This was strong stuff. Liberal organizers speculated that Even had a following in rural Quebec, in the Maritimes, and among certain ethnic communities, especially recent Eastern European immigrants of a conservative Catholic bent.[80]

At first the Trudeau forces opted to ignore such smears in the hope that they would go away. An internal Liberal Party memo made fun of the matter, noting that "cis is against the following: modern art, 'smutty' literature (henry miller and dh Lawrence, notably), fluoridation, the canadian peace research institute, the wall street/communist conspiracy, jews, sex, unicef, unesco, the cbc, disarmament, the un, negroes, miscegenation, and birth control."[81] The author typed in lower case to show that it was all beneath contempt.

Yet Richard Stanbury, the party president, worried about "the 'smut' campaigns which indicate he [Trudeau] is some queer kind of fellow" and thought they were responsible for Liberal fortunes declining in rural ridings as the election campaign progressed.[82] Eventually the Liberals decided that they should counterattack. The accusations of deviant politics and sexuality were so strong in the Lac St-Jean region that Trudeau confronted them directly during his election appearances there. He called them out in speeches in other rural areas as well. "There are all kinds of sick people in our society," he observed on one of these forays. "It is our duty to dis-associate ourselves from this type of garbage."[83]

The question of Trudeau's sexual orientation was aggravated by aspects of his mod style that challenged traditional conventions of masculinity, as well as by his middle-aged bachelor status. His notorious ascot and sandals were a mild version of the provocative androgyny of hippie fashion, but they weren't the only triggers. For example, while being interviewed by the cbc's DePoe at the Château Laurier pool, known in Ottawa as a gay pickup spot, Trudeau reclined in a lounge chair with his chin on the back of a hand supported by a folded wrist, a bit of body language coded fey in the popular culture of the day.

Given the prejudices against homosexuality at the time – the gay liberation movement was only just getting under way – reporting on the questioning of Trudeau's sexual orientation was beyond the pale.[84] It was not possible to say what the most abominable slanders were about, *Le Droit* editorialized, and it did not want to promote them by repeating them.[85] To leave the issue unaddressed, however, was to ignore an Achilles heel in Trudeau's candidacy, so the media addressed it actively, if obliquely, in two ways. The first was to ask Trudeau straight out why he was single, a prompt for Trudeau to provide assurances of his solidarity with the deep-seated heteronormativity of the era. The female *Telegram* reporter who wrote about his encounter with Playboy bunnies, for instance, asked him about marriage.[86] He said he knew people wondered about it, that he'd had a serious relationship once that had almost led to marriage, but that it hadn't worked out. More often he deflected the question with a bit of humour. In the Parliament Hill sequence immediately following his interview at the Château Laurier pool, DePoe asked Trudeau why he'd never married. "I guess I've just never found the right girl," he replied. At other times he replied, "Nobody ever asked me," or "There are so many pretty girls, it's so hard to decide," or "I'm waiting until I find a girl who wants to go to South America for her honeymoon. They all want to go to Europe."[87]

The second way in which the media dealt with the issue was to showcase Trudeau with attractive women. Trudeau obliged by performing heterosexuality. When a reporter asked who would be the hostess at 24 Sussex, if he, a bachelor, were elected, he pointed to the closest young woman, Joyce Fairbairn, a reporter for the *Vancouver Sun*.[88] When a television interviewer asked if he'd hiked solo the previous weekend, he smiled slyly and let it slip that "there was a blonde along."[89] No one asked if the blonde were male. He took Jennifer Rae, a willowy blonde woman young enough to be his daughter, to a diplomatic reception soon after he became prime minister. Predictably, the date made the front pages.[90] He knew what the media needed to make him normal and consistently obliged.

The accusation that he was a communist was, in contrast, based on statements and actions that were on the public record. In this case the press response was remarkable for its lack of critical scrutiny. Rather than disproving the allegation, journalists simply characterized it as a smear and denounced its perpetrators. "Never before in a Canadian election has a prime minister been the subject of so much hatred and innuendo as has been flung at Pierre Elliott Trudeau in the current campaign," declared Peter Newman.[91] Accusations of this sort were also out of bounds because they smacked of McCarthyism. Moreover, since political and sexual deviance were closely linked, to countenance one was tantamount to admitting the other. Any credence given either slur threatened the nationalist project of seeing Canada transformed. Conspicuously ignored by the media, the smear campaign was kept on the margins, circulated among reactionaries primarily by old-fashioned means of communication.

The Trudeau image mended many worrisome schisms in contemporary Canadian society. The national unity crisis was one. Trudeau was bilingualism and biculturalism personified, reconciling the French-English divide. Regional differences were transcended through the widespread support he garnered from nationalists coast to coast, particularly in cities. Though he was middle-aged, Trudeau's image bridged the generation gap by investing him with the most prized characteristics of contemporary youth culture. The ambiguous sexuality intimated by his image undermined gender distinctions and subtly signalled tolerance of alternative sexual orientations. He alleviated mediation anxiety by problematizing the media's role in national politics, in the process collapsing the gap between reality and representation. All these tensions were resolved in the all-encompassing image of the Great Leader.

Trudeau's mod image may have seemed a fantastic concoction, but it served perfectly nationalists' contemporary aspirations. "If I were asked to invent a politician who would come closest to

Canada's needs and desires in 1968, he would come awfully close to Pierre Elliott Trudeau," wrote Charles Lynch.[92] His image served as a sorting mechanism that tested one's sympathy with emergent values. It appealed to "the young, the sophisticated, the urban, the intellectual," noted an Ottawa newspaper editor.[93] In this sense, however, the image was divisive. The mending of so many fracture lines in the body politic came at the expense of splitting Canadians into opposing progressive and traditionalist camps.[94] The Trudeau image might put off the unenlightened, but the march of progress inevitably left some behind. The nation had to move forward. Mod nationalism both prompted and expedited that imperative.

A CBC film crew captures the action of an intense media scrum
during the parliamentary crisis of February 1968.

7

Reel to Real I
The Liberal Leadership Campaign

I feel like a Beatle.
Not that I have anything against the Beatles,
but is this the way to choose a leader?

PIERRE TRUDEAU, *Saturday Night,* 1968

THE MODERN NATION was facilitated by the mass media's ability to foster a sense of collective identity among citizens otherwise divided by region, class, ethnicity, and countless other differences. By the late 1960s television ownership was widespread, its producers were mastering political coverage, and politicians were recognizing that performing for the camera was part of their job. With news footage of events in Ottawa now appearing with little time lag across the country, the national conversation became more pervasive and immediate, increasing people's sense of participation in the imagined dominion.

Voters now knew politicians not just by reading of them in a newspaper or magazine, or hearing them or of them on the radio, but by seeing them on television, a medium that fostered the illusion of a personal encounter. Were onscreen representations as reliable as the more tangible encounters of everyday life? Surely the latter were authentic; the former, comparatively artificial and therefore suspect. The anxiety induced by this incongruity inspired many contemporary experimental film and stage productions, including those at Expo 67 in which film actors left the screen and appeared onstage, transforming the celluloid image into a live actor, only to disappear back into the movie. Pop stars performed a similar transformation. They were known primarily through the media until they went on tour and made the representation real. During election campaigns politicians did the same.

Oddly, fan exposure to celebrities during their personal appearances most often came in a crowd situation that was less up close and personal than encounters through the television screen. The difference in context made up for what was lost in range. The celebrity proved that he or she was real, affirming the authenticity of the relationship with fans, while the fans were reassured that they were genuinely part of something bigger than their directly experienced everyday existence. The distance between the worlds of the celebrity and fan collapsed in a brief communion that resolved the tensions inherent in their mediated relationship. Then the celebrity returned to the screen world. Their appearance in the here and now was significant, but necessarily brief if they were not to be contaminated by the ordinariness of the everyday. The dynamism and excitement of the crowd experiencing the celebrity live was in turn broadcast on television, which transmitted those emotions into the domestic sphere, further conflating tangible and imagined communities. The reel-to-real synthesis was a validation of mass-mediated community that dissipated mediation anxiety, generating waves of relief that propelled the relationship forward.[1]

Canadian political leaders had long toured the country to win support during elections. The appearance in person of the famous man at the grassroots level was a staple ritual of democracy, a gesture symbolically recognizing the sovereignty of the people. In the past, however, tours had not been a prominent feature of leadership campaigns. In 1958, Lester Pearson had campaigned for the Liberal leadership by installing himself in a suite at the Château Laurier and receiving key delegates. He never left Ottawa. When he won on the first ballot, his acceptance speech was broadcast on television. A decade later, the entire convention was staged for television, and the touring feature of general elections had come to characterize leadership campaigns as well. From late February through March 1968, Trudeau travelled twenty thousand miles and made thirty stops as he criss-crossed the country to meet delegates.[2] Once he was positioned as an object of interest by the media, his celebrity attracted crowds to his personal appearances, which

increased media coverage, which increased curiosity and crowds ...
and so it went, in a virtuous cycle of mutually reinforcing event
and representation. The resulting political phenomenon seemed
unstoppable, like "a great god-damned Wagnerian wave," groused
one of his leadership rivals.[3]

The media gaze fell upon the host communities one after another, looping through the national territory and drawing it together.
As Trudeau came into town, locals preened in the national spotlight and the visitation headlined the news. Meanwhile the central
plot line of the leadership campaign rose towards the climax of
the convention in Ottawa in early April, a grand spectacle with a
colourful cast of characters pitted against one another in suspenseful circumstances while the fate of the nation hung in the balance.
It was a reel-world extravaganza that would be watched all across
the country.

The seven-week stretch between Trudeau's declaration of his
candidacy and the convention began with a crisis at the centre of
national affairs. Though Pearson had warned leadership candidates
not to neglect their cabinet duties, many were often on the road
meeting delegates that winter. So it was on February 19, the Monday
following Trudeau's announcement, when the government was
defeated in the House of Commons on a fiscal measure that could
have been interpreted as a nonconfidence vote. The embarrassed
Liberals improvised another vote on a motion declaring that their
defeat had not been a confidence issue. All eyes were on Ottawa as
the drama played out over the last ten days of the month. Pearson
went on television to accuse the Conservatives of playing political
games at the expense of the nation's business. Parliament was transcended and, with Créditiste support, the motion passed. Whereas
some of his leadership rivals had been absent campaigning, Trudeau
was in the Commons when the first vote was lost. In the aftermath
he participated in the government's strategizing and subsequently
defended the Liberals' position vigorously in the House. He came
off looking responsible and engaged.

Trudeau scrubbed a planned trip to Alberta and British Columbia the weekend of February 24-25 because he did not want to risk
missing a sitting of the Commons critical to resolving the crisis
on the following Monday. He did not get away to begin wooing
delegates until after the government was in the clear. As a result,
Trudeau's first leadership campaign outing was not until the evening of Wednesday, February 28, when he drove to Kingston with
local MP Edgar Benson to speak to an overflow crowd of five hundred people and meet with delegates afterwards. In his speech
Trudeau talked at length about participatory democracy. Not yet
used to stump campaigning, he wasn't particularly animated,
repeated himself, and went on a bit too long. It didn't matter.
The crowd loved him. Here, live in the flesh, was the celebrity
as-seen-on-TV.

In Toronto, the St. George Liberal Association had been staging
a series of meetings with the candidates for the Liberal leadership
in the venerable St. Lawrence Hall. Trudeau agreed to appear for
his session on the evening of March 1 (his cabinet colleague Robert
Winters announced his candidacy for the leadership that day,
rounding out the field). It was Trudeau's first appearance in Toronto since he had entered the race two weeks earlier. The four-
hundred-seat hall sold out – the first time in the series this had
happened. The organizers set up an adjoining room with closed-
circuit television, but it sold out too, so they put a TV in the down-
stairs lobby, which quickly overflowed. People continued to arrive
until a crowd of hundreds milled around outside.

When Trudeau showed up he was asked if he could do anything
for those who couldn't get in. "Perhaps we could meet later in
Yorkville," he suggested, titillating the outsiders by alluding to
the local hippie hangout. After the presence glided on, CBC TV
reporter Larry Zolf characterized the atmosphere as "just like a re-
vival meeting."[4]

Inside, Trudeau got a standing ovation merely for walking
through the door. He spoke for half an hour without any dramatic

rhetoric, then sparkled in the question and answer session. Fraser Kelly, the political editor of the *Toronto Telegram*, asked what he would think of an Ontario politician who advocated a constitutional policy opposed by its premier and other leading politicians, by the media, and the church. He was really invoking Trudeau's situation in Quebec. Trudeau replied, smiling, "I'd say he had a lot of guts," and brought down the house. When Warner Troyer of the CBC asked him, "How badly do you want to be Prime Minister?" Trudeau replied, "Not very badly," then continued, "But I can give you another quotation, from Plato – that men who want very badly to head the country shouldn't be trusted."[5] His quick-wittedness and candour, laced with irony, self-deprecation, and erudition, won him laughter and applause. Afterwards he had to run a gauntlet of autograph hunters outside. "If the Toronto reaction is typical of the rest of Canada," concluded Gary Oakes of the *Telegram* the next day, "the other candidates might just as well close their campaign headquarters."[6]

Good organization is usually needed to define a positive image for a candidate. Trudeau's team was not particularly seasoned and had to work out many kinks as it planned and executed his first delegate fishing expeditions. It didn't matter. Just as Trudeau's popularity was a phenomenon that could not have been engineered, it was immune to errant amateurism. Recognizing they had a telegenic candidate, his handlers now steered him away from interviews with the national media, reasoning that he had had enough exposure over the previous few months and that the potential downside of his saying something that could be used against him was greater than the potential upside of anything further he could say. They would, however, have him filmed whenever possible, so his image would continue to appear in the public sphere. As Jim Davey, the Montreal management consultant who was the campaign committee chairman, put it, "We decided to take advantage of any television opportunities offered us. If this meant that a three-man camera crew wanted to ride in Trudeau's 7-seater jet, that would be just fine. Kick out the newsmen."[7] When delegates asked for a closed meeting with Trudeau, his organizers would acquiesce, but then slip a cameraman in to get footage of the excitement in the room.

The Quebec issue remained central. At a Union Nationale fundraiser in Montreal in late February, Premier Johnson accused Trudeau of running down French Canada in a manner reminiscent of Lord Durham, and called him Lord Elliott. Trudeau shot back that "calling me Lord Elliott when his name is Johnson is a ... sticky wicket."[8] Trudeau also attacked Quebec's diplomatic initiatives. That very month Quebec education minister Jean-Guy Cardinal had represented his province at an education conference in Gabon, a tiny equatorial West African republic. The event was attended by France and a dozen or so former French colonies, and the fleur-de-lys flew alongside national flags. Trudeau was all over this issue – he had been responsible for this file from 1966 through 1967 – and he supported Pearson's decision to respond by breaking off diplomatic relations with Gabon.[9]

Terms like the Trudeau "boom," "Trudeauism," or, in French Canada, "Trudeauidolâtrie" were employed to describe the enthusiasm expressed for Trudeau at his public appearances. The one that would stick, "Trudeaumania," was coined by columnist Lubor Zink in the *Toronto Telegram* on March 4. Ironically, he was predicting that Trudeau's popularity was on the wane. "The fad, like Beatlemania, is fading," he claimed.

> Many MPs on both sides of the House who at first succumbed to the psychosis of the tremendous Trudeau build-up by the mass media, now see the Justice Minister as a conceited, tactless, ruthless and dangerous political opportunist whose methods of operation betray the phoniness of his public image of pristine idealism.

Zink meant to ridicule Trudeau by using the term "Trudeaumania." He thought that in the serious realm of politics any allusion to pop culture was a put-down. Instead the media seized on it as a positive descriptor of Trudeau's appeal, and by spring the term was in common journalistic usage.[10]

Throughout March the reel-to-real synthesis consisted of week-days in the Commons in Ottawa, where Trudeau received national political coverage, and weekends packed with appearances in communities across the country and on TV. On the weekend of March 2-3, he toured southern Ontario, followed by two CBC television camera crews. The *Toronto Telegram* ran a front-page story reporting that rival leadership candidate Paul Hellyer led Trudeau among Toronto delegates. So what? The story was overshadowed by a large photo on the same page of Trudeau kissing a young blonde woman. "I'll never wash my face again," she said. "Isn't he wonderful?"[11]

The following weekend, March 9-10, Trudeau's private jet flew west, where he knocked off Lethbridge, Medicine Hat, Edmonton, Calgary, Winnipeg, and Brandon. In Lethbridge, Trudeau was arriving just after John Turner and Paul Hellyer had met with delegates and he crossed paths with Hellyer on his way through the airport as he was departing. Turner had attracted 35 delegates; Hellyer 70. Trudeau's organizers decided to throw his meeting with delegates open to the public, and 600 people showed up.[12] In Medicine Hat, a newspaper columnist noted one of positive pay-offs of the reel-to-real effect:

> Trudeau's biggest accomplishment on his trip to Medicine Hat, and indeed throughout Alberta, was that he convinced people, delegates in particular, that he is real. I don't suppose that many of the delegates had ever met Trudeau before his weekend visit. They have undoubtably read about him, talked about him and seen him on television. Yet I have a feeling that many delegates would have been reluctant, and rightly so, to vote for a man they had never met. Just coming here was perhaps the best thing Trudeau could have done to increase his support in the West.[13]

Locals who expected a wild-eyed radical were surprised to encounter a well-mannered, soft-spoken professorial figure.

Like their Quebec counterparts, the media in the West were skeptical at first about all the fuss over Trudeau. When he generated enthusiastic public responses locally, however, it became news that they reported on. Like the Western premiers, newspaper editorialists had woken up recently to the gravity of the Quebec challenge to Confederation. They now recognized that the national unity crisis was real, and that, compared to the alternatives, Trudeau and official bilingualism might be the best available solution. It then became their duty as opinion leaders to bring their audiences around to this same way of thinking.

Destinations that were within striking distance of Ottawa were targeted for midweek forays when Commons business allowed. On Monday, March 11, Trudeau was interviewed by John Bassett on the CTV television program *Pulse*. On Wednesday, March 13, he travelled to Saint-Basile-le-Grand, on the eastern outskirts of Montreal. He was supposed to carry on to Moncton, but due to foggy conditions made it only as far as Fredericton. The weekend after that, March 16-17, it was Saskatoon and Regina on Saturday, and Vancouver and Victoria on Sunday. In Vancouver, the wife of the president of the Liberal Federation, who supported Hellyer for the leadership, told reporters she was for Trudeau because the party "desperately needed a new image." "And anyway," she concluded, "I think he's sexy."[14] In Victoria, still a crumpets-and-tea royalist town, he was asked about the monarchy, an issue he usually dismissed as not worth worrying about. "I was in Saskatoon the other night and crowned a very lovely queen," he replied with one of his patented shrugs. "So I feel very warm towards the monarchy."[15]

On Thursday night, March 21, Trudeau was in Montreal for a well-attended book launch for *Réponses de Pierre Elliott Trudeau*, a slim volume his friend Gérard Pelletier had put together to repudiate neonationalist insinuations that Trudeau was not a real Québécois. Trudeau had planned to go to Halifax the next day but his flight from Ottawa was cancelled, again due to fog. On Sunday, March 24, he was in northeastern Ontario, visiting Sudbury and North Bay and ending up in Timmins in the evening. Since reports of Trudeau-infatuated females were now an integral part of the narrative, a reporter followed up when a hotel switchboard operator in Sudbury mentioned that "Mary (the desk clerk) shook hands with [Trudeau] and now she's $40 out adding up the cash." "Yes," Mary admitted, "I was so shook up."[16]

The national magazines were now all over the Trudeau phenomenon. *Saturday Night* magazine put Trudeau on its March cover.[17] *Weekend Magazine* devoted a third of a cover in one of its March issues to announce that inside it was running excerpts from *Federalism and the French Canadians*. Peter Gzowski, editor of the *Star Weekly* magazine, decided that his publication should help the Liberals decide who'd be the country's next prime minister by running a series on the candidates. His operating premise was that Canada was getting younger and its politicians were out of touch: "Canadians desperately seek a political leader of a new kind, a leader ... contemporary in mind and spirit, a man of intellect and daring, and above all, a man who welcomes change." Gzowski sent his magazine's national correspondent, Walter Stewart, and the young CBC TV producer Moses Znaimer across the country to talk to Canadian youth about the leadership question. Staff writer Margaret Daly was to look at the style of the candidates, and Gzowski hired Mordecai Richler to write an introductory essay on what ailed Canadian politics. Richler dined with Trudeau and wrote, "This shaky Canadian state, these stormy times, call for a daring man, an original, with imagination and a gift for rhetoric." Although Richler concluded reluctantly that Trudeau didn't have a chance of winning and that John Turner was a more realistic bet for those wanting renewal, the conclusion of Stewart's and Znaimer's investigations was that young Canadians wanted Trudeau. The *Star Weekly* ended its series with Trudeau on the cover of its March 23 issue under the headline "Trudeau: Why Young Canada Feels He'd Make a Great Prime Minister."[18]

Trudeau spent the entire final week of his leadership campaign on the road. It began with a trip to St. John's, where Newfoundland premier Joey Smallwood had arranged for him to be the first federal cabinet minister to address the legislature in regular session. On Tuesday, March 26, he appeared in Rivière-du-Loup, then continued to Quebec City to a jammed Reform Club reception including, according to a male reporter, "women whose faces were rapturous as they listened."[19] A Saint-Jean-Baptiste Society meeting in suburban Charlesbourg was less enthusiastic, but respectful. The day ended with yet another Reform Club meeting in Sherbrooke.

The Quebec media were less overawed by Trudeau than their anglophone equivalents. Newspapers were more likely to report that Trudeau was seen to be a sexy swinger than to promote him as one. There were no front-page photos of Trudeau kissing blondes in the French Canadian press during the winter months.[20] While Québécois could be enthused about Trudeau's appearances, they were not so crazed as audiences elsewhere in the country. Yet even in rural Quebec his reception was, the odd heckler excepted, respectful, and often enthusiastic.[21] Though at first parts of the Quebec federal Liberal Party establishment were resistant to his candidacy – understandably given the required backpedalling on "two nations" – strong-arm tactics and the likelihood he would deliver them to power were bringing them around. Trudeau would end up with the support of a large majority of Quebec delegates.

On March 27, Trudeau hopped on to Saint John, New Brunswick, for a delegate meeting and lunch hosted by the McCain family. Then he was off to Moncton for an afternoon meeting with delegates and, finally, Charlottetown, where Premier Alex Campbell met his plane at the airport with a large and enthusiastic delegation. A PEI housewife had her husband drive her from Summerside to Charlottetown just to see him. After waiting two hours for Trudeau to arrive, she turned down a chance to be introduced, saying only, "I adore that man. I simply adore him."[22]

On Thursday, March 28, Trudeau was in Montreal for a taping of Radio-Canada's popular late evening TV show *Les Couche-Tard*, a dinner with delegates at Rosemère, off the north end of the island, then back downtown for a rally in his Mount Royal riding, where he delighted supporters by breaking into a vaudeville dance step as the band played "Maître Pierre." Since Trudeau's riding was largely anglophone, his seat was as safe as could be. Anglo-Quebeckers did not much like the prospect of being a minority in a province given special status as the homeland of French Canadians. They liked still less the idea of living in a separate Quebec nation-state. Trudeau's defence of federalism was music to their ears.

Given how well Trudeau came across on TV, journalists were surprised to discover he could be boring when delivering a speech live.[23] He hadn't mastered the exaggerative rhetorical mode required to project to a large crowd. Indeed, he was by nature resistant to the necessary histrionics. The problem was worse when he had a set speech on a policy issue, and not so bad when he spoke without notes on a favourite theme such as national unity. He would improve as he became more accustomed to such appearances. Until then the thrill of seeing a celebrity, the aura of his mere presence, carried him through some lacklustre performances. For example, on March 29, the Friday night before convention week, he flew into Toronto for meetings, tapings, and press conferences. In the evening he gave a speech to a crowd of fifteen hundred at the Queen Elizabeth building at the Exhibition grounds. Hundreds of disappointed fans were turned away at the door. His speech was less than riveting, but it didn't seem to matter to the crowd, which thrilled to the experience of seeing the great man. The reel-to-real synthesis worked without much juicing up of the real.

Trudeau's initially dull speechifying was offset by his performance in question and answer sessions or when sparring with the audience, situations where his quick wit carried the day. "I get a great deal of pleasure out of teaching, I suppose," he told a radio interviewer, "of exchanging ideas with people, trying to convince them."[24] On March 30, Trudeau flew to Trois-Rivières and then Arvida. Questioned about the Criminal Code amendments, particularly homosexuality, he replied that Canada had become a pluralistic society. "What about masturbation?" a man shouted. The crowd boggled. "Well" – Trudeau shrugged – "I suppose everyone has his problems." There was relief and wild laughter.[25]

Trudeau usually stopped at local media outlets to tape interviews. The Liberal campaign team knew that the questions would be easy and that the local stations would publicize his celebrity presence in the community. "From the moment he [Trudeau] had entered the race," wrote Peter Newman, "the managers of the electronic media made an instinctive decision that he would be the winner."[26] A media critic pointed out that in a CBC pre-convention TV special that had conducted street interviews to determine the "people's choice" of leader, if the interviewee failed to mention Trudeau, the reporter would follow up immediately by asking eagerly, "What do you think of Mr. Trudeau?"[27]

Excitement about the Liberal convention was building. Usually the leadership had been passed on to an heir apparent: Mackenzie King to Louis St. Laurent, St. Laurent to Pearson. The last wide-open leadership convention had been a half-century earlier, when King won in 1919. The Liberals had a track record of skipping to a new generation for leadership, leaving senior statesmen behind. Great drama lay ahead.

Trudeau spent Monday and most of Tuesday of convention week at his family home in Outremont, holding meetings with aides about strategy. When he arrived in Ottawa on the afternoon of Wednesday, April 3, a wildly enthusiastic mob greeted him at the train station. Hundreds of teenagers carrying handmade signs ("Get that Kennedy feeling with Trudeau," among others) rushed from one side of the station to the other in response to rumours of his entrance, jostling with older fans, delegates, reporters, and camera crews for sight lines. Trudeau made his way through the crowd and into a waiting car, where a television interviewer who rode with him asked him what he thought of the pandemonium. "This kind of popularity is easily lost," he reflected. "Perhaps easily won. Easy come, easy go. I think like most people who get to be known through television, they can get pretty chewed up by the medium."[28]

Mitchell Sharp, once a leading leadership contender, had been hurt by the defeat of his tax bill in February and had subsequently been unable to campaign much because of his responsibilities as minister of finance. Earlier that week he had concluded that he could not win and decided to throw his support to Trudeau. He and Trudeau had chosen this moment to announce his endorsement at a joint press conference. It was another image enhancement for Trudeau. The backing of Sharp, whose WASP stolidity and public service career exuded dependability, reassured those who questioned Trudeau's substance or worried that he was a radical.

With spirits still high from the Sharp endorsement, Trudeau supporters headed for a party hosted by the Quebec Liberals that night at the Chaudière Country Club in Hull, Quebec, across the Ottawa River. Delegates, campaign workers, and the curious flocked to the event. Cars were parked up and down the road for half a mile, and the provincial police arrived on the scene to keep traffic flowing. Inside the club was packed. When Trudeau arrived at eleven, his aides had to form a flying wedge to get him to the stage, which was ringed by a phalanx of cameramen and photographers. From all sides hands stretched out to touch him. He tried to speak, but the sound system was down. It didn't matter. Partiers hoisted him to their shoulders and carried him around. He danced with a young woman for a minute. The energy in the room made him a bit giddy. He sang along with Bobby Gimby's puerile "Ca-na-da" and made inane partygoer comments like "Hi, how are you! Good party!"[29] Then Joey Smallwood appeared and declared, "Pierre is better than medicare – the lame have only to touch his garments to walk again."[30]

A Gallup poll published on the opening day of the convention showed that Trudeau was the public's choice for the Liberal leadership.[31] With all the publicity he had generated, some assumed he would run away with the convention.[32] But that assumption was grounded on the false equivalency of the Liberal Party membership with fashionable opinion. Parties consist of concentric circles

Trudeau and supporters celebrate at Chaudière
Country Club in Hull, Quebec.

of power. At the centre are low-profile apparatchiks who have their hands on the levers of power and the cash box. In the next circle are loyal party workers who operate through riding associations across the country getting out the message and the vote. The next ring includes habitual partisans, many of whom may be party members, though relatively inactive ones. After that is a still more disparate group that vaguely sympathizes with the party and is inclined to support it. The Liberal leadership contest was, strictly speaking, a matter of different cliques from the first group vying for support from the second group. There was still a great deal of resistance to Trudeau among circle two traditionalists who either found him too left-leaning or didn't like having power snatched from them by some johnny-come-lately. According to Maurice Western of the *Winnipeg Free Press*, "suspicion of the stranger was deepened for many delegates by the rapture with which Mr. Trudeau's cause has been embraced by Gordon-ites and near-socialists both within the party and in the general field of information and television."[33] His mod image and all the media hype got their backs up. "They didn't know Trudeau," Richard Gwyn observed. "Worse, in terms of their prospects for patronage, he didn't know them."[34]

Nevertheless, public opinion could trump the party power structure. While Trudeau's travels over the previous month had been ostensibly to allow him to meet delegates, the crowds they attracted served as an object lesson to those delegates of the prospects for power under his leadership. They were in a bind. However much they resented the media's boosting of Trudeau, if it worked for the electorate, they'd be crazy not to go along.[35] His popularity, *Time* reported, was "giving the Liberal delegates a clear signal that he represented the best hope of electoral renewal."[36] The inner circles of the party wanted above all to be in power, and if Trudeau could deliver that, they would put aside their scruples.

In the face of delegate resistance, Trudeau's strategists decided to play things low-key in Ottawa.[37] While other campaigns were gearing up the razzmatazz with cheerleaders, marching bands, and "spontaneous" demonstrations with banners and balloons boosting their candidates, the Trudeau campaign would show that the reel man was real by putting him into direct contact with as many delegates as possible in the short time available before the voting began. As other candidates lurked in their hospitality suites, hoping to ensnare passing delegates, Trudeau circulated, meeting with farmers in the West Block, women at a reception he hosted at the National Library, and Young Liberals at a dance at the Château Laurier. He even dropped by the National Press Club for a drink. A middle-aged woman at the meeting at the National Library became so nervous in asking Trudeau a question that she placed the microphone in her ear. Trudeau playfully answered with his microphone to his own ear.[38]

A section of arena seats was reserved for each of the candidates and their supporters. When the convention opened on Thursday, most campaigns hyped their candidates' arrival in the convention hall with a triumphal procession. Hellyer marched in with his troops and his band blaring, Turner came in pumping hands in a gaggle of big men on campus, Martin shook hands and greeted delegates by name, flashing victory salutes, and Winters waltzed in to the tune of "Walking in a Winter Wonderland." In contrast, Trudeau "[crept] in like Jesus Christ," slipping unheralded into his seat, followed by a few homemade banners and "pretty girls." "It looked like a children's crusade in an age that worships children," wrote Christina Newman.[39] When the crowd caught sight of him there was a roar of excitement.

At the policy workshops on opening day, crowds of delegates followed Trudeau from one session to the next. Wherever he went, people wanted to "touch him as though he were some kind of messiah."[40] The Liberals were gathering to say goodbye to Lester Pearson that evening when news came that Martin Luther King Jr. had been assassinated in Memphis. Inner-city black neighbourhoods in Washington and Chicago erupted in rioting. Coverage of the tragedy and its aftermath dominated the news, but in the middle of it all Ottawa's CJOH-TV broadcast an hour-long interview of Trudeau by *This Hour Has Seven Days* star Patrick Watson. It featured doting close-up shots of Trudeau's eminently watchable face as he pondered questions then delivered thoughtful and lively answers.[41] By the next day there were reports of violence, arson, and looting in Baltimore and Pittsburgh. The Peaceable Kingdom firewall was more important than ever.

The convention, broadcast in colour by the two national networks, was a chaotic kaleidoscope of shifting sights. All the campaigns had young workers, many of them university students. Dressed in coordinated outfits, they greeted delegates, handed out brochures, and staffed hospitality rooms. Merle Shain, a host of CTV's W5, organized the Pierrettes, the young women who were working for Trudeau at the convention. They wore persimmon-orange coloured shifts and matching berets from Montreal's Poupée Rouge boutique. In what one paper called "politics by miniskirt," they had been recruited on the basis of their looks and manners to ensure that they would set off the candidate in an appropriately decorous fashion.[42] They were supplemented with young men, fewer in number, clad in white turtlenecks and orange vests. In addition to these young recruits, the Trudeau campaign attracted many talented women in their mid-twenties. "We were young, we were 'girls' (it was 1968, remember)," recalled Alison Gordon, one of this group. "We had ... recently returned from living in what was then 'Swinging London' and wore miniskirts shorter than some blouses I wear now."[43]

The media took up almost as much space in the convention hall as the delegates. They weren't as numerous, but they had lots of equipment, including bulky television cameras that were placed in prominent positions around the convention floor. One was on an elevated platform directly in front of the podium at centre stage. The power behind the throne was right in front of it, dominating the convention floor and obstructing delegates' views of the action. Outside in the parking lot the media were backed up by trailers full

The leadership rivals recruited teams of young
people and dressed them in distinctive outfits to
brand their campaign and help with convention duties
such as delegate hospitality, cheerleading,
and escorting the candidate. In Trudeau's team,
women outnumbered men and wore
orange dresses from a Montreal boutique.

of technology that relayed the action to the nation. Prominent in their cameras' views of the convention floor were the placards brandished by the different contenders' supporters. Most had the candidate's surname in block letters offset by a field of the campaign's colours. Trudeau had a few different signs, one of which was particularly mod. "Two of us were in charge of all the buttons, posters and other publicity materials for the campaign," Gordon explained.

> I don't remember where I got the idea for it, but I suspect it was based on a similar one of Che Guevara that had hung on the walls of a lot of lefty/hippie communes I'd spent time in. Whatever, I found a picture I thought would work (taken by Boris Spremo at one of Trudeau's speeches), passed it along to a young photographer hanging around who gave it the high-resolution development. Then I began taking it to the political bosses, who, to a man, hated it. But hey, I knew what was what. We sent one down to Trudeau, who said he liked it.[44]

They ordered five thousand. Robert Winters told delegates that "we're choosing a Prime Minister here. It's not a psychedelic experience."[45] But the abstract image of Trudeau's face, defined by shadow, was everywhere, mocking his words.

The Che-style poster was complemented by a drawing of Trudeau by trendy Toronto artist Harold Town that graced the cover of a Trudeau newsletter circulated among delegates. The Trudeau team covered all the bases, responded quickly to new developments, and executed well. Soon after Winters's supporters were spotted sporting lapel buttons proclaiming "It's Winters' Time," Trudeau supporters received a new button reading "It's Spring!"

Friday night was the big night when the candidates made their nomination acceptance speeches. It was their moment in the spotlight before all the delegates, their last chance to make an impression that would convert the uncommitted for the first ballot or draw second-choice votes in subsequent rounds. When it was its candidate's turn to speak, each campaign concentrated its forces for a staged display of enthusiasm, parading its man to the stage amid a crowd of supporters accompanied by music, balloons, streamers, placards, and other colourful hoopla. Trudeau had drawn the second-last spot, so the routine was well established by the time his turn came. Instead of concentrating their forces around Trudeau, his organizers decided to disperse them throughout the crowd. When Trudeau's name was announced, a roar of support rose from the stands. Banners unfurled, Trudeau signs rose in a bristling phalanx up to the rafters, and the candidate made his way to the podium accompanied by only a few young women from his campaign team as a deep and powerful chant of "Troo-dough!" resounded through the arena. Seemingly a spontaneous popular uprising, it was a magical TV moment.

Trudeau was subdued as he spoke about his passion for individual rights. The speech was not rousing, but it conveyed seriousness, substance, and a certain "I am not worthy" humility. Faced with the choice of stage acting for the arena crowd or screen acting for the nation, he chose the latter. He spoke movingly of the death of Martin Luther King. He went on to declare his faith in "the triumph of logic in politics over passion, the protection of individual freedom against the collective tyranny, and a just distribution of the national wealth."[46] It was a mod manifesto for a hip nation. His remarks were deliberately concise to allow for extended applause afterwards. The enthusiastic cheering went on and on after he'd finished. Journalists stood up from their seats and joined in.[47]

The drama of the voting began on the morrow. "Dirty dishes languished in the sink and last week's wash went unattended [as] I followed Pierre Elliott Trudeau's fortunes to the very end on Saturday," wrote a women's page columnist in Quesnel, British Columbia.[48] It was estimated that 17 million Canadians watched or listened to at least part of the final day of the Liberal convention.[49]

Journalists roamed the floor and the stands in search of behind-the-scenes power brokers, wheedled comments out of delegates, and swung boom mikes over the heads of candidates to eavesdrop

Trudeau supporter at the convention, with campaign buttons as earrings. When there was no dramatic action to focus on, news photographers turned their attention to young women.

on their conversations. "Eight camera crews clustered about the Justice Minister," observed Peter Newman, "ignoring most of the other candidates much of the time, giving Trudeau the advantage of built-in excitement and bathing him in a constant halo of artificial light."[50]

First ballot voting began around 1:00 p.m. Troubles with the vote-tabulating machines led to an hour's delay. The candidates sweated it out, anxious to discover their fortunes. Finally, at 2:30, the results were announced:

Trudeau	752
Hellyer	330
Winters	293
Martin	277
Turner	277
Greene	169
MacEachen	165
Kierans	103

With the cards on the table, the game began. Eric Kierans and Paul Martin withdrew from the race and left their delegates free to vote for the candidate of their choice. In his notes for his withdrawal statement, Martin wrote, "I have been caught in the generation gap."[51] Allan MacEachen also withdrew, but too late to have his name taken off the second ballot.

It took another two hours for the delegates to vote again and for the second ballot to be counted:

Trudeau	964
Winters	473
Hellyer	465
Turner	347
Greene	104
MacEachen	11

Trudeau smelling a carnation while sitting in the stands at the leadership convention. In contemporary pop culture, it was typically hippies who stopped to smell the flowers. Trudeau was not only gesturing solidarity with the counterculture; he was also showing himself to be confident enough in his masculinity to mess with gender conventions.

For delegates opposed to Trudeau, Winters, an older establishment figure, had emerged as their best hope to defeat the upstart.
At this point Trudeau needed only another 235 votes to win. The
way things were stacking up, he'd make it unless Winters, Hellyer,
and one other candidate joined forces.

A boom microphone eavesdropped on Secretary of State Judy
LaMarsh as she implored Hellyer to go to Winters lest "that bas-
tard" Trudeau should win. Both Winters and Hellyer met with
Turner and tried to convince him to join them, but he refused. The
third ballot confirmed the trend already in place:

Trudeau	1,051
Winters	621
Hellyer	377
Turner	279
Greene	29

Hellyer's and Winters's support combined added up to 998 delegates. Hellyer made the move to Winters, and the two again tried
unsuccessfully to get Turner to come over to their side. He still refused. The results were announced by Liberal Party president John
Nichol at 8:00 p.m.:

Trudeau	1,203
Winters	954
Turner	195

"Ahh, that's it," said Winters, smiling bravely, "he's got it."[52] Pierre
Trudeau was the leader of the Liberal Party and the next prime
minister of Canada.

"A Modern Man for Canada," declared the headline the next day
in the *Toronto Daily Star*. The modernization project was under way.
"In his comportment, style, and ideas, Pierre Elliott Trudeau appears to be the herald of a new political era, very different from the

At the moment of victory, images of the new
prime minister watched over him.

old," editorialized Cyrille Felteau in *La Presse*. The determining factor for those delegates who were moving from their first choice as the ballots went on, Christina Newman noted, was "a safe-risk split, a division between those who wanted a man for the 1950s and those pushing for a man for the 1970s." "The core of this seemingly casual campaign," she continued, "was a highly controlled machine and a very clever plan, focused on making one feel that a vote against Trudeau was a vote against the Canadian future."[53]

Yet it had been by no means a sure thing because not everyone was in step with the times. Almost half the Liberal delegates had voted against the mod man. Trudeau was fortunate to have had Winters, the most business-friendly candidate in the race, as his final antagonist. If the final ballot had come down to Trudeau versus a more moderate opponent, delegates who thought Winters was too right-wing might have made a different choice. Trudeau was a polarizing figure, winning only by the slimmest of margins on the fourth ballot. "Ah," said a delegate from Cape Breton, "my old woman won't let me in when I go home. This man will never win an election in Nova Scotia. We've just delivered the province to Bob Stanfield."[54]

For much of the media, the victory was a cause for celebration, and metaphorical church bells rang in the newsrooms of the nation. "When ... delegates to the Liberal convention cast their votes on the fourth ballot in favor of Pierre Elliott Trudeau, they made a decision to embark on an adventurous and challenging approach to the future of the nation," declared the editorial in the *Ottawa Citizen*. The hyperbole matched that for Expo 67. According to the *Brandon Sun*, the future would be fun: "We have stopped being deadly dull serious about being Canadians, and have instead come to find pride, even joy, in our identity." The *Whitehorse Star* concurred: "Even from this distance we could sense the excitement of having a new, younger and different type of man at the helm."[55] Trudeau slipped off to Florida for a little R & R after the convention. The media tracked him down, and soon photos of him executing backflips into the hotel pool appeared back home.[56]

Once again there were criticisms that the media had made Trudeau. Former Social Credit leader Robert Thompson attributed Trudeau's rise to supporters in the national television networks of CBC and CTV. He accused them of leading rather than reflecting public opinion and imposing their preferred candidate on the Liberal Party, naming Roy Faibish, Patrick Watson, Merle Shain, and John Saywell as the principal culprits.[57] Frank Underhill, in contrast, saw Trudeau as the creation of the Ottawa press gallery.[58]

Social democrats saw Trudeau as a faux progressive who would siphon off their support, and blamed the media. "Trudeau blurred the critical faculties with his charm and confounded attempts to analyse events by analysing them himself," wrote one such commentator.

> Not the amount of coverage, or the editorial support, but the kind of on-the-spot coverage which Trudeau received, made me think again of B. Traven's description of journalists as pimps, though in this case they weren't even making extra pocket money from their darling's progress.
>
> Trudeau has always been somewhat scornful of the press ... [which] endeared Trudeau to reporters rather than not. And it wasn't long before they were caught up holus-bolus in the old syndrome – chasing the aloof one, making silly asses of themselves, not giving a damn who knew about it, and knowing all the while that their fixation was lacking in solid substance.[59]

Maurice Western penned an extensive article in the *Winnipeg Free Press* that likewise attributed Trudeau's success to his media boosters. "He did not set out to be a colossus," he concluded. "He has been made into one by the avant-garde of the information services."[60]

With victory assured, leading lights in the media began to have pangs of conscience about what they had done. It had all been good fun when they had dared the Liberal party to embrace a novel candidate. But the dare had been accepted. What had they wrought? They were supposed to be professionals reporting objectively on the news, not newsmakers. Besides, there was little news value left in boosting Trudeau – the new opinion leader would be the Trudeauskeptic. Blair Fraser published an article in the April issue of *Maclean's* analyzing the media's role in Trudeau's rise to power, and similar pieces would appear in major national magazines and newspapers in the months that followed.[61] Mediation anxiety within the media themselves now induced self-examination, confession, and renunciation.

Though amusing, the media's contortions to recover its self-respect were by now a sideshow. "The Trudeau myth has an odd effect on the mind," *La Presse* noted. "Like a movie star, the Liberal party leader can't walk down the street without being followed by the curious or his 'fans.'"[62] Now well launched, Trudeaumania would snowball in the weeks ahead.

Sign of the times at a Liberal rally in Montreal, June 21, 1968.
The cartoon character is Linus from Charles Schulz's *Peanuts* comic strip.
Were Canadians looking for adventure, or security?

8

The Just Society, Participatory Democracy, and Other Platformities

There is nothing more attractive to ... Canadians ...
than to be titillated into voting for a radical when deep down
they are comforted by the assurance he is a conservative.

PAUL FOX, March 1968

237

IN THE WAKE of the convention, the Liberal brain trust agonized over whether to call a spring election.[1] Prior to the leadership race the conventional wisdom had been that there would be an election in the fall of 1968, but Trudeaumania changed things. By the time Trudeau was sworn in as prime minister on April 20, the Liberals had polling results showing their support was around 50 percent.[2] They knew that they were enjoying a bump in the polls from all the convention publicity, but even so, 50 percent was a robust number, leaving lots of room for support to dwindle during a campaign while remaining in majority government territory. It was hard to turn down the almost certain prospect of victory.[3]

Parliament resumed on April 23. That afternoon Trudeau left his West Block office by a secret staircase and took a car to Rideau Hall, where he asked the governor general for a dissolution of Parliament. In justifying the election call, Trudeau said, "One tangible but important phenomenon is the change in attitude of many Canadians towards the nature and future of the country ... In my own travels across the country, I have often experienced a feeling of renewed confidence and vigour, particularly among young people."[4] He rationalized it further on the basis that the Progressive Conservatives also had a new leader, and that since the previous election Canada had a new electoral map and nearly a million new voters. He wanted a mandate from the people.[5]

"The master of osculation," said John Diefenbaker, "called Parliament back so he could kiss it goodbye."[6] Otherwise there were few objections to the call. The imagined nation had been convened almost continuously since the centennial year commenced, and this would extend the session only a bit longer to complete national renewal with the installation of a new leader. Liberal offices across the country were besieged with offers to volunteer. In Edmonton, Liberal organizer Mel Hurtig received forty-seven calls in the first hour after the announcement – all from students. One enthusiast "walked in and ceremoniously tore up his NDP card."[7]

Because the Liberals' attention had been focused on the leadership race and convention until just recently, they were not prepared for an election and would have to play catch-up on both fundraising and policy. On the latter front, Trudeau relied heavily at first on progressive-sounding phrases like "the Just Society" and "participatory democracy." He'd employed the Just Society line with increasing frequency during the leadership race. On the podium following the announcement of his victory, Trudeau told the cheering delegates:

Canada must be Unified
Canada must be One
Canada must be Progressive
Canada must be a Just Society[8]

It was an inspiring slogan, but what did it mean?

Trudeau's notion of the Just Society may have originated in his university studies, when he read political philosophy. It is a theme, for instance, in John Stuart Mill's work on utilitarianism, where he asked, "What is a 'just society'?"[9] A friend of Trudeau's, the poet, legal scholar, and Co-operative Commonwealth Federation founder F.R. Scott, had used the expression in his work, but there is no evidence of Trudeau quoting him or otherwise being directly in-fluenced by his use of the term.[10] While it was comparable to Lyndon Johnson's mid-sixties slogan, "the Great Society," Trudeau had been using the term since the late 1950s, including during his Mount Royal constituency campaign in 1965.[11] It may have been an outgrowth of his interest in personalism, a strain of Catholic thought that aimed to reconcile traditional faith with liberal modernity.[12]

Trudeau explained what he meant by the Just Society in an interview with George Bain of the *Globe and Mail* late in May. The Just Society, he told Bain, was "a society in which each individual Canadian was put in a position where he can develop himself to the utmost."[13] Characteristically, then, he defined it in liberal terms, but more specifically in terms of the twentieth-century liberal em-phasis on equality of opportunity promoted by an interventionist state.[14] How did this translate into specific policies? In the interview, Trudeau first connected the Just Society with the amendments to the Criminal Code he had introduced as minister of justice.

> The Just Society means certain things in a legal sense – freeing of the individual so he will be rid of his shackles and permitted to fulfil himself in society in the way which he judges best, without being bound up by standards of morality which have nothing to do with law and order but which have to do with prejudice and religious superstition.

Then he moved on to economics, saying that the Just Society meant alleviating regional economic disparity rather than relying just on social programs targeted at individuals. He wanted to re-duce dependency on the welfare state in economically laggard areas by developing their economies. He rounded out the inter-view by saying the Just Society also meant official bilingualism and updating foreign policy to make sure that it was in line with Canada's current interests.[15]

Meanwhile, the Liberals continued scrambling to devise policy for the campaign. The policy supplements provided for the candidates' handbook relied heavily on quotations lifted from Trudeau's speeches as well as his interview with George Bain, suggesting that policy was for the moment whatever the prime minister was quoted as saying in the newspapers.[16] In early June a paper entitled "The Just Society" was issued under Trudeau's name. Again, the term was characterized in terms of equality of opportunity:

> The Just Society will be one in which all of our people will have the means and the motivation to participate. The Just Society will be one in which personal and political freedom will be more securely ensured than it has ever been in the past. The Just Society will be one in which the rights of minorities will be safe from the whims of intolerant majorities. The Just Society will be one in which those regions and groups which have not fully shared in the country's affluence will be given a better opportunity. The Just Society will be one where such urban problems as housing and pollution will be attacked through the application of new knowledge and new techniques. The Just Society will be one in which our Indian and Inuit population will be encouraged to assume the full rights of citizenship through policies which will give them both greater responsibility for their own future and more meaningful equality of opportunity. The Just Society will be a united Canada, united because all of its citizens will be actively involved in the development of a country where equality of opportunity is ensured and individuals are permitted to fulfill themselves in the fashion they judge best.[17]

This iteration enlarged the list of policies under the Just Society umbrella to include urban development, public transit, affordable housing, participatory democracy, economic development plans, a consumers' code, a faster court system, greater rights for citizens in their dealings with government, and antipollution, anti-inflation, and export development measures. It was wrapped in a commitment to rationality and functionalism in politics and tagged with warnings that those who did not join the parade of progress were doomed to obsolescence.[18]

In the speaker's handbook the Liberals put together for the campaign, "A Just Society" was one of four major headings, along with "A United Canada," "A Prosperous Economy," and "A Peaceful World." Here the Just Society platform was further expanded to include, among the planks already mentioned, auto safety, lower drug prices, revision of the Indian Act, parliamentary reform (including Senate reform), and a charter of rights.[19] The "Liberal Party Policy Statement" prepared that spring by the National Liberal Federation stated that the Just Society involved enhancing "the protection of individual rights and liberties in a society that is becoming increasingly complicated, urbanized and organized," suggesting that it was designed to alleviate some of the ills of modernity. Its means for doing so were to be a charter of rights and the already promised reforms to the justice system.[20]

The noble ring of the Just Society slogan raised expectations of a visionary project. It was a secular call to service for the common good that evoked traditional religious teachings and associated them with the nation.[21] Since it was defined in terms of equality of opportunity, one might have anticipated it would involve some bold new social democratic policies. The building of the welfare state had been one of the Liberals' great postwar accomplishments, rounded out, under Lester Pearson's leadership, with the Canada Pension Plan, the Canada Assistance Plan, a guaranteed supplement to Old Age Security, and medicare. Yet while Trudeau supported these new programs, he had no ambitions to add to the list. He told the media that he thought that the welfare state had expanded as far as it should go for the time being.[22] The economy, after booming for much of the postwar period, had hit a bumpy patch, with inflation and higher interest rates raising concerns. While he believed in social justice, Trudeau was unwilling to drain the treasury in pursuit of it. Early in the campaign, Progressive Conservative leader Robert Stanfield would come out in favour of a guaranteed annual income, which many saw as the logical next step in the construction of the welfare state. Trudeau opposed it.[23] In this context the Just Society was less a vision for the future than a gift-wrapping of the recent past.

In truth, Trudeau was in a bit of a bind because, while he wanted to capitalize electorally on the desire for transformative change, he didn't feel that new spending would be wise. He would repeatedly tell the voters that spring that he wasn't promising any election goodies to win votes, that he wouldn't bribe them with their own tax money. Yet, having trotted out the phrase Just Society, he was obliged to flesh out what he meant by it, especially now that the media was turning on him and levelling criticisms that he was all style and no substance.[24] So, in a bathetic comedown from the lofty heights intimated by the slogan, the Liberals succumbed to the temptation to group a long laundry list of policies under the Just Society heading. The danger in this approach was that the more it came to represent, the less it meant.[25]

There were other ways in which Trudeau failed to live up to his image as an agent of change. When, for instance, lowering the voting age to eighteen from twenty-one became an issue in the campaign, Trudeau at first opposed the idea, telling youth that they should concentrate on their studies, not politics.[26] He did not support abolition of the monarchy because he thought there were more important issues to tackle. He told an interviewer that if he were a young American facing the draft, his initial impulse would be to obey the laws of his country.[27] These were, admittedly, rather minor issues, but the same conservatism was evident on major questions other than the welfare state, such as economic nationalism, Vietnam, and national unity.

Foreign ownership had been one of the most divisive issues in Canada since Walter Gordon had warned in the late 1950s that the Canadian economy was being taken over by American investment.

A few days after the election call, young women admire photos of Trudeau. Or was this a case of a photographer staging a shot by giving them Trudeau photos to admire?

Pearson's attempt to forestall the issue had been the Task Force on Foreign Ownership and the Structure of Canadian Investment, which had recommended a number of protectionist measures. On the same day that Trudeau had announced his candidacy, Gordon held a press conference on the recently released task force report.[28] At his announcement press conference, Trudeau refused to endorse the report, and instead characterized economic nationalism as "an excessive doctrine that tends to work against the best interests of a trading nation like Canada." He stuck with this position. "It's very easy to get rid of foreign capital," he later told one crowd. "Cuba did it in three weeks."[29] He would monitor and regulate foreign capital inflow and encourage Canadian ownership, especially in key areas, but he wasn't about to discourage investment.[30]

He took a passive position on the Vietnam War, saying that Canada couldn't do much to change American policy. Under the circumstances, Canada had to be a good ally and supply arms and resources to its neighbour even if it didn't agree with the war. He told antiwar protesters who wanted him to oppose arms sales that Canada might as well terminate nickel sales too, since the metal ended up in armaments. Were they willing to do that? Had Trudeau really wanted to channel the spirit of the sixties, he would have made common cause with the antiwar movement. Privately, it was said, he opposed the war, but publicly he wasn't prepared to sacrifice political capital to the cause.

National unity was the most significant issue on which Trudeau defended the status quo. In the face of Quebec nationalists' demands, he displayed more sangfroid than any English Canadian politician. His bilingualism and charter of rights reforms were designed to preserve the Canadian federal system in the face of the radical challenge to it presented by Quebec. He not only refuted the special status logic of Quebec politicians, he impugned their motives. Trudeau's forceful rejection of Quebec's claims may have been based on his federalist and liberal antinationalist principles, but it was very attractive to English Canadians for nationalist reasons because it promised to preserve Canada's unity. "For some voters," wrote one journalist, "Mr. Trudeau would offer the unique opportunity to express both a superficial goodwill toward French Canada and a strong reaction against Quebec's rocking the boat."[31] Sometimes this sentiment was expressed less elegantly. Judge J.T. Thorson, a western Liberal, supported Trudeau for the leadership because he would "put Quebec in its proper place."[32] In this he was in agreement with René Lévesque, who described Trudeau as "our Negro King in a sports jacket."[33]

Insofar as Trudeau's political philosophy derived from a liberal ideology that had long been a central organizing doctrine of the Canadian political economy, it was another sign of his conservatism. "Pierre Elliott Trudeau," wrote Ken Dewar in *Canadian Dimension*, "both in the circumstances of his selection as leader and in the nature of his ideas, stands within, not without, the mainstream of Canadian Liberalism." In terms of the Canadian electorate as a whole, this put him smack in the political centre.[34] As Ron Graham has pointed out, the key to understanding Trudeau's politics is context. In the 1950s, when he was opposing the autocratic Duplessis regime in Quebec, his emphasis on democracy, individual rights, and modernization seemed radical. But in post–Quiet Revolution Quebec and in the broader context of 1960s Canada, radicalism meant complete rejection of "the system." In this context, Trudeau's liberalism was relatively conservative.

When the list of Trudeau's conservative positions is totted up, there is much to support the claim made by Paul Fox, a University of Toronto political science professor, that "beneath his dashing image, Pierre Trudeau is a conservative ... That is the source of his appeal to many English Canadians."[35] Trudeau styled himself a pragmatic politician, and, as such, he did not believe wholesale systemic change was either practical or desirable. Reform was a matter of picking and choosing, leaving much intact so that political energy, a scarce resource, could be directed towards priorities for change. Thus the ways in which he was conservative were easy to enumerate.

At the same time it is possible to draw up a counter-list of ways in which he was not conservative. If conservatism is equated with preserving the past, then the label did not fit. Despite his knowledge of history, Trudeau didn't dwell on it. This tendency may have been a result of his experience opposing Duplessis's exploitation of a traditional nationalism that celebrated cultural continuity. In his nomination speech at the convention, he declared, "Liberalism is the only philosophy for our time, because it does not try to conserve every tradition of the past: because it does not try to apply to new problems the old doctrinaire solutions: because it is prepared to experiment and innovate and because it knows that the past is less important than the future."[36] During the election campaign he would repeatedly tell French Canadians to forget past wrongs and look to the future.[37] This orientation perfectly suited Canadian nationalists who wanted to leave behind the old Canada and all of its sins.

The fact that individual freedom was a bedrock principle in Trudeau's thought made it easy to associate him with the progressive spirit of the sixties, which embraced the notion of freedom, albeit in ill-defined and inconsistent ways. ("People Got to Be Free" was a big hit by the Rascals in 1968.) If Trudeau had harkened back to a nineteenth-century classical liberalism of laissez-faire and unfettered capitalism, Fox's conservative label would have been justified. But Trudeau conceptualized freedom in political rather than economic terms. He assigned primacy to politics as a forum for human agency over political philosophies constructed upon theories of economic determinism.[38] He was, as noted above, a twentieth-century liberal who believed the state should provide the equality of opportunity necessary to ensure that individuals could fulfill themselves and participate fully in society. Insofar as this was a concession to egalitarian concerns of political philosophies further left on the political spectrum, it gave him the appearance of some affinity with the more radical elements of the decade. Moreover, although he was in the political centre, the centre was then perceived not as static but as moving leftward over time, in keeping with the metanarrative of progress towards greater liberal democracy. Here the Just Society slogan made a contribution. In implying an ideal to work towards, it reinforced a sense of national temporal momentum towards fulfillment of a noble destiny.

Trudeau's political philosophy fit very nicely with the contemporary needs of Canadian nationalism in other ways as well. Trudeau derided Quebec neonationalism, but in the Canadian context offered a nationalist vision of his own, though he would not have characterized it as such. He maintained that the checks and balances of Canadian federalism, combined with a liberal creed of rights and freedoms, provided an enlightened solution to the challenge of governing diverse populations in the modern world. The principle of freedom offered an efficacious replacement for the traditional romantic nationalism by which Canada had always failed to measure up. Abandoning the futile quest to define Canadians as a homogeneous people, Canadian nationalists were redefining Canada in pluralistic terms, paradoxically making the principle of individual rights the key basis of collective solidarity. Trudeau's proposed charter of rights offered an ideal for Canadians to rally around. As he put it, "Essentially we will be testing – and hopefully establishing – the one-ness of Canada."[39]

Pluralism was the best identity option available to Canadian nationalists at the time. For one thing, it had the virtue of being pragmatic insofar as it reflected demographic reality. If individual freedom was the animating principle of the nation, it mattered little whether it was framed as a tradition of British liberty or codified in a charter of rights; it remained deeply rooted in the dominant ethnic group's heritage. Other cultural markers could be stripped away, but this fundamental principle of political culture remained operative. Even better, individual freedom could be spun as a progressive ideal upon which a new Canada could be constructed.[40] Add in the fact that it could also be deployed to out-flank Quebec's special status claims with a principle that could be presented as morally superior, and the costs – official bilingualism and greater recognition of ethnocultural minorities – were well worth bearing.

What was lost in internal coherence was offset by the potential gains in international status for Canada from being in the van-guard of the international human rights movement. The idea that Canada could continue to earn international plaudits by modelling unity in diversity to a postcolonial world struggling to manage multiethnic states was profoundly seductive. Years earlier Trudeau had written that Canada could be "envied" as "a brilliant prototype for the moulding of tomorrow's civilization," and he would repeat this claim during the 1968 election campaign.[41]

In short, Trudeau's politics were complex and ambiguous. The ways in which he was simultaneously progressive in some ways, stand pat in others, and quite traditional in still others, points to the perils of categorizing with simple labels. One of his decidedly progressive traits was his encouragement of participatory democ-racy. Whereas conservatism is often associated with defending the interests of entrenched elites, Trudeau wanted people to en-gage in politics, to make democracy work by taking responsibility for their futures themselves. To promote this ideal, the Liberal elec-tion campaign materials featured a poster with the Trudeau-as-Che image under the slogan "Come Work with Me."

The sixties were a decade in which protesters assailed trad-itional political leadership as elitist and out of touch, pop art and other experimental aesthetics were undermining traditional high culture, and the interests of the people gained moral authority over the establishment. Whereas in the past the logistical feasibil-ity of mass democracy had been an issue of debate for intellectuals, participatory democracy was now a demand being fought for in the streets and winning the support of a broad public. It had be-come "a kind of panacea for contemporary political discontent."[42]

The huge pent-up pressure for popular participation in politics was accompanied by a conviction that no society that restricted its citizens' access to the political process could be truly just. The political process's insulation from popular input had been a theme of the 1962 Port Huron statement by the Students for a Democratic Society, and "power to the people" was a ubiquitous sixties slogan. The New Left on both sides of the border railed against decision making by remote bureaucracies staffed by entrenched, myopic, self-serving elites. Activists emphasized political organizing at the community level as a mark of commitment to the movement. Grassroots engagement in neighbourhood issues constituted participatory democracy in action. It was a way to circumvent discredited establishment institutions that failed to address people's real needs in their everyday lives.[43]

When Trudeau spoke about what he meant by participatory democracy on his trip to Kingston on February 28, the first outing of his leadership campaign, he said

> Basically, what we try to do in government is to sit down with the people and discuss the facts of the situation ... Politics ... It's a way of working together; it's a way of looking for solutions together. And, if you're a free man, if you're a free people, you don't want to be governed without knowing the reasons why and you don't want solutions fed to you. You want to participate in the solution-making process.[44]

Trudeau was promising a liberal-democratic ideal in which every individual who so desired could get involved and make a difference in national politics. Just how this might work he didn't say.

Probably he couldn't say. No matter how effective and rewarding the participatory ideal was at the local level, making it work on the scale of federal politics was an entirely different matter. The government had already responded to the democratic ferment of the 1960s by trying to engage citizens in decision-making processes. In planning the centennial celebrations it was largely successful in stimulating civic participation and an accompanying sense of belonging to the nation.[45] Yet this had been applied to a unique cultural event, involving unprecedented planning and publicity, not mundane policy making. In the latter context, the logistics of delivering meaningful democratic input into government decision making in a mass democracy were self-defeating: any mechanism devised to do so would inevitably grow more cumbersome the more popular it became, defeating its original purpose.[46] Moreover, if such a mechanism were to work, it raised the dread possibility that the voice of the people might contradict the leadership of the elites. The challenge, then, was how to foster a sense of participation without actualizing it.

With Trudeaumania, it seemed an answer had been found. Modern mass democracy was facilitated by the media's use of the politics of image to engage the citizenry and give people a sense of participation in politics. As Roy Shields of the *Toronto Daily Star* wrote at the time, "Television has made democracy workable ... to gain power these days, a politician has to present himself directly to the people through T.V., a medium that tears the mask from all who dare to appear before it."[47] The media's dissemination of developments in federal politics had created a national phenomenon. Trudeau's supporters, dispersed across the country, engaged in national politics as members of the citizen-audience of a mass-mediated nation, even if their participation was limited to watching on TV. Taking its cue from popular culture, Trudeaumania was participatory democracy in the only practical way it could be conducted on the mass scale of modernity.

Participatory democracy, Trudeaumania-style, intensified in the wake of the Liberal leadership convention. Tourists on Parliament Hill waited outside cabinet meetings to catch a glimpse of Trudeau when he came out. Teenagers hung out at 24 Sussex, hoping for a brush with celebrity. Leaving a cabinet meeting a few days after he was elected Liberal leader, Trudeau was stopped by a blonde girl

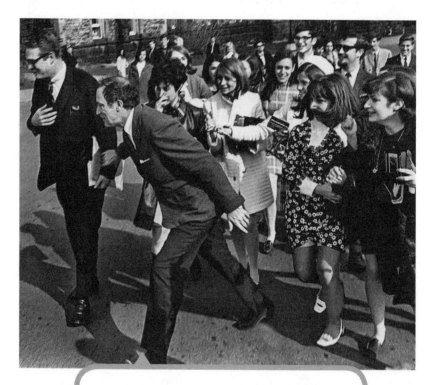

After chatting with a crowd of admiring schoolkids on Parliament Hill on April 22, 1968, an agile Trudeau sprints away, giving the television cameras some good footage for the evening newscast.

wanting a kiss. "Why not?" he replied. "It's spring." Scrummed by reporters afterwards, the girl described the smooch as "Fantastic!"[48] The encounter became a front-page story across the nation. It was the same story a few days later, though this time Trudeau demurely raised his briefcase to block press views of the action.[49] The men who managed the media had decided that the public liked pictures of women fawning over a bachelor playboy politician. The *Vancouver Sun* featured three such encounters in late April and early May, and generated different versions of each for different editions.[50] On April 22, Trudeau was filmed being mobbed by high school students outside the Parliament Buildings. When he broke away from them, loping across the grounds, the kids chased him. This became one of the emblematic scenes of Trudeaumania.

The Liberal campaign strategists understandably decided they could ride Trudeaumania to election victory. Their campaign materials presented Trudeau as "a breakthrough. That's what many Canadians see in Pierre Elliott Trudeau. To them ... he represents a fresh approach – and our chance to become a modern society."[51] Image was the byword, in its general as well as its most literal sense. "All candidates should receive a quantity of pop posters of Trudeau," Liberal headquarters informed the riding associations. "These should be highly sought after."[52] "It appears that the key component of this election will be Mr. Trudeau's personality itself," another Liberal official added. "I would strongly suggest that you tie your candidate's name with Mr. Trudeau's name at every possible chance."[53] Most candidates took this advice. Liberal campaign buttons, which in 1965 had overlooked Pearson, bore only the words "Pierre" or "Trudeau." Thousands of photographs of the new prime minister were distributed to candidates' offices across the country, and his name appeared prominently on almost every Liberal sign or poster.[54] "We Go Trudeau," the lead line on the campaign posters of Norm Cafik, the Liberal candidate in the riding of Ontario, was typical.

Trudeaumania caused a surge of interest and participation in politics that dazzled the media. "In 1968," reported *Maclean's*, "millions of Canadians have suddenly become fantastically interested in, of all things, Canadian politics." They weren't just passively watching either; rather "hundreds of thousands of them have decided to do something about it ... by moving in on existing party structures." In the process many such structures that had been relatively moribund were rejuvenated. Early in the leadership race, the Liberal riding executive in Ottawa West had followed established practice in presenting a slate of delegates to the leadership convention to a members' meeting, only to be assailed by cries of "Railroad!" and demands for the right to nominate from the floor. Surprised and shaken, it acquiesced.[55]

When the Liberals started nominating candidates for the election that spring, the same participatory spirit prevailed. Alberta had elected only two Liberals since 1957; now Liberal party memberships were selling at the rate of four hundred a day. Membership soared in formerly placid riding associations. Nomination contests were lively, with many candidates coming forward and no guarantees for incumbents. Roger Teillet and Maurice Sauvé, two cabinet ministers who were running in new ridings because of redistribution, fell victim to the phenomenon and failed to win nominations. In Minnedosa, Manitoba, 1,200 voting delegates participated in the Liberal nominating convention. In Calgary South, 1,600 showed up. In Ontario's Peel riding it was 3,000. Toronto Davenport became the most spectacular example of the phenomenon. Facilitated by loose membership rules, the riding association grew from some 200 souls to 5,455 in less than two weeks leading up to its nomination meeting.[56] Such eye-popping increases were the result of contenders for the nominations signing up new members, but they wouldn't have been so motivated or successful had Trudeau not been so popular.

Canadians had finally decided, Norman DePoe would observe in *Maclean's* that fall, "that democracy was too important to be left

"Harold, I'm worried about the children ... they've all joined the Liberal party."

As this June 1968 Barron cartoon attests, one way to get people involved in politics and achieve the sixties' ideal of participatory democracy was to borrow from pop culture to create a celebrity politician.

to the politicians."[57] "Politics used to be a marginal activity to which one devoted a certain amount of free time, like the Boy Scouts or the local hospital fund," wrote Peter Newman,

> but suddenly politics is becoming a predominant national concern for people of all ages. Nominations are being fought for as if becoming an MP were one of the most prestigious roles to which a man could aspire; a Canadian political song is near the top of the hit parade; riding associations are besieged with willing workers; editorial writers are hot with partisanship.[58]

Organizers had rented the high school auditorium in Port Perry for the Liberal nomination meeting for the riding of Ontario, only to find it too small for a crowd that overflowed into the halls and out onto the lawn. The Liberal MP for the neighbouring constituency of Durham, Russell Honey, attributed the interest to Trudeau, who "says it like it is ... creating the excitement and desire for participation in politics for the first time."[59]

With Trudeaumania, the media had found a way to present federal politics in a way that made it relevant and engaging. "The television networks have been able to smarten up their techniques of making politics exciting," observed the Liberals' pollsters.[60] The party was attracting formerly disaffected voters who would otherwise have supported a minor party or sat out the entire affair. "I've never been interested in politics before. But I have this feeling that Mr. Trudeau is different from everyone else, something new," explained Lois Cook, a French teacher in London, Ontario, who followed Trudeau into the London Press Club in May.[61] New voters were three times as likely to support the Liberals as the NDP.[62] As usual, Marshall McLuhan had his own unique spin on this development: "[In] all countries, the party system has folded like the organizational chart ... policies and issues are useless for election purposes, since they are too specialized and hot. The shaping of

Herb Gosevich, owner of an Ottawa sports equipment store, capitalized on what he called Trudeau's "mass appeal" by selling "psychedelic" purple and gold "Go Go with Trudeau" sweatshirts. The shirts were illustrated with a toga-clad Trudeau sniffing a flower.

the candidate's integral image has taken the place of discussing particular points-of-view."[63]

Like other aspects of popular culture, celebrity images were efficiently monetized through consumer goods. The Trudeau image, defined in part by his stylish consumption, itself became a commodity. Toronto, the media centre of Canada, also became the epicentre of Trudeau schlock. Homemakers could buy Trudeau tumblers or ashtrays, which sold by the thousands. "Go-Go Trudeau" buttons were equally hot. "Pierre's what's moving at the moment, and that's what we're selling," explained a shop owner. "It's all a part of over-all Trudeaumania."[64]

For the chattering classes, *Federalism and the French Canadians* provided a more substantial token of cultural currency. The English translation sold out and was reprinted three times in the three months following its publication in late February.[65] It was excerpted in magazines and newspapers, and by summer the French and English versions had sold nearly fifty thousand copies combined, making it a runaway bestseller by Canadian standards. Across the land it adorned many a coffee table that spring.[66]

In March, humour columnist Gary Lautens had been the first to draw attention to the disproportionate attention being accorded Trudeau's style of dress:

> The newspapers carry very little about the justice minister's views ... But we do get elaborate descriptions of Trudeau's clothes ... he's described as "mod." What we are actually witnessing is a nationwide fashion show ... Trudeau's clothes have been the talk of the country.[67]

Soon it was possible to put on the Trudeau image by buying clothes like his. "New Look North of the Border" was the headline of a *Life* magazine profile of Trudeau on April 20.[68] In Toronto, a leather-goods manufacturer began making coats and hats like Trudeau's, and a menswear store had a window display proclaiming

"The Trudeau Look." "Suddenly everybody wants to look like Pierre Trudeau," explained a Canadian fashion designer who was planning a fashion show with the same title. CBC host Patrick Watson, it was reported, was just one of many men who had started combing his hair down over his forehead and growing sideburns like Trudeau.[69]

Defined by what he wore, Trudeau in turn became something others wore. There were Trudeau ties. Merchants peddled sweat-shirts with slogans such as "Go Go Trudeau" or "Justice will Triumph." Mod's futurist orientation included celebrating technology by employing unconventional materials like paper and vinyl, brightly coloured or transparent, for women's dresses. Trudeau dresses, made of paper with his image on it, caused a minor sensation. There was something risqué about a woman wearing a man, especially in flimsy material.[70] It was the height of fashion, in the sense of fashion as fad, with its paper material suggesting ephemerality, disposability, and the pleasure of living in the moment at the same time as it signalled the wearer's approval of the worn. Later a cotton print with Trudeau's face on it hit the market and was used as material for women's dresses, skirts, and ponchos. It was even made into pillow cases. The Progressive Conservatives responded by modelling for the media a mod dress to be worn by Stanfield supporters. Tellingly, it did not have the leader's face on it – instead, support for him was declared by a banner worn over the dress. It did not catch on like the Trudeau dresses.

Teenagers looking to decorate their rooms could buy one of ten different posters of Trudeau. A Toronto record store, Half-Beat Harold's, claimed to have sold twenty thousand of them in the last two weeks of May.[71] A poster of Trudeau holding a finger to his lips was the most popular. A young NDP worker accused Kresge's in Toronto's Eglinton Square mall of selling only Trudeau posters and none of Douglas, not to mention Stanfield. "The whole campaign is being conducted in terms of image, not issues," he complained. "Posters of Trudeau have a political impact, and are more

According to this promotional photo for a Toronto boutique on Bloor Street, "Fashions of Trudeau fabric are the latest thing." While the Stanfield poster on the wall (by John Yardley-Jones) provided some partisan balance in this photo, it did not circulate as widely as the "Hail Trudeau, Pierre Power" poster hidden behind the model on the right. (The Trudeau poster is illustrated on p. 328.)

than just merchandise." He organized picketing of the store. The president of the poster company that supplied Kresge's explained that "Trudeau is a cultural phenomenon: the posters aren't political at all." He solved the problem by giving away Douglas posters on request. "I can't sell them," he explained, "nobody wants them. Stanfield doesn't sell well either."[72]

As Trudeau's popularity surged, his image appeared in store windows and on hoardings. In some cases it was multiplied in rows and columns like a huge split screen repeating the same pattern.[73] Whereas Expo's experimental films had bombarded viewers with different images simultaneously, these montages endlessly reproduced the same image. Trudeau was getting the same treatment that Andy Warhol gave celebrities in his silk-screened portraits. Now fodder for the decade's pop culture machinery, the Trudeau phenomenon was duly presented in ways that problematized perception.

Trudeau cultural goods reinforced the reel-to-real synthesis by offering different ways to bring the leading celebrity of the nation tangibly into peoples' lives. Folk singer Allan J. Ryan debuted "PM Pierre" on the Montreal CBC TV show *Seven on Six*, hosted by Laurier LaPierre and Peter Desbarats, three days after the Liberal leadership convention ended. The song was broadcast nationally on CBC Radio's *Russ Thompson Show* on May 9. "Go Go Trudeau," by The Sinners, first played on CHUM Toronto on May 2, was an instant hit, and was played on an hourly rotation thereafter. Ten thousand copies were sold in the first week after its release. Record stores were flooded with requests for it. Taken by surprise, they tried to order stock, only to be told that it was selling so well in Quebec that no copies would be available for Ontario for another three weeks. Once the federal election began, however, authorities ruled that the Trudeau tunes could be construed as partisan advertising, which was strictly regulated during election campaigns, and they disappeared from the airwaves.[74]

Students of Canadian political culture thought Canada particularly prone to the politics of image because of its nonideological, big-tent national parties and relatively high number of swing voters. In the absence of defining issues or radically differing party platforms, these voters tended to decide based on the leader, encouraged by the mass media's proclivity for personifying parties through their leaders. The changing of the guard in the two major parties in the previous few months only accentuated this tendency. Small wonder that Jim Davey, one of the key Liberal planners, mused that the campaign's general theme should be to "publicly ignore personality but privately exploit it."[75]

Yet even as it facilitated the politics of image, the media questioned its complicity in it. One expression of guilt, associated with McLuhan's contention that the electronic media were making modern society more "tribal," was the fear that Trudeau's image marked him as one apart, a superior being, a trope associated with dictators. In one of their columns, Douglas Fisher and Harry Crowe raised concerns about the implications of Trudeau's "strong image in an age that clamours for strong men." They quoted John Kenneth Galbraith's observation that "when problems are numerous, vexatious and incomprehensible ... The press and networks create the master statesman who will see us through."[76] There was a mod riff on this theme at the time in the form of a poster that depicted Trudeau as a Roman emperor, replete with toga and laurel crown, with the slogans "Hail Trudeau" above and "Pierre Power" below in flower-power script.[77] "The politics of style," warned Kenneth McNaught, chagrined at how in Trudeaumania image had trumped social democratic doctrine, "leads directly to the politics of leadership and even of faith ... Nothing could be more perilous in a democracy, however often democracies hanker after such solutions."[78]

Such comments reflected a broader concern among intellectuals about fulfilling the promise of liberal democracy under conditions of modernity. Some of the leading lights of this debate were

This Karsh portrait of Trudeau, taken on November 4, 1968, shows him in the leather coat he often wore while campaigning in the winter of 1968.

scholars from the Frankfurt School in Germany who had fled to the United States as the Nazis consolidated their hold on power in the 1930s. This experience made them particularly interested in and qualified to comment on one of the great political riddles of the age: How did a supposedly civilized modern Western society give rise to one of the most brutal dictatorships in history? Frankfurt School alumni applied sociological theory and Freudian psychoanalytical theory to provide answers. Freud's pseudo-scientific approach provided a socially acceptable pretext and form for talking about sex that had been titillating the chattering classes for decades, so basic Freudian concepts had by this time become well-established in popular culture. Their influence suggested that some sinister and atavistic instinct lurking deep in the human psyche was to blame. Former Frankfurt School member and neo-Freudian Erich Fromm had argued in his book *Escape from Freedom* that authoritarianism was a refuge from the alienation induced by modernity. It sold millions of copies in the postwar period.[79] The follower's devotion to the great leader was of a piece with the belonging of the individual to the nation: both loyalties provided a sense of belonging. Better to locate oneself securely if submissively than to float freely in an atomistic and meaningless liberal modernity. If McLuhan was right that television was retribalizing society, then Trudeau was chieftain of an electronic clan. From this perspective, his penchant for wearing a Nazi-style full-length leather coat was ominous.

Few Canadians seriously worried about the rise of a strongman, but mediation anxiety was widespread beyond the media. The *Star Weekly* reported that it found "suspicion of dark dealings among Canada's communicators" among the young in every city its reporters visited in Canada. In Sackville, New Brunswick, they were told that "Trudeau is being created by you guys ... Three months ago, he didn't even exist." A secretary in Toronto told a journalist, "I like Trudeau, he impresses me very much, but I have this feeling that he is being sold to us by the mass media, and that he may not be what he appears."[80]

Yet Trudeau was ahead of the crowd on this issue. He was often critical, even contemptuous, of the media. This cynicism may have originated in Duplessis-era Quebec, where he observed a press complicit with what he saw as a corrupt, exploitative regime. In *Federalism and the French Canadians* he had written, "Mass media, to the extent that they claim to reflect public opinion, constitute a vehicle for error, if not indeed an instrument of oppression. For my part, I have never been able to read newspapers without a sense of unease." They "follow their customers and are therefore always lagging behind reality," he claimed.[81] Word went around early on in his tenure as justice minister that he would flip quickly through the news clippings that were handed to him, looking bored. He said that when he saw a camera he was "tempted either to wave at it or thumb my nose at it."[82]

Trudeau had a long history of performing critical distance. At parties he would slip away from the chatter and stand on his head in the corner.[83] In the public eye he performed entertaining stunts that set him apart from the pack. From the moment the media spotlight fixed on him in 1967 he took pains to demonstrate his detached perspective by drawing attention to the mediation of the studio or the scrum. His playacting conveyed a knowing cynicism about TV, highlighting its role as an intermediary between him and the public. His penchant for questioning the premises of interviewers' questions fulfilled the same function. Trudeau dramatized his awareness of the mediated nature of politics by stepping out of his assigned role within the artificial frame applied by the media.

In a culture that longed for authenticity, Trudeau performed it convincingly. "Sartre calls personality an enterprise," one commentator noted at the time. "You cultivate yourself, and you make of yourself what you are in the world. You are a project to yourself ... Mr. Trudeau has made of himself what he is ... you can call it elegant, flexible, creative, he has verve, he's laconic, he's civilized, he's urbane, he's all these things."[84] In a world where one's "real" self and one's image were confused, and the latter was increasingly vital to success, Trudeau seemed to have figured it all out and gotten well ahead of the game. He surfed to power on the politics of image while maintaining a bemused, detached perspective on the very forces propelling him forward.

The result was a candidate who could be seen as an antidote not just to mediated democracy but to the general malaise of modernity. If the *Montreal Star* were to be believed,

> he restores to each of us a sense of individual worth. We are no longer insignificant members of a mob, all running in the same direction because our leaders tell us to … He wants … to release us from servility to mass machines created by others, from the dominance of self-appointed elites who think they know better than we do what is good for us … This is why we would like to see him have his chance, to see him try to develop his "Just Society" or at least a society more just than we have had.[85]

"His great concern is said to be with the alienated and isolated individual," wrote another journalist in a similar vein. "In a sense he has been adopted by a society unhappy with grey corporatism and worried about the burgeoning all-embracing bureaucracy, and puzzled if not fearful over the coming dehumanized, technological culture."[86]

On the face of it these comments were curious. Back in the 1950s, Trudeau had recommended liberal modernity as the solution to the problems of Quebec, and he now represented the same attractive prospect to Canada as a whole. At the same time he evinced a quintessentially modern mindset with his calls for rationality and functionalism in Canadian politics. Nevertheless, his image as a rugged individualist aligned him with the countercultural rebellion against conformity and other ills of modernity.[87] His cynicism about the media reinforced this impression. In 1968 these impressions resonated with modern Canadians more than his political philosophy or policy positions.

Lisa and Marlin Kurz pose on Yonge Street in downtown Toronto in their "Justice Will Triumph" sweatshirts, March 27, 1968.

Ironically, the representation of Trudeau as a radically free individual was the driver of the politics of image that in turn made participatory democracy practicable on the mass scale of the modern nation-state. "One of the chief paradoxes of the 1960s," Howard Brick has written, "was the coincidence of devotion to the ideal of authenticity – of discovering, voicing, and exercising a genuine whole personality freed from the grip of mortifying convention – and fascination with the ways of artifice, with the calculated techniques of image making or 'the games people play.'"[88] While Trudeau's image embodied the promise that he would modernize Canada, it simultaneously promised that he would heal what ailed modernity by restoring an authenticity and community that supposedly had made life meaningful in some imaginary, long-lost, premodern Golden Age.

The Just Society and participatory democracy slogans were key signifiers of this project. They served Canadian nationalism by providing respectively a sense of purpose for and participation in a meaningful modern mass polity. "For many of us," Trudeau had declared in his nomination speech at the convention,

> the world of today stands on the threshold of a golden age. By building a truly just society, this beautiful and rich and energetic country of ours can become a model in which every citizen will enjoy his fundamental rights, in which two great linguistic communities and people of many cultures will live in harmony, and in which every individual will find fulfilment.[89]

Here was an aspirational ideal that gave the nation a reason for being and a goal to strive towards. It facilitated national unity by casting French Canada's cultural survival as a matter of equal rights rather than special treatment, while at the same time equating it with the minority rights of other ethnocultural groups. It appealed to national status by suggesting that Canada could become a model to the world. It countered modern alienation with meaningful participation in this national project. The Just Society and participatory democracy were also effective campaign slogans because they gratified nationalists' wish to be morally superior to the United States and promised to fulfill their desire for national transformation.[90] Nationalists could envision the "city upon a hill" mantle passing from the United States to the Peaceable Kingdom. The Just Society would be just north of the border.

At the end of Trudeau's big day in Toronto on June 19, 1968, an excited crowd of more than six thousand people greeted him at the Centennial Arena in North York. According to the *Toronto Daily Star*, Trudeau was almost pulled off the platform and had to be held on to by James Walker (left), Liberal candidate in York Centre, and former Toronto mayor Phil Givens (second from left), Liberal candidate in York West.

9

Reel to Real II
The Federal Election Campaign

Jim has a concept of platform which is quite radically
different from anything that has been done before and
which should be exactly in the image of Mr. Trudeau.

SENATOR RICHARD STANBURY[1]

271

"**THIS IS THE** electronic election," declared a TV critic, citing a television producer's opinion that television coverage of politics had finally come into its own in 1968.[2] While television was adapting itself to politics, politics was adapting itself to television, and the 1968 election was planned with its needs in mind. The reel-to-real phenomenon that had distinguished the leadership race would become even more pronounced during the election campaign. The leader's tour resembled a pop star going on the road, except that Trudeau hit multiple communities a day, jetting in and out of town in a whirlwind. His arrival and his departure were important parts of the show. The people were now the direct target market, not an indirect audience as they had been when the purported target was convention delegates. When they gathered to welcome Trudeau, they formed crowds that generated in microcosm the feelings of solidarity, loyalty, and excitement that came with the more abstract belonging to nation.[3] At each stop, television crews recorded the action and played it back to the national audience, stitching one community after another into the national fabric.

The Liberal team planned for the campaign to unfold in three stages. For the first few weeks after the election was called on April 23, Trudeau would remain in Ottawa, attending to the nation's business and appearing statesmanlike. He would make a few appearances, but the emphasis would be on getting Canadians accustomed to him as prime minister and associating him with the prestige of the office. Stage two would be the leader's tour, commencing May 21. Trudeau would criss-cross the country, making campaign swings through particular regions over one or two days. Stage three, in the last few days before the June 25 election, would be a series of rallies in larger cities to generate big crowds and wide publicity that would make it look as if Trudeau were riding to victory on the crest of a swelling wave of popular support.

Trudeau's appearances were designed for television, which demanded engaging visuals and short, simply themed, dramatic reports.[4] Rather than sticking Trudeau in static indoor events where a succession of local worthies introduced one another ad nauseam before the candidate took the stage, his visits would be outdoors, showcasing the candidate and allowing him to be seen and touched. Advance men scoped out the best camera angles and set things up accordingly. Events were staged to get images into the news of the candidate amid crowds roiling with emotion. Breaks were built into the schedule after each event to allow journalists to file their stories.[5]

Trudeau was always photographed and filmed with the local candidates so they could invoke his local presence in their subsequent publicity efforts. He also did interviews with local media, as he had during the leadership race.[6] Policy was to be soft-pedalled, though Trudeau would make some announcements at press conferences to ward off the criticism that the Liberals had no policy.

The tone was established with the handful of appearances Trudeau made in the first stage of the campaign. To show he was a man of the people, Trudeau went to a Canadiens playoff game against the Chicago Black Hawks on April 27. Fans shouted, "We want Béliveau," "We want Lemaire," and "We want Trudeau." It ended well, with Montreal winning in overtime, sending the team to the Stanley Cup playoffs.[7] On May 17, Trudeau was back in Montreal to open Man and His World, the attempt to reinvent Expo 67 as a permanent exposition. In its report of the event, the

Trudeau is scrummed following his announcement that there would be a federal election, April 23, 1968.

Toronto Daily Star highlighted a "mob of screaming girls" who began "fighting to kiss him, touch him or get his autograph."[8]

In the second week of May, Trudeau visited Vancouver, White-horse, Yellowknife, and Edmonton. He drew crowds on all of these stops. At the University of Alberta in Edmonton, he and United Nations secretary-general U Thant were given honorary degrees. Thousands gathered at Edmonton's city hall to see Trudeau presented with a Klondike hat and cane by the mayor. As he left, the crowd pressed in and Trudeau was mobbed. At first police managed to hold people off, but as Trudeau tried to gain his car, they closed in, pushing and shoving to get at him. Two of his aides were thrown against the car and Trudeau himself barely managed to squeeze in the door.[9]

It was the same on May 19, when Trudeau hit four shopping malls in the Toronto suburbs. "I was to take the Prime Minister to the airport so I was trying to go with him to his car," recorded party president Richard Stanbury,

> but we no sooner stepped out of the meeting room than he was mobbed by a tremendous crowd of people and it was almost impossible to stay anywhere near him ... The day in Toronto was a tremendous success. During the morning, the Prime Minister visited three ridings, mainstreeting and going through shopping centres, always followed by great crowds of people.[10]

The success was a foreshadowing of things to come.

Trudeau's leader's tour officially began on May 21 with a swing through small-town southwestern Ontario. When he flew into London, he was met by screaming girls. For the reporter on the scene, it was "reminiscent of the wild, almost mindless mobbing of the Beatles in their heyday." The next day "a teen-aged Indian girl draped a woven cloth necklace and amulet around his neck and swore it contained a love potion."[11] This was traditional Tory territory, yet in every town Trudeau visited he was greeted by ebullient crowds, signed countless autographs, was kissed repeatedly, had flowers presented to him, thrown at him, and shoved into his face, and was applauded when he switched from English to French. The most colourful aspect of Trudeau's receptions, Peter Newman wrote, was "the hordes of teeny-boppers, running with long manes blowing like banners in the wind, full of vitality, excitement, laughter, shrieking in a kind of wild ecstasy that rises to a squawk when one of their number is kissed."[12] Trudeau's opponents attributed the ardour with which he was received to feckless kids who'd been let out of school for the occasion and were, they pointed out, not old enough to vote.[13] Evidently the local school authorities were Liberals. In fact there were people of all ages in the crowds, but the dynamism and excitement that the young generated was a political organizer's dream.

Trudeau's welcoming committee in London had included "Trudeau's True Pets," an irregular bevy of teenyboppers who screamed and jostled for kisses as he worked his way to his car. This kind of spontaneous organization gave the Liberals an idea. In order to channel the youthful enthusiasm for Trudeau into constructive channels – and "keep alive the swinging image" of the new PM – they organized Action Trudeau groups in every riding under the direction of a young party worker, Michael Ignatieff.[14] Liberal headquarters sent the riding organizations instructions on appropriate outfits so there would be visual consistency to Trudeau youth across the country. When he arrived, the girls acted as reception committees, honour guards, and cheerleaders. "It was politics in the mod style," reported Anthony Westell of a Trudeau visit to a shopping plaza in Burnaby, British Columbia. "Action Trudeau girls in orange-and-white minidresses formed a chorus line on the platform. A go-go singer in a dress made of black and white plastic squares joined with metal fastenings urged the 3,000 crowd to 'Blow your Mind.'"[15] Equipped with buttons bearing the Pierre-as-Che image as well as special orange campaign materials, the Action Trudeau squads were put to work canvassing for their local candidates. Liberal headquarters claimed there were four thousand Action Trudeau members in 240 of the 264 federal ridings.

Every Liberal candidate wanted to have Trudeau visit his or her riding. The strategists naturally wanted to concentrate on swing ridings where his visit might make a difference, which meant, unfortunately, that loyal Liberal ridings generally got shafted.[16] Trudeau was working hard, running flat out all day for many days in a row. On the southwestern Ontario campaign swing he made eight stops in one day, a pace that proved unsustainable. Without enough sleep or quiet time to himself, the candidate got grumpy. His handlers dialled back the schedule, planning to get perhaps five appearances per day out of him, fewer if one involved a major speech.[17]

On May 22, Trudeau was in Montreal for his constituency nomination meeting, which packed seven hundred Liberals into a hall, leaving fifteen hundred outside brandishing placards proclaiming "Do it, Trudeau, Do it, Trudeau" and "Trudeau is a Happening."[18] Then he was off to Winnipeg to give a speech to the Canadian Club. He avoided the cavernous Winnipeg Auditorium, where Robert Stanfield had appeared earlier in the week, and made appearances at four shopping centres instead, with three hours in between to tape television interviews.[19] At the Conservative rally, in contrast, former premier Duff Roblin had spoken so long that the CBC broadcast went off the air before viewers got a chance to see the Tory leader speak.[20]

In populous areas Trudeau got around by car; elsewhere he would hop by air from one community to the next. The Liberals had chartered a DC-9 from Air Canada. Unlike Stanfield's plane, it was large enough to accommodate network television crews. After landing, Trudeau would give a brief speech to party workers at the airport, then be driven in a motorcade (or "cavalcade" as the Liberals liked to call it) to a prearranged crowd scene, often at a shopping plaza or main street – centres of consumerism where all the latest fashions were found. He would walk into the crowd and slowly make his way to the stage, where he would make another short speech, perhaps take questions, and then mingle with the people again before being driven back to the airport. His speeches were simple, emphasizing national unity and idealizing Canada as a country that did not discriminate on the basis of ethnicity or language. He always spoke briefly in French in English Canada and in English in French Canada. He made few promises and constantly warned that people should not expect handouts or subsidies from any government he headed. He talked of the future, that it was to be welcomed, that Canada must not hesitate to change but rather get out ahead of the curve. The themes were hope and confidence, that Canadians could do almost anything if they worked together with goodwill and collective resolve.

Trudeau's handlers constantly had to be vigilant that an enthusiastic local partisan didn't hijack their schedule. One warned that

> the local people ... are quite apt to slip "happenings" whereupon arrival at airport, for example, or upon driving through a town, there will be a magically gathered crowd of several hundred with a flat bed truck and sound system happening to be right in front of them ... The locals will screw you if they get the chance, of course from the best of motives.[21]

The same tactic worked for opponents. At the end of his day in Winnipeg, Trudeau was confronted by a hostile group of students with questions about Canada's complicity in Vietnam, the voting age, and tax reform. He got up on the back of a truck with a megaphone and asked for time to explain his position on each of these issues. He had to put down hecklers as he sparred with the boisterous crowd, which at times applauded but also groaned and jeered. "Anarchy, fun, hostility, one-upmanship. A heady mixture," observed one reporter.[22] Trudeau had come face to face with radical dissent. By engaging in a dialogue with the students he managed – if just barely – to avoid coming off as a reactionary establishment figure.

Saturday, May 25, found Trudeau blitzing small towns across southern Ontario again. In Newmarket, just north of Toronto, he dropped in by helicopter on a crowd of four thousand. Here as elsewhere he was "gaped at, flower-bedecked, sung to, applauded,

Trudeau seems to enjoy the excitement of the crowd in this shot, although on one occasion he told a friend that he only smiled because it was all so ridiculous.

The photograph suggests that it wasn't enough to have just the candidate himself, live in the flesh – his image had to accompany him; indeed, multiple images of him seemed to be required to signify his importance.

Or did the extensive web of signification take on a life of its own, rendering its referent irrelevant?

heckled, admired."[23] Then he got into a convertible for a motorcade to a rally in Markham, led by a platoon of motorcycle police. The local paper pronounced it the biggest local political event of the century.[24]

"It's just like a president or something," said one woman as she watched his motorcade pass. She wasn't alone in this observation – many pundits, chief among them Larry Zolf, equated the Liberal campaign's focus on the leader with Americans' idolization of the presidency and pronounced it out of keeping with the Canadian parliamentary tradition.[25] Interestingly, this critique was just as pronounced in French Canada as in English Canada.[26] Tapping into deep-seated fears of American domination, the criticism offered a principled objection to the Trudeau candidacy, particularly for those opposed to modernization. Yet it was entirely logical that the two political systems were becoming more alike, for both were modern mass-mediated societies in which democratization was accompanied by a politics of image focused on party leaders.

Trudeau's dashing to and fro was calculated to make him look, well, dashing. A decade earlier, John Diefenbaker had criss-crossed the country by train, conducting a traditional whistle-stop campaign of a type that could be traced all the way back to Wilfrid Laurier. Now everything was accelerated by new technology. "The schedule attempts to create an impression of movement around the country and an opportunity of dealing with new issues rather than having the old ones get stale by staying in one region too long," explained Gordon Gibson.[27] Television coverage featured footage of convertibles, helicopters, and jets, or Trudeau deplaning after another miraculous descent.[28] Symbolically, Trudeau's DC-9 was twice as fast as Stanfield's DC-7C turboprop. Stanfield hadn't even joined the jet age. At one campaign stop, Stanfield was photographed on a stagecoach, the type of publicity that only heightened the contrast between his campaign and Trudeau's.[29]

Sometimes Trudeau's trip into town was dispensed with and the campaign event was staged entirely at the airport. This was the case in Dauphin, Manitoba, where Trudeau spent barely more than

This photo of Progressive Conservative leader Robert Stanfield, taken at a Calgary shopping centre on May 24, 1968, appeared in newspapers across Canada. Did editors run it because it was picturesque or because it fit with preconceptions that Stanfield was old-fashioned? Local officials often gave party leaders regionally appropriate headgear, like the Stetson Stanfield is wearing here, as props for photo ops, yet photographs of Trudeau wearing a funny hat neither circulated widely nor stuck as defining images of Trudeaumania.

a quarter of an hour. He spoke briefly about agricultural policy and multiculturalism – then it was "up, up and away!"[30] The risk that he would be seen as just dropping in, not really caring about a community, was offset by the dynamic associations of the airport setting.

If Trudeau could materialize by helicopter, all the better. In Newfoundland, he arrived at a church this way, literally descending upon the congregation from the heavens.[31] When he did the same at a rally in Victoria's Beacon Hill Park, one of the organizers recalled proudly that "it was just like the Second Coming, because he flew in right against the sun. He dropped out of the sky, and after his speech, he just disappeared again."[32]

Visitation by aviation facilitated the reel-to-real synthesis. Having the star appear and disappear suddenly was part of the show, highlighting his other-worldiness and impressing the locals with his command of the wonders of modernity. Trudeau spent more time moving than stationary, his body propelled hither and yon like an action hero on amphetamines.

On the first Sunday of his leader's tour, May 26, Trudeau toured the lower St. Lawrence, then the following day headed east out of Montreal towards the Eastern Townships. Separatists had heckled him the day before at Matane and Rimouski, and now he encountered more at Fort Chambly.[33] Some were posing as Trudeau supporters and bore placards saying "Trudeau, get the frogs to speak white," "We are losing our patience, Look out Frogs," and "Down with stupid Frenchmen." Trudeau responded with an attack on all those who sowed hatred and intolerance. Another claimed to be a homosexual and bore a placard thanking Trudeau for his Criminal Code amendments. This presented a challenge to the PM. He chose to chastise the placard bearer, saying that the whole point of the legislation was that sexuality should be private – the state didn't want to be in his bedroom.[34] Separatists also showed up in Sherbrooke that evening to heckle him during his speech.[35] Some observers thought their attacks backfired because they got Trudeau riled up, prompting fiery responses that impressed listeners.[36]

Trudeau was drawing substantial crowds in Quebec cities. This was true not just in Montreal and Quebec City, but smaller centres like Trois-Rivières, where seven thousand attended his rally, and Sherbrooke, where the turnout was over three thousand.[37] Rural Québécois turned out in smaller numbers. They were curious about Trudeau because of all the fuss about him, but tended to take a skeptical, wait-and-see attitude. He was yet another emissary from Montreal, and they were suspicious of the modern city and its ways. They wanted to hear about bread-and-butter issues, not abstract talk about the constitution. For those who held to residual Catholic values, Trudeau was suspect for liberalizing divorce, abortion, and homosexuality. For older rural residents, his swinger image made him an alien from another planet.[38] It was, of course, the combination of these factors that fuelled the smear campaign against him. Rival party leaders denounced it, but often local candidates did nothing to refute the rumours that Trudeau was a communist of questionable sexual orientation. Copies of the issue of *Vers Demain* that attacked Trudeau were found in Créditiste candidates' offices in rural Quebec.[39]

Less traditional Québécois were willing to give Trudeau a chance. While the political elites tended to have set positions, the majority of people were open to changing their views in response to shifting circumstances. The Trudeau candidacy had the effect of siphoning off support for systemic change among centrist nationalists. Trudeau was himself living proof of his own argument that French Canadians could make it in Canada, and many Québécois were proud that one of them had ascended to the highest political office in the land. Trudeau offered a model that was an attractive alternative to sheltering in a fortress Quebec.[40] His formula for protecting French Canadian culture with official bilingualism and a charter of rights was a reasonable option that had the advantage of being more likely to be realized and less risky than experiments with redistributing powers.

This Québécois political calculus was more complicated still. The Liberal Party's tradition of alternating between English and

French Canadian leaders recognized French Canada's influence in Confederation. Having a French Canadian as prime minister, the latest in a long line of French Canadian prime ministers, contradicted the Quebec neonationalist claim that French Canadians had always been a subjugated underclass, while reinvigorating age-old tactics of la survivance. The Quebec electorate had long displayed a propensity for supporting strong provincial-rights regimes in Quebec City while at the same time sending committed and influential federalists to Ottawa. Though incongruous at first glance, the strategy sensibly played one level of government off against the other. In Ottawa the French Canadian bloc could exploit the party system, boosting one party into power in return for protection of its interests, while in Quebec City a doctrine of provincialism extracted maximum benefits from Ottawa. In supporting Trudeau, Québécois were following this tradition, playing the system with a sophistication worthy of experts in game theory.

As a result, a Québécois could be a French Canadian nationalist and a Canadian nationalist at one and the same time, or, alternatively, a French Canadian nationalist who was federalist for practical reasons. Quebec sovereignty carried a considerable economic risk, whereas Trudeau's policy of official bilingualism promised opportunities for francophones in the federal public service. Moreover, the modernization agenda implicit in Trudeau's candidacy was entirely commensurate with the post–Quiet Revolution modernization of Quebec. As the campaign progressed, Trudeau was even more explicit about his one Canada, two languages opposition to special status, and his reception in Quebec grew warmer, even outside of Montreal.

After his Quebec swing, Trudeau moved on to the Maritimes. On the evening of Saturday, May 30, his party – and the seventy-odd journalists who were covering him – landed at Canadian Forces Base Shearwater, outside Halifax. A crowd of a thousand greeted him, and spectators lined the route to his hotel downtown.[41] The next day he hit a couple of shopping centres, then headed off to Kentville and Yarmouth. This was Stanfield country, and rural, so the locals managed to keep their mania in check. Still, the next day's Halifax paper featured a front-page photo of Trudeau with a young woman who wanted his autograph. Inside the paper was a full-page photo spread including a shot of another young woman kissing him.[42]

"The more you think about it," proclaimed one Tory banner, "Stanfield is the man."[43] This slogan might have worked if elections were thoughtful affairs. Stanfield tried everything he could think of to get some traction. He couldn't criticize Trudeau's policies because he had few, he couldn't criticize the Liberal record because they had a new leader, he couldn't offer a bold new plan because he was too responsible and the voters wouldn't have bought it anyway, and he couldn't wow them with his personality because he was neither charismatic nor a great orator. One of his campaign slogans, "Sock It to Them," evoked the hosiery manufactured by his family firm more than the spirit of the sixties. "In the era of the flower-power and kissing cuties, he's clearly miscast," wrote Frank Jones of the *Toronto Daily Star*.[44]

Trudeau's campaign was mod, those of his rivals traditional. When Stanfield or Tommy Douglas came to town, he was greeted by a bagpiper in a kilt or a brass band.[45] One Tory audience was serenaded with "Pack Up Your Troubles in Your Old Kit Bag," a First World War chestnut that automatically dated them. The Liberals, in contrast, would have a folk or pop band entertain the crowd at a shopping centre while waiting for Trudeau to arrive. The musicians were all young and groovy. The Liberals' "mad mod election campaign" full of "exploding color and excitement," one reporter wrote, was "like looking at a psychedelic film."[46]

Both opposition parties tried to make the economy the issue and blame the Liberals for inflation and higher interest rates, but Trudeau preached careful stewardship of the treasury and effectively blunted that attack. Stanfield, meanwhile, had made promises that seemed to involve greater spending. "There is no Santa Claus," Trudeau admonished an audience. "The Government must not fool the people by promising things and pretending they can be paid for without increased taxation. We do not think taxes should rise."[47] He used a variation of this line in his speeches time and time again during the campaign.

Tommy Douglas read the writing on the wall and admitted publicly that the NDP could not win the election. He hoped for a minority Parliament in which his party would hold the balance of power. The NDP concentrated on the fifty ridings the party thought it had a chance of winning. Its platform emphasized state intervention to address issues that directly affected the average working person, including a national housing program to ease unemployment and the high cost of home ownership, a price review board to keep corporate profits in check, and implementation of the recommendations issued by the Task Force on Foreign Ownership and the Structure of Canadian Investment. Though the NDP should have been well placed, with its left-wing platform, to capitalize on the progressive bent of the sixties, it suffered from having a leader who seemed old and passé like Pearson and Diefenbaker. The campaign put Douglas into a convertible and drove him up Main Street, but the multitudes did not flock to him as they did to Trudeau.

At Trudeau rallies, the camera would track across a sea of humanity surging around the candidate, whose composure positioned him as the calm at the eye of the storm. Footage of his arrival at a shopping centre typically featured screeches, shots of girls, overcome by emotion, jockeying for a kiss, kids jumping up and down in excitement, adults straining for a sightline, a thicket of arms outstretched towards the stage.[48] This material was compelling viewing. The crowds seethed with power and anarchic potential, and the viewer was challenged to discern what others found so intriguing about the figure at the centre of it all. What the viewer did not see was the periphery or, for that matter, any scenes where the action was less dramatic or people were acting more or less normally. Yet, in keeping with the maxim that the camera did not lie, its selective field of view was presented as objective fact.

To what extent the excitement about Trudeau was attributable to him alone, and to what extent he had stumbled into the lead role in a contemporary pop culture phenomenon, was up for debate. De Gaulle's progress from Quebec City to Montreal had elicited a similar response the year before. The same phenomenon was evident in the United States, where political events had taken a dramatic turn. After Senator Eugene McCarthy began campaigning successfully for the Democratic nomination on an anti-war platform, Bobby Kennedy jumped into the race in mid-March. In a move unprecedented for a sitting president, Lyndon Johnson announced at the end of the month that he had decided not to run for reelection rather than risk splitting his party over the war issue. Kennedy began to get a response similar to Trudeau's in his primary appearances, with enthusiastic crowds thronging his motorcades. He too had charisma and pretty coeds as campaign workers, although his campaign was targeted more specifically towards the poor and marginalized. He promised visible minorities integration into the American mainstream while offering middle-class whites the dream of a return to Camelot.

Like Trudeau, Kennedy was handsome, youthful, and articulate, and appealed to the spirit of the times with the promise of transformative change. Knowlton Nash, sent to cover the phenomenon for the CBC, believed the enthusiastic crowds Kennedy was attracting were unprecedented in US political history.[49] If anything, they were even crazier than those that greeted Trudeau. While Trudeau was kissed incessantly and lost his watch and the odd hair to an overenthusiastic fan, Kennedy lost his watch, his jacket, his shoes, even his socks. The impulse to get a souvenir as tangible proof of contact with the celebrity world put the candidate's safety at risk. During one motorcade an enthusiastic supporter pulled RFK right out of the convertible he was riding in, leaving him with a fat lip and a chipped tooth.[50] Was it something about the times? Kennedy tried to explain it in political terms, telling Nash, "People are concerned about the poverty, the violence, and Vietnam." But he added,

"Others have seen your picture on the cover of magazines and think it's a lark."[51] Whatever the reason, as Canadians watched both campaigns unfold that spring, for once their domestic programming rivalled the American offering.

The first Gallup poll of the campaign north of the border, taken in the first two weeks of May and reported in the second-last week of the month, confirmed the Liberals' preelection polling. It had them at 50 percent support among decided voters, with the Tories trailing at 29 percent (down 4 percent since 1965), the NDP down 2 percent to 16 percent, and Social Credit at 5 percent.[52] In the second Gallup poll, published in the last week of May, support for the Conservatives held steady, but the Liberals had lost four points, primarily to inroads by Créditistes in Quebec.[53] Créditiste leader Réal Caouette had been able to capitalize on a number of plant closures to press home his standard critique that the economic elites were screwing the little guy.

Some journalists were now criticizing Trudeau for "simply presenting himself to allow the crowds to touch the hem of his robes." "I sense … disenchantment," fretted the party president.

> In the early stages of the campaign they were willing to accept the huge crowds as evidence of his being new and exciting. However, that kind of news has begun to pall. They are looking for him to say something new and exciting. The Press give the impression that he is saying nothing and our policy papers have indicated to those who are looking for change that he is not going to change much.[54]

The policy papers to which Stanbury referred had been distributed to Liberal candidates at the end of May. Whereas the 1965 platform had called for medicare, a war on poverty, and educational initiatives, the eighty planks in the new platform included no new social welfare programs, and, apart from enhanced regional development, no major expenditures.[55]

The problem with talking policy was that when Trudeau did it, the audience got bored, and listened politely but without enthusiasm. Still, the accusations that he was all style and no sub-stance continued to dog him. "The Trudeau campaign is, in effect, a throwaway when you think of the man's intellectual capacities and the range of his mind as demonstrated before he committed him-self to the role of the showbiz campaign, showing himself to the hero-hungry people," complained Charles Lynch. "All the people want to do is look at Trudeau, and have him mingle with them, and get the autograph of the man who got so famous so fast."[56]

What criticisms of this sort overlooked was that Trudeau had an issue, and a big, winning issue at that: national unity.[57] He had fought the battle within the Liberal Party and seen his staunch fed-eralist position prevail against the drift towards special status; now he took the same position to the people. Quebec's diplomatic ambi-tion, demonstrated most dramatically by the Gabon affair, was one of his targets. At a press conference in Ottawa on May 8, Trudeau said he was seeking a mandate to challenge Quebec's pretensions in foreign policy. Unless the issue were confronted, he warned, Canada would be surrendering a key part of its sovereignty with-out a fight. In case anyone missed his message, he repeated it in a speech in Montreal on May 15, declaring that "when a foreign country wants to talk to Canada, there is only one address: Ottawa." Trudeau deployed his favourite argumentative technique, *reductio ad absurdum*, asking what if, for instance, Acadians wanted to attend such a conference – who would determine this, Gabon? If so, "we would have the Gabonese deciding on the development of the French fact in Canada."[58] He repeated earlier warnings that if France, which he suspected was behind the invitation from Gabon, tried the same stunt itself, Canada would break off relations with it, just as it had with Gabon.

The Quebec issue put the PCs and the NDP in a pickle. They needed seats in Quebec not just to win the election but to sup-port their claims to being national parties. The Conservatives were down to seven seats in the province from their high of fifty under Diefenbaker in 1958. The NDP had yet to elect an MP in Quebec. Since they had English Canadian leaders, the two opposition

'Then he swept me into his arms and said, "What are we going to do about de Gaulle?"'

Editorial cartoonist James Reidford solicits a chuckle by linking teenybopper affairs of the heart with weighty foreign affairs.

parties turned to prominent Québécois to help represent their parties in the province.

The Tories' man was Marcel Faribault, Premier Johnson's chief constitutional adviser for the previous six months. Wooed by Stanfield, he resigned as president of Trust Général du Canada and, on May 14, announced he was running for the Progressive Conservatives. Stanfield apparently sealed the deal by telling Faribault that he could express himself freely on the issue of Quebec and the constitution. His recruitment was regarded as a coup for the Conservatives due to his business credentials and status as a credible French Canadian with a firm position on the constitutional issue.[59] Faribault was a federalist but wanted constitutional reform along two nations lines. This included conceding the province's right to an international presence on issues under its jurisdiction and recognition of Quebec as the homeland of French Canada, which implied some kind of special status.[60] His position was not out of line with party policy as it had been articulated, albeit in more general terms, at the Conservative convention the previous fall, but the range of opinion on the issue within Tory ranks made a certain ambiguity on this point expedient.

Trudeau wasted no time in attacking Faribault's position. "If you identify one nation, in the sociological sense, with one province and its government," he argued, "you are well on the way to admitting that the province speaks for French Canada. Then you've gone a long way down toward special status, associate statehood, or independence for the province."[61] On his visit to Sherbrooke on May 27, Trudeau fleshed out one of his counterproposals: a six-point position on bilingualism, which he presented as the price of Canadian unity. Meanwhile he attacked the Tories effectively with the accusation that Stanfield was not forthcoming in western Canada about what Faribault was advocating in Quebec.

The Liberals eventually ran a television ad that accused Stanfield of subscribing to the two nations views of Faribault. Stanfield reacted angrily, demanding that Trudeau disavow "these lies and distortions. I have never advocated two nations. I have never advanced special status."[62] Trudeau said that he'd have the ads withdrawn if Stanfield would state that he did not favour the two nations concept, then went ahead and withdrew them anyway, contenting himself with saying that the Tories had a "two policy policy."[63]

The NDP's predicament with the Quebec issue was roughly the same as that of the Conservatives: Quebec NDP leader Robert Cliche talked special status, while elsewhere in Canada federal party leader Tommy Douglas emphasized new social programs that would entail a more interventionist federal government. The apparent discrepancy wasn't as obvious as among the Conservatives, because Cliche stayed in Quebec and spoke mostly in French. Nevertheless, when in NDP territory, Trudeau denounced it as "a waffling, hypocritical party of confusion and double-talk which had never had the 'guts' to face up to the problem of national unity."[64]

On the Quebec issue, Trudeau represented stability through the preservation of symmetrical federalism. His hard line on national unity resonated all the more amid the uncertainties of the day. The counterculture continued to challenge all that was decent and dear to the hearts of the God-fearing and right-thinking. Hippies refused to get a job or even, some critics contended, take a bath. South of the border, anti-Vietnam protests were in full swing that year, with university campuses roiled by marches and sit-ins. Meanwhile a fissure had appeared in the Iron Curtain, threatening to destabilize the Cold War equilibrium. In Czechoslovakia, President Alexander Dubček had recently announced a ten-year program of liberalization that would bring greater freedom of the press, freedom of speech, and freedom of movement, limitations to the power of the secret police, an increased economic emphasis on consumer goods, and the possibility of a federalization of the country's two nations, Czechs and Slovaks. Though anxiety-inducing, the Prague Spring appeared to be a good thing insofar as it might liberate the country from Soviet tyranny. What would the Soviets do? The world watched and waited.

In Sweden, Poland, Germany, France, Spain, and Italy, student protests led to chaos in the streets that spring. Authorities generally overreacted in their crackdowns, generating broad public sympathy for the students. Violent police repression of student protests in Paris mobilized progressives who joined the students in the streets, clashing with gendarmes in pitched battles. Televised scenes of police brutality won the protesters still more sympathy and further reinforced their ranks. On Monday, May 13, over a million people marched in Paris. Workers joined in, occupying factories, until about two-thirds of the total national workforce, some ten million people, were on strike. There were fears that the communists would use the unrest as a springboard to revolution. The government was shaken, and at one point, when President de Gaulle left the country, appeared to be collapsing. Things began to calm down only when late in the month Prime Minister Georges Pompidou orchestrated dissolution of the National Assembly, bringing on a national election.[65] These events, widely publicized as they unfolded throughout the month of May, suggested that one possible outcome of sixties liberations was a descent into chaos.

Then came shocking news. After winning the California primary on Wednesday, June 4, Bobby Kennedy was shot by a lurking gunman while leaving his victory party at the Ambassador Hotel in Los Angeles. A candidate of change and social justice upon whom millions had pinned their hopes was mortally wounded and died the next day. All the expectations he'd raised were dashed. Coming, as it did, so soon after the assassination of Martin Luther King Jr., it was too much. American civilization appeared desperately sick.

When news of Kennedy's death came on the morning of June 5, Trudeau was in Montreal attending the funeral of André Laurendeau, who, his friends believed, had worked himself to death on the bilingualism and biculturalism commission. As Trudeau left the church in Outremont, he was confronted by separatist hecklers and cries of "Traitors! Go back to Ottawa." In Sudbury the following day, Trudeau threw away his prepared speech and spoke with feeling about Laurendeau and his commitment to tolerance and diversity.

> I felt the best way I could pay homage to my friend Laurendeau would be to come to a city such as yours which has given testimony to the ability of Canadians to work together and to live together in peace and harmony. We see confrontations which are taking the forms of violence. We see racial strife in the United Kingdom. We see great outbursts of civil disorder in France. We see great cities in the United States being torn apart by racial strifes, by poverty, and we have to reflect that, in Canada, we are indeed a very fortunate nation.[66]

Canada had so far escaped bloodshed, yet it would not be immune "if we tolerate the language of violence or hate. We have seen bombs go off, and we have seen groups appeal to hate and civil disorder."[67] Trudeau angrily equated Kennedy's killer with separatist terrorists in Quebec. Instead of violence, rational means of change must be sought, "venues of reason, of discussion, of dialogue, that will permit us to find these solutions." "We can only reflect on the frailty of human beings and the societies they build together," he mused.[68]

Lester Pearson was in the audience, and phoned Marc Lalonde, his former assistant, to tell him it was "the best political speech he had ever heard."[69] The next day, June 7, in the northern Quebec town of Rouyn, Trudeau lit into a handful of teenage separatist hecklers, yelling at them that "the men who killed Kennedy are purveyors of hate like you."[70] This was strong language – indeed, rhetorical overkill – for putting down a bunch of kids, but no one criticized him. Canadians seemed willing to let him vent. Indeed, in the context of all the doom and gloom elsewhere, Canadians took comfort that their pop star politician continued to appear in public and might well mingle with them soon.

Trudeau's campaign combined the excitement of crowds with assurances of order. Senator David Croll told his audience in Bowmanville, Ontario, that

> Prime minister Trudeau has inspired the young people of Canada … Look around and contrast this with what is happening in other countries. A revolt is going on. In the United States, Columbia University is locked up. There are riots at the Sorbonne in Paris. Students are fighting in Germany and Italy, and there is even student restlessness and rebellion in Great Britain.
>
> Here, Trudeau is a bridge between generations. He tells it as it is, and young people listen to him, believe, and become actively involved in this election.[71]

In the disconcerting context of the spring of 1968, Trudeau's repeated declarations on the hustings that we must be one and we must move forward together were not mere platitudes; they were reassurances that addressed profound anxieties then preying on people's minds.

On June 7, Trudeau repaired to Harrington Lake, the prime ministerial retreat in the Gatineau Hills north of Ottawa, to prepare for the joint CTV-CBC television debate scheduled for the evening of Sunday, June 9. The debate proved to be a dull affair. For the first televised leaders' debate in Canadian history, the networks, fearful that their medium would be criticized for trivializing solemn affairs of state, devised a staid format. The leaders answered the same questions one at a time. There was no opportunity for interruptions, objections, sparring, or any of the personality-driven drama that made for good television. Trudeau came off as aloof, even bored by the proceedings.

Mediation anxiety soothsayer Marshall McLuhan criticized the format of the debate in a letter to Trudeau. "The witness box cum lectern cum pulpit spaces for the candidates was totally non-TV," he argued.[72] Commentators were surprised that Trudeau had not

Trudeau greets supporters during a rally at
Place Ville Marie in Montreal, June 21, 1968. Check out
the number of cameras capturing his image and note
how an image captured earlier appears on posters in
the crowd. The live appearance is a critical yet
exceptional episode for fans in their ongoing mass-
mediated relationship with the star.

come off better, but the result was consistent with his previous performances – he was at his best in the cut and thrust of wide-open debate or interview, not in delivering set-piece speeches, where his delivery was flat unless he got riled up. According to a survey published by the *Toronto Daily Star* on June 12, most Canadians thought Douglas won the debate. Nevertheless, Trudeau "came out ahead of the game," according to one observer, because he projected an image of a solid, responsible, respectable politician," which reassured those put off by "the 'swinger' image that has dogged him throughout his campaign."[73]

After the debate, Trudeau was back on the campaign trail, resuming his frenetic criss-crossing of the country. In his earlier Ontario campaigning, he had attracted large audiences in smaller centres: 3,000 in Oakville, 5,000 in Burlington, 4,000 in Markham, 5,000 in Stouffville. He continued to be a draw. In early June, Trudeau went from the prairies (4,000 in Dauphin, Manitoba, 3,000 in Yorkton, Saskatchewan, and 12,000 in Regina, more than Diefenbaker in his prime), to Cape Breton (5,000 waiting for his late-night arrival in Sydney, Nova Scotia), to Prince Edward Island (4,000 in traditionally Tory Charlottetown) and back to Ontario for a swing from Toronto down to St. Catharines, then back to Hamilton, where 18,000 showed up to hear him speak.[74]

Trudeau's handlers continued to shamelessly exploit his photogenic potential, and he always obliged. Knowing that the campaign was wearing on him, one of them suggested that he get some exercise by going for a swim at the hotel he was staying at in Oakville on June 14. The press was tipped off, and when Trudeau appeared a battery of lenses was trained on him. Instead of fleeing, or doing just a couple of laps for the sake of appearances, Trudeau climbed onto the diving board and put on a show, performing flips and dives. He invited a young woman who was watching to join him, and, when she declined, saying she had no bathing suit, suggested that Marilyn Monroe would have gone in without one. Then he politicized the display. "Here's the Stanfield dive," he announced, hobbling up to the end of the board and toppling off. Then he did

Trudeau's diving exhibition at an Oakville hotel pool on June 14 was front-page news across Canada and the United States the next day. It was illustrated with photographs such as this one and headlined by phrases such as "Trudeau Makes a Splash." Action shots engage audiences, and Trudeau provided plenty of action.

the "Douglas dive," which consisted of striding confidently down the board into thin air. For Caouette, he did a perfect somersault. As Trudeau signed autographs, another woman appeared on the pool deck. She was, of course, attractive, bikini-clad, and blonde. After she dove in, one of the photographers shouted, "Go get her, tiger!"[75]

The next day Trudeau was pictured soaring in midair off the diving board on front pages across the continent.[76] It was hard to imagine another Canadian political figure who could appear publicly in a bathing suit and not become an object of ridicule. Stanfield and Douglas could not compete in this game. As one voter said of Stanfield, "Il n'a pas de sex appeal."[77]

The Liberals now had the results of a new private poll, more extensive than there had been time for before the election call. The big news was that their numbers were holding up. The pollster's analysis had lots to say about the impression Trudeau was making on Canadians and how to exploit this in the campaign, but for the most part it reinforced the Liberal approach to date. Its most notable finding was that Trudeau, "an exciting new personality on the Canadian political scene," was not in need of exposure: 93 percent of Canadians knew who he was. He was also associated strongly with transformation: "Pierre Trudeau is looked upon as the man to usher in a new era in Canadian government. He can enhance this strength by ushering in a new era in Canadian politics ... the Canadian electorate ... is grasping for movement. Pierre Trudeau must make certain that voting decisions are based on this."[78] Trudeau's cabinet colleagues, who knew rural Canada, had earlier cautioned against such an approach. Joe Greene had observed that the "large cities and the rest of Canada are two different worlds, not only politically but in so many other ways" and suggested they run different campaigns in each. Allan MacEachen agreed, recommending a seasoned operator who knew the Maritimes to run the Liberal effort there. But the numbers were in the cities, and strategy was geared accordingly.[79]

The day after his pool party, Trudeau had a big blowout with campaign co-chair John Nichol as he was being dropped off at 24 Sussex

Drive. With the election seemingly in the bag, he balked at having to maintain his hectic pace on the campaign trail. Nichol insisted, and Trudeau got angry but finally relented.[80] So off he went, back to British Columbia, Alberta, Saskatchewan, and Ontario. By the time he hit Fort William, Ontario, on June 18, he'd travelled 27,500 miles, spoken at 118 shopping centres in 84 ridings, visited 113 towns, and shared the platform with 122 different Liberal candidates. He'd done five swings through Ontario, four through Quebec, two in each of the western provinces and Nova Scotia, and one in each of the remaining provinces.[81]

All that remained was stage three, the dramatic build-up to election day. On June 19, Trudeau hit Toronto, where organizers had pulled out all the stops to set the stage for a scene of full-blown Trudeaumania. "When we started our planning three weeks ago, we knew Stanfield would be here some time in the last week of the campaign, and it was a safe bet the Tories would go for the traditional kind of indoor political rally where you pump your people in by the busload," explained a youthful Liberal organizer. "We decided to forgo all that, and try for something a little more genuine – an open-air event which would draw not only committed Liberals but the uncommitted and the curious – the kind of people who might be swayed just by the sight of the Prime Minister. They publicized the rally metro-wide, distributing 10,000 posters, 10,000 placards, 10,000 buttons, and 107,000 handbills saying "Come and Greet Pierre Elliott Trudeau."[82]

Bobby Gimby led Trudeau's ticker-tape parade up Bay Street in full view of the Toronto business elite. Meanwhile a pop band and a folk group entertained the crowd waiting for him in Nathan Phillips Square, in front of Toronto's futuristic new city hall. By lunchtime the throng had swelled to fifty thousand people. "Trapped in it, the only way you could chart Trudeau's course without a periscope was by watching for the sudden thrust of cameras at arm's length and listening for the orgiastic squeals of the teenage girls who suddenly found him heading their way," reported one journalist.[83] The event was "not a political rally at all," Peter Newman observed, "but some kind of public rite, new and strange to the Canadian electoral process."[84]

Two more events were held in the suburbs that afternoon. As Trudeau switched cars, a crowd gathered instantly, and "he had to shout and mug for them, departing with a Gallic shrug."[85] Ten thousand people showed up to see him in Scarborough's Centennial Park, dwarfing organizers' expectations. Another sixty-five hundred packed into North York Centennial Arena to hear him at his last stop. Altogether, more than sixty-eight thousand people turned out for him in Toronto that day.[86]

Trudeau's subsequent big-city events became a triumphal march towards election day. On June 21, he flew into Montreal for a home-town rally. His open-air campaign bus overheated on the way in from the airport, but instead of letting breakdown become a meta-phor for his campaign, Trudeau got out and danced with a young woman, generating action for the cameras.[87] When he arrived downtown, he received an "ecstatic reception" from a crowd of thirty-five thousand at a rally in Place Ville Marie, inspiring him to deliver what reporters thought was one of his best speeches of the campaign. "Gripping the microphone while waving one hand in the air, Mr. Trudeau exploded into a non-stop, emotion [sic] oration ... that appeared to hold his audience momentarily spellbound."[88] "It wasn't really Trudeaumania that struck Montreal," George Radwanski explained,

> but rather Trudeauphilia – a vast outpouring of friendliness towards the Prime Minister.
>
> The screaming teeny-boppers were there, all right, but they were a highly-vocal minority ... About three-quarters of the crowd that overflowed Place Ville Marie for Mr. Trudeau's noon appearance were people of voting age ... They were interested, curious, sympa-thetic, perhaps excited – but certainly not hysterical ... Above all, they were receptive.[89]

When his bus broke down en route to his big
rally in Montreal on June 21, Trudeau found a
dance partner and swung into action,
creating another upbeat scene for the media.

It was a good turnout for a political rally, even if it paled in comparison with other popular enthusiasms. When the Habs had won the Stanley Cup a month earlier, 600,000 cheered their victory parade in Montreal.[90]

On June 23, Trudeau was in Winnipeg, riding in a convertible as marshal of the Red River Parade that opened the Red River Exhibition. Then he went on to Vancouver, where 12,500 came out to his rally. A final Gallup poll, published in the *Toronto Daily Star* on June 22, showed the Liberals at 42 percent, with the Tories down to 26 percent, the NDP at 16 percent, and other parties at 5 percent support. Eleven percent of voters were still undecided, but they could not close the gap between the two major parties even if they all voted PC.[91]

On the last morning of the campaign, June 24, Trudeau went to the Montreal suburb of St. Laurent to campaign for Jean-Pierre Goyer, the Liberal candidate for Dollard. Trudeau talked about this "incredibly rich and beautiful country" and the importance of keeping it together. "The fundamental question of the campaign is our future as a united country," he declared, "one Canada, one nation with two languages, no special privileges to any province, no *statut particulier*."[92] He went on to the riding of Duvernay, where Eric Kierans was running. Then he took a helicopter to Sainte-Hyacinthe, a south-shore textile town, to support Maurice Sauvé's reelection bid. "Our home is not just Quebec," he told the crowd. "Our home, *chez-nous*, is not just the province of Quebec. It's the whole of Canada."[93]

Trudeau had come a long way over the previous year. The plot line of his ascent to power was like something out of romance fiction. The story had begun with a marginal awareness of someone interesting, moved quickly to passionate engagement, then escalated to the climax of the election. "Life imitates art," television producer Richard Nielsen observed, "and no medium in history creates the taste for real-life drama that TV does."[94]

But there was still one more plot twist to come. Weeks before, Trudeau had accepted an invitation to attend the Saint-Jean-

In the closing days of the campaign, Trudeau visited Winnipeg to appear in the Red River Parade.

Baptiste parade in Montreal on election eve. After his encounters with separatist hecklers during the campaign, he must have anticipated the possibility of a confrontation at the parade. Given recent events south of the border, he probably asked himself whether he would be in the crosshairs of a rifle scope. Indeed, several anonymous calls said he'd be assassinated if he showed up. The week before the parade, Pierre Bourgault, leader of the separatist Rassemblement pour l'Indépendance Nationale, urged a wildly cheering crowd of supporters to go to the parade to protest against Trudeau, the "traitor" and "sellout." Police feared that a full-scale riot was in the cards.[95] Was Parisian-style anarchy coming to the streets of Montreal? Would Canada's political saviour be martyred by extremists? Trudeau was forewarned.[96] But he went anyway.

On the eve of election day, Trudeau stood up to separatist rioters
at the Saint-Jean-Baptiste parade in Montreal in a dramatic scene
played out on national television.

10

Split Electorate
The Political Work of Mod

Canada has crossed a psychological watershed ...
We have broken out of the flatlands of the past
and now move ahead to the promise
of the unexplored but rising ground ahead.

EDITORIAL, *Victoria Times*, June 26, 1968

307

THE PARADE IN Montreal on Saint-Jean-Baptiste Day, a traditional French Canadian holiday, usually consisted of decorated floats crewed by costumed characters, along with marching bands in their polyester finery, celebrity representatives of worthy causes waving from open convertibles, and clowns working the crowd. It was a family event to which parents brought their children, a summer community festival that took advantage of the long hours of daylight at the summer solstice.

1968 would be different. June 24 was muggy, with the threat of a thunderstorm hanging in the air. The VIP stand for the parade was in front of the Montreal Public Library on the east side of Sherbrooke Street, a few blocks north of downtown, facing La Fontaine Park. Opposite it was an observers' stand where newsmen and cameramen gathered. At this pinch point the parade had to funnel between the two structures.

The parade was scheduled to pass the reviewing stand around 9:30 in the evening, when darkness would be settling in. An hour earlier the sidewalks were already packed with spectators. Meanwhile a crowd of separatists gathered in the park. They shouted anti-Trudeau slogans: "Tru-deau au pot-eau" (Trudeau to the post, as in for a firing squad) and "Le Qué-bec aux Qué-bé-cois." Riffing on Trudeau's "lousy French" comment, others proclaimed "Lousy ones! Get rid of your lice! Don't vote! Lice to Ottawa!"

Police moved through the crowd to keep it from concentrating its force. Occasionally they'd pack a demonstrator off in a paddy wagon. They also lined the street to keep the demonstrators from disrupting the parade. Around 9:30, a pop bottle sailed through the air and smashed at the feet of the police lined up on the street. Then a couple more. This put the police on edge, and they got more aggressive with the demonstrators, hauling more of them off and handling them roughly. The VIPs, including Trudeau, began to file into the reviewing stand as the lead floats of the parade hove into view down the street. Then rioters rushed the police line. Helmeted riot police armed with clubs appeared on the scene, and the hitherto scattered skirmishes escalated into a pitched battle. The protesters, supplemented by hellraisers looking for cover under which to wreak havoc, threw bottles, some containing acid, paint, or kerosene, and swung at police with two-by-fours and crowbars. The police fought back, swinging their clubs liberally. A couple of policemen got separated from their comrades and were badly beaten.

Tires screeched as police vehicles and ambulances raced around, sirens wailing, taking out the casualties and arrests and bringing in reinforcements. Pierre Bourgault appeared, urging on his forces. He was pleased to be hoisted immediately onto the shoulders of supporters, then dismayed when they turned out to be plainclothes cops who promptly packed him away in a paddy wagon. Mounted police in riot gear arrived and charged repeatedly into the protesters, forcing them to retreat off the street into the shelter of trees in the park. The parade started to go by, crunching through the broken glass. In the park and the streets behind it clashes continued. Rioters smashed car windshields and overturned police cars, setting one on fire.

Just before eleven, a separatist incursion compromised one end of the police line protecting the VIP stand. The parade paused, stranding a marching band and a green Mustang convertible in front of the reviewing stand. One rioter got within throwing range and heaved a pop bottle at the VIPs. Everyone in the stand ducked, covering their heads with their hands as it smashed into the library portico behind them. Then another projectile came in. In the face of this assault, Mayor Jean Drapeau and his wife, who were sitting beside Trudeau, leaned over, urging him to get out of harm's way. Other VIPs, including Premier Daniel Johnson and Archbishop Paul Grégoire, beat a retreat, and Drapeau ushered his wife to safety.

The prime minister's RCMP bodyguards pulled him to his feet and back towards shelter. Trudeau shook them off with an angry gesture and sat down defiantly at the front of the stand, leaning forward to watch the parade as it began to move again. In the media stand across the street, journalists forgot their professional commitment to objectivity, leapt to their feet, and cheered him. He waved back, then quickly turned his attention back to the parade. The police, embarrassed by their lapse, tore into the demonstrators and beat them with abandon, bringing the drama to a sickening conclusion.[1]

The television cameras captured the whole affair, albeit within their limited focus on the street and the reviewing stand. Although election coverage was blacked-out for the forty-eight hours before the polls opened, news was news, and Trudeau's last stand was broadcast nationwide just in time for the vote the next day. A Liberal organizer guessed it was "worth 40,000 votes in Toronto alone." Dalton Camp considered this a gross understatement.[2] A nun who ran into Trudeau the next day told him she was thankful he wasn't killed. "How could I have been?" he replied. "I was sitting beside the archbishop."[3]

On election day, Trudeau voted in Montreal, then journeyed to the Château Laurier in Ottawa to follow the election results on television in a suite of rooms rented by the party. Guests included his family, the Pearsons, his political staff, party officials, and Patrick Watson. The early returns from eastern Canada were not encouraging. Despite Joey Smallwood's support, the Liberals lost to the Conservatives six of the seven seats they had formerly held in Newfoundland. Nova Scotia stayed Tory, as predicted, and the Liberals went from two seats in the province to one, Allan MacEachen's Cape Breton riding, where he barely squeaked in. Prince Edward Island, considered a bellwether province, stayed all Tory, four for four. In New Brunswick, where the Liberals had six seats going in, they dropped one to the Conservatives.

But the rich harvest of ridings in central Canada was yet to come. What about Quebec, where Trudeau had outraged the ruling elites with his staunch federalist position? The Liberal popular vote shot up eight percentage points over 1965 to 53.6 percent, by far the highest level of support the party received in any province. The Conservatives lost seats, dropping from seven to three, with Marcel Faribault going down to defeat. Yet this loss did not translate into gains for the Liberals, because the Créditistes went from eight to fifteen seats, all in rural Quebec, leaving the Liberals with fifty-six Quebec MPs, the same number they had going in.

Then came Ontario, another populous, seat-rich province. Here the Liberals trounced the opposition, winning sixty-three of eighty-eight seats, gaining at the expense of both the Conservatives and the NDP. In the Trudeaumania production centre, Toronto, the PCS were completely shut out. At this point the Liberals were on pace to match their 1965 seat total. If they were to make a majority it would come thanks to the West.

In Manitoba, where they had won only a single seat in 1965, five of the thirteen ridings went Liberal. The Liberals hadn't won a seat in Saskatchewan in the previous election. Now they got two, with the NDP taking six and the Conservatives five. Alberta elected fifteen Conservatives and four Liberals, enough to give the Liberals a majority in the House of Commons. British Columbia would be the icing on the cake. In 1965 it had elected seven Liberals, nine NDP, three Conservatives, and three Social Credit; this time the Liberals won fifteen seats, including one at the expense of NDP leader Tommy Douglas, while the NDP won seven. The Conservatives and Social Credit were shut out.

In short, the Liberals had lost support in the Atlantic provinces, but held their position in Quebec, won big in Ontario and British Columbia, and also gained seats on the Prairies. The final standings were Liberals – 154, Conservatives – 72, NDP – 22, Créditiste – 14, and Independents – 1. The Liberals got 45.5 percent of the popular vote, up five percentage points from the previous election. The Conservatives polled 31 percent, down a point from 1965. The NDP too dropped a point, from 18 percent to 17 percent. A total of 7,984,654 Canadians cast ballots, a record number that reflected the one million baby boomers who were newly eligible to vote. Voter turnout was 75.7 percent, solid but not exceptional for that era.[4]

What did these results say about the impact of Trudeaumania? Trying to draw sweeping conclusions from election results is a dicey business. To begin with, there are diehard partisans who vote for their party no matter what. Then there is the appeal of the local candidate, regardless of the national leadership. Moreover, regional and local concerns – something as parochial as getting a new bridge – can trump all else in a constituency battle. The first two-thirds of an article on the election in a small-town BC paper, for example, covered the local MP's outrage at the federal government's failure to come through with funding for a major highway in the region. Only then did it quote him on the larger campaign, and that reference consisted of a warning about the false blandishments of national politics:

> In 1958 the Canadian people were sold a bill of goods in the form of Diefenbakerism. We accepted Mr. Diefenbaker on trust alone without regard to his performance. We were never more disappointed in our political lives … Now we are being asked to accept Trudeauism with the same blind faith. In fact it is probably the same high priced advertising agency that handled the campaign for Diefenbakerism that is now handling Trudeauism. We were bitten once we can't afford to be bitten again.[5]

Another consideration is that a certain portion of voters were simply clued out. When asked the main factor in their thinking about the election, 13 percent of residents in Toronto's Davenport riding complained about the state of local roads, sewers, and other issues that fell under municipal jurisdiction.[6] In short, so many variables have to be taken into account from one riding to the next that any conclusions about voters' choices are necessarily speculative and must be carefully hedged.[7]

Nevertheless, some general patterns were evident in the 1968 election results. First of all, Trudeaumania was clearly not a mania in the sense of a contagion that swept through most of the populace. The Liberals' share of the popular vote increased by five percentage points from 1965. While enough to give them a majority government, this increase was hardly evidence of a mass phenomenon. It is significant too that Liberal support, which peaked around 50 percent with the customary bump enjoyed in the wake of a leadership convention, declined almost five percentage points during the campaign. In other words, Trudeaumania did not snowball towards election day. Throughout the campaign the Liberals were fighting to lose as little as possible of the soft support they had at its start.[8]

Still, a gain of five percentage points is significant, particularly in a first-past-the-post voting system. On the face of it, the gain was the difference between Lester Pearson's minorities and the majority government that had eluded him. Yet even this conclusion has to be hedged. Had the electoral redistribution of 1966 taken place before the 1965 election, Pearson would have had a majority. If he had run against Robert Stanfield rather than John Diefenbaker, however, the Tories' new leader probably would have stolen Liberal votes.[9] In speculating about what may have been, the what-ifs always accumulate and gum up the works. In general terms, however, it is safe to say that Trudeaumania allowed the Liberals to hold on to their base, offset the impact of new leadership in the Progressive Conservative Party, capture a large proportion of swing voters, and even win over some Canadians who usually voted for rival parties.[10] No doubt the Trudeau image lost them some votes too, but on the whole they benefited from the trade-off.

When voters were asked about the issues that mattered to them, most raised perennial economic concerns such as inflation, unemployment, government spending, and high taxes. Yet these did not become defining issues of the election. The economy was strong in 1968, and no significant differences between the major parties on economic policy emerged to dominate the campaign. Those polled mentioned other issues as well – abortion, women's rights, divorce, Vietnam, pollution, foreign ownership, business power, whither contemporary youth – but none of these either crystallized into a major focus of the campaign or gave any one party a distinct advantage.[11]

On one issue, however, the Liberals enjoyed supremacy. Their polling found that nationalist issues separated Trudeau from the pack. One poll included questions about which leader would do best on a particular file. On the nationalist concern of "improving Canada's position in the world," Trudeau was the first choice of 62 percent, with Stanfield trailing badly at 26 percent and Douglas at 8 percent. On national unity, Trudeau scored 76 percent, compared with 16 percent for Stanfield and 6 percent for Douglas. Significantly, Torontonians were more concerned about national unity than other Canadians. Commenting on the national unity results, the pollster noted, "Over the years we have never found this issue as important to Canadians as the press would have you believe or perhaps as important as it should have been." Nevertheless, those who shared the press's national unity worries overwhelmingly preferred Trudeau.[12]

A sidelight on the national unity issue is that Trudeau did not seem to lose any support in Quebec because of his hard-line federalism. Claude Ryan rejected the suggestion that the 53.6 percent popular vote for the Liberals in Quebec represented an endorsement of Trudeau's constitutional position, attributing it instead to the province's support for a native son.[13] Interestingly, however, in the Liberals' private polling, 67 percent of those polled agreed with the statement that "the province of Quebec is asking too much" in constitutional negotiations, a number that held up in Quebec. The Liberals were also strongly supported by French Canadian minorities outside Quebec, whose interests were in line with Trudeau's constitutional and bilingualism policies.

What made Trudeaumania a "mania" was not the extent of the contagion, but rather the strength of the engagement that Trudeau inspired among his supporters. Those who liked Trudeau liked him a lot. Many of Trudeau's fans "became intensely interested in politics for the first time" and displayed that interest publicly.[14] In this sense the allusion to Beatlemania, which saw wild displays of enthusiasm from fans, was apt.

The Pearson Liberals had appealed more to educated, prosperous urbanites in higher-status occupations than to any other demographic groups. Trudeaumania enhanced this appeal. Analysis of the election results bears out the abundant anecdotal evidence that Trudeau supporters were disproportionately urban, well educated, affluent, and, if not young, at least youthful in spirit. In the eighty-five urban constituencies in Montreal, Toronto, Vancouver, Edmonton, Calgary, Winnipeg, Hamilton, Ottawa, and Quebec City, the Liberals jumped from 42.1 percent of the vote in 1965 to 52.5 percent, which gave them sixty-six urban seats, or 78 percent of the urban ridings.[15] Liberal support reflected an urban-rural split, with cities going Liberal while rural areas of Quebec, the Maritimes, and the Prairies remained relatively immune to Trudeaumania. In fact, the more distant from a large city or more isolated the rural area, the less likely it was to support Trudeau. In Quebec, for example, the Créditistes won in isolated ridings like Beauce and Rouyn-Noranda.

Class and Liberal support were also correlated. The Liberals' polling showed that Trudeau was most popular among those in the upper middle classes, and least popular among the poor. Breaking this down further, Trudeau seemed to appeal most to the professional-managerial class. He garnered strong but slightly less support from white-collar workers and small business people. He was distinctly less popular among blue-collar families.[16] As political scientist John Meisel observed in his study of the election results, Trudeau's supporters were "the most industrialized, urbanized, technocratic and managerial Canadians ... the Liberal party can be thought of as being most progressive or 'modern,' in the sense of appealing most to those elements in society which feel at home in the so-called 'advanced,' urbanized and highly technological world usually associated with urban North America."[17] This appeal was illustrated in the gains the Liberals made at the expense of the NDP. In British Columbia and Ontario, the NDP lost to the Liberals in more affluent ridings but held on to its working-class constituencies. Evidently upper-class NDP supporters were more susceptible to Trudeau's charms than its lunch-bucket crowd.

The 1968 election was the first in which any baby boomers were old enough to vote. Trudeau was perceived as more youthful than his rivals, and Gallup numbers showed that Trudeau won the Liberals more new supporters among Canadians in their twenties than among any other age group. Only in the over-fifty age bracket did support for the Liberals decline compared with 1965.[18] Yet the Liberal advantage among the young was not all that large. Moreover, despite all the highly publicized kissing of Trudeau, women did not vote for the Liberals any more than did men. In fact, they showed a slight preference for the Conservatives, while men voted NDP more than women.[19] This outcome reinforces the point that the mania was a mania due to its intensity among a select group, not because it affected most of the population. The kissing was a way for Trudeau's female supporters to signal he was an agent of change by associating him with the sexual revolution and the sixties cultural liberations of which it was a part.

Being modern affected support for Trudeau more than either one's age or one's sex.[20] Prosperous, highly educated urbanites

FASTEN YOUR SEAT BELTS

In Duncan Macpherson's rendering the day after the election, the flirtation, the thrill of the chase, and the courtship were over. Canada had made a lasting commitment and was setting off on a new stage of life.

were involved in the modern world more than poorer rural Canadians, for whom tradition and local culture offset outside influences. The modern versus traditional split could be seen in voters' attitudes towards controversial questions of the era. Those who remained immune to Trudeau's charms had values that disposed them to resist the liberations of the sixties. Trudeauphiles were tolerant of ethnocultural minorities, homosexuality, and divorce; Trudeauphobes reacted negatively to all three. Trudeauphiles opposed the death penalty; Trudeauphobes supported it. Trudeau's mod supporters were also more knowledgeable about and engaged in federal politics than their compatriots. "Liberal voters ... showed themselves to be the most progressive, liberal, secular and politically interested and to feel politically effective," John Meisel noted in his analysis of the election results. "Support for Mr. Trudeau's party varied directly with religiosity, moral liberalism, interest in foreign affairs, greater importance being attached to the central government, interest in the election, a sense of efficacy, general optimism about the future and economic expectations; it varied inversely with authoritarianism, respect for law and order ... and cynicism."[21] Denizens of modernity identified more strongly with the national community because their identity derived less from being rooted in any particular local community. Not only were they engaged in federal politics, they felt that they had particular influence in that sphere. Its instability throughout the sixties bothered them, making them feel insecure, and they longed for a majority government to bring calm and order to national affairs.[22]

Media commentary at the time portrayed the election as a contest between the past and the future. The *Peterborough Examiner* editorialized that in electing Trudeau, Canada "tossed tradition in the trash-can and took off in a new direction."[23] Larry Zolf wrote impishly that "Canadians were no longer Uriah Heepish but rather Great Forward Leapish."[24] Channelling mod nationalism, a writer in London's *Spectator* magazine exulted that "it was as if Canada had come of age, as if he himself singlehandedly would catapult the country into the brilliant sunshine of the late 20th century from the stagnant swamp of traditionalism and mediocrity in which Canadian politics had been bogged down for years."[25] Pent-up forces had been unleashed, and the nation had been rejuvenated in one magnificent *coup de foudre*.

A survey conducted in Hamilton during the last ten days of the election campaign showed that while Trudeau was perceived more favourably than the other leaders, he was also the most polarizing. Ambiguous feelings about him were low.[26] Traditionalists viewed his mod image with suspicion. Among the most conservative, his image provoked a Trudeauphobia that saw him as communist, homosexual, or both. This was true in Quebec as well as in English Canada.[27] Trudeaumania functioned as a litmus test for one's sympathy with emergent values. The more rural, uneducated, aged, or poor you were, the less likely you were to be blowing kisses at Pierre Trudeau in the spring of '68.

Trudeau was a wedge candidate, and sex was the thin edge of the wedge. His supporters pushed his mod image hard, gambling that it would split the electorate in their favour. And it did, producing a chunk of votes just large enough to deliver a majority. The trendy, educated, and affluent urbanites had their way by forcing the issue. As ideological leadership it was less than subtle: the elites worked in concert openly and aggressively to promote their interests over the resistance of less privileged elements of society. They had no scruples about leaving the rural, unplugged, residual culture behind.

While the election results showed clearly who Trudeau's supporters were, to understand how this cohort's voting power was consolidated behind him requires a review of how political events unfolded during the previous six months. The rise of Trudeaumania in this period provides an instructive case study of how elites conspire in a mass-mediated modern democracy. Both "elite" and "conspire" are loaded words that conjure up images of political bosses plotting in smoke-filled backrooms. But the processes that drove Trudeaumania were not so simple, morally or logistically. The professional-managerial class made its way in the world by operating the complex technologies and bureaucracies of modernity. Process was its forte. Empowered by their media, cultural, and political literacy, Trudeau's supporters conspired by reading events, anticipating how they would unfold, and intervening to ensure things would go the way they wanted. Participatory democracy was an effective vehicle for their class interests.

Was Trudeau a creation of the media? That was a common charge. Certainly the media were not innocent bystanders. They had disproportionate influence because they were cultural producers with privileged access to the communications systems that bound the far-flung nation together. Journalists liked to see themselves as proxies for the public interest, yet they were immersed in the national political scene far more than their audience, living and breathing its gossip every day. Naturally, they tried to humanize their beat by draping the amoral mechanics of state in the romantic garb of nation. Overexposure made them more impatient than most Canadians with the desultory Ottawa scene. They were also influenced by professional competition to identify the next big thing and the commercial imperative to win audience share. In sponsoring the kissing campaign that launched Trudeau, the media were responding to these pressures. They found in Trudeau a figure who fit their needs and helped him on his way to fulfilling them.

Yet the media could not have made Trudeau without a complicit audience. Audience reception theory stresses that recipients of media messages filter them through their own beliefs, experiences, and interests, rejecting many, negotiating the meaning of others to fit with their world views, and accepting uncritically only those that confirm their prejudices. A substantial segment of the media's audience thought much the same way as the media did because, like them, it was part of Canada's modern professional-managerial middle class. Trudeaumania was not a simple case of the media foisting Trudeau on a hoodwinked public. An influential segment of the public thought along the same lines.

While the media may not be able to brainwash audiences, they do have the power to determine what is and is not news. With Trudeau, the media did what scholars agree they do best: agenda setting. They shone the spotlight on him and made him news. Then they presented him in a fashion calculated to appeal to like-minded Canadians. After identifying Trudeau as a possible solution to the nation's challenges, they characterized him as a mod man for the times, dashing, exciting, and fun, sporting both sexual sizzle and cosmopolitan panache. They pushed him until they had helped make him prime minister. At that point they backed off and re-dedicated themselves to their journalistic ideals (not to mention the careerist imperative to be the first to break a story, which for some meant criticizing the media's role in Trudeau's rise). By then, however, the Trudeau juggernaut was rolling and didn't need their boosting any more.

The broader Trudeauphile constituency then sustained the mania through established institutions, practices, and communications channels. Trudeau supporters used mod to brand their cause and exploited the predictable, participatory, and theatrical rituals of electoral politics to maximize their influence. Mod hailed audiences in a way that forced them to choose between the past and the future. Youth and sex, the hallmarks of the Trudeau image, challenged Canadians to embrace emergent values. "Pierre, with the ladies, racin' a Mercedes," would father a new era in national life.[28] There was no need to spell out this promise in the measured rhetoric of a political speech: the mod style said it all. Best of all, it made politics fun – jejune, upbeat sex and youth chatter beat the dull rhetoric of constitutional conferencing hands down.

As political theatre, Trudeaumania had it all: a compelling protagonist, a suspenseful plot, rife with complications, and audience participation. Federal election campaigns were participatory rituals in which belonging could be performed. Trudeau's supporters were better acquainted with the rules and practices of electoral politics than most Canadians and better attuned to the media cues about how to join in. Within this framework they worked together, not through tight organization, but rather by improvisation in response to circumstances as events unfolded. Shared values and civic competencies provided the basis for concerted action. They participated in the national drama as media-literate citizen-actors who anticipated and worked collectively towards a happy ending.

The baby boomers among them were particularly conversant in contemporary popular culture. They had grown up participating in the latest fads. When they were kids it had been Daniel Boone coonskin caps; when they were preteens it had been whatever dance craze was then sweeping the continent. "Come on and take a chance, and get-a with this dance," commanded the singer of "The Wah-Watusi." And they did. The baby boomers were used to having their collective indulgences presented as daring deviations from social convention. Attuned to media prompts about the latest style, they were adept at adapting quickly.[29]

Trudeau's ability as a screen actor established him early on as leadership material.[30] Telegenic and articulate, he came across well on TV, running the gamut of emotions from shy to snide, indifferent to passionate. On top of that, he provided the visual action television demanded: interesting gestures, flips off a diving board, slides down banisters, boogying beside a broken campaign bus, a fake fall down a staircase. In a made-for-TV campaign, Trudeau gave good TV.

As for plot, the events of 1967 established a problem in need of resolution. Then along came a mysterious stranger. This raised an intriguing prospect: Could he sweep aside all obstacles, vanquish all rivals, and carry the day? Would Miss Canada be seduced and carried off into the sunset by the romantic hero? The answer would be found through a leadership race and then an election campaign, political rituals that provided a predictable trajectory of events. Matters would be resolved within limited time frames that would climax in votes. The knowledgeable professional-managerial middle class knew how this chapter in the national narrative would play out and what they needed to do to get the result they desired.

The leadership and election campaigns provided a long-running series of occasions for the reel-to-real ritual that was an increasingly prominent feature of postwar popular culture. It involved crowd formation, public displays of enthusiasm, and spectacle improvised in emulation of models such as the pop concert, the protest march, and street theatre.[31] These occasions provided local audiences with confirmation that they mattered, that their man was real, and that their identification with the nation was authentic. Being part of the crowd was exciting and generated feelings of security and belonging. The experience provided a visceral sense of community that counteracted mediation anxiety and modern alienation. In the context of a national election campaign, it was easy to conflate the intense, first-hand crowd experience with membership in the larger, imagined community of the nation. Each Trudeau appearance was publicized, providing subsequent crowds with an example of how to behave.[32] Even those who never demonstrated their enthusiasm for the candidate in public could still follow the unfolding storyline through the media, identify with what they saw, and ultimately make it real in the polling booth.

Either way, Trudeau's supporters participated collectively in a drama that unfolded within a predictable temporal framework defined by established rituals of Canadian political culture. They had the political literacy required to understand how leadership campaigns and general elections unfold and what they could do to influence the process. As they played along, Trudeau's public appearances became dots connecting a plot line that rose towards a climax – first the Liberal leadership convention and, a while later, election day.

The flip side of the organizing advantages of the Trudeauites was that more traditional Canadians, who were oriented more towards their local and regional communities, were relatively disorganized and dispersed. They didn't commune through the mass media. As a result they did not cohere as effectively as a national political force. Instead they fought a defensive, rearguard action in isolated redoubts.

In short, Trudeau's supporters leveraged their modern competencies in media, culture, and politics to make history together. The process worked so well that towards the end their cause took on an air of triumphal inevitability. The moral of the story was that to the literate go the spoils. Yet even as they communed through the mass media to achieve their goals, they were anxious about modernity generally and their mass-mediated simunation in particular. The media were necessary tools of national collective life, but were their representations real? Could they be trusted? Mediation anxiety was an increasingly common feature of contemporary public discourse.

In this respect Trudeau proved himself a superior candidate. He discomfited journalists by making it known that he didn't think much of them. He teased them, preying on their consciences by suggesting that they had created him. He spoke of circumventing the media to speak directly to the people, pointing up the media's intermediary role. He dramatized his awareness of the mediated nature of national politics by stepping out of his assigned role within the frame applied by the media. His playacting conveyed a knowing cynicism about TV and highlighted its interpolation between him and the public, suggesting that he was more substantial than the media circus around him. His image was made by mocking the image making, by satirizing the drama in which he starred even as it unfolded, by questioning the role of the media in a process that it increasingly mediated.

Did the media resent this? Quite the contrary. His contempt for them worked to his advantage. Reassured by his stagey lack of artifice, they did his PR for him. The candidate's ability to address and ameliorate mediation anxiety was yet another way in which he exuded the sixties virtue of authenticity. His supporters were more immersed in mass media and popular culture than most Canadians and thus more afflicted by mediation anxiety. Trudeau connected through the media both directly and ironically with an audience of increasingly self-conscious media consumers. Trudeau and the Trudeauphiles communed in their shared distrust of their means of communication with one another even as they used it expertly to achieve their mutual goal.

In terms of contemporary pop culture, Trudeaumania was Beatlemania with the promise of Camelot at its end. Two formative pop experiences from the early 1960s were recycled and repurposed within the Canadian political arena. In this light Trudeaumania may be regarded as an embarrassing symptom of a colonial propensity for slavish imitation. Canada had been inundated by continental mass culture for so long that nationalists perennially despaired of its ever having a distinctive culture of its own. The way events unfolded in 1968, however, suggests that the country had a distinctive political culture. Trudeaumania was an instance of Canada borrowing from the broader popular culture to rejuvenate its political culture, in the process accommodating the 1960s demand for a more participatory, responsive politics that was otherwise unattainable in a mass democracy.

In December 1969, long after the initial exhilaration of Trudeaumania had faded, Trudeau would receive a highly publicized visit from John Lennon and Yoko Ono. Earlier that year Lennon had recorded "Give Peace a Chance" during a bed-in with Ono in Montreal, and now they were touring the world to promote peace. Who better to help with this quest than the philosopher king of the Peaceable Kingdom? Canadians were flattered that their prime minister warranted the call, and gratified that Lennon afterwards told reporters that Trudeau was a beautiful person and that there would be world peace if more leaders were like him. It did not strike anyone as

The stars align: John Lennon and Yoko Ono
meet with Trudeau, December 22, 1969.

incongruous that Canada's middle-aged prime minister would be consorting with one of the Beatles. The star of Trudeaumania fit naturally within the wider sixties celebrity cosmos.[33] Norman DePoe had hinted as much when he wrapped up CBC TV's 1968 election coverage, signing off with a world-weary "Good night Marshall McLuhan wherever you are."[34]

Trudeau à la mode mod, courtesy of cartoonist John Yardley-Jones.

After the Love-In
The Lingering Effects of Peak Nationalism

Social images are one thing and social realities another.
Yet the two are not completely separate. Social images are
not entirely fictional characters with only a coincidental likeness
to a real society living or dead. Often the images can be
traced to an earlier historical period, its golden age perhaps,
which, thanks to historians, is held up, long after it has been
transformed into something else, as a model way of life.

JOHN PORTER, *The Vertical Mosaic*

PRIOR TO PIERRE Trudeau's arrival centre stage on the Canadian political scene, a consensus about the nature and needs of the nation was forming among leading voices in the national conversation. What they wanted, not surprisingly, was a nation in their own image. They were impatient with the federal politics of the 1960s because first John Diefenbaker, then Lester Pearson, had promised transformative change, yet Parliament had instead fallen under a grey pall of petty scandals, sordid partisan bickering, and old-fogeyism. They sympathized with the restless spirit of the sixties insofar as it meant liberation from the dead hand of the past. At the same time, they were frightened by the twin spectres of continentalism and separatism.

The first six months of 1968 saw protest, confrontation, violence, and destruction escalate throughout the Western world. There were even outbreaks within the gates of the Peaceable Kingdom. The counterculture was increasingly outrageous, abandoning any pretence of social critique to embrace provocation for its own sake. In the United States these provocations were splitting mainstream politics between reactionaries who adopted a bunker mentality and moderates who still hoped to accommodate dissent through judicious reform.[1] Political assassinations cruelly snuffed out hopes for deliverance through visionary leadership.

These developments created space for Canada to stake out a position to the left of the United States. Canadians redefined their national identity by being more responsive to contemporary critiques of the establishment than their neighbour to the south. According to nationalist identity theory, Canada was untainted by the blights then afflicting the American republic. Nationalists caricatured the United States as racist, militaristic, chauvinistic, authoritarian, and imperialistic, and in contrast cultivated the myth of Canada as a gentle, tolerant, orderly Peaceable Kingdom in harmony with sixties values of peace and love. Their hopes for Canada were pumped up first by the centennial and Expo 67, then by Pierre Trudeau, "our permanent Expo,"[2] who promised to open politics to popular participation and make Canada a Just Society. Later in 1968 Americans would confirm the differences between the two countries by electing Richard Nixon president.

The imperative of modernization presented the classic political dilemma of how to manage it to bring progress without destabilizing social order. The mod style was well suited to this purpose. Trudeau's image channelled the iconoclasm of the sixties, making the Liberals appear more in tune with the spirit of the times than their rivals, and invoking the pleasure and excitement of change undergirded by assurances that it offered no threat to the status quo.

Scratch the surface of Trudeaumania's mod hype and you found stability assurance. The most obvious instance was Trudeau's defence of federalism. On the Quebec issue Trudeau confronted forces that invoked the causes of decolonization and national liberation in keeping with the spirit of the times. He countered them by characterizing Quebec nationalism as an illiberal, retrograde force. But this wasn't the only example. He pledged no new spending. He proposed no new social programs to enhance the welfare state – indeed, he felt it had gone as far as it should for the moment. His popularity implicitly promised a return to stable majority government, like Canada had back in the 1950s.

The image of the celebrity politician stabilized a number of worrisome fissures in the body politic. Trudeau the perfectly bilingual and bicultural Canadian embodied a reconciliation of French Canada and English Canada. Regional differences were transcended through the solidarity of his modern urban supporters from coast to coast. Trudeau's mod youthfulness bridged the generation gap and accommodated, if only superficially, the radical youth challenges of the sixties. His supposed irresistibility to women superficially reconciled the sexes, while his androgynous gestures undermined gendered polarities and hinted at public acceptance of sexual orientations other than heterosexuality. Trudeau's appearances across the country alleviated anxiety about the mass-mediated nature of national life. Those who had not seen him live could purchase and display Trudeau merchandise as another way to bring the nation tangibly into their lives.

Trudeau's liberalism, long a dominant political ideology in Canada, was another assurance of stability. One might have expected that in the context of the sixties it would be villainized as a core feature of the establishment. But liberalism is a protean dogma, and the sixties were ideologically incoherent, so liberal freedom could be sold as a solution rather than the problem. The key liberal value of freedom was, after all, entirely congruent with fundamental sixties impulses. Freedom informed the postwar human rights movement and attendant sixties liberations from discrimination based on colour, sex, or sexual orientation. It also inspired the sexual revolution and lifestyle liberations of the counterculture. Trudeau's liberalism offered a principled, multipurpose answer to many issues besetting late-sixties Canada. By emphasizing individual freedom, Canada could refute the collectivist premises of Quebec's sovereignty ambitions, differentiate itself from a United States that was increasingly portrayed as repressive, and redefine Canadian identity in pluralistic terms, paradoxically making the principle of individual rights the key marker upon which collective identity could be based. Trudeau's liberalism sliced through various Gordian knots entangling the Canadian nation-building project, freeing it to move into the future with a new clarity and nobility of purpose.

Nevertheless, many inconsistencies coexisted at the heart of Trudeaumania. Trudeau the antinationalist became the darling of Canadian nationalists. Trudeau the advocate of individual freedom was raised to power by groupthink. Trudeau the rational advocate of functional politics rode an emotional wave of support into office. Trudeau the devout liberal democrat generated a cult of personality redolent of atavistic longings for a strongman. Trudeau ridiculed the media even as it empowered him. Trudeau would cure the ills of modernity by modernizing. All such contradictions were overlooked in pursuit of the greater goal of national renewal.

In the end, what did it all matter? Were there any significant, long-term effects of Trudeaumania?

Astute political analysts have argued that the 1968 election was not particularly momentous. Though Trudeaumania helped the Liberals win a majority government, the five percentage points by which their share of the popular vote increased from the previous election was hardly overwhelming. Moreover, the election did not reconfigure the political landscape by fashioning a new coalition of voters that realigned party support. Pearson's Liberals had appealed to the growing modern, urban, professional-managerial class, and so did Trudeau's, only more so.[3] These arguments, well grounded in polling data and the pattern of election results across the country, are convincing as far as they go.

Yet the significance of '68 lies elsewhere – in the imagined life of the nation. The nebulous nature of this change means that gauging the extent of Trudeaumania's impact involves leaving the firm ground of empirical facts for a comparatively speculative foray. Drawing conclusions about the influence of a certain concept of national identity is fraught with difficulty because no research methodology can definitively prove the effects of such abstractions. The longer the time period elapsed since Trudeaumania, the greater becomes the challenge of proving its long-term influence. Yet the temptation to address this issue is irresistible because echoes of peak nationalism can be heard to this day, suggesting a structure of feeling characterizing the *longue durée*. What

follows is a provisional argument that Trudeaumania was a formative episode in Canadian nationalism that had an enduring influence on national identity.[4]

With Trudeau's elevation to power, nationalists believed that
Canada had been permanently changed. The Peaceable Kingdom
had been transmuted from identity theory into a government with
the power to make Canada a unique nation-state. In subsequent
decades the promise of Canada as a kinder, gentler America would
be often be betrayed. Yet the myth was so comforting and deep-
seated that it was impervious to mere facts. It represented a greater
truth – what Canadians wanted to believe about themselves.

In the short term, Trudeaumania gradually faded. In the months
after the 1968 election, the media reverted to its customary oppositional stance. Trudeau could no longer get away scot-free when he
said something harsh or mean-spirited. In August, when asked
about his position on the civil war raging in Nigeria, Trudeau asked
flippantly, "Where's Biafra?" and was roundly criticized. At a Liberal
fundraiser in Winnipeg the following December, he asked rhetor-
ically, "Well, why should I sell the Canadian farmers' wheat?" and
much indignant protest followed. The bloom was off the rose; the
thorny bits, now exposed, suggested that Canada might have to
suffer the odd prick. Trudeau's star power continued to shine, if
less brightly, and that and nostalgia ensured that there would always be a Trudeaumania of sorts.[5] But it would never again be as
influential or promising as it was in 1968.

During the October Crisis, Trudeau's tough-guy persona trumped
his highly touted credentials as a civil libertarian. He gave police a
free hand to round up suspected members or sympathizers of the
Front de Libération du Québec and hold them without laying charges, a violation of fundamental civil liberties. In retrospect the episode was recognized as an egregious abuse of state power. At the
time, however, public opinion backed the government's extreme
measures to keep the peace. It was a point of pride for Canadians
that their Peaceable Kingdom was a sanctuary that had previously
been relatively free of terrorist violence. The FLQ discredited itself

and its violent tactics by murdering Pierre Laporte, diverting separatist energies back into duly constituted political processes. The
upshot was a situation in which, observers marvelled, the destruction of Canada was pursued peacefully within the system.

In 1972 Trudeau had a much rougher electoral outing, and the
Liberals were again reduced to a minority government. Despite
the setback, Trudeau spent fifteen and a half years at the head of
government, impressive longevity for a Canadian prime minister.
He implemented his 1968 national unity agenda. He passed official
languages legislation to offset Quebec nationalists' claim that a
Quebec nation-state was necessary to protect French Canadian
rights, and managed thereafter to keep Quebec separatism at bay.
He introduced a multiculturalism policy that fleshed out the unity
in diversity approach to national identity. Eventually he even patriated the constitution with his long-promised Charter of Rights and
Freedoms. He governed centre-left, practising state intervention
and accumulating deficits long after such practices had been
demonized by a resurgent classical liberalism that had become the
new common sense of private-sector elites by the end of his time
in power.[6]

Yet Trudeaumania was not just about Trudeau. As Richard Gwyn
has suggested, it could have been called Canada-mania.[7] Trudeaumania was the means by which the peak nationalism of the 1960s,
emboldened by the glories of the centennial and Expo 67, remade
the nation. Canada subsequently displayed its distinct new identity in its response to major international trends of the late twentieth century.

The antiestablishment challenges and leftward leanings of the
sixties had galvanized right-wing opposition. Amid the dismay
and confusion of economic turmoil in the 1970s, the right saw its
opportunity to regain lost ground and began propagandizing on
multiple fronts to discredit Keynesianism and state intervention.
Neoliberals preached a radical reduction in the size of government,
a return to a laissez-faire reliance on unfettered markets, and
a rigorous anti-inflationary monetary policy. They excoriated

public debt and enjoined governments to balance their books. They attacked the welfare state as ruinously expensive and blamed its social programs for undermining the work ethic. If governments would only go away and let the invisible hand of the market wield its magic, they preached, efficiency and productivity would return, bringing back prosperity and progress.[8]

In the United Kingdom and the United States, this approach quickly gained credibility. Margaret Thatcher came to power in 1979 determined to break the unions, kick people off the dole, and get Britain working again. In the United States, Ronald Reagan became president in 1981 on the strength of similar nostrums. After Trudeau retired in 1984, pundits expected the subsequent federal election would feature a swing to the right to bring Canada into ideological alignment with its senior partners in the anglosphere. The new government, whether Liberal or Conservative, would introduce program and budget cuts to eliminate deficits and work towards paying down the public debt. Then came a surprise: the majority of the Canadian electorate was unreceptive to deficit discourse. During the 1984 election campaign it became clear that a politician who talked the neoliberal line risked being characterized as mean-spirited and un-Canadian. Fearful of losing votes, both Prime Minister John Turner and Conservative leader Brian Mulroney backed away from their policies of fiscal retrenchment. If buttonholed on the topic, they would talk vaguely of their concerns about the sustainability of the government's mounting debt. Otherwise they soft-pedalled the issue.

Soon after winning that election, Mulroney tried to deindex old age pensions from inflation but had to back down in the face of public protests. He had more luck in pursuing deregulation of industry and privatization of government enterprises. He even managed to win the 1988 election with his free trade gambit. Notably, however, the majority of voters in that election voted against free trade, in part at least because of the threat it presented to the imagined nation's identity. Canadians, it seemed, were still resistant to the neoliberal virus that had infected Britain and the United

States long before. Not until 1993, almost a decade and a half after the election of Margaret Thatcher in Britain, did the continuous neoliberal discourse have sufficient effect that a Canadian government felt it was politically possible to cut programs aggressively and balance the budget.

The constitutional crises of the 1980s provided further evidence of how deeply Canadian political culture was rooted in the 1960s. When Brian Mulroney sought ratification of the Meech Lake Accord, fierce opposition arose to its description of Quebec as a distinct society. Pierre Trudeau returned to the public spotlight to oppose the deal, arguing for the equality of provinces in a symmetrical federal system, just as he had in 1968. It wasn't just Trudeau's logic that carried the day, however. Many Canadians passionately opposed the Meech Lake vision of Canada as unpatriotic. For them the concept of Canada that had been entrenched by the formative events of the late sixties *was* Canada.

The 1995 referendum saw Quebec nationalism come tantalizingly close to prevailing over that concept of Canada, foregrounding the narrative of two irreconcilable nationalist agendas. Yet the two solitudes were also twin solitudes.[9] In the wake of the Quiet Revolution, social democratic nationalism was a dominant strain in Quebec politics that eventually found its political home in the Parti Québécois. Canadian nationalists were but a half-step behind in modernizing, differentiating, and solidifying group identity by veering left. Indeed, Trudeau was an agent of cross-pollination who came out of the Quebec social democratic stream and helped make that happen. He had wanted a just society without nationalism but ended up stuck with the nationalism, albeit in its Canadian rather than its Québécois form.

With neoliberal achievements such as trade liberalization, deregulation, and spending cuts, Canada lost much of the sovereignty required to design national institutions and legislation according to Canadian values and began sliding down a slippery slope towards policy harmonization with other Western capitalist democracies. By the new millennium, many of the key identity markers developed in the 1960s to differentiate the Peaceable Kingdom from the United States offered less of a contrast. The Canadian army's peacekeeping missions were now eclipsed by its status as a belligerent in Afghanistan. The welfare state was restrained in growth. After Barack Obama's health care plan was signed into law in 2010, Canadian medicare, though still far more comprehensive, was less useful as a symbol of Canadian distinctiveness. US cities that had been riven by racial tensions and torched by rioters had risen from the ashes, reducing Canadian cities' self-congratulatory margin of superiority. Canadians continued to take comfort in being immune to American gun culture, but nevertheless experienced their share of gang shootings and deadly rampages by crazed gunmen. Whereas there had been a long tradition of state intervention in Canadian history, now trade agreements constrained the government from actions in support of Canadian enterprises both private and public. Increasingly, beer company advertising rather than federally subsidized cultural producers performed the minstrelsy of national identity.

Canadian nation building, Peaceable Kingdom–style, was on hold, yet the myth endured. Like another holdover from the sixties, the Playtex "Cross Your Heart" bra, it displayed a remarkable capacity to lift and separate with no visible means of support. When polled in succeeding decades, Canadians still articulated values that distinguished them from Americans, sustaining the idea that Canada was a kinder, gentler America.[10] Ironically, Quebec was a bastion of social democratic values that helped define and preserve Canadian exceptionalism.

It is easy to poke holes in this argument. It is a confection of baby boomer nostalgia and left-nationalist idealism. There is no such thing as a collective essence that endures over decades. Nations are always aborning or coming of age because these are just metaphors for periodic identity tune-ups. Quebec nationalism is as vital and legitimate as Canadian nationalism, and the current state of play between them is neither preordained nor final. Budgets are real, and not balancing the books becomes a problem whatever a government's politics. We live in a postnational world in which the idea of Canada isn't so much problematic as it is irrelevant. Take your pick, combine your favourites, or add in some of your own.

On the other hand, just after this book was submitted for publication a new Trudeau came to power, conjuring flashbacks of 1968. Those who'd seen the steely glint of authoritarianism in the mania for Trudeau could now fear not just dictatorship, but hereditary dictatorship. During the interregnum there had never been another moment in which cultural ferment and nationalist excitement redefined Canadian identity. It was as if the sixties formulation of it still permeated the torpid substrata of collective consciousness, awaiting only the warmth of sunny ways to coax it out of hibernation. When Trudeau the Younger pronounced "Canada is back" in 2015, the ice slowly melting off the Peaceable Kingdom glistened. As the Beatles sang back in the sixties,

It's been a long cold lonely winter.
Here comes the sun.

NOTES

PRELUDE: KISS POWER!

1 Library and Archives Canada (LAC), Canadian Broadcasting Corporation, Television: Kines from Parc, Toronto, *The Way It Is*, June 16, 1968, consultation copy VI 8402-0047.

2 LAC, CTV Television Network, CTV News, "Trudeau," n.d., consultation copy VI 8011 0054; CBC Archive Sales/Archives Radio-Canada, "Trudeau Junket, Pierre Trudeau Takes a Whistlestop Tour of Southwestern Ontario Ridings," May 21, 1968; "Trudeau National, Pierre Trudeau Campaigns in Ontario," May 25, 1968; "Trudeau Maritimes, Trudeau Speaks to a Crowd in the Maritimes," May 31, 1968; "Trudeau Five, Pierre Trudeau Campaigns in British Columbia, Penticton," June 4, 1968; "Trudeau Elexen III, Trudeau Campaigns in Newfoundland," June 2, 1968.

3 Ryan won the 1968 Lloyd E. Moffat Memorial Award in the "Best Originality and Creativity in Canadian Recording" category. See "Sock It to Me Trudy ...?" *Toronto Telegram*, May 10, 1968; interview with Allan J. Ryan, Ottawa, February 22, 2004; email communication from Allan J. Ryan, March 11, 2016.

4 "Rock Fans in Spin over New Hit – 'Go Go Trudeau,'" *Toronto Daily Star*, May 3, 1968.

5 Martin Sullivan, *Mandate '68: The Year of Pierre Trudeau* (Toronto: Doubleday, 1968), 295.

6 Sheila Gormely, "A Swinger with Oomph," *Toronto Telegram*, February 16, 1968.

7 Quoted in John English, *Just Watch Me: The Life of Pierre Elliott Trudeau, 1968-2000* (Toronto: Knopf, 2009), 20. The title of this chapter is taken from "Kiss Power: Trudeau Speculates That Political Buss May Save Canadian Youth from the Fate of Becoming Dropouts from Society," *Globe and Mail*, May 27, 1968).

8 Gary Oakes, "Trudeauism Sweeps into an Excited Ontario," *Toronto Telegram*, March 4, 1968.

9 Canadian Press, "Blonde or Brunette? Oui Says Pierre," *Calgary Herald*, March 11, 1968.

10 Gary Oakes, "Trudeauism Sweeps into an Excited Ontario," *Toronto Telegram*, March 4, 1968.

11 "The Election: Leading from Strength," *Time* (Canadian edition), May 31, 1968, 11.

12 George Radwanski, *Trudeau* (Toronto: Macmillan, 1978), 106; Canadian Press, "Hairy Ordeal: Prime Minister Trapped, Loses Some Wisps to Children," *London Free Press*, May 23, 1968.

13 Gary Dunford, "'The Poor Dear Must Be Pooped,' Trudeau Fan," *Toronto Daily Star*, June 20, 1968.

14 *The Way It Is*, June 16, 1968.

15 Susan Danard, "Trudeaumania Engineer Loved His Job, the Man," *Victoria Times-Colonist*, September 30, 2000.

16 *Time* advertisement, *Globe and Mail*, July 4, 1968.

17 LAC, Canadian Broadcasting Corporation, Television: Kines from Parc, Toronto, *The Way It Is*, May 26, 1968, consultation copy VI 8402-0046.

18 Attributed to Dalton Camp in Paul Rutherford, *When Television Was Young: Primetime Canada 1952-1967* (Toronto: University of Toronto Press, 1990), 430.

19 George Bain, "Canada Has a Case of Trudeaumania," *New York Times*, June 16, 1968.

20 The "Kiss me Pierre ... but run my country Bob" bumper sticker is pictured with David Kilgour in "The Election: Magnetism and Calm," *Time* (Canadian edition), June 14, 1968, 12. It's mentioned too in Anthony Westell, "Pierre Trudeau's Two-Pronged Attack on the Voters," *Globe and Mail*, June 12, 1968, and pictured in CBC Archive Sales/Archives Radio-Canada, "Trudeau Five: Pierre Trudeau Campaigns in British Columbia," June 4, 1968.

21 Gayle S. Stever, "1989 vs. 2009: A Comparative Analysis of Music Superstars Michael Jackson and Josh Groban, and Their Fans," *Journal of Media Psychology* 16, 1 (2011): 3-5; Daniel Cavicchi, "Loving Music: Listeners, Entertainments, and the Origins of Music Fandom in Nineteenth-Century America," in *Fandom: Identities and Communities in a Mediated World*, ed. J. Gray, C. Sandvoss, and C.L. Harrington (New York: New York University Press, 2007), 235-249.

22 The word "mania" conjures up images of mass excitement and infectious folly. In recorded history manias have taken varied forms. Many have been religious, featuring divine revelations and mass conversions. Economists have long been interested in manias because they have been a feature of speculative behaviour in capitalist societies, from the Tulip Mania in seventeenth-century Holland or the South Sea Bubble in seventeenth-century Britain to the dot-com boom of the late twentieth century. Since the field of economics is too dismal to explain such bizarre phenomena, scholars have turned to psychology and sociology for insights into why free individuals prefer stampeding in herds to exercising independent judgment. In the political context, manias have been associated with crowd psychology and mass society theory, fields rife with pessimistic conclusions about whether the promise of liberal democracy can be fulfilled. In all of these cases, "mania" evokes an enthusiasm that spreads rapidly and widely through society. A mania seems to take on a life of its own, inviting descriptive metaphors of viral contagion.

INTRODUCTION: SEX AND THE BODY POLITIC

1 In studying television and social change during this period in the United States, Aniko Bodroghkozy has described a Gramscian "crisis of authority" in which hegemony failed, at least temporarily, to co-opt dissident voices (Bodroghkozy, *Groove Tube: Sixties Television and the Youth Rebellion* [Durham, NC: Duke University Press, 2001], 16). In Canada, however, authority seems to have appropriated emergent values and moved on. This may have been a function of nationalist interest in affirming Canadian nationhood by asserting an identity distinct from that of the United States. In any case, the contrast suggests the significance of the national context in which social change occurs.

2 The female enthusiasm evident in Beatlemania has been explained in terms of the limited options for sexual expression available to young women in the early 1960s. The hypocrisy of contemporary sexual mores placed huge pressures on young single women. They were supposed to bend but not break under amorous male advances, burdening them with the stressful responsibility of negotiating desire and morality. Fandom was a way to express the former without violating the latter. As one study put it, "Bad kids became juvenile delinquents, smoked reefers, or got pregnant. Good kids embraced the paraphernalia, the lore and the disciplined fandom of rock 'n' roll. For girls, fandom offered a way not only to sublimate romantic and sexual yearnings but to carve out subversive versions of heterosexuality" (Barbara Ehrenreich, Elizabeth Hess, and Gloria Jacobs, "Beatlemania:

Girls Just Want to Have Fun," in *The Adoring Audience: Fan Culture and Popular Media*, ed. Lisa A. Lewis [New York: Routledge, 1992], 99-100). Fan phenomena such as Beatlemania were also a public demonstration of female power. In a society in which middle-class women's gendered destiny was to be a wife, homemaker, and mother, one of the few prerogatives allowed them was the choice of a mate. Teenage girls had a brief period of free agency prior to adult conformity. The excitement of the crowd and the thrill of the chase made up an intensely emotional experience that bonded them with both their immediate posse and the larger fan base of which it was a part. The emotion powerfully shaped an identity – ephemeral perhaps, but deeply felt – that was independent of the family.

3 "In 1967," writes Barbara Freeman, "the transition in leadership between women's club feminism and radical feminism had barely begun in Canada" (Freeman, *The Satellite Sex: The Media and Women's Issues in English Canada, 1966-1971* [Waterloo, ON: Wilfrid Laurier University Press, 2001], 23). The Royal Commission on the Status of Women was appointed in February 1967 but did not report until 1970, and feminist critiques of a patriarchal society had yet to attain any significant profile in public discourse. The exception was the women's magazine *Chatelaine*, in which editor Doris Anderson mixed traditional women's fare such as fashion and recipes with advocacy for women's issues. It is interesting to note that in 1968 two risqué songs that dealt with different facets of women's contemporary sexual predicament, the Supremes' "Love Child" and Merrilee Rush's "Angel of the Morning," became hits.

4 The age of Trudeau's female fans was an ambiguous variable. Blair Fraser, the national political correspondent for *Maclean's*, observed that "women of all ages were particularly enthusiastic" (Fraser, "The Sudden Rise of Pierre Trudeau," *Maclean's*, April 1968, 65). Adolescent "teenyboppers" were the most boisterous and demonstrative in their pursuit of Trudeau. Yet older women were also fans insofar as they too sought a direct encounter with him at his public appearances. Sometimes their political rationale for preferring Trudeau was ignored by the media, which preferred to portray them as smitten by his charms. At the same time, they displayed great enthusiasm for Trudeau, if more decorously than their juniors, and many expressed their preference for him in romantic terms.

5 Roland Marchand, *Advertising the American Dream: Making Way for Modernity, 1920-1940* (Berkeley: University of California Press, 1985), 66.

6 Erin Hurley, *National Performance: Representing Quebec from Expo 67 to Céline Dion* (Toronto: University of Toronto Press, 2011), 53-57; Yasmeen Abu-Laban, "Introduction," in *Gendering the Nation-State: Canadian and Comparative Perspectives* (Vancouver: UBC Press, 2008), 11-12; Jill Vickers, "Gendering the Hyphen: Gender Dimensions of Modern Nation-State Formation in Euro-American and Anti- and Post-colonial Contexts," in Abu-Laban, ed., *Gendering the Nation-State*, 40-45; and Janine Brodie, "Putting Gender Back In: Women and Social Policy Reform in Canada," in Abu-Laban, ed., *Gendering the Nation-State*, 167-68. In pop culture manias the object of desire was always male. This would hold true when the phenomenon migrated into the political arena.

7 I am drawing on Anthony D. Smith for these categories but simplifying his schema somewhat for the sake of brevity. See Smith, *The Nation in History: Historiographical Debates About Ethnicity & Nationalism* (Hanover: University Press of New England, 2000).

8 See chapter 1 of John A. Armstrong, *Nations before Nationalism* (Chapel Hill, NC: University of North Carolina Press, 1982), for a discussion of the role of symbols and myths in nationalism. The difference between constructionists and perennialists on this point is that the former, in keeping with their belief that nations are a wholly modern phenomenon, regard invocations of pre-modern nations as cases of reading the present in the past. The latter, in contrast, contend that there have been socio-political formations akin to the

modern nation in the past and that the ethnic origins of modern nations, though distorted and embroidered for present-day purposes, are not wholly fictive.

9   Alienation has been expanded to include anomie, anonymity, apathy, and atomization, which together constitute the "five As" of modern malaise (John Durham Peters, *Speaking into the Air: A History of the Idea of Communication* [Chicago: University of Chicago Press, 1999], 28).

10 Benedict Anderson, *Imagined Communities: Reflections on the Origin and Spread of Nationalism* (London: Verso, 1983); Michael Billig, *Banal Nationalism* (London: Sage, 1995).

11 Larry Pratt and Matina Karvellas, "Nature and Nation: Herder, Myth and Cultural Nationalism in Canada," *National History* 1, 1 (1997): 59-77.

12 Ernest Renan, "Qu'est-ce qu'une nation?" in *Nationalism*, ed. John Hutchinson and Anthony Smith (Oxford: Oxford University Press, 1994).

13 Homi Bhabha, "Introduction," in *Nation and Narration* (London: Routledge, 1990), 1-7. See also Edward Said, *Culture and Imperialism* (London: Chatto and Windus, 1993), xiii.

14 Gene Allen and Daniel Robinson touch on this point in the introduction to their recent anthology of scholarship on Canadian communications history, noting that "the public sphere and the nation constitute different types of socio-political spaces, and both may be usefully linked back to the idea of dissemination. They are not only spaces to which messages are disseminated by particular media, but spaces that are *brought into existence* by this dissemination" (Allen and Robinson, eds., *Communicating in Canada's Past: Essays in Media History* [Toronto: University of Toronto Press, 2009], 9) [emphasis in original]. For an overview of how twentieth-century thinkers have grappled with the role of mass communications in modern society, see Peters, *Speaking into the Air*, 10-31.

15 Craig Calhoun, *Nationalism* (Minneapolis: University of Minnesota Press, 1997), 3.

16 Many definitions of postmodernity see it as a distinct cultural era successive to modernity. See, for example, Perry Anderson, *The Origins of Postmodernity* (London: Verso, 1998), 78-92. In contrast, Ien Ang writes, "If the Enlightenment project of modernity was based on a belief in the possibility of a world singularly organized around the principles of universal reason, rationality and truth, then postmodernity signals not so much a radical end of the modern era, its wholesale supersession and negation by an alternative set of beliefs, but rather an awareness and recognition of the political and epistemological limits of those principles – what Lyotard (1984) has called the loss of master narratives" (Ang, *Living Room Wars: Rethinking Media Audiences* [London: Routledge, 1996], 2). Although there is no room here to argue this point, I contend that modern epistemology continued to characterize the dominant culture.

17 Jean-François Lyotard, *The Postmodern Condition: A Report on Knowledge*, trans. Geoffrey Bennington and Brian Massumi (Minneapolis: University of Minnesota Press, 1984), xxiv; Perry Anderson, *The Origins of Postmodernity* (London: Verso, 1998), 24-25.

18 Jean Baudrillard, *Simulacra and Simulation*, trans. Sheila Faria Glaser (Ann Arbor: University of Michigan Press, 1994), 1-42. Baudrillard's notion of simulation reflects the contribution to postmodernism made by semiotics, a field of linguistics focused on the relationship between language (signifier) and reality (signifier). The way in which the signifier denotes the signified is necessarily arbitrary, which leads to the conclusion that human attempts to represent any underlying reality are deeply flawed.

When a modern metanarrative becomes a depthless simulacrum, it is ripe for postmodern critique. Pointing out rhetoric-reality gaps is a venerable critical practice. In the postmodern view, however, the misrepresentation that is the object of such critique is neither episodic nor consciously willed but rather systematized, a prevailing condition rather than an aberrant deviation from normal practice.

19 Warren Sussman, "Introduction" and "Personality and the Making of Twentieth-Century Culture," in *Culture as History: The Transformation of American Society in the Twentieth Century* (New York: Pantheon, 1985), xxii, 277-80. In the 1950s the term "identity" was coined as a way to discuss the individual's sense of belonging in an alienating modernity. Over time the scholarly consensus moved from a conception of identity as immutable to one that understood identity as fluid, changing form as the individual's context shifted.

20 By the late twentieth century, modernity's dependence on the mass media was becoming harder and harder to ignore. Canadian media historian Mary Vipond's reflections on how mass society communicates and is constituted are instructive:

> John B. Thompson argued in his 1993 book *Media and Modernity* that the development of the media was "interwoven in fundamental ways" with other developmental processes to constitute modernity itself. The media are central agencies of self- and community-formation in the modern world. Quite simply, the mass media have been one of the major social and political forces in modern societies. Through them we gain much (although certainly not all) of our access to the outside world, much (although again not all) of our entertainment, much (although not all) of our socialization. We live, and have lived since the turn of the twentieth century at least, in a mediatized world.
>
> We cannot fully understand that world unless we study, *as objects in and of themselves*, the media in general and broadcast media in particular. To put it another way, as various traditional social institutions such as churches, voluntary organizations, and local communities have withered away throughout the late twentieth century, the mass media, and again I would specify television (and at the end of the century, the internet), have grown in influence – indeed, have thrived. Politics, leisure, education, interpersonal communication – I could go on and on – have all been fundamentally transformed in the last century by the flourishing of the broadcast media. We need to know *their* history to understand *our* history. (Vipond, "The Historiography of Canadian Broadcasting," in Allen and Robinson, *Communicating in Canada's Past*, 239)

21 For a discussion of this phenomenon in Western democracies more generally, see John Simons, "Popular Culture and Mediated Politics: Intellectuals, Elites and Democracy," in *Media and the Restyling of Politics: Consumerism, Celebrity and Cynicism*, ed. John Corner and Dick Pels (London: Sage, 2003), 171-89.

22 For generations, scholars have noted the Canadian nation's dependence on transportation and communications systems to bind together disparate parts of a vast territory. Indeed, the prominence of such technologies in the development of the Canadian state led to a distinctively Canadian tradition of communications theory. See the discussion of Harold Innis and the Laurentian thesis in Chapter 2, and Robert Babe, "Foundations of Canadian Communication Thought," *Canadian Journal of Communication* 25, 1 (2000): 19-37.

This tradition of viewing Canada as a communicative community can also be traced back to Karl Deutsch, who argued that nationalism depends not so much on shared characteristics as on "a functional definition of nationality" in which "membership in a people essentially consists in wide complementarity of social communication. It consists in the ability to communicate more effectively, and over a wider range of subjects, with members of one large group than with outsiders" (Deutsch, *Nationalism and Social Communication* [New York: John Wiley and Sons, 1953], 71, 97). Subsequent nationalism theory has expanded upon Deutsch's argument. See, for example, Anderson, *Imagined Communities*, 44-45; Anthony D. Smith, *Nationalism and Modernism* (London: Routledge 1998), 138-40; David Morley, "Broadcasting and the Construction of the National Family," in *The*

Television Studies Reader, ed. Robert C. Hall and Annette Hill (London: Routledge, 2004), 418-20.

Canadian historians have increasingly incorporated these insights into their analyses of Canada's development. In *Citizens and Nation*, for example, Gerald Friesen periodizes Canadian history in terms of dominant communications regimes and writes of conversation being constitutive of community. In his discussion of postwar English Canadian nationalism, José Igartua characterizes the English Canadian nation as a "communicational community" (Friesen, *Citizens and Nation: An Essay on History, Communication, and Canada* [Toronto: University of Toronto Press, 2000]; Igartua, *The Other Quiet Revolution: National Identities in English Canada, 1945-1971* [Vancouver: UBC Press, 2006], 4).

At the same time, historians have been leery of ascribing magical powers to the media. They caution that new technologies are necessarily incorporated into existing cultural practices and institutional power structures. Technologies may change the way things work in certain specific ways, but claims that they revolutionize society in and of themselves are suspect, and close study is required to determine exactly what their effects may be. For commentary that qualifies technological determinism in this way, see Robert Cupido, "The Medium, the Message and the Modern: The Jubilee Broadcast of 1927," *International Journal of Canadian Studies* 26 (2002); Paul Rutherford, *When Television Was Young: Primetime Canada, 1952-1967* (Toronto: University of Toronto Press, 1990), 483-95; Jeff Webb, "Technologies of Communication and the Canadian State," *Acadiensis* 27, 2 (1998): 142-50. John Fiske and John Hartley argue that "television is a human construct, and the job that it does is the result of human choice, cultural decisions and social pressures. The medium responds to the conditions within which it exists. It is by no means natural for television to represent reality the way it does" (Fiske and Hartley, *Reading Television* [London: Methuen, 1978], 5).

23 Considerable scholarship comparing politics to business focuses on parties building a "brand" and "selling" certain policies to the electorate. This leads to extensive analyses of marketing strategies and the targeting of voters through demographic segmentation enhanced by the infometrics of the digital age. Less attention has been paid to politics as a unique kind of business, show business, wherein the emphasis is not on profiting from the manufacture, marketing, and sale of a commodity but rather on creating a celebrity who delivers empathetic performances to ingratiate herself with the electorate (see John Street, "The Celebrity Politician: Political Style and Popular Culture," in *Media and the Restyling of Politics: Consumerism, Celebrity and Cynicism*, ed. John Corner and Dick Pels [London: Sage, 2003], 94-96).

24 James Carey's work on the ritualistic elements of communication is relevant in this regard. He emphasizes the ways in which the media provide structure, including temporal structure, for their audiences' participation in the life of the collective. This perspective is unlike the dominant approach in the field of communications, which focuses on the ways in which media representations reflect and reproduce power relations. See Carey, *Communication as Culture* (New York: Routledge, 2009), 11-28.

25 Early crowd theory posited a process of contagion whereby individual responsibility and rationality were lost in the excitement of the crowd. "It is one of the most revealing, purely sociological phenomena that the individual feels himself carried by the 'mood' of the mass," wrote German sociologist Georg Simmel in 1917 (Simmel, "Fundamental Problems of Sociology [Individual and Society]," in *The Sociology of Georg Simmel*, ed. K.H. Wholff [New York: Free Press, 1950], 35, quoted in Christian Borch, *The Politics of Crowds: An Alternative History of Sociology* [Cambridge: Cambridge University Press, 2012], 1).

One of the big questions of the time was whether liberal democracy was feasible on a mass scale: if given the vote, would the masses be able to exercise it responsibly?

According to crowd theory, the answer was no. Since mobs were susceptible to suggestion, they were potentially a powerful tool for unscrupulous demagogues. The rise of fascism in Germany seemed to confirm these fears.

Although later scholars challenged the conviction held by the pioneers of crowd psychology that crowds were irrational, affect theory has recently reinvigorated the notion that crowds can transmit some sort of emotional contagion. Affect theorists are studying whether the ways that a person tends to mimic and replicate facial expressions, postures, movements, and exclamations of others in close physical proximity cause them to "'catch' their emotions" (Janice R. Kelly, "Mood and Emotion in Groups," in *Blackwell Handbook of Social Psychology*, ed. Michael A. Hogg and Scott Tindale [Malden, MA: Blackwell, 2001], 169). The term "mimetic communication" has been used to describe a "synchrony of facial expressions, vocalizations, postures and movements with those of another person" that occurs in group interactions (Elaine Hatfield, John T. Cacioppo, and Richard L. Rapson, *Emotional Contagion* [Cambridge: Cambridge University Press, 1994], 5, cited in Anna Gibbs, "After Affect: Sympathy, Synchrony and Mimetic Communication," in *The Affect Theory Reader*, ed. Melissa Gregg and Gregory J. Seigworth [Durham, NC: Duke University Press, 2010]). Affect theorist Teresa Brennan, among others, uses the term "entrainment" to denote a "process where human affective responses are linked and repeated." She suggests entrainment could be based on the stimulation of a person's senses by the bombardment of smells, touches, sounds, and images in a crowd. She further suggests that a crowd can generate quite specific moods, because hormonal stimulation causes humans to emit pheromones that in turn stimulate similar hormonal responses in others. The upshot is that the feeling of "something in the air" is quite literally true (Brennan, *The Transmission of Affect* [Ithaca, NY: Cornell University Press, 2004], 52-53, 68-73).

26 I've chosen to use the term "journalist" rather than "media worker" because it was journalists whose names were most closely attached to media texts. However, I use the term broadly, intending it to encompass producers, editors, designers, and other collaborators directly involved in the meaning-making processes of the media.

27 Since the airwaves are public property, the state regulates the media within its territory. By the mid-twentieth century, when the electronic media had the technical and financial capacity to form networks across the country, they were called national networks because their audience was deemed congruent with the nation. Broadcasting economics dictate that an appeal be made to as broad a public as possible to maximize audience size, and thus advertising revenue and profits. Consequently, the audience was interpellated as a "nation." Since all residents of the land were nominally Canadian, this was an appeal to which all might respond. In providing the main channels of communication within which the discourse of the communicative community took place, the mass media were one of the makers of the Canadian nation.

28 Pierre Bourdieu characterized the "new petite bourgeoisie" as consisting of "all the occupations involving presentation and representation." He included "'the cultural intermediaries' of advertising, journalism, marketing, public relations and the modern – or rather, postmodern – media and culture generally" (Bourdieu, *Distinction: A Social Critique of the Judgement of Taste* [Cambridge, MA: Harvard University Press, 1984], 359).

29 Nor did they graduate into the enduring collective memory of Trudeaumania. Many of the images reproduced in these pages continue to perform political work by sustaining public memory of Trudeau. The fact that they are mostly black and white rather than colour reinforces the sense that they come from a formative period of contemporary Canada's pre-history.

30 As one student of the nationalizing effects of the media has put it, "think of it as a graduated incline, in which fuller membership depends, among other things, on particular

types and amounts of media consumption" (Morley, "Broadcasting and Construction," 421).

31 Barbara Ehrenreich and John Ehrenreich, "The Professional-Managerial Class," *Radical America* 11, 2 (1977): 7-32. For extensive critiques of the Ehrenreichs' thesis, see Pat Walker, ed., *Between Labour and Capital* (Boston: South End Press, 1979). The concept of the professional managerial class has interesting parallels with the long-standing German denotation of *Bildungsbürgertum*, a middle class whose status derives from education and expertise and which believes in meritocracy and continuous self-improvement.

32 Alvin Goulder includes this condition among his set of propositions about what he calls "the New Class": "With the spread of public schools, literacy spreads; humanistic intellectuals lose their exclusiveness and privileged market position, and now experience a status disparity between their 'high' culture, as they see it, and their lower deference, repute, income and social power. The social position of humanistic intellectuals *particularly in a technocratic and industrial society*, becomes more marginal and alienated than that of the technical intelligentsia. The New Class becomes internally differentiated" (Goulder, *The Future of Intellectuals and the Rise of the New Class* [New York: Seabury Press, 1979], 4; see also 65). Emphasis in original.

33 The plot line of Trudeaumania was conventional in ways beyond just the leadership convention and could easily be foreseen by all participants. Various formulations have been put forward since classical times to explain the basic components of a dramatic plot, but in its simplest form it involves an opening that introduces a situation that demands attention, consequent action rising to a climax that may or may not resolve the situation, and then a falling off of action towards the end. Sociologist Victor Turner developed the concept of "social drama" to describe the way in which societies work through problems following a predictable pattern. Whether Turner's "social drama" is a case of life imitating art or vice versa is a classic chicken-and-egg question. See Elizabeth Bell, *Theories of Performance* (London: Sage, 2008), 87-92, 105-10.

34 "The right of an imagined community to arbitrate is established (though for a time only; and always merely until further notice) in proportion to the amount and intensity of public attention forced to focus on its presence; 'reality,' and hence also the power and authority of an imagined community, is the function of that attention" (Zygmunt Bauman, *Intimations of Postmodernity* [London: Routledge, 1992], xx).

35 As David Morley puts it, "Sociability, by definition, can only ever be produced in some particular cultural (and linguistic) form – and only those with access to the relevant forms of cultural capital will feel interpellated by and at home within the particular form of sociability offered by a given programme" (Morley, "Broadcasting and Construction," 422).

CHAPTER 1: THE SIXTIES, MODIFIED

1 The term "the sixties" uses the chronological decade as shorthand to evoke an era characterized by protest movements and a countercultural challenge to the status quo that emerged from and then subsided into bracketing periods of relative conformity. Since the sixties were not an arbitrarily calendarized period but rather a particular *zeitgeist*, scholars debate passionately when they began and ended. Some argue for a "long sixties" that started in the 1950s and didn't tail off until the 1970s. Others see the essence of the decade encompassed by shorter periodizations, but never quite agree on which period is most critical. For the purposes of understanding Trudeaumania, it is enough to recognize 1968 as a year in which the sixties were in full flood.

2 The portrayal of the 1950s as conformist typically involves a Cold War–conditioned ideological toeing of the line, an enthusiastic embrace of materialism in rededication to the American Dream, and a suburbanizing society that literally put everyone in the same

boxes. This portrayal has been challenged by historians who have diligently revealed the roots of the 1960s rebellions in the 1950s. The salient point, however, is that from the point of view of sixties progressives, the fifties were a conformist era.

3 The term "counterculture" was introduced by Theodore Roszak in an article in the *Nation* on March 15, 1968, and he later published a book entitled *The Making of a Counter Culture*. Arthur Marwick argues that the term misleadingly applies a nonexistent unity to the various alternative subcultures of the sixties, and that it is more misleading still because it suggests as well a Marxist dialectical progress that did not in fact exist (Marwick, *The Sixties: Cultural Revolution in Britain, France, Italy, and the United States, c. 1958-c. 1974* [New York: Oxford, 1998], 10).

4 I've taken a bit of a chronological liberty here, because "Something in the Air" didn't chart until the summer of 1969. The description of the sixties that follows focuses first on how the decade unfolded in the United States, then turns to a consideration of how developments in Canada compared with, and were affected by, those in the United States. To the extent that they were both part of a shared North American culture, the sixties affected the two countries in similar ways. Since the United States was the superpower Cold Warrior and also seen as the fountainhead of modernity, the establishment that radicals railed against was more that of the United States than Canada. Since US news, public affairs, and popular culture were widely disseminated in Canada, the American experience was, to an extent, also experienced in Canada. One obvious differentiating factor was that Canadians saw events in the United States as American first and foremost, and thus affecting them only indirectly.

5 Aniko Bodroghkozy, *Groove Tube: Sixties Television and the Youth Rebellion* (Durham, NC: Duke University Press, 2001), 5-9.

6 Terry Anderson, *The Sixties* (New York: Pearson Longman, 2007), 120-25.

7 United Nations, "Preamble," "The Universal Declaration of Human Rights," http://www.un.org/en/documents/udhr/.

8 Aniko Bodroghkozy, *Equal Time: Television and the Civil Rights Movement* (Urbana: University of Illinois Press, 2012), 2-7.

9 The protest ethos of civil rights and anti-nukes inspired other social critiques. Rachel Carson's 1962 bestseller, *Silent Spring*, detailed how indiscriminate pesticide use was devastating wildlife, providing more evidence of how the dynamic duo of capitalism and technocracy had produced a blinkered, arrogant form of power that pursued deviant agendas with a skewed appreciation of the public good and zero accountability. Air and water quality became pressing issues because anyone could see that pollution was adversely affecting peoples' quality of life and threatening their health. Industries that released poisonous effluent into water systems or belched noxious fumes from their smokestacks became targets for protest. This emerging environmental movement provided yet another indictment of how big business, big government, and big science could combine to mess things up on a grand scale

10 Marwick, *Sixties*, 18.

11 Barbara Ehrenreich, Elizabeth Hess, and Gloria Jacobs, "Beatlemania: Girls Just Want to Have Fun," in *The Adoring Audience: Fan Culture and Popular Media*, ed. Lisa A. Lewis (New York: Routledge, 1992), 86-98.

12 The idea that a man could not control his sexual urges was evident as well in "Young Girl," Gary Puckett and the Union Gap's big hit in 1968, which was about an adult male being tempted by an underage female. It was at the top of the CHUM Chart, the list of top hits published by the influential Toronto radio station 1050 CHUM, during the Liberal convention in April.

13 Anderson, *Sixties*, 12.

14 "Sex and selling had been part of consumer culture for most of the century, but whereas advertisers used sexual allusion to sell products, Hefner and others reversed the order and sold sex with slick packaging and mass marketing" (David Steigerwald, *The Sixties and the End of Modern America* [New York: St. Martin's Press, 1995], 171).

15 Paul Rutherford, *When Television Was Young: Primetime Canada 1952-1967* (Toronto: University of Toronto Press, 1990), 50.

16 Daniel Boorstin, *The Image: Or, What Happened to the American Dream* (New York: Athenaeum, 1961), 183. Writing about the moral panic over subliminal seduction in this period, Charles Acland describes mediation as "the wonderful and frustrating fact that something is always in the way every time we communicate" (Acland, *Swift Viewing: The Popular Life of Subliminal Influence* [Durham, NC: Duke University Press, 2011], 30).

17 Guy Debord, *The Society of the Spectacle* (Berkeley, CA: Bureau of Public Secrets, 2014), 2. I am indebted to Paul Rutherford, who is working on a history of advertising, for several of the preceding references.

18 See Lyn Speigel and Michael Curtin, eds., *The Revolution Wasn't Televised: Sixties Television and Social Conflict* (New York: Routledge, 1997), 224-26, for American examples of television being viewed as a "guilty pleasure" by the "upscale viewer" earlier in the decade. Peter Dahlgren speaks of a "lingering discomfiture in some circles over its 'television-ness'" (Dahlgren, *Television and the Public Sphere: Citizenship, Democracy and the Media* [London: Sage, 1995], 48). See also Raymond Williams, *Television, Technology and Cultural Form* (London: Routledge, 1975), particularly chapter 5, "Effects of the Technology and Its Uses."

Concern about mediation was part of a broader anxiety about modern mass society that saw in it many forces threatening to the individual fulfillment and agency promised by liberal democracy. These forces included a consumer capitalism whose messages permeated the media, promoting a materialism that critics believed ultimately unfulfilling, a "dumbing-down" of the populace instead of its edification through the media's pursuit of the largest possible audience, and a blinkered worship of technological progress as an intrinsic good. For background, see Philip Massolin, *Canadian Intellectuals, the Tory Tradition, and the Challenge of Modernity* (Toronto: University of Toronto Press, 2001), 3-19; Leonard Kuffert, *A Great Duty: Canadian Responses to Modern Life and Mass Culture* (Montreal: McGill-Queen's University Press, 2003), 12-23.

19 "The Playboy Interview: Marshall McLuhan," *Playboy*, March 1969, Marshall McLuhan Center on Global Communications website, http://www.mcluhanmedia.com/m_mcl_inter_pb_01.html.

20 Donald Peacock, *Journey to Power: The Story of a Canadian Election* (Toronto: Ryerson, 1968), 16. Bryan Palmer explores the McLuhan phenomenon in tandem with Trudeaumania in "Celebrity and Audacity: Marshall McLuhan, Pierre Elliott Trudeau, and the Decade of the Philosopher King," chap. 5 in *Canada's 1960s: The Ironies of Identity in a Rebellious Era* (Toronto: University of Toronto Press, 2009).

21 Paul Neubauer, "Marshall McLuhan and the '60s New Media Debate: A Survey of Effects," in *The Sixties Revisited: Culture-Society-Politics*, ed. Jürgen Heideking, Jörg Helbig, and Anke Ortlepp (Heidelberg: Universitätsverlag Winter, 2001), 113. McLuhanism was so pervasive that even Eugene Whelan, MP for the rural Ontario riding of Essex South, would draw on McLuhan's cultural currency to make a point (Library and Archives Canada [LAC], R 12069, Roméo LeBlanc fonds, vol. 403, file 10, Liberal Caucus Meeting, April 24, 1968).

22 Hugh MacLennan, *Cross-Country* (Edmonton: Hurtig, 1972; reprint of Toronto: Collins, 1949), xvi.

23 Cara Spittal, "The Diefenbaker Moment" (PhD dissertation, University of Toronto, 2011), 4. One issue in interpreting Diefenbaker's use of TV is that later conventional wisdom

accepted that television is an intimate medium into which the histrionics of classical oratory exemplified by Diefenbaker do not translate well. It may be that at this moment in
the development of television, when screens were small, broadcasting was in black and
white, and production values were relatively low, the intimacy factor had not yet asserted
itself fully and traditional stage rhetoric worked, indeed, was necessary to project through
the intermediary noise.

24 36th Annual Couchiching Conference, Program 3, July 31, 1967, and Program 4, August 1,
1967, as cited ibid., 142.

25 Owram, *Born at the Right Time*, 190.

26 Ibid., 207. In his analysis of Toronto's Yorkville neighbourhood, Stuart Henderson argues
that it was more heterogeneous than portrayed in the media and notes the media's weakness for presenting it as a hippie enclave in conflict with the establishment (Henderson,
Making the Scene: Yorkville and Hip Toronto in the 1960s [Toronto: University of Toronto
Press, 2011], 25). Aside from whatever desire hippies had to flock together, social commentators seemed to find it convenient, or psychically reassuring, to segregate them spatially,
containing them so they would not infect the rest of society.

27 According to Beth Bailey, the term "sexual revolution" was in use by 1963 (Bailey, "Sexual
Revolution(s)," in *The Sixties: From Memory to History*, ed. David Farber [Chapel Hill:
University of North Carolina Press, 1994], 237).

28 Owram, *Born at the Right Time*, 198; Marcel Martel, "Law versus Medicine: The Debate over
Drug Use in the 1960s," in *Creating Postwar Canada: Community, Diversity, and Dissent, 1945-
1975*, ed. Robert Rutherdale and Magda Fahrni (Vancouver: UBC Press, 2007), 323.

29 LAC, Canadian Broadcasting Corporation, Television: Two-Inch Quad Videotapes for
Deposit, *The Way It Is*, "Drug Show: Nancy Green and Pierre Trudeau," recorded January
25, 1968, broadcast February 11, 1968, consultation copy VI 8202-0025.

30 Ibid.

31 One of the decade's most successful rock groups, the Doors, took their name from
The Doors of Perception, a 1954 book by Aldous Huxley that detailed his experiences while
taking mescaline. Huxley in turn took his title from William Blake's poem "The Marriage
of Heaven and Hell," which included the lines, "If the doors of perception were cleansed
every thing would appear to man as it is, Infinite / For man has closed himself up, till he
sees all things thro' narrow chinks of his cavern." Huxley had not been content to see his
drug trip as a simple case of perception altered physiologically. For him the experience
took on spiritual dimensions.

32 Alice Echols described the counterculture's political philosophy as a "laissez-faire libertar-
ianism" (Echols, *Shaky Ground: The Sixties and Its Aftershocks* [New York: Columbia University
Press, 2002], 50).

33 Joan Didion, *Slouching Towards Bethlehem*, quoted in Steigerwald, *Sixties and the End*, 183.

34 Roy Shields, "'No Contest,' as Trudeau Tops Berton," *Toronto Daily Star*, March 21, 1968.

35 Sean Mills, *The Empire Within: Postcolonial Thought and Political Activism in Sixties Montreal*
(Montreal: McGill-Queen's University Press, 2010).

36 Palmer, *Canada's 1960s*, 198-200.

37 "The defining battle of the sixties was a cultural civil war that pitted a traditional culture
born in an age of scarcity against a new culture that was more appropriate to the age of
affluence," argues David Steigerwald. "Traditional culture ... comprised a set of values
shaped by need and want: self-denial, the work ethic, and a faith in technological progress" (Steigerwald, *Sixties and the End*, 154).

38 As Steigerwald puts it, "The more the mainstream press worried over the hippies, the
more young people sought to emulate them. Behind the energies of many cultural entre-

preneurs, the hippies became trend-setters and their 'style' ballooned, as Todd Gitlin has written, 'into a whole cultural climate'" (ibid., 183). The Gitlin reference comes from his book *The Sixties: Years of Hope, Days of Rage*.

39 LAC, Canadian Broadcasting Corporation, Television: Kines from Parc, Toronto, *The Way It Is*, June 16, 1968, consultation copy VI 8402-0047.

40 See Roberta Lexier, "'The Backdrop against Which Everything Happened': English-Canadian Student Movements and Off-Campus Movements for Change," *History of Intellectual Culture* 7, 1 (2007): 1-18.

41 Ian Mackay, *Rebels, Reds, Radicals: Rethinking Canada's Left History* (Toronto: Between the Lines, 2005), 184.

42 Ian Milligan, *Rebel Youth: 1960s Labour Unrest, Young Workers and New Leftists in English Canada* (Vancouver: UBC Press, 2014), 45-58, 64-80.

43 Alice Echols writes that "the counterculture was always more complicated – edgier, darker, and more tied to the dominant culture – than most anyone at the time could see" (Echols, *Shaky Ground*, 18).

44 Germaine Greer, "Mozic and the Revolution," quoted in Gerard J. DeGroot, *The Sixties Unplugged: A Kaleidoscopic History of a Disorderly Decade* (Cambridge, MA: Harvard University Press, 2008), 395.

45 Ibid., 396.

46 Ibid., 394. Steigerwald emphasizes that a mainstream culture that exhibited a bland, conformist deference to authority continued to run strong throughout the sixties. See Steigerwald, *Sixties and the End*, 154.

47 Acland, *Swift Viewing*, 224.

48 Thomas Frank, *The Conquest of Cool: Business Culture, Counterculture, and the Rise of Hip Consumerism* (Chicago: University of Chicago Press, 1997). Frank lays out his argument in the first chapter and expands it in the rest of the book. See Henderson, *Making the Scene*, 23, for an insightful discussion of how the counter- and mainstream cultures interacted. Arthur Marwick argues that "the various counter-cultural movements and subcultures, being ineluctably implicated in and interrelated with mainstream society while all the time expanding and interacting with each other, did not *confront* that society but *permeated* and *transformed* it." He points out that the counterculture was itself dependent on private enterprise. The evils of capitalism applied to multinational corporate behemoths, not to small hippie businesses. "Most of the movements, subcultures, and new institutions which are at the heart of sixties change were thoroughly imbued with the entrepreneurial profit-making ethic," he observes, listing as examples "boutiques, experimental theatres, art galleries, discotheques, nightclubs, 'light shows,' 'head shops,' photographic and model agencies, underground films, pornographic magazines." These enterprises leveraged the cultural capital of their countercultural credibility, weaving hemp into gold (Marwick, *Sixties*, 10-13). Emphasis in original.

49 Aurora Wallace, "Girl Watching at Expo 67," in Rhona Richman Keneally and Johanne Sloan, *Expo 67: Not Just a Souvenir* (Toronto: University of Toronto Press, 2010), 120.

50 Christine Jacqueline Feldman, "*We are the Mods*": *A Transnational History of a Youth Subculture* (New York: Peter Lang, 2009), 1. See also Stuart Hall and Tony Jefferson, eds., *Resistance through Rituals: Youth Subcultures in Post-war Britain* (London: Hutchison, 1975); DeGroot, *Sixties Unplugged*, 167-76.

51 Both in *Maclean's*, August 20, 1966.

52 Helen Meyer, "The Modish Male," *Canadian/Star Weekly*, January 21-28, 1967.

53 Helen Meyer, "Strikingly Simple, Simply Striking," *Canadian/Star Weekly*, April 29-May 6, 1967.

54 Frank, *Conquest of Cool*, 190.

55 LAC, Canadian Broadcasting Corporation, Television: Kines from Parc, Toronto, *The Way It Is*, November 3, 1968, consultation copy VI 8402-0052. CBC TV avoided hard rock, preferring relatively mellow tracks such as a jazz version of Dylan's "Lay Lady Lay," the Judy Collins version of "Both Sides Now," or the Beatles' "Magical Mystery Tour."

56 See Dominique Clément, "Canada's Rights Revolution," chap. 2 in *Canada's Rights Revolution: Social Movements and Social Change, 1937-1982* (Vancouver: UBC Press, 2008).

57 The environmental movement that arose out of the 1960s also had a significant impact on a number of fronts. It changed people's thinking and through moral suasion altered many wasteful and ecologically damaging practices. It convinced governments to pass laws to protect the environment, to create agencies to regulate industrial environmental practices, and to develop environmental assessment processes to vet development projects.

58 For a study of contemporary liberalism that argues that the American public is far more liberal now than it was before the sixties, with individual "rights, choice and self-expression" now prevailing in spheres like the family and religion where they had formerly been subordinate to communal values, see Robert Booth Fowler, *Enduring Liberalism: American Political Thought since the 1960s* (Lawrence: University Press of Kansas, 1999), ix-x, xiii, 244.

CHAPTER 2: CONSTRUCTING THE PEACEABLE KINGDOM

1 Frank Underhill, "Foreword," in *Nationalism in Canada*, ed. Peter Russell (Toronto: McGraw-Hill, 1966), xvii.

2 Stephen Azzi, *Walter Gordon and the Rise of Canadian Nationalism* (Montreal: McGill-Queen's University Press, 1999), 64, 99-110, 160-65; Melville Watkins, *Foreign Ownership and the Structure of Canadian Industry: A Report of the Task Force on the Structure of Canadian Industry* (Ottawa: Privy Council Office, 1968). See also Library and Archives Canada (LAC), MG 32 B 44, Walter Gordon fonds, vol. 37, file 6, Walter Gordon, "Address to the Junior Board of Trade," Toronto, October 19, 1965, cited in Ryan Edwardson, "'Kicking Uncle Sam Out of the Peaceable Kingdom': English-Canadian 'New Nationalism' and Americanization," *Journal of Canadian Studies* 37, 4 (2003): 131-50; Walter Gordon, *A Choice for Canada: Independence or Colonial Status* (Toronto: McClelland and Stewart, 1966).

3 Canada, *Report of the Royal Commission on National Development in the Arts, Letters and Sciences* (Ottawa: King's Printer, 1951), 18. See also Ryan Edwardson, *Canadian Content: Culture and the Quest for Nationhood* (Toronto: University of Toronto Press, 2008).

4 Robin Mathews and James Steele, *The Struggle for Canadian Universities* (Toronto: New Press, 1969); Jeffrey Cormier, *The Canadianization Movement: Emergence, Survival, and Success* (Toronto: University of Toronto Press, 2007); Paul Axelrod, *Scholars and Dollars: Politics, Economics, and the Universities of Ontario, 1945-1980* (Toronto: University of Toronto Press, 1982).

5 The "unity in diversity" slogan was by then pervasive enough to become the title of a history textbook. Published in 1967, it was notable for having both French and English Canadian historians as authors (Paul Cornell, Fernand Ouellet, and Marcel Trudel, *Canada: Unity in Diversity* [Toronto: Holt, Rinehart and Winston of Canada, 1967]). Donald Peacock discusses how Pearson wrote this concept into the Queen's speech to Canada on New Year's Eve at the opening of Canada's centennial year (Peacock, *Journey to Power: The Story of a Canadian Election* [Toronto: Ryerson, 1968], 4-5). The idea was sufficiently popularized to be used as a tourism sales pitch. See, for instance, Doris Hopper, "Canadian Mosaic is World in Miniature as Various Cultures Thrive," *Montreal Gazette*, June 1, 1968.

6 Hugh MacLennan, *The Colour of Canada* (Toronto: McClelland and Stewart, 1967), 9, 15.

7 For an example of a writer's self-consciousness about playing this role, see Hugh MacLennan, "After 300 Years, Our Neurosis Is Relevant," in *The Price of Being Canadian*, ed. D.B. Hamlin, 7th Winter Conference, Canadian Institute of Public Affairs (Toronto: University of Toronto Press, 1961), repr. in William Kilbourn, *Canada: A Guide to the Peaceable Kingdom* (Toronto: Macmillan 1970), 9.

8 Sigmund Freud coined this phrase, and more recently Michael Ignatieff employed it to provide insight into the conflict in the Balkans in the 1990s. Anton Blok points to Pierre Bourdieu's insight that those who are closest to us are those from whom we have to try hardest to differentiate ourselves (Ignatieff, "The Narcissism of Minor Difference," in *The Warrior's Honor: Ethnic War and the Modern Conscience* [New York: Metropolitan Books, 1998], 36-37, 48-53, 61-62; Blok, "The Narcissism of Minor Difference," *European Journal of Social Theory* 1, 1 [1998]: 33-56). Nationalism theorists generally agree that groups tend to identify themselves less by identifying internal similarities than by emphasizing their differences from other groups (John A. Armstrong, *Nations Before Nationalism* [Chapel Hill: University of North Carolina Press, 1982], 5.)

9 Joseph Levitt, "English Canadian Nationalists and the Canadian Character, 1957-1974," *Canadian Review of Studies in Nationalism* 12, 2 (1985): 223-38.

10 Carl Berger, *The Writing of Canadian History: Aspects of English-Canadian Historical Writing Since 1900* (Toronto: University of Toronto Press, 1986). The classic statement of the continental destiny argument was Goldwin Smith, *Canada and the Canadian Question* (Toronto: Hunter Rose, 1891).

11 Maurice Charland, "Technological Nationalism," *Canadian Journal of Political and Social Theory* 10, 1 (1986): 196-220.

12 Trudeau himself explained Canada in terms of the Laurentian thesis in the 1968 election campaign (Brian Shaw, ed., *The Gospel According to Saint Pierre* [Richmond Hill, ON: Simon and Schuster, 1969], 213). The downside of this interpretation was that it implied an internal mercantilism serving eastern interests, a characterization that, however accurate, was not likely to be appreciated by denizens of the hinterlands.

13 Hugh MacLennan, "The Canadian Character," in *Cross-Country* (Edmonton: Hurtig, 1972; reprint of Toronto: Collins, 1949), 44. MacLennan's idea could be updated to include Indigenous peoples (an omission from the original that was telling of its times), draft dodgers, Vietnamese boat people, and so on, ad infinitum. In this formulation was a germ of the unity in diversity idea, which could, of course, be tracked back earlier still to the "new nationality" rhetoric of the fathers of Confederation. The "nation of losers" idea would be echoed by subsequent commentators, including, for example, Mordecai Richler, who once described Canada as "a holding tank filled with the disgruntled progeny of defeated peoples" (quoted in Nino Ricci, *Pierre Elliott Trudeau* [Toronto: Penguin, 2009], 11).

14 W.L. Morton, *The Canadian Identity* (Toronto: University of Toronto 1961), 93.

15 Ibid., 108-14. Again, the absence of any mention of Indigenous peoples was typical of the times. "The discovery and occupation of Canada was separate and distinct from the discovery and occupation of the Americas," Morton would write elsewhere, signalling his essential sympathy with the Laurentian thesis (Morton, "The Northern Frontier: Key to Canadian History," in Kilbourn, *Canada: A Guide*, 282).

16 Morton, *Canadian Identity*, 111.

17 Northrop Frye, "Conclusion," in *The Literary History of Canada*, ed. Carl Klinck (Toronto: University of Toronto Press 1976), 821-49.

18 Ian Angus, *The Border Within: National Identity, Cultural Plurality, and Wilderness* (Montreal: McGill-Queen's University Press, 1997), 31-33.

19 William Kilbourn, "The Quest for the Peaceable Kingdom," in *The Making of the Nation: A Century of Challenge* (Toronto: The Canadian Centennial Publishing Company, 1965), 120-24.

20 Philip Kokotailo, "Creating the Peaceable Kingdom: Edward Hicks, Northrop Frye, and Joe Clark," in *Creating the Peaceable Kingdom and Other Essays on Canada*, ed. Victor Howard (East Lansing: Michigan State University Press, 1998). See Judy Torrance, *Public Violence in Canada, 1867-1982* (Montreal: McGill-Queen's University Press, 1986), 104-5, for "trickle down" reiterations of the Peaceable Kingdom theme. Interestingly, Hugh MacLennan had characterized Canada as pacifistic relative to the United States in the 1940s, using an unfortunate metaphor of Canada as the feminine "good wife" to the manly United States (*Cross-Country*, 5). See also Heike Härting and Smaro Kamboureli, "Introduction: Discourses of Security, Peacekeeping Narratives, and the Cultural Imagination in Canada," *University of Toronto Quarterly* 78, 2 (2009): 659-61.

21 In keeping with the progressive spirit of the 1960s, securing the moral high ground involved abandoning most traditional moral regulation and embracing liberation. The late 1960s was a time "when Canada was invited to begin to think of itself as a liberal, tolerant, and permissive society. This new relation to pleasure and the state was to be central to a new Canadian identity" (Patricia Cormack and James F. Cosgrave (in *Desiring Canada: CBC Contests, Hockey Violence, and Other Stately Pleasures* [Toronto: University of Toronto Press, 2011], 4).

22 Al Purdy, ed., *The New Romans: Candid Canadian Opinions of the U.S.* (Edmonton: M.G. Hurtig, 1968). William Kilbourn would gather together his favourite essays on Canadian identity in a volume called *Canada: A Guide to the Peaceable Kingdom*, and adapt his 1965 essay as the introduction to the volume. Key identity concepts were elaborated in the following essays: Barbara Ward, "The First International Nation"; Ronald Bryden, "How to Live on the Margin"; Larry Zolf, "Boil Me No Melting Pots"; Melville Watkins, "Technology in Our Past and Present"; Gad Horowitz, "Red Tory"; Neil Compton, "Cancult and the CBC"; and Hugh MacLennan, "After 300 Years, Our Neurosis Is Relevant."

23 A.B. McKillop, *Pierre Berton: A Biography* (Toronto: McClelland and Stewart, 2008), emphasizes how Berton established himself as a brand. See also Rae Fleming, *Peter Gzowski: A Biography* (Toronto: Dundurn, 2010). These two biographies provide insight into influential Toronto journalists and nationalists, and the circles they moved in.

24 For more insight into the Canadianization efforts of Toronto publishers, see Ruth Panofsky, *The Literary Legacy of the Macmillan Company of Canada: Making Books and Mapping Culture* (Toronto: University of Toronto Press, 2012); Sandra Campbell, *Both Hands: A Life of Lorne Pierce of Ryerson Press* (Montreal: McGill-Queen's University Press, 2013); and Janet Friskney, *New Canadian Library: The Ross-McClelland Years, 1952-1978* (Toronto: University of Toronto Press, 2007).

25 LAC, Canadian Broadcasting Corporation, Television: CBOT Film Library, *The Hill* [The Press], April 1, 1968, consultation copy VI 8202-0069. The host, former member of Parliament Frank McGee, called the national press gallery "a powerful force in Canadian politics." The script was written by Douglas Fisher, a former NDP MP who was then a national affairs columnist.

26 Ibid.

27 Gene Allen, *Making National News: A History of Canadian Press* (Toronto: University of Toronto Press, 2013), 228.

28 John Porter, *The Vertical Mosaic: An Analysis of Social Class and Power in Canada* (Toronto: University of Toronto Press, 1965), 1.

29 Kilbourn, *Making of the Nation*, 124.

30 On this point, see McKillop, *Pierre Berton*, 441-48, and Fleming, *Peter Gzowski*, 123-76.

31 John English, *Citizen of the World: The Life of Pierre Elliott Trudeau* (Toronto: Knopf, 2006), 438. See also LAC, MG 26 Q10-1, John Turner fonds, vol. 4, file 9, *The Pierre Berton Show*, March 22, 1967, in which John Turner, who always sought the centre of the political spectrum, advocated all these policies.

The complementarity of nationalism and the desire to make Canada a superior North American form of democracy would be epitomized in the formation in 1969 of the Waffle, a wing of the NDP that banded together in support of a program of nationalism and socialism for Canada. The logic of the combination lay in the conviction that in a capitalist economy Canada would always be subordinate to the United States. Socialism was required because the power of the state was necessary to offset foreign capital if Canada was to be truly independent. In this formulation, socialism also gave Canada a morally superior raison d'être. In pre-Waffle 1968, some nationalists were of a socialist bent, but far more were relatively moderate social democrats. From the standpoint of establishing a distinct national identity, full-blown socialism was unnecessary; it was sufficient simply to be slightly more social democratic than the United States.

32 Mordecai Richler, "Why We Need Him," *Star Weekly*, March 2, 1968.

33 Peter C. Newman would write that "it was the Vietnamization of the United States that finally brought about the Canadianization of Canada" (Newman, "Our American Godfather," *Maclean's*, November 1972, 25, quoted in Robert Wright, "From Liberalism to Nationalism: Peter C. Newman's Discovery of Canada," in *Creating Postwar Canada: Community, Diversity, and Dissent, 1945-1975*, ed. Robert Rutherdale and Magda Fahrni (Vancouver: UBC Press, 2007), 127.

34 For a discussion of nationalist Canadian New Left resistance to US imperialism, see David S. Churchill, "Draft Resisters, Left Nationalism, and the Politics of Anti-Imperialism," *Canadian Historical Review* 93, 2 (2012): 227-60.

35 Hugh Hood, "Where the Promise Comes From," *Toronto Daily Star*, December 9, 1967; repr. as "Moral Imagination: Canadian Thing," in Kilbourn, *Canada: A Guide*, 29-35; 35.

36 "How can a conservative not feel sympathy with their [the New Left's] outrage against the emptiness and dehumanization that North American society produces?" asked George Grant (Grant, "A Critique of the New Left," in *Canada and Radical Social Change*, ed. Dimitrios I. Roussopoulos [Montreal: Black Rose Books, 1973], 57). See Hood, "Where the Promise Comes From," for another expression of this affinity. See also Leonard Kuffert, *A Great Duty: Canadian Responses to Modern Life and Mass Culture* (Montreal: McGill-Queen's University Press, 2003), 232. This sort of alliance against the contemporary configuration of modern society was uneasy because conservatives tended to bemoan a past lost to modernity, whereas progressives were more likely to believe in progress towards some future solution to be attained through more or different application of modern techniques.

37 In English Canada, José Igartua argues, the notion of British liberty offered a starting point from which tolerance evolved and eventually largely prevailed over ingrained prejudices (Igartua, *The Other Quiet Revolution: National Identities in English Canada, 1945-71* [Vancouver: UBC Press, 2006], 223-24).

38 Gad Horowitz, "Tories, Socialists and the Demise of Canada," *Canadian Dimension*, 2, 4 (May 1965): 12, 15. Robertson Davies would later make the same point by calling Canada a "socialist monarchy." This observation appears in his novel *Murther and Walking Spirits* (Toronto: McClelland and Stewart, 1991), 41, and in interviews of Davies in preceding years.

39 "Ottawa's Action Generation," *Monetary Times*, April 1967.

40 Ramsay Cook, "Of Instant Books and Instant Prime Ministers," *Tamarack Review* 49 (1969): 64-80. For more on this mood in the press, see Stephen Clarkson and Christina McCall, *Trudeau and Our Times*, Vol. 1, *The Magnificent Obsession* (Toronto: McClelland and Stewart, 1990), 97.

41 Christina Newman, "This Month: Ottawa Letter – The Inglorious End of an Era," *Saturday Night*, February 1968, 9.

42 The crises included the Gordon budget, the furniture scandals, the Rivard case, the Munsinger affair, and the flag debate. See Bryan Palmer, *Canada's 1960s: The Ironies of Identity in a Rebellious Era* (Toronto: University of Toronto Press, 2009), 77-109; Stephen Azzi, "The Nationalist Movement in English Canada," in *Debating Dissent: Canada and the Sixties*, ed. Lara Campbell, Dominique Clément, and Gregory S. Kealey (Toronto: University of Toronto Press, 2012), 213-30; Robert Bothwell, Ian Drummond, and John English, *Canada Since 1945: Power, Politics and Provincialism* (Toronto: University of Toronto Press, 1981), 293-301, 326-27.

43 Kenneth McRoberts, *Misconceiving Canada: The Struggle for National Unity* (Don Mills, ON: Oxford University Press, 1997), 64-68.

44 Denis Smith, editorial, *Journal of Canadian Studies* I, I (1966): 1-2. See also Hugh MacLennan, "After 300 Years." According to nationalism theorist John Hutchinson, it is common for cultural nationalists to advocate regeneration to modernize the nation. See John Hutchinson, "Cultural Nationalism and Moral Regeneration," in *Nationalism*, ed. John Hutchinson and Anthony Smith (Oxford: Oxford University Press, 1994), 122-31. This piece is an excerpt from John Hutchinson, *The Dynamics of Cultural Nationalism* (London: Allen and Unwin, 1987), 12-19, 30-36.

45 Dalton Camp, "The Trouble with the Tories (and the Liberals Too)," *Weekend*, November 1966, 11.

46 Peter Newman, "Digging for Soul: The People Take Over the Election," *Vancouver Sunday Sun*, June 1, 1968.

47 LAC, Canadian Broadcasting Corporation, Television: CBOT Film Library, *Twenty Million Questions*, "The Young Contenders," March 30, 1968, item number 268119. Here again the counterculture informed the establishment game of politics. "Throughout the decade the notion that change was imminent and that it could spring from the elements of youth culture is a pervasive and recurring theme," writes Doug Owram (Owram, *Born at the Right Time: A History of the Baby Boom Generation* [Toronto: University of Toronto Press, 1996], 209). Looking back, Pierre Berton wrote "in 1967, a better world seemed to beckon ... we looked forward with anticipation" (Berton, *1967: The Last Good Year* [Toronto: Doubleday, 1967], 365-66). Stephen Clarkson and Christina McCall, drawing on Max Weber's concept of "alienation potential," argue that Canadian society at the time had developed the preconditions for a dramatic change of leadership: "There had grown up among the younger or more progressive a defiant optimism that some as yet unidentified change would soon transform the country. Once the old, with their fusty ideas, their antiquated attachments, their foolish fears, had been swept out of power, and the young with their energy and strength had been swept in, love, love, love – or something very much like it in the form of a more democratic, more open government and a more equitable, more compassionate, more intellectually alive society – would prevail" (Clarkson and McCall, *Magnificent Obsession*, 97). Later they add: "As a collective, Canadians knew that the country needed to grow into another stage of nationhood, but they were uncertain about how to proceed" (114-15). All of this evidence that there was a feeling that substantial change was in the works brings to mind Antonio Gramsci's belief that societies occasionally experienced a "crisis of authority" which could lead to the emergence of charismatic "men of destiny" as political leaders (Gramsci, *Selections from the Prison Notebooks*, ed. and trans. Quintin Hoare and Geoffrey Nowell Smith [London: Lawrence and Wishart, 1971], 210, 276).

48 This was, of course, a long-standing trope in Canadian and other nationalist discourse. Back in the 1940s, journalist Bruce Hutchison had written that "My country ... is ... the

wild confusions and restless strivings of a boy who has passed his boyhood but is not yet a man" (Hutchison, *The Unknown Country: Canada and her People* [New York: Coward-McCann, 1942], 3). In the spring of 1968, Arnold Edinborough quoted this passage from Hutchison in *Saturday Night* magazine and continued the anthropomorphic metaphor, cataloguing how "we" have changed (Edinborough, "The Idea of Canada," *Saturday Night*, April 1968, 27-28). In the 1960s, Canadian nationalists were inordinately fond of the coming-of-age metaphor and, insofar as they were hard at work remaking the nation in their own image, their use of it was apt enough. Leerom Medovoi alludes to this trope:

> As scholars of international law have shown ... the doctrine of sovereignty is itself based upon what is sometimes called the 'domestic analogy,' in which the liberal individual's natural rights are writ large, so that each state is itself conceived as an individual among other individuals, equally entitled by natural law to self-determination. State sovereignty therefore acts as the projection of individual liberty onto the level of the body politic. Insofar as identity likewise moves from the individual's achievement of psychopolitical autonomy to an analogous one sought by the figure of the collectivity, it mirrors the political idea of sovereignty. (Medovoi, *Rebels: Youth and the Cold War Origins of Identity* [Durham, NC: Duke University Press, 2005], 7)

Medovoi sees the teenager as a key site of modern America's struggle to differentiate itself from rival authoritarian systems. By celebrating adolescent rebellion, a Fordist society could make room for individual agency by assigning it to the formative coming-of-age period preceding the individual's inevitable assimilation into a conformist adult world. If this notion were applied to Canada at the time, it bolsters the proposition that there was a mutually reinforcing relationship between youth rebellion and nationalism in 1960s Canada. One could interpret the acting-out of sixties nationalism as a stage of adolescent rebellion prior to Canada's submission to its destiny as a junior partner in the American empire.

CHAPTER 3: CELEBRATING THE SIMUNATION

1 Helen Davies, *The Politics of Participation: Learning from Canada's Centennial Year* (Toronto: MASS LBP, 2010).
2 Gary R. Miedema, *For Canada's Sake: Public Religion, Centennial Celebrations, and the Re-making of Canada in the 1960s* (Montreal: McGill-Queen's University Press, 2005), 68.
3 Under the Federal/Provincial Confederation Memorial Program, the commission offered up to $2.5 million to each province to erect a centennial building in its capital city. The results included a new provincial archives in Victoria, British Columbia, the Manitoba Cultural Centre in Winnipeg, and the Ontario Science Centre in Toronto. The commission also put millions into cultural facilities in Ottawa, most notably the new National Arts Centre.
4 Library and Archives Canada (LAC), RG 20-1, Advertising Books of the Canadian Government Office of Tourism, "Speaking of Canada," special centennial campaign, 1966-67.
5 Miedema, *For Canada's Sake*, 70.
6 Other events that would have happened anyway, like the Pan-Am games in Winnipeg (July 22-August 7), the Calgary Stampede, and the Canadian Armed Forces Tattoo, were rebranded as part of the centennial celebrations (LAC, RG 20, 1987-88/040 24, "Centennial Canada: Aglow with Festivities in '67," Canadian Government Office of Tourism special centennial campaign 1966-67).
7 Quoted in Frank Rasky, "CA-NA-DA," *Star Weekly/Canadian Magazine*, June 10-17, 1967, 3.

8 Penny Williams, "The Hit Song That's Rocking All Ca-na-da," *Maclean's*, February 1967, 2-3.

9 LAC, RG 20-1, Advertising Books of the Canadian Government Office of Tourism, special centennial campaign 1966-67, "Speaking of Canada." Theorists of nationalism invariably point to the importance of the past in forming a sense of collective identity in the present. Benedict Anderson described the nation as "a sociological organism moving calendrically through homogeneous, empty time" (Anderson, *Imagined Communities: Reflections on the Origin and Spread of Nationalism* [London: Verso, 1983], 26).

10 LAC, RG20-1, Advertising Books of the Canadian Government Office of Tourism, special centennial campaign 1966-67, "Centennial Canada: Aglow with festivities in '67."

11 The Canadian edition of *Time* magazine reported the total attendance for the train and caravan as 10,026,900, or almost half the population ("The Centennial: Annus Mirabilis," *Time* [Canadian edition], January 5, 1968, 9). According to *Time*, attendance statistics compiled for the Confederation Train and Caravan when its tour was half-finished showed that 38 percent of Canadians had seen the display. However, in Quebec the attendance ratio was 5.5 percent.

12 Misao Dean, "The Centennial Voyageur Canoe Pageant as Historical Re-enactment," *Journal of Canadian Studies* 40, 3 (2006): 43-67.

13 The editorial went on, "1967 has become, for ourselves and for the world, a firm assertion of our late-blooming self-knowledge and self-confidence ... Canadians have a right to be excited about this symbol of our maturing as a nation ... in this land which Providence stretched from sea to sea we have a great inheritance. The Canadian people have grown rich by sharing their legacy of culture and faith. Our celebrations should stimulate pride in our ancestors, faith in ourselves, confidence in our neighbors, and above all great hope in our national future" ("What Expo Really Is: A Coming-of-Age Party," editorial, *Maclean's*, January 1967, 4).

14 Davies, *Politics of Participation*, 176.

15 Moshe Safdie, *Beyond Habitat* (Montreal: Tundra Books, 1986), 66, quoted in Isabelle Massicotte, "The Architecture of Expo 67: National Identities and the Signs of Time" (MA thesis, Carleton University, 2003), 35. See Massicotte for a fuller discussion of Expo architecture and space planning.

16 Miedema, *For Canada's Sake*, 126-27; Sonya Macdonald, "Expo 67, Canada's National Heterotopia: A Study of the Transformative Role of International Exhibitions in Modern Society" (MA thesis, Carleton University, 2003), 133.

17 David Anderson and Viviane Gosselin, "Private and Public Memories of Expo 67: A Case Study of Recollections of Montreal's World's Fair, 40 Years after the Event," *Museum and Society* 6, 1 (2008): 12.

18 Eva-Marie Kroller, "Expo '67: Canada's Camelot?" *Canadian Literature* 152/153 (1997): 48.

19 Erin Hurley, *National Performance: Representing Quebec from Expo 67 to Celine Dion* (Toronto: University of Toronto Press, 2011), 32-33.

20 Walter Gray, "Pearson Rebukes Him – Now ... De Gaulle Going Home," *Toronto Daily Star*, July 26, 1967; Lester B. Pearson, *Words and Occasions: An Anthology of Speeches and Articles Selected from His Papers* (Toronto: University of Toronto Press, 1970), 277.

21 David Meren, *With Friends Like These: Entangled Nationalisms and the Canada-Quebec-France Triangle, 1944-1970* (Vancouver: UBC Press, 2012), 121, 239.

22 Myra Rutherdale and Jim Miller, "'It's Our Country': First Nations' Participation in the Indian Pavilion at Expo 67," *Journal of the Canadian Historical Association* 17, 2 (2006): 148-73.

23 Kroller, "Expo '67: Canada's Camelot?" 44.

24 Ibid.

25 Davies, *Politics of Participation*, 107.

26 Kroller, "Expo '67: Canada's Camelot?" 39.

27 Wendy Michener, "Where's It All Happening This Year? In Film, Baby," *Maclean's*, June 1967, 93.

28 Quoted ibid., 127.

29 John Lownsbrough, *The Best Place to Be: Expo 67 and Its Time* (Toronto: Allen Lane, 2012), 135.

30 *Labyrinth* was the subject of an article the previous year in *Maclean's* (Wendy Michener, "Through a Multi-Screen Darkly," *Maclean's*, September 17, 1966, 57-58). For recent analyses, see Ben Highmore, "Into the Labyrinth: Phantasmagoria at Expo 67," in *Expo 67: Not Just a Souvenir*, ed. Rhona Richman Kenneally and Johanne Sloan (Toronto: University of Toronto Press, 2010), 125-42; Seth Feldman, "Minotaur in a Box: The Labyrinth Pavilion at Expo 67," in *Reimagining Cinema: Film at Expo 67*, ed. Monika Kin Gagnon and Janine Marchessault (Montreal: McGill-Queen's University Press, 2014), 26-45.

31 Johanne Sloan, "Kaleidoscope," in Gagnon and Marchessault, eds., *Reimagining Cinema*, 56.

32 Michener, "Where's It All Happening?" 93.

33 Pierre Berton, "By God, We Did It! And Generally We Did It Well," *Maclean's*, June 1967, 3.

34 All quoted in Kroller, "Expo '67: Canada's Camelot?" 36.

35 Both quoted in Davies, *Politics of Participation*, 14.

36 Both quoted in Richard Gwyn, *The Northern Magus: Pierre Trudeau and Canadians* (Toronto: McClelland and Stewart, 1980), 61.

37 Quoted in Lownsbrough, *Best Place to Be*, 216. See also Sonya Macdonald, who comments, "Like the point of passage that occurred for a teenager in primitive societies, Expo was for Canada a space of crisis where a significant transformation was to occur" (Macdonald, "Expo 67, Canada's National Heterotopia," 106-7).

38 Quoted in Kroller, "Expo '67: Canada's Camelot?" 36.

39 Robert Fulford, *Remember Expo: A Pictorial Record* (Toronto: McClelland and Stewart 1968), 9.

40 Peter C. Newman, "It Could Change the Whole Direction of Canada's History," *Montreal Star*, April 28, 1967, quoted in Lownsbrough, *Best Place to Be*, 3. In his book on 1960s politics, published in 1968, Newman elaborated: "The nationalistic fervour that Walter Gordon had never personally been able to stir in Canadians erupted of its own accord during celebrations marking the 1967 centennial year. It was a brief shimmering season in the long wash of history, a mass rite that managed to expose the latent patriotism in even the most cynical Canadians, leaving them a little embarrassed at their sentiment, a little surprised by their tears. It was a wild, happy, crazy year" (Newman, *The Distemper of Our Times: Canadian Politics in Transition: 1963-1968* [Toronto: McClelland and Stewart, 1968], 423-24).

41 "Shall We Ever Be the Same Again?" *Chatelaine*, July 1967, 3. Harry Bruce observed, "It gave Canadians a sense of unabashed pride in themselves and their country. Maybe we've changed forever" (Bruce, "So Long 67 You Were a Very Good Year," *Canadian Magazine*, December 30, 1967).

42 Peter Desbarats, "It Sang What Was Hidden in Our Hearts," *Montreal Star*, October 30, 1967, quoted in Lownsbrough, *Best Place to Be*, 218.

CHAPTER 4: A LIBERAL TO WATCH

1 Joseph Campbell, *The Hero with a Thousand Faces*, 2nd ed. (Princeton, NJ: Princeton University Press, 1968; first published 1949), 37. Nino Ricci also alludes to this idea in his *Pierre Elliott Trudeau* (Toronto: Penguin, 2009), 42.

2 The Gzowski article mentioned incidents, such as Trudeau throwing a snowball at Stalin's statue in Moscow and attempting to row to Cuba, that would be widely cited by journalists in 1968 as examples of Trudeau's élan (Rae Fleming, *Peter Gzowski: A Biography* [Toronto: Dundurn, 2010], 103-4). When the Canadian Political Science Association and the Association of Canadian Law Teachers focused their 1964 annual meetings on the future of French-English relations in the wake of the Quiet Revolution, they invited

Trudeau to write on federalism from a French Canadian perspective. His essay was published along with the other proceedings as "Federalism, Nationalism, and Reason" in *The Future of Canadian Federalism*, ed. P.A. Crépeau and C.B. Macpherson (Toronto: University of Toronto Press, 1965), 16-35. Though they did not meet until 1961, historian Ramsay Cook knew of Trudeau through his writings in the mid-1950s. Cook, however, was much more interested in Quebec than the average English Canadian, or, for that matter, the average English Canadian historian (Cook, *The Teeth of Time: Remembering Pierre Elliott Trudeau* [Montreal: McGill-Queen's University Press, 2006], 11).

3 Pierre Elliott Trudeau, "We Need a Bill of Rights, Not a New Version of the BNA Act," *Maclean's*, February 8, 1964, 24-25.

4 Pierre Elliott Trudeau, "The New Treason of the Intellectuals," in *Federalism and the French Canadians* (Toronto: Macmillan, 1968), 178. The original French version of this essay had been published in *Cité Libre* in April 1962.

5 Kenneth McNaught, "The National Outlook of English-Speaking Canadians," in *Nationalism in Canada*, ed. Peter Russell (Toronto: McGraw-Hill, 1966), 70.

6 Earlier, Pearson had been moving towards special status for Quebec. The "two nations" view of Canada was part of the terms of reference of the Royal Commission on Bilingualism and Biculturalism, and he said on the CBC in 1964 that "we must recognize that Quebec in some vital respects is not a province like the others but the homeland of a people." This was just one of many such statements he made before Trudeau got his ear. This approach was realized in practice by deals allowing Quebec to opt out of federal programs. In 1966, Pearson's position began to change, and his operating premise became that special status would reinforce the two solitudes and ultimately undermine Confederation. See Donald Peacock, *Journey to Power: The Story of a Canadian Election* (Toronto: Ryerson, 1968), 117, 122-23.

7 Stephen Clarkson and Christina McCall, *Trudeau and Our Times*, Vol. 1, *The Magnificent Obsession* (Toronto: McClelland and Stewart, 1990), 100-1; David Meren, *With Friends Like These: Entangled Nationalisms and the Canada-Quebec-France Triangle, 1944-1970* (Vancouver: UBC Press, 2012), 175; John English, *Citizen of the World: The Life of Pierre Elliott Trudeau* (Toronto: Knopf, 2006), 435.

8 Canadian Press, "Liberal to Watch," *Lethbridge Herald*, February 2, 1967.

9 I use the term "memorable" because television insider Richard Nielsen, producer of CBC's *The Public Eye*, stated that Trudeau had not appeared on English-Canadian television at all in this period (Nielsen, "Let's *See* Our Politicians at Work," *Maclean's*, September 1968, 36-37). Yet Trudeau and Pelletier had been interviewed by Pierre Berton soon after their election to the House of Commons (LAC, Pierre Elliott Trudeau fonds, R11629-0-8-E, Series 20, Vol 25, file: Correspondence/Correspondance 1966 partie 1, "The Pierre Berton Show: Pierre Elliott Trudeau–Gérard Pelletier Interview"). There may well have been other appearances as well.

10 Library and Archives Canada (LAC), Canadian Broadcasting Corporation, Television: CBOT Film Library, *Twenty Million Questions*, March 16, 1967, Trudeau, Pierre Elliott – Interview, consultation copy V1 9310 0048.

11 Canadian journalists of the day were inordinately impressed by sports cars. Around the same time Canadian Press ran a piece entitled "New Cabinet Minister Has Yen for Sports Cars," which declared that Trudeau was the most unconventional Canadian justice minister ever (Ken Clark, "New Cabinet Minister Has Yen for Sports Cars," *Lethbridge Herald*, April 12, 1967).

12 CBC Archive Sales/Archives Radio-Canada, *Newsmagazine*, "Minister on the Move: The Many Lives of Pierre Elliott Trudeau," May 16, 1967.

13 LAC, CBC TV, Norman DePoe fonds, Film, 1967, Norman DePoe on Pierre Trudeau: outtakes," Consultation Copy VI 8211-10037. Usually the statue at which Trudeau reputedly threw a snowball in Moscow was of Stalin, not Lenin as DePoe had it.

14 Claude Ryan, "As Others See It: English Canada Is 'Astonishingly Naive' about Quebec," *Toronto Daily Star*, April 21, 1967. Ryan would return to the "messiah" theme in response to Trudeau's emergence as a national political phenomenon in 1968.

15 Peter C. Newman, "Ottawa Reels to Trudeau's New Tune," *Toronto Daily Star*, April 25, 1967.

16 Jack Batten, "Rating the Ottawa Press Gallery," *Saturday Night*, January 1968, 21.

17 Douglas Fisher was one of the more prominent commentators on national affairs at the time. With Harry Crowe, a history professor, he co-authored a column on national politics that appeared in the *Toronto Telegram* and three other newspapers. A former NDP MP (he had defeated C.D. Howe in Thunder Bay in 1957), he was disliked by many of his press gallery colleagues who felt he'd treated them shabbily when he'd been a politician. His sources included the NDP caucus, Diefenbaker Tories, and Liberals who were not in the innermost councils of power and not happy about it. He appeared frequently on CTV public affairs shows.

18 Donald Peacock, a former press gallery journalist who became a political assistant on the Hill in 1964, noted that after first meeting Trudeau in 1966, "the writer took every chance to observe Trudeau and his performance … increasingly impressed by his obvious ability and potential appeal … Would it be possible – even conceivable – that Trudeau might succeed Lester Pearson as Prime Minister?" (Peacock, *Journey to Power*, 155).

19 Edith Iglauer, "Profiles: Prime Minister/Premier Ministre," *New Yorker*, July 5, 1969, 50.

20 "Trudeau Dressed for House," *Calgary Herald*, July 7, 1967. Apparently Trudeau was known for wearing an ascot and sandals, if not in the House, then around Parliament, because when he'd been sworn in as justice minister Pearson had joked that someone had guessed he was being named to cabinet because he was wearing a tie that day. "And shoes," John Turner added. (J.R. Walker, "Quebec Swingers in Cabinet," *Calgary Herald*, April 4, 1967). In some versions of this exchange it was a reporter who added the shoes comment ("Trudeau et Chrétien entrent au Cabinet," *Le Devoir*, April 5, 1967).

21 Meren, *With Friends Like These*, 162-80.

22 Pierre-Elliott Trudeau, "L'évolution constitutionelle: Une nouvelle déclaration des droits de l'homme serait le meilleur point de départ d'une véritable réforme," *Le Devoir*, September 6, 1967. The initial reports in *Le Devoir* viewed the Bar Association speech as a welcome indication that Trudeau had shifted his position and was now willing to talk about the constitution. Following the press conference, however, Claude Ryan weighed in with an editorial that took him to task for calling two nations "une connerie" and "une grande fumisterie intellectuelle" (Ryan, "L'attitude déplorable de M. Pierre-Elliott Trudeau," editorial, *Le Devoir*, September 8, 1967).

23 Kenneth McRoberts, *Misconceiving Canada: The Struggle for National Unity* (Don Mills, ON: Oxford University Press, 1997), 50-53.

24 "Robert Cliche: Trudeau induit en erreur le Canada anglais," *Le Devoir*, July 4, 1967.

25 James Ferrabee, "Policy Group Backs Deux-Nations," *Montreal Gazette*, September 6, 1967; McRoberts, *Misconceiving Canada*, 48.

26 "PM Curbs 4 Ministers on Race for Leadership," *Globe and Mail*, November 10, 1967.

27 "The Statistical Breakdown," *Toronto Daily Star*, October 7, 1967.

28 Frank Howard, "Sweeping New Powers Advocated for Quebec," *Globe and Mail*, October 11, 1967. Lévesque's plan called for separation as a sovereign state, then reassociation in a common market. The Liberal conference sent it for "further study" because it was deemed too extreme. Lévesque walked out of the conference on Saturday night after delegates

endorsed special status but stopped short of accepting separatism. "Lévesque Quits as Party Turns Back on Separatism," *Globe and Mail*, October 16, 1967.

29 Roger Newman, "Special Status Plans Lack Logic, Trudeau Says," *Globe and Mail*, October 13, 1967.

30 Roger Newman, "Separatism a Retreat, Pearson Tells Quebec," *Globe and Mail*, October 23, 1967.

31 Ronald Lebel, "Much Larger Quebec Estates-General Goal," *Globe and Mail*, November 27, 1967.

32 "Johnson: Un nouveau fédéralisme canadien; De Gaulle: Un Québec souverain au Canada," *Le Devoir*, November 28, 1967.

33 Anthony Westell, "French-English Equality Essential to Save Canada, B-B Report Says," *Globe and Mail*, December 6, 1967.

34 Alexander Ross was the author of this article, which was balanced with "And Why It Can't Happen," by Blair Fraser. See *Maclean's*, December 1967, 80, 12.

35 LAC, Canadian Broadcasting Corporation, Television: Kines from Parc, Toronto, *The Way It Is*, December 10, 1967, consultation copy VI 8402 0036.

36 See, for example, Louis O'Neill, "Les moyens de communication sociale, courroies de transmission des objectifs prioritaires en vue d'un développement harmonisé," *La Presse*, May 25, 1968.

37 Blair Fraser, "The Sudden Rise of Pierre Trudeau," *Maclean's*, April 1968, 65.

38 Lewis Seale, "Trudeau Gaining Quebec Backing for Leadership," *Globe and Mail*, January 4, 1968.

39 Cook, *Teeth of Time*, 41.

40 In October 1966, Pearson had told Liberal Party organizer Richard Stanbury and Senator John Nichol that he planned to resign after the centennial celebrations were over, in late 1967 or early 1968 (LAC, MG 32 C 5, Richard Stanbury fonds, vol. 13, file 1: Diary, unnumbered diary notes for May 1968).

41 Peacock, *Journey to Power*, 106.

42 Michael Gillan, "Hellyer, Sharp, Martin Favourites as PM Quits, Calls Convention," *Globe and Mail*, December 15, 1967. Richard Gwyn tells the story of how Roy Faibish, a CBC producer, who had read Trudeau and followed his pronouncements, cornered him at a Rockcliffe dinner party and told him he had to run for the sake of the country. This was on December 14, the day Pearson announced his resignation. Trudeau later wrote to Faibish and thanked him for "talking me into it" (Gwyn, *The Northern Magus: Pierre Trudeau and Canadians* [Toronto: McClelland and Stewart, 1980], 66).

43 John Saywell, ed., *Canadian Annual Review for 1968* (Toronto: University of Toronto Press, 1969), 17; Martin Sullivan, *Mandate '68: The Year of Pierre Trudeau* (Toronto: Doubleday, 1968), 274. This quotation appears in both sources.

44 Blair Fraser, "Backstage in Ottawa: Why Liberals Almost Wish Dief Were Back," *Maclean's*, December 1967, 7. As of October, even Liberal insider Keith Davey hadn't considered Trudeau as a possible candidate for the leadership (English, *Citizen of the World*, 447).

45 Its coverage of the contest began with an expression of dismay at the usual suspects for the Liberal leadership. See "La course commence," *La Presse*, December 15, 1967; "La course au leadership libéral: Une fournée d'aspirants à la succession de Pearson, mais aucun d'eux ne semble être le candidat de l'heure," *La Presse*, December 26, 1967. The latter part of the second headline suggests the editors may have had a more timely candidate in mind.

46 "How the Pros Assess the Liberals," *Star Weekly*, January 6, 1968.

47 Marcel Pépin, "M. Pierre Elliott-Trudeau," editorial, *Le Droit*, December 21, 1967. Pépin wrote of Trudeau's intellectual gifts and praised his work in Parliament, administrative ability, clarity of vision, imagination, bilingualism, and pragmatism. Pépin was comforted to know that there was a high-quality French Canadian candidate available if Marchand

decided not to run. A couple of weeks later Pépin published an opinion piece in *Le Devoir* that did not mention Trudeau by name but portrayed the contemporary Canadian scene as needing someone like him to perpetuate Expo and move the country ahead. See Marcel Pépin, "Le Canada de 1968 en quête du'un chef," *Le Devoir*, January 4, 1968.

48 CBC Digital Archives, CBC Television News, December 21, 1967. See http://www.cbc.ca/ archives/categories/politics/rights-freedoms/trudeaus-omnibus-bill-challenging -canadian-taboos/theres-no-place-for-the-state-in-the-bedrooms-of-the-nation.html.

49 "Trudeau's one-liner is repeated endlessly because it has allowed Anglo-Canadians to feel modern, liberated from a colonial past" argue Patricia Cormack and James F. Cosgrave in *Desiring Canada: CBC Contests, Hockey Violence, and Other Stately Pleasures* (Toronto: University of Toronto Press, 2011), 4.

50 Gwyn, *Northern Magus*, 64, notes that Martin O'Malley of the *Globe and Mail* had coined the phrase in an earlier unsigned editorial: "Obviously, the state's responsibility should be to legislate rules for a well-ordered society. It has no right or duty to creep into the bed-rooms of the nation" ("Unlocking the Locked Step of Law and Morality," *Globe and Mail*, December 12, 1967).

51 Norman DePoe, "Why the Knife-Wielders in the Ottawa Press Gallery Will Soon Start Carving Up Trudeau," *Maclean's*, October 1968, 3.

52 "What can I add," asked *Canadian Dimension's* media columnist, "to the thousands of col-umn inches already written about television's role in Pierre Elliott Trudeau's convention victory, and about newspaper comments on television's role, and about television's com-ments on newspaper comments on television's role...?" (Richard Dahrin, "The Media and the Rise of P.E. Trudeau," *Canadian Dimension* 5, 5 [June-July 1968]: 5).

53 Nielsen, "Let's *See* Our Politicians."

54 Quoted in Newman, "Ottawa Letter."

55 Blair Fraser, "The Sudden Rise of Pierre Trudeau," *Maclean's*, April 1968, 65.

56 Christina McCall-Newman, *Grits: An Intimate Portrait of the Liberal Party* (Toronto: Macmillan, 1982), 108-9. Ramsay Cook relates how a *Toronto Daily Star* story by Val Sears and Ron Haggart gave him credit for the petition when the real forces behind it were the Teitelbaums (Cook, *Teeth of Time*, 41). See also Douglas Stuebing, John R. Marshall, and Gary Oakes, *Trudeau: A Man for Tomorrow* (Toronto: Clarke Irwin, 1968), 9; Saywell, *Canadian Annual Review*, 14; Christopher Young, "No Gimmick, No Messiah," *Ottawa Citizen*, Feb-ruary 18, 1968; Ben Tierney, "Trudeau and Turner," *Edmonton Journal*, March 22, 1968.

57 "The Liberals: The Eighth Man," *Time* (Canadian edition), January 26, 1968, 7.

58 When discussing plans for the leadership convention, Liberal officials took care to ensure the proceedings would be television-friendly. One of the organizers even pro-posed that the convention feature "psychedelic props such as Expo-type films, etc." Stanbury recorded that Dan Coates, the party's research director, had gone to Washington and "says he has learned a good deal from the Democrats and Republicans" (LAC, MG 32 C 5, Richard Stanbury fonds, vol. 13, file 1: Diary pp. 1-99 [+6 pp. unnumbered diary notes for May 1968], "68" p. 2.).

59 Nielsen, "Let's *See* Our Politicians," 37.

CHAPTER 5: COY WONDER

1 John English, *Citizen of the World: The Life of Pierre Elliott Trudeau* (Toronto: Knopf, 2006), 449.

2 Richard Nielsen, "Let's *See* Our Politicians at Work," *Maclean's*, September 1968, 37.

3 Pierre-C. O'Neill, "Trudeau a entrepris en grand secret une tournée des capitales de l'Ouest," *Le Devoir*, January 19, 1968; "Trudeau Sent on Unity Mission," *Montreal Gazette*, January 19, 1968. In his biography of Pearson, John English writes that Pearson wanted the tradition of alternation between English and French Canadian leaders to continue,

and did a lot to assist Trudeau's candidacy (English, *The Worldly Years: The Life of Lester Pearson* [Toronto: Vintage, 1992], 382-84.

4 Quoted in Peter Newman, "Professors, Writers Support Trudeau," *Ottawa Journal*, January 13, 1968.

5 Martin Sullivan, *Mandate '68: The Year of Pierre Trudeau* (Toronto: Doubleday, 1968), 294.

6 Edith Iglauer, "Profiles: Prime Minister/Premier Ministre," *New Yorker*, July 5, 1969, 51.

7 Peacock, *Journey to Power*, 190, 192; "The Liberals: Waiting Game," *Time* (Canadian edition), February 2, 1968, 9.

8 Library and Archives Canada (LAC), CTV Television Network, *One Canada! Two Nations?* February 4, 1968, consultation copies V1 8301-0058, V1 9708-0002; "Johnson accuse Trudeau de partisanerie," *Le Devoir*, January 30, 1968.

9 Quoted in John Saywell, ed., *Canadian Annual Review for 1968* (Toronto: University of Toronto Press, 1969), 18.

10 Blair Fraser, "The Sudden Rise of Pierre Trudeau," *Maclean's*, April 1968, 67.

11 LAC, MG 32 C 5, Richard Stanbury fonds, vol. 13, file 1, Diary, pp. 1-99 (+6 pp. unnumbered diary notes for May 1968), January 28, 1968.

12 Peacock, *Journey to Power*, 200.

13 Claude Ryan, "Les deux 'événements' du congress libéral," *Le Devoir*, January 29, 1968. *Le Devoir* also chastised Trudeau for his empire-building comment; this was, it claimed, provocative name-calling that closed down dialogue (Vincent Prince, "A propos du 'petit empire' québécois," *Le Devoir*, January 31, 1968).

14 Christina McCall-Newman, *Grits: An Intimate Portrait of the Liberal Party* (Toronto: Macmillan, 1982), 112. René Lagarde, a Quebec Liberal organizer who lost his executive position after the Trudeau forces voted in a new executive at the January convention, complained that Marchand had ridden roughshod over proper procedures and "trampled democracy" to get his way; he compared Trudeau to Hitler. Lagarde published a ninety-six-page booklet entitled "The Old Guard Was Railroaded" and distributed it to Liberal delegates. See Robert McKenzie, "Quebec Pamphlet Hits Trudeau," *Toronto Daily Star*, March 21, 1968, and "Trudeau Arm-Twisting Charged," *Toronto Telegram*, March 26, 1968. See also Sullivan, *Mandate '68*, 304, 324.

15 "The Liberals: The Eighth Man," *Time* (Canadian edition), January 26, 1968, 7.

16 Val Sears, "How Trudeau Dazzled the Quebec Liberals," *Toronto Daily Star*, January 29, 1968.

17 *One Canada! Two Nations?* February 4, 1968.

18 LAC, MG 31 D 112, Norman DePoe fonds, vol. 7, file 10, Trudeau, Pierre Elliott – Clippings, brochures, transcript of DePoe interview, 1968, transcript of CBC *Newsmagazine* – January 23, 1968.

19 "Federalism: On to the Summit," *Time* (Canadian edition), February 2, 1968, 10.

20 LAC, Canadian Broadcasting Corporation, Television: Kines from Parc, Toronto, CBC News Special Presentation: The Ottawa Conference on the Constitution, February 7, 1968, consultation copies V1 8211-0052, V1 8211-0053, V1 8211-0061, V1 8211-0062.

21 "Federalism: An End and a Beginning," *Time* (Canadian edition), February 16, 1968, 10.

22 The main exceptions were the Maritime press, which regarded regional economic development as directly connected with constitutional renewal, and the *Winnipeg Tribune*, which viewed the charter as a sellout to American-style democracy (LAC, R 12069 Roméo LeBlanc fonds, vol. 402, file 15, Conclusions of meetings of the Constitutional Conference/Conférence sur le constitution January 31-February 13, 1968, "Report on Press Coverage of the Constitutional Conference").

23 *Le Devoir* gave voluminous coverage to the conference. The paper's editors were encouraged by Ontario and New Brunswick's openness to bilingualism and approved the federal

proposal to entrench linguistic rights by amending the constitution, but warned that a charter of rights should not be pursued before the constitutional reform process dealt with the Supreme Court. Le Devoir also deplored the failure of the conference to acknowledge the need for special status for Quebec. Quebec City's L'Action warned that despite all the encouraging signs, Ottawa could not be trusted to protect French Canadian culture – only a strong Quebec could do that (ibid.).

24 Frank Underhill, "The WAY We Choose Is Out of Date," Toronto Daily Star, March 2, 1968.

25 Peter Newman, "C'est la télévision qui sauvera la Confédération," La Presse, February 7, 1968. Translated by the author.

26 Maurice Western, "The Trudeau of the Image Makers," Winnipeg Free Press, April 4, 1968.

27 La Presse, April 4, 1968, cited in George Radwanski, Trudeau (Toronto: Macmillan, 1978), 104.

28 Lubor Zink, "Trudeau's Spontaneous Support May Not Be So Spontaneous," Toronto Telegram, January 31, 1968. Zink's reference to a "neutralist state" invoked the wish for Canada to be an honest broker in international affairs, a foreign policy stance that informed the peacekeeping myth (see, for example, James Minifie, Peacemaker or Powder-Monkey: Canada's Role in a Revolutionary World [Toronto: McClelland and Stewart, 1960]). Trudeau would capitalize on this sentiment by calling for a review of Canadian foreign policy in his election platform.

29 Editorial, Toronto Telegram, January 30, 1968; "No Trudeau Plot," editorial, Toronto Telegram, January 31, 1968. For the internal politics of the Telegram on this affair, see LAC, R5588-0-X-E, John D. Harbron fonds, vol. 4, file 4, Election Campaign, 1968.

30 "Une nation erronée?" letter to the editor, La Presse, February 1, 1968. See also Bernard Dubé, "Brainwashing and the CBC," Montreal Gazette, May 18, 1968.

31 Both quoted in Dominique Clift, "To the French-Canadian Press Trudeau Is as Objectionable as Diefenbaker," Toronto Daily Star, March 21, 1968. During a press conference following his convention victory, Trudeau said that he'd adopted his famous "reason over passion" dictum to contradict Wilfrid Laurier's observation that French Canadians had no opinions, only sentiments. He was trying to encourage more rationality in Québécois political culture (LAC, Pierre Elliott Trudeau fonds, R11629-0-8-E, Series 13, Vol. 25, File: Press Conferences/Conférences de presse, January 19–May 8, 1968, "Transcript of Press Conference with Pierre E. Trudeau, National Press Building, Ottawa, April 7, 1968").

33 For Claude Ryan's response to the emergence of Trudeau's candidacy, see his articles: "La course au leadership libéral: simples conjectures," Le Devoir, January 15, 1968; "M. Marchand ou M. Trudeau," Le Devoir, January 17, 1968; "Deux communautés linguistique ou deux sociétés?" Le Devoir, January 27, 1968; "La vielle tentation du Canada anglais," Le Devoir, February 1, 1968; "M. Trudeau suivra-t-il le courant?" Le Devoir, February 10, 1968; "Les ambiguités de la candidature de M. Trudeau," Le Devoir, February 17, 1968. Le Devoir gave the constitutional issue extensive in-depth coverage in the lead-up to the Quebec Liberal meeting; see in particular its January 19 and January 20 editions.

34 "Discussions with delegates at the weekend convention confirmed the suspicion that rural Quebecers don't find Trudeau anywhere near as attractive as do more sophisticated Montrealers" (Gordon Pape, "Trudeau Bandwagon Shifted into High at Convention," Montreal Gazette, January 30, 1968). Although some small papers that were closely associated with the Catholic Church took strong stands against Trudeau, on the whole rural papers in Quebec, like those elsewhere in Canada, largely ignored federal politics. Their beat was local, and, with some exceptions, they did not risk alienating readers by taking sides.

35 LAC, Canadian Broadcasting Corporation, Television: Two-Inch Quad Videotapes for Deposit, The Way It Is, "Drug Show: Nancy Green and Pierre Trudeau," recorded January 25, 1968, broadcast February 11, 1968, consultation copy VI 8202-0025.

36 LAC, Susan Dexter fonds, CTV TV, W5, Sound, Trudeau, Pierre Elliott – Interview, March 29, 1968, consultation copy A1 2003-09-0008.

37 Canadian Press, "'Improve Lousy French' – Trudeau," *Montreal Gazette*, February 15, 1968.

38 Geoffrey Stevens, "How They Stand at the Halfway Mark," *Globe and Mail*, February 13, 1968.

39 "Une petition du Québec invite Trudeau à poser sa candidature," *Le Devoir*, February 15, 1968; "80 p.c. du caucus appuie Trudeau," *La Presse*, February 14, 1968.

40 Charles Lynch, "Image Unleashed," Southam News Service, February 13, 1968.

41 Quoted in Saywell, *Canadian Annual Review*, 21.

42 Robert Miller, "Trudeau: The Hip Saviour?" *Toronto Daily Star*, February 16, 1968.

43 Peter Newman "Are We Ready for a Leader Who'll 'Tell It Like It Is'?" *Toronto Daily Star*, February 17, 1968.

44 Quoted in Saywell, *Canadian Annual Review*, 21-22.

45 Lubor Zink, *Trudeaucracy* (Toronto: Toronto Sun Publishing, 1972), 2.

46 In a *Maclean's* article on the impact of colour TV, Marshall McLuhan suggested that colour might be as important as the medium itself, while Carleton journalism professor T. Joseph Scanlon reported that students who watched colour TV were more affected by what they watched. Said Scanlon, "Color could change our attitudes about politicians and government and society. It could change our government ... the effects of media are mysterious and uncharted" (Jon Ruddy, "When Is TV Not TV? When It's in Colour," *Maclean's*, August 1967, 2).

47 *The Pierre Berton Show*, "The Liberal Image – Liberal Leadership Race," March 8, 1968.

48 Peter C. Newman, "Canada Is in a Ferment, Digging for Its Soul ...," *Toronto Daily Star*, June 1, 1968.

49 Donald Peacock, *Journey to Power: The Story of a Canadian Election* (Toronto: Ryerson, 1968), 258.

50 Margaret Daily, "Will Norman DePoe be Our Next Prime Minister?" *Star Weekly*, February 24, 1968.

CHAPTER 6: POP GOES THE IMAGE

1 "A Matter of Image," *Maclean's*, March 1968, 34-35. Along the same lines, a graduate student in Toronto, Rick Alway, told a journalist, "The funny thing is that I agree with many of the stands Martin has taken – for Medicare, for instance – but ... I just don't like his style" (Walter Stewart, "Why Young Canada Has No Time for the Old Guard," *Star Weekly*, March 9, 1968).

2 Ian Ward, "Trudeaumania and Its Time: The Early Use of TV for Political Communication," *Australian-Canadian Studies* 19, 1 (2001): 2.

3 Three of television's leading qualities, as identified by John Corner, are that it is (i) electronic, (ii) visual, and (iii) mass/domestic in character, i.e., it penetrates deeply into everyday life to give a sense of immediate connectedness to far-off events (Corner, *Critical Ideas in Television Studies* [Oxford: Clarendon, 1999], 4). See also David Taras, *The Newsmakers: The Media's Influence on Canadian Politics* (Scarborough, ON: Nelson, 1990), 156; Mat Atkinson, *Our Master's Voices* (London: Methuen, 1984), 174-76.

4 Leslie Miller, "Rating the Talking Heads," *Globe Magazine*, March 30, 1968.

5 The term "charisma" was used frequently in 1968, but was not as central to the discussion about Trudeau then as it would later be. See, for instance, Anthony Westell, "Is Charisma the Key to Solving the Trudeau Mystery?" *Globe and Mail*, February 12, 1968; Library and Archives Canada (LAC), Pierre Elliott Trudeau fonds, R11629-0-8-E, films and broadcasts, Accession number 1976-0067, CJCB, Sydney, Nova Scotia, Donovan, Neil – Interview

(interviewer Ann Terry), April 13, 1968, consultation copy AI 2005-01-0021. A journalist suggested to Trudeau at the St. Lawrence Hall meeting in Toronto that he was the victim of an "implosion of charisma" (CBC Archive Sales/Archives Radio-Canada, "Special – What Happened Here," *The Public Eye*, "Trudeau," March 26, 1968). His biographers, Stephen Clarkson and Christina McCall, would later write:

> What Trudeau had displayed that winter and spring – as projected by the print and television journalists who were presenting him as the answer to the public's hopes and fears – was an impressive number of the attributes that Weberian scholars have isolated as the prerequisites of political charisma: an element of foreignness, some obvious imperfections of feature and character, elevated social station, a sexual mystique, a facility to dramatic self-presentation, an unusual style of living, and, above all, an extraordinary calling or vocation and along with it, the fighting stance of the crusader preaching social change (Clarkson and McCall, *Trudeau and Our Times*, Vol. 1, *The Magnificent Obsession* [Toronto: McClelland and Stewart, 1990], 111-12)

6 "He was able to leap all barriers, to act a bit like a political superman, because television gave him the necessary boost," concludes Paul Rutherford (Rutherford, *When Television Was Young: Primetime Canada 1952-1967* [Toronto: University of Toronto Press, 1990], 433). See also John Duffy, *The Fights of Our Lives: Elections, Leadership, and the Making of Canada* (Toronto: HarperCollins, 2002), 240; Douglas Stuebing, John R. Marshall, and Gary Oakes, *Trudeau: A Man for Tomorrow* (Toronto: Clarke Irwin, 1968), 75.

7 LAC, Columbia Pictures Television Canada fonds, *The Pierre Berton Show*, "The Liberal Image – Liberal Leadership Race," March 8, 1968, consultation copy VI 9210-0018. The panellists were Fraser Kelly, Blair Fraser, and Douglas Fisher.

8 LAC, MG 31 D 156, Marshall McLuhan fonds, vol. 39, file 34 – Trudeau, Pierre 1968, Marshall McLuhan to Pierre Trudeau, June 12, 1968.

9 Westell, "Is Charisma the Key?"

10 Quoted in Bryan Palmer, *Canada's 1960s: The Ironies of Identity in a Rebellious Era* (Toronto: University of Toronto Press, 2009), 169.

11 Quoted in Martin Sullivan, *Mandate '68: The Year of Pierre Trudeau* (Toronto: Doubleday, 1968), 313.

12 LAC, Canadian Broadcasting Corporation, Television: Kines from Parc, Toronto, *The Way It Is*, May 26, 1968, consultation copy VI 8402-0046; George MacFarlane, "The Image Problem," *Globe and Mail*, April 22, 1968.

13 "Canadians Hear the Truth ... From a Bilingual Patriot," editorial, *Vancouver Sun*, June 24, 1968, repr. in *The Trudeau Decade*, ed. Rick Butler and Jean-Guy Carrier (Toronto: Doubleday, 1979), 40.

14 "Canada's Next Prime Minister," *New York Times*, April 8, 1968.

15 Margaret Daly, "A Realist, an Intellectual and a Man of Action," *Star Weekly*, March 23, 1968. Trudeau, the *Toronto Daily Star* wrote enthusiastically, "is believable ... the viewer, if it is on television, or the reader, is left with the impression that the man is talking straight, that he believes what he is saying, that he is willing to share that open belief with the electorate of this country. He inspires not the confidence of pat solutions, but the certainty that he will face problems without prejudice" (February 17, 1968, quoted in John Saywell, ed., *Canadian Annual Review for 1968* [Toronto: University of Toronto Press, 1969], 22).

16 These and other observations of how Trudeau came across on television are based on close viewing of the various archived television programs cited elsewhere in these notes.

17 Rutherford, *When Television Was Young*, 431.

18 See John English, *Citizen of the World: The Life of Pierre Elliott Trudeau* (Toronto: Knopf, 2006), 256-67; George Radwanski, *Trudeau* (Toronto: Macmillan, 1978), 103. Richard Gwyn also noted how Trudeau performed for the cameras: "Trudeau turned out to have qualities no one had counted on: the instincts of a consummate actor. He would wave to the crowds looking endearingly bashful, an impish little-boy half grin on his face, as a signal to the audience that he knew, and they knew, and each knew the other knew, that he wasn't all that bashful. It was a delicious matinée idol bit of teasing, that made the adoring crowds work all the harder to evoke from him a full smile, in public confession of how much he was enjoying himself" (Gwyn, *The Northern Magus: Pierre Trudeau and Canadians* [Toronto: McClelland and Stewart, 1980], 68).

19 These performances can be found in CBC Archive Sales/Archives Radio-Canada, *Newsmagazine*, "Minister on the Move: The Many Lives of Pierre Elliott Trudeau," May 16, 1967; CBC Digital Archives, "Trudeaumania: Dancing Trudeau," from *The Way It Is*, June 29, 1969, http://www.cbc.ca/archives/entry/trudeaumania-dancing-trudeau. See also Donald Peacock, *Journey to Power: The Story of a Canadian Election* (Toronto: Ryerson, 1968), 288. Bernard Dubé, "Trudeau–Pratfall and All," *Montreal Gazette*, April 9, 1968, describes the staircase stunt, which apparently had been filmed two weeks before for *The Way It Is*.

20 *Montreal Star*, May 30, 1968, quoted in Saywell, *Canadian Annual Review*, 49.

21 Quoted in Peacock, *Journey to Power*, 259.

22 Christina Newman, "This Month – Ottawa Letter," *Saturday Night*, May 1968, 7. Ken Dewar noted the historical proclivity of Liberal prime ministers to anoint their successors and suggested that Pearson had done the same: "Most of the men chosen in this manner had another quality in common: they were relatively new men, who, having entered the party hierarchy at a high level, succeeded to the leadership in preference to the old party hacks" (Dewar, "Pierre Elliott Trudeau and the Liberal Party: Continuity and Change," *Canadian Dimension* 5, 5 [1968]: 7).

23 Gwyn, *Northern Magus*, 68. "Canadians thought of Paul Martin, or even of Paul Hellyer, in the context of Mackenzie King. They thought of Pierre Trudeau as a man for this season, uncontaminated and uninhibited," explained Lester Pearson in his memoirs (*Mike: The Memoirs of the Rt. Hon. Lester B. Pearson*, vol. 3, 1957-1968 [Toronto: University of Toronto Press, 2015; first published 1975], 327).

24 "Old Guard Backlash," editorial, *Edmonton Journal*, April 2, 1968, repr. in Butler and Carrier, *Trudeau Decade*, 12.

25 Pierre Elliott Trudeau, *Federalism and the French Canadians* (Toronto: Macmillan, 1968), xix.

26 This was on March 19, after Trudeau had called Bennett a "provincialist" during his swing through British Columbia the previous weekend (Canadian Press, "Bennett Calls Pierre Trudeau a 'Playboy,'" *Toronto Daily Star*, March 20, 1968).

27 Douglas Fisher, "John Turner: Yes, He Does Sweat and Swear," *Executive* 14, 4 (April 1972): 62. See also David Steigerwald, *The Sixties and the End of Modern America* (New York: St. Martin's Press, 1995), 178.

28 John Street, "The Celebrity Politician: Political Style and Popular Culture," chapter 5 in *Media and the Restyling of Politics: Consumerism, Celebrity and Cynicism*, ed. John Corner and Dick Pels (London: Sage, 2003), 96-97.

29 Donovan, Neil – Interview, April 13, 1968.

30 The changing of the generations was part of the narrative. Blair Fraser talked about Trudeau's ascot raising eyebrows "in the sober precincts of Ottawa's Rideau Club, where certain elderly members had harrumphed indignantly when Trudeau appeared as somebody's guest, wearing his Ascot tie" (Fraser, "The Sudden Rise of Pierre Trudeau," *Maclean's*, April 1968, 65).

31 Alisdair Dow, "Trudeau: Trend to Tomorrow's Society," *Toronto Daily Star*, December 23, 1967.

32 George Bain, "A Prudent Bet," *Globe and Mail*, April 4, 1968. In its analyses of the political implications of popular culture, cultural studies has been sensitive to the significance of style in denoting identity in subcultures, but has paid scant attention to the significance of style in political culture. Nor has political science focused much on fashion as a form of political communication (Street, "Celebrity Politician," 96).

33 "He Points to Joyce as Hostess Choice," *Vancouver Sun*, April 4, 1967.

34 All news reports here as quoted in Peacock, *Journey to Power*, 259. Dalton Camp believed that intellectualism was a characteristic that Kennedy had brought into the political mainstream (Camp, "The Trouble with the Tories (and the Liberals Too)," *Weekend*, November 1966).

35 Denis Harvey, Michael Hanlon, and John Miller, "Trudeau and Stanfield on Movies, Luck, Women ... Things Like That," *Canadian*, June 22, 1968, 7.

36 Stan Fischler, "Here's the Newest Trudeau Fan Club – In New York City," *Toronto Daily Star*, March 21, 1968.

37 After Trudeau became prime minister, Canadian Press ran a story titled "Impressions of Trudeau by Seven Women Friends" that gave personal glimpses, all flattering, of the new PM. One told of how he'd asked for some time to unwind when he'd arrived at her place for dinner. She expected he wanted a quick catnap, but discovered him standing on his head, practising yoga (*Lethbridge Herald*, May 21, 1968).

38 LAC, Susan Dexter fonds, CTV TV, W5, Sound, Trudeau, Pierre Elliott – Interview, March 29, 1968, consultation copy A1 2003-09-0008.

39 Roy Shields, "Which Image ... Is Really US?" *Toronto Daily Star*, June 22, 1968.

40 Jay Walz, "Trudeau Conjures Up a 'Perpetual Expo 67,'" *New York Times*, n.d. (likely April 1968), in LAC, MG 31 D112, Norman DePoe papers, file 7: Trudeau, Pierre Elliott, 1968 – Clippings, brochures, transcript of DePoe interview. Indeed, many commentators have maintained that Trudeau would not have been possible without Expo 67. "The last time, perhaps the only time we dared to dare greatly together was Expo '67," Richard Gwyn would write. "Trudeau is an icon of that summer of excellence" (Gwyn, *Northern Magus*, 19). Bryan Palmer describes Trudeaumania as "the pyrotechnics of a Canadian identity struggling to be born, shooting wildly out of the euphoria that had, for some, begun with the architectural imagination of Expo '67" (Palmer, *Canada's 1960s*, 169).

41 Larry Martin, "Maureen in 'Trudeau Troupe,'" *Canadian Champion*, April 10, 1968.

42 "Who Says Pierre Elliott Trudeau Is All That Hot? Writers and Editors Just About Everywhere, That's Who," *Maclean's*, September 1968, 3. The March 13 edition of the *London Evening Standard* ran a half-page feature calling Trudeau "the most exciting politician this side of the Atlantic Ocean." On the eve of the Liberal leadership convention, the US TV show *The Huntley-Brinkley Report* ran a Trudeau profile (Peacock, *Journey to Power*, 226). See also John David Hamilton, "Canada's Swinging Egghead," *New Statesman*, April 12, 1968.

43 Scott Young, "Does Only Bachelorhood Lie Behind the Admiration of Pierre Trudeau?" *Globe and Mail*, May 21, 1968. See also Peter Newman, "Pierre Elliott Trudeau redonne au Canada l'esprit vivant de l'Expo 67," *La Presse*, April 8, 1968.

44 *The Way It Is*, May 26, 1968. Whenever Trudeau offered up anything personal like this, he would slide it into the conversation in passing, not boastfully, and the journalist, grateful for anything personal from someone so private, lapped it up.

45 Westell, "Is Charisma the Key?"

46 David Waters, a journalist at the *Montreal Gazette*, found many parallels between the hero archetype and Trudeau's reception. He cited Beowulf, Hamlet, Lawrence of Arabia, and

Jesus Christ as examples of heroes whose lives fit this pattern (Waters, "Mythology, Mr. Trudeau, and … Us," *Montreal Gazette*, April 20, 1968).

47 CBC Archive Sales/Archives Radio-Canada, *Twenty Million Questions*, "The Young Contenders," March 30, 1967. Among the clichés commonly cited to prove that politicians must appeal to youth or else fail in this "young country," the commonest was to say "half the population of Canada is under 25," Blair Fraser noted, but he then proceeded to contest this assertion: "The statement is almost true, but in political terms it is quite without meaning," because only 1.4 million of those under twenty-five were old enough to vote. Among 11.2 million voters they amounted to 12.5 percent of the total, or roughly one in eight. Two-thirds of the electorate was over the age of thirty-five. Moreover, youth wasn't a political bloc. University students tended to be left of centre, but they were a small minority in their age group (Fraser, "Backstage in Ottawa: Why Political Strategists Could Hardly Care Less about the 'Under-25' Vote," *Maclean's*, June 1968, 1). Fraser wasn't taking into account, however, the contribution that non-voting youth could make to Trudeau's image through their public displays of enthusiasm for him.

48 Quoted in Peacock, *Journey to Power*, 260.

49 Fischler, "Newest Trudeau Fan Club."

50 Ibid., 262.

51 George Bain, "Canada Has a Case of Trudeaumania," *New York Times*, June 16, 1968.

52 Stuebing, Marshall, and Oakes, *Trudeau: A Man for Tomorrow*, 91.

53 Peter Braunstein, "Forever Young: Insurgent Youth and the Sixties Culture of Rejuvenation," in *Imagine Nation*, ed. Peter Braunstein (New York: Routledge, 2002), 243, quoted in Stuart Henderson, *Making the Scene: Yorkville and Hip Toronto in the 1960s* (Toronto: University of Toronto Press, 2011), 15. Henderson discusses how "hipness was conferred in wildly different ways and was accessible to most anyone through a variety of identity performances" (14-15). According to one commentator at the time, the contemporary meaning of the term "swinger" was "someone between the 30th and 50th year, who in fact is still so open-minded, so liberal, so emotionally liberal … that they can think, talk and communicate with the young" (Donovan, Neil – Interview April 13, 1968).

54 Bain, "Canada Has a Case."

55 Beth Bailey, "Sexual Revolution(s)," in *The Sixties: From Memory to History*, ed. David Farber (Chapel Hill: University of North Carolina Press, 1994), 238.

56 Allan MacEachen was also a bachelor, but for some reason his single status didn't make him sexy. R.B. Bennett and Mackenzie King had been bachelors, but they hadn't earned the same status as sex objects (Young, "Only Bachelorhood?").

57 Allan Fotheringham, "Turner's Biggest Problem Is to Convince Delegates," *Vancouver Sun*, March 25, 1968.

58 CBC Archive Sales/Archives Radio-Canada, "Special – What Happened Here," *The Public Eye*, "Trudeau," March 26, 1968.

59 CBC Digital Archives, CBC Television News, December 21, 1967, http://www.cbc.ca/archives/entry/omnibus-bill-theres-no-place-for-the-state-in-the-bedrooms-of-the-nation.

60 Douglas Marshall, "Okay, so he's no swinger. BUT …," *Maclean's*, March 1968, 23.

61 See Renaude Lapointe, "Une expérience passionnante," *La Presse*, April 25, 1968; MacFarlane, "The Image Problem." That week the *Times* of London took notice of the Canadian election call under the headline "Trudeau Image Hard to Beat" (April 25, 1968).

62 LAC, Canadian Broadcasting Corporation, Television: CBOT Film Library, *Newsmagazine*, "Countdown to Liberal Leadership Convention," April 2, 1968, consultation copy VI 8203-0109.

63 LAC, Canadian Broadcasting Corporation, Television: CBOT Two-Inch Video Inventory – Tapes on Deposit, *Twenty Million Questions*, "The Style Is the Man Himself," September 9, 1968, consultation copy V1 8506-0104.

64 LAC, Canadian Broadcasting Corporation, Television: Kines from Parc, Toronto, *The Way It Is*, April 7, 1968, consultation copy V1 8402-0043.

65 "Trudeau Magic Needed in Edmonton," *Calgary Herald*, June 7, 1968.

66 Lubor Zink, "'Pragmatism' – Or Just Plain, Old-Fashioned 'Deceit'?" *Toronto Telegram*, May 14, 1968. The Canadian Intelligence Service publication *On Target, A Weekly Review of News Highlights, Background Information, Observation and Comment* (no. 36, May 20, 1968) reprinted the column.

67 "80,000 visiteurs dès le depart," *La Presse*, May 18, 1968.

68 *Canadian Intelligence Service*, 18, 3 (1968) in LAC, R5727-2-5-E, Liberal Party of Canada fonds, vol. 1084, file: Communications, hate/smear campaign; Peter C. Newman, "The FACTS and FICTIONS of the Trudeau Smears," *Toronto Daily Star*, June 15, 1968. CIS had in fact started in on Trudeau soon after his elevation to cabinet the previous year (LAC, Pierre Elliott Trudeau fonds, R11629-0-8-E, Series 20, Vol 25, Correspondence/Correspondance 1967 partie 1 "Fabian Socialists Taking Over Ottawa," *Canadian Intelligence Service*, May 1967).

69 "Macdonald Says Big Money behind Smear-the-PM Plot," *Toronto Daily Star*, June 15, 1968; Stuebing, Marshall, and Oakes, *Trudeau: A Man for Tomorrow*, 89-91, 166.

70 "Trudeau Spearing Fabian Takeover," *Canadian Intelligence Service*, March, 1968, in LAC, R5727-2-5-E, Liberal Party of Canada fonds, vol. 1084, file: Communications, hate/smear campaign; Jon Ruddy, "Ron Gostick Makes a Living Telling People Trudeau is a COMSYMP. You'd Be Amazed How Many People Believe Him," *Maclean's*, November 1968, 108c. Later Gostick followed up in *On Target*. See Gostick, "Our Nasty Campaign against Trudeau," *On Target, A Weekly Review of News Highlights, Background Information, Observation and Comment* (no. 28, March 25, 1968), and Gostick, "Many 'Converts' to Attend Liberal Convention," *On Target, A Weekly Review of News Highlights, Background Information, Observation and Comment* (no. 29, April 1, 1968), both in LAC, R5486-20-1-E, Blair Fraser and family fonds, vol. 3, file: Trudeau leadership win, articles, speeches, and clippings.

71 LAC, R11600, Lubor Zink fonds, vol. 16, file 3, Trudeau file, n.d. (2/2).

72 "The Smear Pamphlets," editorial, *Lethbridge Herald*, June 24, 1968.

73 Ron Haggart, "Martin Office Mail List Aided Smear: Trudeau Men," *Toronto Daily Star*, 3 April 1968, cited in Thirstan Falconer, "Governing the 'Government Party': Liberal Party of Canada Leadership Conventions of 1948, 1958 and 1968" (MA thesis, University of Waterloo, 2012), 82. Trudeau's backers blamed Paul Martin's campaign for its distribution, but it denied any involvement.

74 LAC, R5727-2-5-E, Liberal Party of Canada fonds, vol. 1084, file: Communications, hate/smear campaign, "Candid Comment" by Bob Thompson, MP, "Pierre Elliott Trudeau – No. 11." See also Stuebing, Marshall, and Oakes, *Trudeau: A Man for Tomorrow*, 90.

75 Frank Jones, "Trudeau Hits Back at 'Hate Literature' Linking Him to Reds," *Toronto Daily Star*, June 14, 1968.

76 Peter Regenstreif, "A Rural Row to Hoe," *Winnipeg Free Press*, May 31, 1968.

77 English, *Citizen of the World*, 466; McCall-Newman, *Grits*, 113-14. McCall-Newman believed the rumours started in English Canada and were later picked up in French Canada. In February, before Trudeau had even announced, there were anti-Trudeau cartoons in circulation. One "smearingly" connected Trudeau to abortion and homosexuality (Peacock, *Journey to Power*, 225).

78 Claude Henault, "An Anti-Trudeau Propaganda War Turns Vicious," *Montreal Gazette,* June 15, 1968. See also Frank Howard, "Right-Wing Quebec Group Identifies PM with Communism, Perversion, Subversion," *Globe and Mail,* June 8, 1968.

79 LAC, R5727-2-5-E, Liberal Party of Canada fonds, vol. 1084, file: Communications, hate/smear campaign, Louis Even, "Elliott-Trudeau, A Pro-Soviet, Pro-Castro, Pro-Mao; Wants to Turn Canada into a Socialist Country Like China," *Vers Demain* 29, 5 (1968).

80 LAC, R5727-2-5-E, Liberal Party of Canada fonds, vol. 1084, file: Communications, hate/smear campaign, Memorandum, June 11, 1968.

81 LAC, R5727-2-5-E, Liberal Party of Canada fonds, vol. 1084, file: National Campaign Committee.

82 LAC, R5727-2-5-E, Liberal Party of Canada fonds, vol. 1084, file: Policy − Platform, "Strategy Notes − May 4, 1968," "Memo, Stanbury to Lalonde, June 4, 1968"; LAC, MG 32 C 5, Richard Stanbury fonds, vol. 13-1, file 1: Diary pp. 1-99 (+6 pp. unnumbered diary notes for May 1968), May 21, 1968.

83 LAC, R12069, Roméo LeBlanc fonds, file: Campagne electorale de 1968/Election Campaign 1968, April 24-June 18, and vol. 4, file 02-13, Trudeau–Montague [PEI]; John English, *Just Watch Me: The Life of Pierre Elliott Trudeau, 1968-2000* (Toronto: Knopf, 2009), 22.

84 A work on affect and TV in Canada by Marusya Bociurkiw maintains that Trudeau was gay, or, at least, bisexual. "Trudeau's frequently alleged bisexuality was an open secret," Bociurkiw writes. His "predilection for gay icons such as Barbra Streisand" helped "queer his image." "The newspapers coyly played along," she continues. "Endless photos of Trudeau in capes and femmy hats were printed and reprinted." Since nations are masculine constructions, Bociurkiw maintains, Canada's inability to be a real nation makes it queer. Thus Trudeau's rise to power signified "the becoming-queer of the national body; the becoming-national of the queer" (Bociurkiw, *Feeling Canadian: Television, Nationalism, and Affect* [Waterloo: Wilfrid Laurier University Press, 2011], 115). Trudeau's "queerness" is, however, the starting point for her analysis, which does not concern itself with proof of his sexual orientation.

85 Marcel Gingras, "Basses attaques contre M. Trudeau," *Le Droit,* June 17, 1968.

86 Sheila Gormely, "A Swinger with Oomph," *Toronto Telegram,* February 16, 1968.

87 Merle Shain, "Trudeau: His Own Man, but What's He Like?" *Chatelaine,* September 1968, 124.

88 "He Points to Joyce as Hostess Choice," *Vancouver Sun,* April 4, 1967.

89 *The Way It Is,* May 26, 1968. Blondes seemed to have additional currency in the sexiness department. Women were always judged in terms of their appearance, and were described by male reporters as blonde, striking, statuesque, and so on. See also Stuebing, Marshall, and Oakes, *Trudeau: A Man for Tomorrow,* 54.

90 "The Election: First Round to Trudeau," *Time* (Canadian edition), May 17, 1968, 14.

91 Newman, "FACTS and FICTIONS." Charles Lynch claimed that one of the results of the smear campaigns was that any criticism of Trudeau was suppressed (Norman DePoe, "Why the Knife-Wielders in the Ottawa Press Gallery Will Soon Start Carving Up Trudeau," *Maclean's,* October 1968, 3).

92 Charles Lynch, "Why I'm So Uneasy," Southam News Service, June 21, 1968, repr. in Butler and Carrier, *Trudeau Decade,* 38-39.

93 Christopher Young, "Turner in Action," *Ottawa Citizen,* March 16, 1968.

94 In his analysis of the centennial celebrations, Gary Miedema describes Canadian elites as pushing an agenda more progressive than the values of the general Canadian populace. He argues that "the ability of political and cultural elites to harness the reformist optimism of the 1960s must be recognized as one of the most important features of that decade" (Gary R. Miedema, *For Canada's Sake: Public Religion, Centennial Celebrations, and the*

Re-making of Canada in the 1960s [Montreal: McGill-Queen's University Press, 2005], 205). At Expo such leadership divided traditional and progressive religious groups in much the same way as Trudeaumania would later split the electorate (ibid., 199).

CHAPTER 7: REEL TO REAL I

1   The part played by the kissing females in this process is worthy of note. They were performing a gender role, certainly, but to what end? Their gendered performance got them in the news, and that exposure made them a force in the campaign. By leveraging stereotypes about women they gained power that they could then use to change those stereotypes.

2   Peter Newman, *The Distemper of Our Times: Canadian Politics in Transition: 1963-1968* (Toronto: McClelland and Stewart, 1968), 458.

3   "The Liberals," *Time* (Canadian edition), March 8, 1968, 10-11. *Time* printed "god-damned" as "g.d." The candidate's name was not mentioned.

4   CBC Archive Sales/Archives Radio-Canada, "Special – What Happened Here," *The Public Eye*, "Trudeau," March 26, 1968.

5   Edith Iglauer, "Profiles: Prime Minister/Premier Ministre," *New Yorker*, July 5, 1969, 52.

6   Quoted in Donald Peacock, *Journey to Power: The Story of a Canadian Election* (Toronto: Ryerson, 1968), 266.

7   Martin Sullivan, *Mandate '68: The Year of Pierre Trudeau* (Toronto: Doubleday, 1968), 312.

8   "Trudeau Accuses His Accuser," *Ottawa Journal*, February 27, 1968.

9   David Meren, *With Friends Like These: Entangled Nationalisms and the Canada-Quebec-France Triangle, 1944-1970* (Vancouver: UBC Press, 2012), 176-79.

10 Lubor Zink, "Trudeaumania Seems to be Fading on Parliament Hill," *Toronto Telegram*, March 4, 1968. The paper used the term in a headline just a month later (John Marshall, "A Wraparound Display of Trudeaumania," *Toronto Telegram*, April 6, 1968). The term popped up in the liberal-leaning *Toronto Daily Star* on May 4, two weeks into the general election campaign. It appeared in the *Vancouver Sun* on May 11. The *Globe and Mail* held off using it until May 19. *Le Devoir* avoided it, while in *La Presse* it appeared on May 27. The term also suited the journalists' self-image because it reinforced their professional positioning as detached observers of the passing scene, bemusedly chronicling the antics of the masses with knowing superiority, even though they had primed the public for exactly such a response.

11 "Hellyer Tops Trudeau in Metro Poll," *Toronto Telegram*, March 4, 1968.

12 Marian Bruce, "Low-Key Trudeau Steals the Show," *Calgary Herald*, March 11, 1968.

13 Myron Johnson, "A Majority of One," *Medicine Hat News*, March 13, 1968.

14 Peacock, *Journey to Power*, 258.

15 Newman, *Distemper of Our Times*, 456.

16 Frank Jones, "Timmins Gives Trudeau Biggest-Ever Turnout," *Toronto Daily Star*, March 25, 1968.

17 Robert Stanfield's aide Hugh Segal wrote to the editor objecting to the special treatment, saying that he'd "rather have a stodgy P.M. who can bend on policy than a gyrating P.M. who does not" ("Letters," *Saturday Night*, July 1968). Surprisingly, *Chatelaine* magazine, under the feminist editorship of Doris Anderson, had little to say about Trudeau or Trudeaumania from the fall of 1967 through to the summer of 1968. The Royal Commission on the Status of Women in Canada was appointed in the winter of 1967 and began its hearings in the spring of 1968, and *Chatelaine*'s political content focused on it.

18 Trudeau ran strongest among young Ontarians but far outdistanced his closest contenders in all regions of the country. See "A Man for Today," and Mordecai Richler, "Why We Need Him," *Star Weekly*, March 2, 1968; Walter Stewart, "Why Young Canada Has No Time

for the Old Guard," and Margaret Daly, "The Old Guard: Why One Young Writer Sees Them as Men for Yesterday," *Star Weekly*, March 9, 1968; "Intellect, Honesty and Guts," *Star Weekly*, March 16, 1968; and Margaret Daly, "A Realist, an Intellectual *and* a Man of Action," *Star Weekly*, March 23, 1968. A large ad for the March 16 issue featuring a photo of Trudeau ran earlier that week in the newspapers that carried the magazine.

19 Peacock, *Journey to Power*, 273.

20 *Le Devoir* was resolutely high-minded and concentrated on the issues rather than fluff like the kissing campaign. The exception that proved the rule was a piece featuring photographs of the three best-looking men in Canada as decided by the female listeners of Radio-Canada's *Place aux Femmes*. Trudeau placed third, after Quebec politician Marcel Masse and Quebec broadcaster Jacques Boulanger (*Le Devoir*, February 15, 1968, 11). *La Presse* eschewed photos of female Trudeau fans kissing him until after the Liberal leadership convention. It then ran some photos of Trudeau kissing or being kissed by attractive young women, but carefully balanced them with similar coverage of Robert Stanfield, Tommy Douglas, and Réal Caouette of the Ralliement des Créditistes, though in the last two cases the kisses were dutiful greetings by female party members trying to give their leaders the same attention Trudeau attracted spontaneously.

21 William Boyd, "In Rural Quebec, They Like Pierre," *Toronto Telegram*, February 16, 1968.

22 Peacock, *Journey to Power*, 257-58. Again, it should be kept in mind that this anecdote was told by a male reporter and circulated among a predominantly male media corps.

23 "He's at his best away from the howling mobs, at press conferences where he is transformed into a first-rate teacher who can turn tentative, vaguely articulated questions into something intelligent, reworking them so that each answer becomes a lucid lecture, a precis of the problem at hand, its ramifications, his policy on it, other possible solutions and the difficulties involved" (Peter C. Newman, "Even This Early It Looks Like a Liberal Sweep," *Toronto Daily Star*, May 25, 1968). See also Gary Oakes, "Trudeau's a Blah Speaker, a Marvellous Mingler," *Toronto Telegram*, May 18, 1968.

24 Library and Archives Canada (LAC), Susan Dexter fonds, CTV TV, W5, Sound, Trudeau, Pierre Elliott – Interview, March 29, 1968, consultation copy A1 2003-09-0008.

25 Sullivan, *Mandate '68*, 325.

26 Peter Newman, *Distemper*, 458.

27 Richard Dahrin, "The Media and the Rise of P.E. Trudeau," *Canadian Dimension* 5, 5 (1968): 6.

28 LAC, Canadian Broadcasting Corporation, Television: CBOT Two-Inch Video Inventory – Tapes on Deposit, *Twenty Million Questions*, "The Style is the Man Himself," September 9, 1968, consultation copy V1 8506-0104. Larry Zolf later wrote amusingly, and pointedly, on this aspect of Trudeaumania:

> What Trudeau wanted from Canadians was a commitment to his views based on conviction, not passion – a commitment derived from a careful reading of *Federalism and the French Canadians*. Rather than an emotional Beatleswoon response to his mere physical presence ... What the paparazzi never knew (and still don't) was that Trudeau never really enjoyed the charisma phase of his political career. The irrational aspects of it all went against the very grain of his rational, scholarly, one could almost say scholastic nature. The irrational aspects of Trudeaumania were too close to the kind of thoughtless quest-for-authority politics he had fought against in Duplessis' Quebec for so many years. (Zolf, *Dance of the Dialectic* [Toronto: James Lewis and Samuel, 1973], 35)

29 LAC, Canadian Broadcasting Corporation, Television: Kines from Parc, Toronto, *The Way It Is*, April 7, 1968, consultation copy V1 8402-0043.

30 Newman, *Distemper of Our Times*, 460.

31 "Trudeau – et de loin," *La Presse*, April 3, 1968.

32 Ian Macdonald, "Runaway Trudeau Victory Shapes Up at Convention," *Vancouver Province*, April 4, 1967.

33 Maurice Western, "Mr. Trudeau Reassures the Party," *Winnipeg Free Press*, April 8, 1968.

34 Richard Gwyn, *The Northern Magus: Pierre Trudeau and Canadians* (Toronto: McClelland and Stewart, 1980), 69.

35 *The Way It Is*, April 7, 1968.

36 "The Liberals: A Man Who Demands Risks," *Time* (Canadian edition), April 12, 1968, 10. The Trudeau campaign newsletter presented the results of a number of opinion surveys in which Trudeau trounced rival candidates, and reported that "the job of translating the public opinion polls into delegate votes is moving into high gear" (Victoria College Archives, University of Toronto, Keith Davey fonds, 36, Box 017 [15] Liberal Convention – 1968, "Pierre Elliott Trudeau – Ontario Committee – Campaign Report #1, March 1, 1968).

37 Pierre-C. O'Neil, "Conseils pratiques pour faire d'un P.E. Trudeau le chef du parti libéral," *Le Devoir*, April 27, 1968.

38 John English, *Citizen of the World: The Life of Pierre Elliott Trudeau* (Toronto: Knopf, 2006), 470; Peacock, *Journey to Power*, 295.

39 Christina Newman, "This Month – Ottawa Letter," *Saturday Night*, May 1968, 7. The previous quotes are from Frank Walker, editor of the *Montreal Star*. See also Peter Newman, *The Distemper of Our Times: Canadian Politics in Transition: 1963-1968* (Toronto: McClelland and Stewart, 1968), 461.

40 Stephen Clarkson and Christina McCall, *Trudeau and Our Times*, Vol. 1, *The Magnificent Obsession* (Toronto: McClelland and Stewart, 1990), 111.

41 Maurice Western, "The Trudeau of the Image Makers," *Winnipeg Free Press*, April 4, 1968; see also Patrick Watson's contribution in *Pierre: Colleagues and Friends Talk about the Trudeau They Knew*, ed. Nancy Southam (Toronto: McClelland and Stewart, 2005), 107.

42 As the convention planning document put it, "They have been chosen because they are very good looking, bright, well-educated, bilingual, courteous and charming. We will have 30 girls and 20 boys of this calibre, recruited in Toronto, Ottawa and Montreal" (Clara Thomas Archives and Special Collections, York University, Donald Stovel Macdonald fonds, 2012-010, box 009, file: Liberal Party Convention Planning – 1968 2012-010/009 [2], Confidential: Report on Convention Planning). See also Rose-Anne Giroux, "La politique passe par la mini-jupe," *La Presse*, April 5, 1968. Canadian Press circulated a photo of the Pierrettes that appeared in newspapers across the country. See, for example, "Color Liberally Splashed on City," *Ottawa Citizen*, April 3, 1968. In another context these young women were referred to as the Trudeau Troupe (see Chapter 6, n42). The parallels to Expo 67 hostesses were striking, especially the criteria for selection (Aurora Wallace, "Girl Watching at Expo 67," in *Expo 67: Not Just a Souvenir*, ed. Rhona Richman Kenneally and Johanne Sloan, [Toronto: University of Toronto Press, 2010], 110-12).

43 Alison Gordon, "Inventing Trudeaumania Many Springs Ago," *Ottawa Citizen*, April 30, 1988. See also Alison Gordon, "Into Power," in *Trudeau Albums*, ed. Karen Alliston, Rich Archbold, Jennifer Glossop, Alison Maclean, and Ivon Owen (Toronto: Penguin Studio, 2000), 38-43.

44 Alison Gordon, "Inventing Trudeaumania Many Springs Ago."

45 "Would Sell Air Canada, Other Crown Companies If Elected, Winters Says," *Globe and Mail*, April 6, 1968.

46 Quoted in John Saywell, ed., *Canadian Annual Review for 1968* (Toronto: University of Toronto Press, 1969), 27, 68.

47 Dahrin, "The Media and the Rise," 6.

48 Mabel Richards, "Facts and Fancies," Quesnel (BC) Cariboo Observer, April 11, 1968.

49 Norman DePoe, "The New Politics – 1: Suddenly, Everybody's Anxious to Belong to a Party – But How Long before the Fever Cools Down?" Maclean's, July 1968, 1.

50 Peter Newman, Distemper, 458-59. See also LAC, CTV Television Network, The Liberal Leadership Convention, April 6, 1968, consultation copies V1 8302-0006, V1 2004-03-0055.

51 Saywell, Canadian Annual Review, 27. Lloyd Henderson hasn't been included in this account. Considered a nuisance candidate, he polled zero votes on the first ballot.

52 Sullivan, Mandate '68, 353.

53 Christina Newman, "This Month – Ottawa Letter," Saturday Night, May 1968, 9. Newman described the Trudeau back rooms: "Their campaign headquarters were not a slap-happy crew of star-gazers but a highly organized group caught up in 'critical flow charts,' computer analyses of delegate preferences and a spy system that had infiltrated observers into other candidates' camps." See also LAC, Canadian Broadcasting Corporation, Television: Kines from Parc, Toronto, The Way It Is, June 16, 1968, consultation copy V1 8402-0047.

54 Paul Fox, "The Liberals Choose Trudeau – Pragmatism at Work," Canadian Forum, May 1968.

55 "On to Trudeau's 'Just Society,'" editorial, Ottawa Citizen, April 8, 1968; "Trudeau's Victory," Brandon (MB) Sun, April 8, 1968; "The New Man," Whitehorse (YT) Star, April 8, 1968. All of these references are reprinted in The Trudeau Decade, ed. Rick Butler and Jean-Guy Carrier (Toronto: Doubleday, 1979), 15-22.

56 Pierre-C. O'Neil, "Pierre Trudeau a été 'vu' à Fort Lauderdale (Floride)," Le Devoir, April 16, 1968; Blair Fraser, "Backstage in Ottawa: Why Political Strategists Could Hardly Care Less about the 'Under-25' Vote," Maclean's, June 1968.

57 "... des partisans politiques à Radio-Canada et à CTV," La Presse, April 8, 1968

58 Frank Underhill, "The WAY We Choose Is Out of Date," Toronto Daily Star, March 2, 1968.

59 Dahrin, "The Media and the Rise," 6.

60 Maurice Western, "The Trudeau of the Image Makers," Winnipeg Free Press, April 4, 1968. "The producer," Nielsen observed, "is forced to apply the same standard – audience acceptance – to both factual and fictional material. He is apt, therefore, to soup up our public life and to supply drama at the expense of clarity." He added, "Television not only made Trudeau the people's choice at the Liberals' April convention; it made him the choice of the party Establishment ... TV made his candidacy irresistibly attractive" (Nielsen, "Let's See Our Politicians at Work," Maclean's, September 1968).

61 For another example of this phenomenon, see LAC, Canadian Broadcasting Corporation, Television: Kines from Parc, Toronto, The Way It Is, November 3, 1968, consultation copy V1 8402-0052.

62 "Le 'mythe Trudeau,'" La Presse, April 18, 1968. Translated by author. Trudeau's papers for this period include correspondence that provides another indication of Canadians' excitement about his rise to power and the interest it generated across the country. There are missives from self-important experts with political advice, people who had met him once and now presumed close friendship, students expressing solidarity as a lark, elderly ladies who said they were praying for him, job-seekers, and cranks enclosing self-published pamphlets on topics ranging from the economy to metaphysics. The letters and telegrams include cryptic warnings about the Bolshevik menace, invitations to speak at local book clubs, samples of poetry and song, and advice on cabinet appointments. (LAC, Pierre Elliott Trudeau fonds, R11629-0-8-E, Series 7, Vol 734, files: General – Miscellaneous – Before April 22, 1968 – Not indexed – [Parts A-W]).

CHAPTER 8: THE JUST SOCIETY, PARTICIPATORY DEMOCRACY, AND OTHER PLATFORMITIES

1 "Even before the new prime minister was chosen a group of senior Liberals had prepared a set of 'position papers' making the case for an immediate election," wrote Blair Fraser (Fraser, "Backstage in Ottawa: Can Pierre Trudeau Resist the Pressures for an Early Election – Or Will He Even Want To?" *Maclean's*, May 1968, 2). There were pros and cons on both sides. An early election call could capitalize on the convention publicity. And, provided the Liberals were victorious, an election would outflank Premier Daniel Johnson in Quebec by giving Trudeau a mandate to deal with him. If Johnson called an election first, the shoe would be on the other foot. The party bagmen were, however, against an immediate election because it would be difficult to raise money for it so soon after the convention (Library and Archives Canada [LAC], MG 32 C 5, Richard Stanbury fonds, vol. 13, file 1: Diary, May 1968). When Quebec followed up on the Gabon affair by sending Education Minister Jean-Guy Cardinal to Paris on April 19 to attend a conference to which Canada had not been invited but at which the other participants were all sovereign states, Trudeau saw this as an issue that he could fight an election over (John Saywell, ed., *Canadian Annual Review for 1968* [Toronto: University of Toronto Press, 1969], 31-32; John English, *Just Watch Me: The Life of Pierre Elliott Trudeau, 1968-2000* [Toronto: Knopf, 2009], 23).

2 LAC, MG 32 C 5, Richard Stanbury fonds, vol. 13-1, file 1: Diary pp. 1-99 (+6 pp. unnumbered diary notes for May 1968), Sunday, April 21, 1968; LAC, R5727-2-5-E, Liberal Party of Canada fonds, vol. 1119, file: A Quick Telephone Survey of the Political Climate in Canada – Research Services Ltd., April 1968.

3 LAC, MG 32 C 5, Richard Stanbury fonds, vol. 13-1 [file 1]: Diary pp. 1-99 (+6 pp. unnumbered diary notes for May 1968), Monday, April 22, 1968.

4 Saywell, *Canadian Annual Review*, 32.

5 "The Election: Into the Finals," *Time* (Canadian edition), May 3, 1968, 11.

6 "Trudeau Master of Osculation: Diefenbaker," *Globe and Mail*, April 25, 1968.

7 "The Election: Into the Finals," *Time* (Canadian edition), May 3, 1968, 11.

8 CBC Digital Archives, "Pierre Trudeau: 'Canada must be a just society,'" http://www.cbc.ca/archives/entry/pierre-trudeau-canada-must-be-a-just-society; originally broadcast as "The Style Is the Man Himself," September 9, 1968. Interestingly, Eric Kierans had talked in his nomination speech of the "gentle society," and Allan MacEachen of the "compassionate society." Such phrases had contemporary currency (LAC, Pierre Elliott Trudeau fonds, R11629-0-8-E, films and broadcasts, Accession number 1976-0067, CJCB, Sydney, Nova Scotia, Donovan, Neil – Interview [interviewer Ann Terry], April 13, 1968, consultation copy AI 2005-01-0021).

9 Dennis P. Hollinger, *Choosing the Good: Christian Ethics in a Complex World* (Grand Rapids, MI: Baker Books, 2002), 166.

10 John English, *Citizen of the World: The Life of Pierre Elliott Trudeau* (Toronto: Knopf, 2006), 329. Max and Monique Nemni maintain that Trudeau took his Just Society notions from his experience in England in 1948, a time when the Labour government had performed miracles, achieving high employment despite demobilization, and introducing medicare, legal aid, workers' compensation, retirement pensions, unemployment benefits, and maternity leave. It had also nationalized resource industries and the Bank of England (Nemni and Nemni, *Trudeau Transformed: The Shaping of a Statesman, 1944-1965* [Toronto: McClelland and Stewart, 2011], 87).

11 Bryan Palmer, *Canada's 1960s: The Ironies of Identity in a Rebellious Era* (Toronto: University of Toronto Press, 2009), 171. See also George Bain, "Canada Has a Case of Trudeaumania,"

New York Times, June 16, 1968, in which Bain quotes at length his interview with Trudeau on the Just Society that appeared in Bain, "A Conversation with the Prime Minister (II)," *Globe and Mail*, May 22, 1968.

12 Richard Gwyn quotes from Trudeau's *Memoirs* to make this point (John English, Richard Gwyn, and P. Whitney Lackenbauer, eds., *The Hidden Pierre Trudeau* [Ottawa: Novalis, 2004], 10).

13 Bain, "Conversation." See also Donald Peacock, *Journey to Power: The Story of a Canadian Election* (Toronto: Ryerson, 1968), 334. John English characterizes the Just Society as follows: "Its contours were thinly sketched and its foundations, apart from a commitment to the rights of individuals to make their own decisions, were barely visible" (English, *Just Watch Me*, 4). See also Piergiorgio Mazzachio, "Editorial: The Lame Policies of a 'Just Society,'" *Le Devoir*, October 26, 1968, repr. in Rick Butler and Jean-Guy Carrier, eds., *The Trudeau Decade* (Toronto: Doubleday, 1979), 74; LAC, Pierre Elliott Trudeau fonds, R11629-0-8-E, Series 13, Vol. 25, file: Press Conferences/Conférences de presse, May 10–July 31, 1968, "Transcript of the Prime Minister's Press Conference," May 23, 1968.

Although this discussion focuses on what the Just Society meant in 1968, the concept lived on long after. The Charter of Rights and Freedoms adopted with patriation of the constitution in 1982 would be interpreted as the fulfillment of Trudeau's Just Society slogan. In 1968, however, a charter did not have pride of place in the policy platform or the campaign.

In her profile of Trudeau, published a year later, Edith Iglauer quoted him as follows:

> Justice is the problem – the one about which I have been concerned the most, stated the most, thought the most. I guess most of the authors I've read crystallize my particular idea of virtue – that justice is a cornerstone of the society I live in, the basis of all human relations in the family or the state. I was not dreaming the Just Society up as a catchword or a cliché ... To me, it summed up the total of the relationships in a society of free men. The Just Society is the kind of society freedom would establish. Looking ahead, I don't think a state can say "Here's a state, a package imposed on you. A Just Society is one toward which every citizen must work, and the first condition of such a society is that of respecting the liberty of individuals ... I've always dreamt of a society where each person should be able to fulfill himself to the extent of his capabilities as a human being, a society where inhibitions to equality would be eradicated. This means providing individual freedom, and equality of opportunity, health, and education, and I conceive of politics as a series of decisions to create this society. (Iglauer, "Profiles: Prime Minister/ Premier Ministre," *New Yorker*, July 5, 1969, 53-54, 60)

Much later, Iglauer would add, "The concept of a Just Society was never merely a convenient phrase; it was the inspiration for Trudeau's deepest feelings. He believed that the ever-widening gulf between rich and poor at home and in undeveloped countries should be reduced. He thought it was government's responsibility to provide equal status, equal opportunity, and fair treatment for all" (Iglauer, "Pierre Trudeau: Champion of a Just Society," *Americas* 53, 1 (2001): 57. See also Thomas S. Axworthy and Pierre Elliott Trudeau, eds., *Towards a Just Society* (Markham, ON: Viking, 1990), 4-5, 357, 360; Pierre Elliott Trudeau, *Conversations with Canadians* (Toronto: University of Toronto Press, 1972).

14 The Just Society was, in other words, another way of expressing twentieth-century liberalism's concern for equality of opportunity. This was garden-variety twentieth-century liberalism, in which the state intervened in the market with social programs designed to offset disadvantages of social condition or misadventure that might disadvantage individuals through no fault of their own.

15 Bain, "Conversation." Elsewhere Trudeau said, "We must strike at the root of economic disparity, putting behind us the easy subsidized solutions of the past. It is our intention … to further the process whereby people in the less affluent regions will develop their own economic affairs in order to provide a firm basis for future prosperity" (Saywell, *Canadian Annual Review*, 46).

16 LAC, R5727-2-5-E, Liberal Party of Canada fonds, vol. 1056, file: Candidates' Handbook Supplement, Election '68.

17 LAC, R5727-2-5-E, Liberal Party of Canada fonds, vol. 1056, file: "Platform Papers–Election 1968: 'The Just Society,' 'Trudeau,' 'A United Canada,' etc. See also Official Statement by the Prime Minister, "The Just Society," June 10, 1968, in *The Essential Trudeau*, ed. Ron Graham (Toronto: McClelland and Stewart, 1998), 16-20. *Le Devoir* and *La Presse* both published this paper. See Pierre Elliott Trudeau, "La juste société," *Le Devoir*, June 13, 1968. The Native rights movement was just getting under way in 1960s Canada, and, as suggested here, the Liberals were approaching it in the same way as they approached Quebec, i.e., equal rights for all rather than collective rights for minorities. This approach would prove controversial, but that is another story; in 1968 the rights of Indigenous peoples did not figure prominently in the federal election campaign. For background see Palmer, *Canada's 1960s*, 388-408.

18 Peacock, *Journey to Power*, 334-38.

19 LAC, R5727-2-5-E, Liberal Party of Canada fonds, vol. 1056, file: Speaker's Handbook.

20 LAC, R5727-2-5-E, Liberal Party of Canada fonds, vol. 1056, file: Policy – Platform, "Strategy Notes – May 4, 1968."

21 Donald Smiley, "Political Images," *Canadian Forum*, July 1968, 75.

22 Trudeau seemed to think that the costs of these new programs would have to be gauged and absorbed before any new social programs could be afforded, which was conventional wisdom at the time ("The Liberals: A Man Who Demands Risks," *Time* [Canadian edition], April 12, 1968), 13.

23 Roy Shields, "'No Contest,' as Trudeau Tops Berton," *Toronto Daily Star*, March 21, 1968.

24 Ramsay Cook claimed that Trudeau soon regretted having introduced the Just Society slogan because it became "his own albatross" (Cook, *The Maple Leaf Forever: Essays on Nationalism and Politics in Canada* [Toronto: Macmillan, 1971], 27). One of the redeeming features of the Just Society slogan was that it tapped into a rich vein of contemporary popular culture. The legal system was regularly assailed by sixties activists, making "justice" a contemporary catchphrase. The figure of the judge was commonly ridiculed as a pompous old buffoon who personified all the hypocrisy, arrogance, and incompetence of the establishment. Early in 1968, *Rowan and Martin's Laugh-In*, the popular mod comedy TV show, ran a routine called "Here Come de Judge" in which an African American (sometimes Sammy Davis Jr.) played a ridiculous rhyming, jive-talking judge figure. It became wildly popular. The phrase was on hipsters' lips that spring, and songs with that title were climbing the hit parade. Later that year General Motors would call a version of its 1969 Pontiac GTO muscle car "The Judge." Seemingly anything to do with justice had pop currency.

25 "The platform has a good potential, but is not very specific," Senator Stanbury noted, attributing its failings to "the Prime Minister's belief that specific promises must not be made unless they can be kept, and a further warning that no promises can be kept if they involve spending money unless they fall into the classification to correct regional disparities or poverty" (LAC, MG 32 C 5, Richard Stanbury fonds, vol. 13-1, file 1: Diary pp. 1-99 [+6 pp. unnumbered diary notes for May 1968], Tuesday, May 21, 1968).

26 "Canada's Next Prime Minister, Pierre Elliott Trudeau," *New York Times*, April 8, 1968.

27 LAC, Susan Dexter fonds, CTV TV, W5, Sound, Trudeau, Pierre Elliott – Interview, March 29, 1968, consultation copy AI 2003-09-0008.

28 Gary Oakes, "Trudeau Attacks Gordon's Policy," *Toronto Telegram*, February 16, 1968.

29 "Liberals: Man Who Demands Risks," *Time* (Canadian edition), April 12, 1968, p. 13.

30 W5, Trudeau, Pierre Elliott – Interview, March 29, 1968.

31 Stan McDowell, "The Man from Quebec," *Winnipeg Free Press*, February 15, 1968.

32 Larry Zolf, *Dance of the Dialectic* (Toronto: James Lewis and Samuel, 1973), 35.

33 Quoted in Martin Sullivan, *Mandate '68: The Year of Pierre Trudeau* (Toronto: Doubleday, 1968), 302. Trudeau's biographer, John English, argues that "Trudeau's rise to national political power was fundamentally a response, first by the Liberal Party and then by many Canadians, to Quebec's new challenge to Confederation (English, *Just Watch Me*, 8).

34 Ken Dewar, "Pierre Elliott Trudeau and the Liberal Party: Continuity and Change," *Canadian Dimension* 5, 5 [June-July 1968]: 7). On the conservative or liberal question, Ron Graham argues, "All his talk of the individual, decentralized power, and the end of the nation-state may have come from the left in Quebec in the 1950s, but because of the differences in Canada's two political cultures, it certainly sounded as if it were coming from the right in English Canada in the 1960s." Graham sees Trudeau as a nineteenth- rather than a twentieth-century liberal. However, he notes that a paramount principle for Trudeau was to "create counterweights." In this regard, the state's role in creating a modicum of equality of opportunity was such a counterweight. Moreover, "he wasn't afraid to have the state intervene when necessary for good liberal reasons, such as providing the social conditions that would give weak individuals as much chance as strong ones to fulfil themselves" (Graham, *One-Eyed Kings: Promise and Illusion in Canadian Politics* [Toronto: Collins, 1986], 35-38).

35 Paul Fox, "Trudeau: The Eternal Nay Is Not Enough," *Toronto Daily Star*, March 9, 1968. Fox, a University of Toronto political science professor, made this comment, and the comment that heads this chapter, in a review of *Federalism and the French Canadians*. He also remarked, "Well bravo, Edmund Burke! Whether or not Trudeau likes it and despite the fact he considers it a silly exercise, Quebec is on fire with nationalism and passionately involved, like a new nation, with fulfilling itself" (ibid.).

36 Quoted in Peacock, *Journey to Power*, 293.

37 Brian Shaw, ed., *The Gospel According to Saint Pierre* (Richmond Hill, ON: Simon and Schuster, 1969), 163; Saywell, *Canadian Annual Review*, 51. Interestingly, this orientation was yet another way in which Trudeau fit the mould of the archetypal hero. "There is one thing nearly all the versions of the myth share," David Waters noted in the *Montreal Gazette*. "They are never reactionary. They do not look back to preserve, so much as they symbolize a visionary hope of a way through a critical phase" (Waters, "Mythology, Mr. Trudeau, and ... Us," *Montreal Gazette*, April 20, 1968).

38 For a discussion of the "primacy of politics" as an indicator of a social democratic disposition, see Kenneth Dewar, "The Social Democracy Question," ActiveHistory.ca, http://activehistory.ca/papers/the-social-democracy-question.

39 Pierre Elliott Trudeau, "Toward a Constitutional Bill of Rights," *Canadian Forum*, October 1967, 158. This article was an excerpt from the speech Trudeau delivered to the Canadian Bar Association on September 4, 1967. Herein lay his liberal rejoinder to Quebec's claims for special status: a guarantee of individual freedoms that would become the fundamental principle of Canadian federalism. Herein too lay a paradox that would endure: the liberal individualism Trudeau advanced to counter Quebec nationalism would be embraced as a hallmark of Canadian identity and a bulwark of Canadian nationalism. Interestingly, this was yet another way in which Trudeau fit the messiah myth. Joseph Campbell had written that "the great deed of the supreme hero is to come to the knowledge of ... unity in multiplicity and then to make it known" (Campbell, *The Hero with a Thousand Faces*, 2nd ed. [Princeton, NJ: Princeton University Press, 1968; first published 1949], 37, 40).

40 *Saturday Night* editor and Trudeau-booster Arthur Edinborough wrote, "Surely [Canada] is to grow together as a nation dedicated to freedom, to the rule of law and to the provision of opportunity to every member of our society" (Edinborough, "The Idea of Canada," *Saturday Night*, April 1968, 27). See José Igartua, *The Other Quiet Revolution* (Vancouver: UBC Press, 2006), 12-15, 223, for a discussion of the idea of British liberty and how it transformed into civic nationalism in the 1960s. The way in which the contemporary political elite went about reforming Canada in a British manner, even as it ostensibly abandoned Canada's British identity, is described in depth in C.P. Champion, *The Strange Demise of British Canada* (Montreal: McGill-Queen's University Press, 2010).

41 In an article originally published in *Cité Libre* in April 1962 and reprinted in *Federalism and the French Canadians*, Trudeau wrote:

> The die is cast in Canada; there are two ethnic and linguistic groups; each is too strong and too deeply rooted in the past, too firmly bound to a mother culture, to be able to swamp the other. But if the two will collaborate inside a truly pluralistic state, Canada could become the envied seat of a form of federalism that belongs to to-morrow's world. Better than the American melting pot, Canada could offer an example ... to all those ... who must discover how to govern their polyethnic populations with proper regard for justice and liberty. (Pierre-Elliott Trudeau, "The New Treason of the Intellectuals," in *Federalism and the French Canadians* [Toronto: Macmillan, 1968], 178-79)

This passage was quoted in the Trudeau leadership campaign publicity materials (Clara Thomas Archives and Special Collections, York University, Donald Stovel Macdonald fonds, 2012-010, box 009, file: Trudeau leadership campaign – 1968). See also Shaw, *Gospel According to Saint Pierre*, 44. Pearson, perhaps reflecting Trudeau's influence, had made this point in a speech the day after announcing his retirement (Peacock, *Journey to Power*, 122-23). It was also expressed in the work of centennial planners; see Gary R. Miedema, *For Canada's Sake: Public Religion, Centennial Celebrations, and the Re-making of Canada in the 1960s* (Montreal: McGill-Queen's University Press, 2005), 69.

42 Terrence E. Cook and Patrick M. Morgan, eds., *Participatory Democracy* (San Francisco: Canfield Press, 1971), 21. See also Richard Flacks, "On the Uses of Participatory Democracy," *Dissent* 13 (November 1966): 701-8, and Colin Crouch, "The Chiliastic Urge," *Survey* 69 (October 1968): 57.

43 Sean Mills, *The Empire Within*, 173.

44 Quoted in Saywell, *Canadian Annual Review*, 23.

45 Miedema, *For Canada's Sake*, 47, 70–71.

46 For a discussion of the problems of translating participatory democracy from the local to the national scale, see C.B. Macpherson, *The Life and Times of Liberal Democracy* (Oxford: Oxford University Press, 1977), 94-98.

47 Quoted in Peter Newman, *The Distemper of Our Times: Canadian Politics in Transition: 1963-1968* (Toronto: McClelland and Stewart, 1968), 69.

48 "Pourquoi pas? C'est le printemps," *La Presse*, April 18, 1968.

49 Germain Dion, "Le style Trudeau," *Le Droit*, April 22, 1968.

50 See the following articles in the *Vancouver Sun*: "Pierre, Blond, Kiss in Hospital," April 17, 1968; "Kissing Advice," May 6, 1968; "An Autograph and a Kiss," May 11, 1968, and a front-page photo of Trudeau kissing an eighteen-year-old, captioned "Trudeau Trademark," on the same date.

51 LAC, R5727-2-5-E, Liberal Party of Canada fonds, vol. 1056, file: Election Campaign – April – 1968; Public Relations – Miscellaneous Material, "Profile of the Hon. Pierre Elliott Trudeau, Leader of the Liberal Party." The Liberal brain trust took seriously the idea that

the mass media offered a means of fulfilling participatory democracy in modern times. Arrangements were made for Trudeau insiders to meet with Marshall McLuhan to discuss such matters in the fall of 1968 (LAC, Pierre Elliott Trudeau fonds, R11629-0-8-E, Series 7, Vol. 737, file: 319 to 391.843, Coded 1968-1969, Backlog - Prior to 15 September 1969, 1968-1969).

52 LAC, R5727-2-5-E, Liberal Party of Canada fonds, vol. 1056, file: Election Campaign 1968 Radio + TV Time [Copies] - Public Relations, "Memorandum from Ian Howard to Allan O'Brien, April 23, 1968, Re: The Role of the Public Relations Department in a General Election."

53 LAC, R5727-2-5-E, Liberal Party of Canada fonds, vol. 1056, file: Election Campaign - 1968 Public Relations Ian Howard - May, Ian Howard to Betty Trainor, May 20, 1968.

54 Norman DePoe, "The New Politics - 1: Suddenly, Everybody's Anxious to Belong to a Party - But How Long before the Fever Cools Down?" *Maclean's*, July 1968.

55 Ibid.

56 "The Election: Political Spring," *Time* (Canadian edition), May 17, 1968, 13; Saywell, *Canadian Annual Review*, 40.

57 Norman DePoe, "Why the Knife-Wielders in the Ottawa Press Gallery Will Soon Start Carving Up Trudeau," *Maclean's*, October 1968, 3.

58 Peter C. Newman, "Canada Is in a Ferment, Digging for Its Soul...," *Toronto Daily Star*, June 1, 1968.

59 "Honey Credits Trudeau with Arousing Interest in Canadian Politics," *Canadian Statesman*, May 15, 1968.

60 LAC, R5727-2-5-E, Liberal Party of Canada fonds, vol. 1084, file: Policy - Platform, "Strategy Notes - May 4, 1968."

61 Peacock, *Journey to Power*, 257.

62 LAC, R5727-2-5-E, Liberal Party of Canada fonds, vol. 1119, file: A Quick Telephone Survey of the Political Climate in Canada - Research Services Ltd., April 1968.

63 Quoted in Joe McGinnis, *The Selling of the President, 1968* (New York: Trident Press, 1969).

64 Paul King, "King of Postermania," *Globe and Mail*, May 29, 1968.

65 Ramsay Cook, *The Teeth of Time: Remembering Pierre Elliott Trudeau* (Montreal: McGill-Queen's University Press, 2006), 63.

66 As a standard of comparison for this success, it should be noted that when René Lévesque published his separatist tract, *An Option for Quebec*, in late January, it sold fifty thousand copies in the first three weeks following its release (Michel Roy, "'Option-Quebec' paraitra a Paris et a Toronto," *Le Devoir*, February 2, 1968).

67 Gary Lautens, "Trudeau: Do the Clothes Make the Prime Minister?" *Toronto Daily Star*, March 22, 1968.

68 Gilbert D. Moore, "New Look North of the Border: Close Up - Pierre Trudeau, Canada's Next P.M.," *Life*, April 20, 1968, in LAC, MG 31 D 156, Marshall McLuhan fonds, vol. 90, file 17: Trudeau - clippings, n.d., 1968, 1969.

69 Marie Moreau, "Canadian Designer Plans 'Trudeau Look' Show," *Toronto Daily Star*, May 16, 1968. See also Marie Moreau, "Dressed-up Casuals - The Trudeau Look," *Toronto Daily Star*, March 14, 1968.

70 CBC Archive Sales/Archives Radio-Canada, PET Shop [Winnipeg], May 25, 1968; LAC, R1300-77, e004413880, paper dress from Pierre Trudeau's 1968 Liberal leadership campaign. Political paper dresses were popular south of the border that year as well, with versions produced both for Richard Nixon and Bobby Kennedy. There was also a Trudeau dress made from a cotton fabric with his face printed on it in a repeated pattern (see "Trudeau Campaign Dress," *Quebec Chronicle-Telegraph*, June 8, 1968). The Progressive Conservatives countered with dresses of their own. However, they didn't have Stanfield's

image on them. Instead a sash proclaiming "I'm for BOB" or some such message was worn over the dress.

71 Eric Dennis, "Postermania: Bob, Pierre Pin-Up Boys," *Halifax Chronicle-Herald*, May 31, 1968.

72 "Pickets Demand Kresge's Sell NDP Posters," *Globe and Mail*, June 4, 1968; John Kelsey, "Kresge's Capitulates, Removes PM Posters," *Globe and Mail*, June 5, 1968.

73 Marshall McLuhan clipped one such photo for his Trudeau file (LAC, MG 31 D 156, Marshall McLuhan fonds, vol. 39, file 48, Trudeau, Pierre – notes, clippings).

74 "Go Go Trudeau Record Soaring on the Hit Parade," *Toronto Telegram*, May 3, 1968. See also "Pas de 'Go Go Trudeau' à R.-Canada," *La Presse*, May 18, 1968; "The Election: Political Spring," *Time* (Canadian edition), May 17, 1968, 13.

75 LAC, R5727-2-5-E, Liberal Party of Canada fonds, vol. 1056, file: National Campaign Committee – General Election 1968, May-June 1968, Campaign Minutes Policy Committee Meeting: May 9, 1968. The original document misspells "publicly" as "publicity." The images of other leaders had embodied values that were highly valued at the time. In the era of postwar consensus, for example, Canadians had elected Louis St. Laurent, whose temperament nicely fit the times. It made sense that the sixties would give rise to a Trudeau. Richard Gwyn observes that John A. Macdonald, Wilfrid Laurier, and John Diefenbaker were charismatic, and suggests that personality politics may provide a substitute for the lack of a political centre or central political issues in Canada (Gwyn, *The Northern Magus: Pierre Trudeau and Canadians* [Toronto: McClelland and Stewart, 1980], 19).

76 Harry Crowe and Douglas Fisher, "The Swing Is to a Swinging PM," *Toronto Telegram*, March 16, 1968.

77 LAC, Canadian Broadcasting Corporation, Television: Kines from Parc, Toronto, *The Way It Is*, June 16, 1968, consultation copy VI 8402-0047; Paul King, "King of Postermania," *Globe and Mail*, May 27, 1968; Eric Dennis, "Postermania."

78 Kenneth McNaught, *Saturday Night*, August 1968, 7. As Jeremy Black has noted, "the cult of personality, and the associated sense of historical mission, was very pronounced in the totalitarian regimes" (Black, *Using History* [London: Hodder Arnold, 2005], 70).

79 See Lawrence J. Friedman, *The Lives of Erich Fromm: Love's Prophet* (New York: Columbia University Press, 2013), 97-118, 156-83; Mark Kurlansky, *1968: The Year That Rocked the World* (New York: Ballantyne, 1964), 108-9.

80 "Intellect, Honesty, and Guts," *Star Weekly*, March 16, 1968.

81 Pierre Elliott Trudeau, *Federalism and the French Canadians* (Toronto: Macmillan, 1968), xxii.

82 Dusty Vineberg, "Just Call It a Fantastic Weekend," newspaper clipping [*Montreal Star*], n.d. [probably the week of April 7, 1968], in LAC, MG 31 D 112, Norman DePoe fonds, vol. 6, file 1: Liberal Leadership Convention 1968 – Brochures, clippings.

83 Douglas Stuebing, John R. Marshall, and Gary Oakes, *Trudeau: A Man for Tomorrow* (Toronto: Clarke Irwin, 1968), 51.

84 Donovan, Neil – Interview, April 13, 1968.

85 "The Rights of Man," editorial, *Montreal Star*, June 22, 1968, repr. in Butler and Carrier, *Trudeau Decade*, 40. Harry Crowe and Douglas Fisher also thought the Trudeau image offered this promise:

> It is not merely a revolt against the traditional style of politics in Canada, it is a revolt against politics itself. And even more than being rescued from politics, an increasing percentage of our people wish to be rescued from themselves ... If they have jobs, families, obligations, they cannot physically run off to Yorkville. But they can do it symbolically in a leader who they create out of their dreams ... A bachelor, wealthy, a judo expert, immensely confident, literate, unconventional,

unabashed by great affairs of state, in fact, slightly bored by them – the great dream of male and female suburbia. And on top of all that he will tell the Quebeckers to go jump in Lac St. Jean. (Crowe and Fisher, "Swinging PM").

86 Waters, "Mythology, Mr. Trudeau."

87 As Ron Graham noted, Trudeau was "by temperament an individualist and an iconoclast" and a "loner" (Graham, *One-Eyed Kings*, 35-36).

88 Howard Brick, *The Age of Contradiction: American Thought and Culture in the 1960s* (New York: Twayne, 1998), 66.

89 Quoted in Peacock, *Journey to Power*, 293.

90 A confidential handbook given out to Liberal candidates described the campaign in terms of the nation's progress: "Our people have come alive with pride in themselves and their nation. We indeed accomplished near miracles with Expo and our other centennial celebrations. And we are determined to keep our nation together and working towards the goal of a just society, with a prosperous economy in a united Canada, contributing to a peaceful world" (quoted in Saywell, *Canadian Annual Review*, 47).

CHAPTER 9: REEL TO REAL II

1 Library and Archives Canada (LAC), MG 32 C 5, Richard Stanbury fonds, vol. 13-1 [file 1]: Diary pp. 1-99 (+6 pp. unnumbered diary notes for May 1968), Thursday, May 2, 1968. The Jim in question was Trudeau advisor Jim Davey.

2 Roy Shields, "Which Image ... Is Really US?" *Toronto Daily Star*, June 22, 1968. "In terms of the media, the 1968 election represents a historic divide," John English notes (English, *Just Watch Me: The Life of Pierre Elliott Trudeau, 1968-2000* [Toronto: Knopf, 2009], 18). See also David Taras, *The Newsmakers: The Media's Influence on Canadian Politics* (Scarborough, ON: Nelson, 1990), 156.

3 Carol Johnson, "The Politics of Affective Citizenship: From Blair to Obama," *Citizenship Studies* 14, 5 (2010): 495-509; Mabel Berezin, "Secure States: Towards a Political Sociology of Emotion," in "Sociological Review Monograph Series: Emotions and Sociology," ed. Jack Barbalet, special issue, *Sociological Review* 50, S2 (October 2002): 33-52.

4 R. Jeremy Wilson, "Media Coverage of Canadian Election Campaigns: Horse-Race Journalism and the Meta-campaign," *Journal of Canadian Studies*, 15, 4 (Winter 1980-81): 56-69, 62; LAC, R5727-2-5-E, Liberal Party of Canada fonds, vol. 1084, file: Policy – Platform "Strategy Notes – May 4, 1968."

5 LAC, R5727-2-5-E, Liberal Party of Canada fonds, vol. 1056, file: Advance Team Check List for Prime Minister's Tour – May 18-June 24, 1968 – and other related material; Canadian Press, "PM Likes Open Air," *Winnipeg Free Press*, May 25, 1968. Richard Stanbury noted, "The vision of him going through and meeting with the people, I am satisfied, is the right one for us to portray throughout the campaign, and it is the best possible media for him" (LAC, MG 32 C 5, Richard Stanbury fonds, vol. 13-1 [file 1]: Diary pp. 1-99 [+6 pp. unnumbered diary notes for May 1968], Saturday, May 18). "The idea, as it has been applied in Ontario, is to get to as many places as possible and be seen, or better still, touched, by as many people as possible" (John Dafoe, "How Pierre Power Stacks Up against Local Issues in Lakeshore," *Globe and Mail*, May 24, 1968). "The whole Liberal campaign has been cast with an eye to letting Trudeau be seen and touched by the greatest number" (George Bain, "Canada Has a Case of Trudeaumania," *New York Times*, June 16, 1968).

6 LAC, R12069, Roméo LeBlanc fonds, vol. 4, file 2: Campagne électorale de 1968/Election Campaign 1968, April 24-June 18, memorandum for the prime minister from Gordon Gibson, May 6, 1968.

7 Gilles Terroux, "On veut Béliveau, on veut Trudeau, c'est Lemaire qui devient la vedette," *La Presse*, April 29, 1968.

8 "Mob of Screaming Girls," *Toronto Daily Star*, May 18, 1968.

9 Joyce Fairburn, "Trudeau Big Draw at Edmonton Stop," *Winnipeg Free Press*, May 13, 1968. The crowd was estimated variously as three thousand and five thousand. "Giggling Youngsters Mob PM," *Edmonton Journal*, May 13, 1968.

10 LAC, MG 32 C 5, Richard Stanbury fonds, vol. 13-1 [file 1]: Diary pp. 1-99 (+6 pp. unnumbered diary notes for May 1968), Saturday, May 18, 1968.

11 Gerry Toner, "Teens Mob Trudeau at London Airport," *London Free Press*, May 21, 1968; Gerry Toner, "Trudeau Sails through Area," *London Free Press*, May 22, 1968.

12 Peter C. Newman, "Even This Early It Looks Like a Liberal Sweep," *Toronto Daily Star*, May 25, 1968.

13 A Union Nationale organizer explained, "So you think this Trudeaumania is real? Well, I'll tell you that it's no[t] ... It's all newspaper and television stuff. You do it with kids out of school with no vote" (Dominique Clift, "'Trudeaumania? Bah – It's All Done with Kids,' Says Union Nationale Man," *Toronto Daily Star*, May 30, 1968).

14 "Liberals Now Recruit Swingers for Trudeau," *Vancouver Sun*, May 28, 1968.

15 Anthony Westell, "Trudeau Discovers Niche with Final Swing in B.C.," *Globe and Mail*, June 18, 1968; Martin Sullivan, *Mandate '68: The Year of Pierre Trudeau* (Toronto: Doubleday, 1968), 399.

16 On May 22, Stanbury reported that they were "re-organizing the P.M.'s tour, on the basis of swing ridings. Found almost immediately that we were wasting at least half-a-day in Northern Quebec on safe Liberal seats" (LAC, MG 32 C 5, Richard Stanbury fonds, vol. 13-1, file 1: Diary pp. 1-99 [+6 pp. unnumbered diary notes for May 1968], May 22, 1968).

17 LAC, R5727-2-5-E, Liberal Party of Canada fonds, vol. 1056, file: Prime Minister's Election Tour 1968, "Prime Minister's Election Tour"; John Sawatsky, *The Insiders: Government, Business, and the Lobbyists* (Toronto: McClelland and Stewart, 1987), 30.

18 Sullivan, *Mandate '68*, 389.

19 "This is an essential ingredient of the new politics," wrote Peter Newman approvingly. "The appeal is piped directly into the voters' homes, immeasurably multiplying the effectiveness of a tour of this nature" (Newman, "PM Looks Like Winner," *Winnipeg Free Press*, May 25, 1968).

20 "The Election: Leading from Strength," *Time* (Canadian edition), May 31, 1968, 11-12.

21 LAC, R5727-2-5-E, Liberal Party of Canada fonds, vol. 1056, file: Prime Minister's Election Tour 1968, "Prime Minister's Election Tour."

22 Ken Clark, "Trudeau Trades Barbs with Youthful Crowd," *Dauphin* (MB) *Herald*, May 24, 1968.

23 Newman, "Even This Early."

24 "Trudeau the Star of Liberal Rally," *Stouffville* (ON) *Tribune*, May 30, 1968.

25 Ibid.; Larry Zolf, "Trudeau Ran for President – and Won," *Toronto Daily Star*, June 26, 1968.

26 In a caption accompanying a front-page photo of Trudeau girls at the Liberal convention, *Le Devoir* suggested that such razzmatazz was American ("Un concours de beauté?" *Le Devoir*, April 3, 1968). *La Presse* observed that the similarities between the campaigns of Robert Kennedy and Trudeau showed how Canada was becoming just like the United States ("Variations sur le theme 'Kennedy,'" *La Presse*, April 2, 1968).

27 LAC, R5727-2-5-E, Liberal Party of Canada fonds, vol. 1084, file: Prime Minister's Tour 1968, Gordon Gibson, "Memorandum for the Prime Minister."

28 LAC, Canadian Broadcasting Corporation, Television: Kines from Parc, Toronto, *The Way It Is*, June 16, 1968, consultation copy VI 8402-0047.

29 "Western Hero," *Globe and Mail*, May 25, 1968. Marshall McLuhan clipped this photograph for his files, perhaps recognizing the symbolism of Stanfield's conveyance (LAC, MG 31

D 156, Marshall McLuhan fonds, vol. 90, file 17: Trudeau – clippings, n.d., 1968, 1969). Trudeau did some of these obligatory photo-op campaign stunts as well – wearing a Klondike hat in Edmonton, for example – but somehow these images did not come to define his public image (see "Le Grand Bison blanc de l'Est," *La Presse*, May 24, 1968).

30 "Prime Minister Visits Dauphin," *Dauphin (MB) Herald*, June 12, 1968. Dauphin was a PC riding. The crowd was described as large, but no screaming teenyboppers were noted. A photo featured the local Liberal candidate's matronly wife pinning a boutonnière on Trudeau's lapel upon arrival. Neepawa and Portage La Prairie, Manitoba, and Kapuskasing, Ontario, were similar drop-in destinations.

31 *The Way It Is*, June 16, 1968.

32 Susan Danard, "Trudeaumania Engineer Loved His Job, the Man," *Victoria Times-Colonist*, September 30, 2000. Or, as Anthony Westell put it, Trudeau created "the anticipatory excitement of a god descending from the sun into the midst of his people" (quoted in J. Murray Beck, *Pendulum of Power* [Scarborough, ON: Prentice Hall, 1968], 402).

33 Fernand Beauregard, "La ville de Duplessis fait bon accueil à Trudeau," *La Presse*, May 27, 1968.

34 Stan McDowell, "Trudeau Attacks Racists," *Winnipeg Free Press*, May 28, 1968; Fernand Beauregard, "De séparatistes conspuent Trudeau," *La Presse*, May 28, 1968.

35 "Rural Quebec Gives Trudeau His First Really Cool Reception," *Toronto Daily Star*, May 27, 1968. "It is generally felt among separatists that the only reason for Trudeau's support in English Canada is the belief that he – a French Canadian – is the best way of putting French Canadians back in their place" (Andrew Salwyn, "Separatists to Face Trudeau, Riot Feared," *Toronto Daily Star*, June 21, 1968).

36 The *La Presse* reporter wrote that the separatists at Fort Chambly and Sherbrooke (they didn't appear at the towns Trudeau stopped at in between) actually helped Trudeau's cause. He was patient with them, refuted their arguments, and had the crowd, which had, after all, come to hear him, on his side (Beauregard, "De séparatistes conspuent").

37 Beauregard, "La ville de Duplessis"; Marcel Pépin, "M. Trudeau aime les accrochages avec les manifestants," *Le Droit*, May 28, 1968. "We are calling it two provinces," said Quebec Tory organizer Brian Mulroney, "the province of Quebec and the province of Montreal" ("The Election: Edgy Mood," *Time* [Canadian edition], June 14, 1968, 13).

38 The biggest difference in reception was between small-town Ontario and small-town Quebec. When Trudeau swung through southwestern Ontario, for example, his reception was as wildly enthusiastic as it was in the cities. The explanation perhaps was that small-town Ontario, or that part of it at least, was better connected with its many urban centres and thus more modern in outlook.

39 Claude Henault, "An Anti-Trudeau Propaganda War Turns Vicious," *Montreal Gazette*, June 15, 1968.

40 See, for example, Renaude Lapointe, "Où est notre fierté nationale?" *La Presse*, April 11, 1968. On Claude Ryan's continuing opposition to Trudeau, see Dominique Clift, "Trudeaumania Stirs Quebeckers – to the Point of Trudeauphobia," *Toronto Daily Star*, June 17, 1968. Peter Desbarats believed that "Québécois have their own brand of Trudeaumania, as the election showed, based on racial affinity, personal admiration and the old deep-rooted respect for the intellectual elite" (Desbarats, "Quebec Letter," *Saturday Night*, August 1968, 10).

41 "Trudeau Woos N.S.," *Halifax Chronicle-Herald*, May 30, 1968.

42 "Nova Scotia Campaign – Trudeau Style," *Halifax Chronicle-Herald*, May 31, 1969.

43 "The Election: Magnetism and Calm," *Time* (Canadian edition), June 14, 1968, 12.

44 Frank Jones, "Silent Bob Stanfield Stalks West – Leaving Crowds Underwhelmed," *Toronto Daily Star*, May 23, 1968.

45 *The Way It Is*, June 16, 1968.

46 *Ottawa Citizen*, May 31, 1968, quoted in Beck, *Pendulum of Power*, 402-3.

47 "The Election: Leading from Strength," *Time* (Canadian edition), May 31, 1968, 11. However, there were exceptions. At Rimouski, Trudeau joined Forestry Minister Maurice Sauvé and Premier Daniel Johnson in signing a $258 million rural development pledge, largely funded by the federal government. He also promised a new department of regional economic expansion to stimulate economic development in the Maritimes ("The Election: First Round to Trudeau," *Time* [Canadian edition], May 17, 1968, 14; Stan Fitzner, "Three-Fold Thrust Proposed by Trudeau to Rid Inequalities," *Halifax Chronicle-Herald*, June 1, 1968). On top of this came a pledge of $17 million for a new ferry to cross the Bay of Fundy between Saint John and Digby (Stan Fitzner, "New Digby-Saint John Ferry Service Promised by Trudeau," *Halifax Chronicle-Herald*, May 31, 1968).

48 *The Way It Is*, June 16, 1968.

49 LAC, Canadian Broadcasting Corporation, Television National News Library, No. 68 [Kennedy Campaign], March 28, 1968, consultation copy V18310-0100.

50 "A Bruise and a Chipped Tooth," *Toronto Telegram*, May 3, 1968.

51 LAC, Canadian Broadcasting Corporation, Television: Newsworld Off-Air, Sense of History (Re-broadcast of a *Newsmagazine* segment from 1968), ISN 284680.

52 "The Election: Leading from Strength," *Time* (Canadian edition), May 31, 1968, 11.

53 "The Election: Magnetism and Calm," *Time* (Canadian edition), June 14, 1968, 11.

54 LAC, R5727-2-5-E, Liberal Party of Canada fonds, vol. 1084, file: Policy – Platform, "Strategy Notes – May 4, 1968," memo, Richard Stanbury to Marc Lalonde, June 4, 1968.

55 John Saywell, ed., *Canadian Annual Review for 1968* (Toronto: University of Toronto Press, 1969), 47.

56 Charles Lynch, "Masterpiece or Malfunction?" *Ottawa Citizen*, June 1, 1968.

57 Cy Gonick, editor of *Canadian Dimension*, wrote: "One theme has dominated the election so far – national unity and the content of federalism ... Trudeau's strong position on "the French-Canadian question," after all, had a great deal to do with his being catapulted into the leadership of the Liberal Party" (Gonick, "English-Canada and Special Status," *Canadian Dimension* 5, 5 [June-July 1968]: 4).

58 "The Election: An Issue Joined," *Time* (Canadian edition), May 24, 1968, 11.

59 Marcel Faribault had been one of Trudeau's university professors, and they had been friends since then. (Fraser, "Backstage in Ottawa: Can Pierre Trudeau Resist the Pressures for an Early Election – Or Will He Even Want To?" *Maclean's*, May 1968, 2). Faribault had been at the Tories' 1964 "Thinkers' Conference" in Fredericton to talk about the two founding nations, and had been influential in getting a committee of the Conservative party to support a two nations policy going into its 1967 convention. For his constitutional views, see Marcel Faribault, "Vers un nouvel ordre constitutionnelle," *Le Devoir*, February 21 and 22, 1968.

60 Fred Schindeler, "The Election," *Canadian Forum*, July 1968.

61 Quoted in Saywell, *Canadian Annual Review*, 49.

62 The Election: Into the Stretch," *Time* (Canadian edition), June 21, 1968, 7.

63 Canadian Press, "Trudeau Repudiates Adv't," *Medicine Hat News*, June 20, 1968. Since the Tories had put Stanfield's name and Faribault's name on the pontoons of a helicopter they were using, Trudeau also said they had a "two pontoon policy" ("Trudeau Halts 'Quebec Ad'; Again Challenges Tories," *Calgary Herald*, June 20, 1968).

64 Carman Cumming, "Trudeau Tackles NDP, Hecklers," *Dauphin* (MB) *Herald*, June 12, 1968.

65 Arthur Marwick, "'1968' and the Cultural Revolution of the Long Sixties (c. 1958-1974)," in *Transnational Moments of Change: Europe 1945, 1968, 1989* (Lanham, MD: Rowman and Littlefield, 2004), 81-94.

66 Brian Shaw, ed., *The Gospel According to Saint Pierre* (Richmond Hill, ON: Simon and Schuster, 1969), 118.

67 "The Realm: 'A Shadow over All of Us,'" *Time* (Canadian edition), June 14, 1968, 11.

68 *The Way It Is*, June 16, 1968.

69 English, *Just Watch Me*, 25.

70 Duart Farquharson, "Angry Trudeau Assails Separatists at Rally," *Calgary Herald*, June 7, 1968.

71 "Senator Praises Trudeau for Leadership Qualities, Ability to Communicate," *Canadian Statesman*, June 19, 1968.

72 LAC, MG 31 D 156, Marshall McLuhan fonds, vol. 39, file 34: Trudeau, Pierre 1968, McLuhan to Trudeau, June 12, 1968. See also Jean-Pierre Fournier, "Les grands défauts du débat: la durée, l'interprétation, la grande solennité," *Le Devoir*, June 10, 1968.

73 "MacDuff Ottawa Report," *Springfield Leader*, June 18, 1968; "Did the TV 'Debate' Have to Be So Dull?" editorial, *Toronto Daily Star*, June 10, 1968.

74 Mel Hinds, "Trudeau Wins Regina Crowd," *Regina Leader-Post*, June 11, 1968; "Trudeau Speaks to Large Crowd," *Dauphin* (MB) *Herald*, June 12, 1968; "The Election: Into the Stretch," *Time* (Canadian edition), June 21, 1968, 7.

75 John Walker, "Trudeau Makes a Big Splash," *Ottawa Citizen*, June 15, 1968; Bob Burtt, "Mobbed at Plaza: Pierre Gets in the Swim," *Canadian Champion* (Milton, ON), June 19, 1968. He told newsmen he was not a swinger but a hippie: "That is H.I.P., Honesty in Politics, and that is what I stand for" (Burtt, "Mobbed at Plaza").

76 Sawatsky, *Insiders*, 32-33. The instigator of this stunt was Bill Lee, Paul Hellyer's executive assistant and leadership campaign head, whom the Trudeau forces had recruited to run their election campaign. Lee later orchestrated a similar stunt with Trudeau on a trampoline at a Vic Tanney's gym in Oshawa. See also "Trudeau Makes a Splash," *Globe and Mail*, June 15, 1969, clipping in LAC, MG 31 D 156, Marshall McLuhan fonds, vol. 90, file 17: Trudeau – clippings, n.d., 1968, 1969.

77 "The Election: Magnetism and Calm," *Time* (Canadian edition), June 14, 1968, 13.

78 LAC, R5727-2-5-E, Liberal Party of Canada fonds, vol. 1120, file: A Survey of Voter Opinion in Canada – Research Services Ltd., June 1968. Whereas the previous survey for the Liberals had been done by telephone, this one was done in person by trained interviewers, who conducted eighteen hundred interviews between May 4 and 11. Of course, the pollster's analysis was not news. Attentive observers, journalists among them, said the same thing publicly. Weeks earlier Peter Newman had written, "The real key is change – this Canada wants. They believe Trudeau will bring them a fresh, new approach. They like his style. If the campaign ... stresses youth, energy, and change then the Liberals can win on June 25 – and very possibly with a majority" (Peter C. Newman, "Canada Is in a Ferment, Digging for Its Soul ...," *Toronto Daily Star*, June 1, 1968).

79 LAC, R5727-2-5-E, Liberal Party fonds, vol. 1084, file: Communications, J.J. Greene to John Nichol, April 29, 1968; Allan MacEachen to Richard Stanbury, April 7, 1968. Ignoring this advice, the Liberals used a Toronto advertising agency to run a national campaign rather than subcontracting regions to regional agencies (see Joseph Wearing, *The L-Shaped Party: The Liberal Party of Canada, 1958-1980* [Toronto: McGraw-Hill Ryerson, 1981], 101).

80 Richard Gwyn, *The Northern Magus: Pierre Trudeau and Canadians* (Toronto: McClelland and Stewart, 1980), 70.

81 LAC, R5727-2-5-E, Liberal Party of Canada fonds, vol. 1056, file: Prime Minister's Campaign Tour 1968, "From Dan [Coates] to Dick [Stanbury], Statistics – Prime Minister's Election travels, May 17 to June 18, 1968."

82 John Burns, "How a Hip PM Filled the Square," *Globe and Mail*, June 20, 1968.

83 Patrick Scott, "Trudeaumania in Toronto: 'For Four Minutes I Was Literally Swept off My Feet,'" *Toronto Daily Star*, January 29, 1968.

84 Peter Newman, "Trudeau's Toronto Rally a Great One – If He Hadn't Opened His Mouth," *Toronto Daily Star*, June 20, 1968.

85 Gary Dunford, "'The Poor Dear Must Be Pooped,' Trudeau Fan," *Toronto Daily Star*, June 20, 1968.

86 Frank Jones, "Trudeau Repudiates Ads Saying Tories Want Two Nations," *Toronto Daily Star*, June 29, 1968.

87 "The Image: Where It's From," *Montreal Gazette*, June 22, 1968; "Trudeau Trips the Light Fantastic for Montrealers," *New York Times*, June 22, 1968.

88 Brian Stewart, "Throngs Jam pvm at Noon for Trudeau," *Montreal Gazette*, June 22, 1968.

89 George Radwanski, "Trudeaumania? No, It Was a Love-In," *Montreal Gazette*, June 22, 1968.

90 "600,000 personnes acclaiment les héros," *La Presse*, May 14, 1968.

91 Canadian Institute of Public Opinion, "Last Poll Shows Liberals Holding Their Lead," *Toronto Daily Star*, June 22, 1968.

92 Sullivan, *Mandate '68*, 5.

93 Ibid., 6.

94 Richard Nielsen, "Let's *See* Our Politicians at Work," *Maclean's*, September 1968, 37.

95 Andrew Salwyn, "Separatists to Face Trudeau, Riot Feared," *Toronto Daily Star*, June 21, 1968.

96 Edith Iglauer, "Profiles: Prime Minister/Premier Ministre," *New Yorker*, July 5, 1969. "To back out," Martin Sullivan explained, "would have been to give the nationalists and separatists a tremendous moral victory" (Sullivan, *Mandate '68*, 3).

CHAPTER 10: SPLIT ELECTORATE

1 Martin Sullivan, *Mandate '68: The Year of Pierre Trudeau* (Toronto: Doubleday, 1968), 12; cbc Archive Sales/Archives Radio-Canada, June 24, 1968, Trudeau – Baptiste Parade; Edith Iglauer, "Profiles: Prime Minister/Premier Ministre," *New Yorker*, July 5, 1969, 52. There were 123 injuries, including 43 policemen. Bourgault and 291 demonstrators were arrested. The French Radio-Canada commentator at the Saint-Jean-Baptiste parade was accused of pro-separatist bias by hundreds of irate listeners and suspended by the cbc, which prompted a job action by fellow francophone news staff. As a result Radio-Canada carried no French-language election coverage (John Saywell, ed., *Canadian Annual Review for 1968* [Toronto: University of Toronto Press, 1969], 434).

2 "A Voyage of Self-Discovery," *Time* (Canadian edition), July 5, 1968, 11.

3 Frank Jones, "How Could I Get Killed Next to the Archbishop?" *Toronto Daily Star*, June 25, 1968.

4 Voter participation in 1968 was about the postwar average, but slightly higher than in 1965, when turnout was 74.8 percent. Only the subsequent election, in 1972, would draw more voters (76.7 percent) before participation rates started trending downward to around 60 percent in the twenty-first century (Elections Canada, "Voter Turnout at Federal Elections and Referendums," http://www.elections.ca/content.aspx?dir=turn& document=index&lang=e&section=ele).

A survey conducted in three ridings in Hamilton during the lead-up to election day found that 85 percent of those surveyed were "very interested" or "interested" in the election campaign, with 45 percent saying they were more interested in 1968 than they had been in the previous election. Party leadership was the most frequent explanation for their interest, and analysis of the results suggested that they meant Trudeau rather than the other party leaders. The authors of the study concluded that Trudeau won votes from many Canadians who didn't usually vote (Gilbert R. Winham and Robert B. Cunningham, "Party Leader Images in the 1968 Federal Election," *Canadian Journal of Political Science* 3, 1 [1970]: 44. These results were from one urban Ontario riding, and they are at odds with the level of voter turnout overall. Perhaps Trudeau motivated voters who usually did not vote to cast ballots for the Liberals, while demotivating those who usually voted for other parties.

5 "Seeks Re-Election," *Nechako Chronicle* (Vanderhoof, BC), May 16, 1968.

6 John Doig, "... But Sometimes the Ferment Loses Its FIZZ," *Toronto Daily Star*, June 1, 1968.

7 Patrice Dutil and David MacKenzie, in their analysis of the results of the 1911 election, go riding by riding to show that local issues often mattered more than the grand debates over Reciprocity and the Naval Bill that national historians associate with the campaign. See Dutil and MacKenzie, *Canada 1911: The Decisive Election that Shaped the Country* (Toronto: Dundurn, 2011), 253-79.

8 According to a poll conducted for the Liberals in May, they were then at 49 percent, with the Conservatives at 29 percent and the NDP at 15 percent. At that time undecided voters were down to 13 percent from 25 percent in an April poll. The Liberals' 49 percent support was just a slight drop from 50 percent the previous month (Library and Archives Canada [LAC], R5727-2-5-E, Liberal Party of Canada fonds, vol. 1120, file: A Survey of Voter Opinion in Canada – Research Services Ltd., June 1968).

9 Blair Fraser, "Why Political Strategists Could Hardly Care Less about the 'Under-25' Vote," *Maclean's*, June 1968, 1. Redistribution helped the Liberals because, in keeping with continuing urbanization, it gave more representation to Canadian cities. If the 1965 election had been run with the new 1968 constituency boundaries, the Liberals would probably have won 136 seats rather than the 131 out of 265 seats they won that year. This analysis is possible because while the riding boundaries changed, the polls stayed the same.

10 While partisans voted for their party regardless of leader, uncommitted voters tended to vote for the party whose leader they preferred (Winham and Cunningham, "Party Leader Images," 53).

11 When the pollsters aggregated "mentions" of specific issues under broader categories, they identified taxes and spending as the primary issue, mentioned by 48 percent of the respondents, with some secondary issues, such as inflation and housing, in the 20 percent range, and "French Canadian problems" mentioned by 14 percent (LAC, R5727-2-5-E, Liberal Party of Canada fonds, vol. 1120, file: A Survey of Voter Opinion in Canada – Research Services Ltd., June 1968).

12 Ibid. The survey of voters in Hamilton, Ontario, similarly found that issues were not closely tied to respondents' opinions of the party leaders, with the exception of "respondents who mentioned 'French-English unity' being significantly favourable towards Trudeau" (Winham and Cunningham, "Party Leader Images," 47-48).

13 Claude Ryan, "Le scrutin de mardi et la tension entre les deux nationalismes," *Le Devoir*, June 27, 1968.

14 Saywell, *Canadian Annual Review*, 39.

15 The Liberals also made gains in rural areas, going from 35 percent to 41 percent of the vote. Most of these gains were in regions closest to Canada's largest cities. Conservatives held their ground in the Maritimes but lost rural ridings everywhere else, while in rural Quebec the Ralliement des Créditistes benefited from rural suspicion of what Trudeau represented.

16 LAC, R5727-2-5-E, Liberal Party of Canada fonds, vol. 1120, file: A Survey of Voter Opinion in Canada – Research Services Ltd., June 1968. Ontario was a bit of an exception; larger

numbers of the upper class and the better educated supported the Conservatives there.

17 John Meisel, *Working Papers on Canadian Politics*, 2nd ed. (Montreal: McGill-Queen's University Press, 1975), 38.

18 Saywell, *Canadian Annual Review*, 65-66; Winham and Cunningham, "Party Leader Images," 41. John Meisel claimed that the Liberals "did not have a consistently greater appeal to any age group" and Winham and Cunningham concurred, but the Gallup numbers showed that Liberal support declined as the age of the voter increased (Meisel, *Working Papers*, 12; Winham and Cunningham, "Party Leader Images," 49).

19 Winham and Cunningham, "Party Leader Images," 48; Meisel, *Working Papers*, 12; W.L. White, R.H. Wagenberg, and R.C. Nelson, *Introduction to Canadian Government and Politics* (Toronto: Holt, Rinehart and Winston, 1972), 77. Paul Stevens's analysis in the *Canadian Annual Review for 1968* drew upon Gallup polls and showed that women supported Trudeau slightly more than men, by 48 percent to 45 percent. However, this had also been true for Pearson in 1965. Trudeau attracted five percentage points more support from each sex, i.e., his leadership did not attract a disproportionate increase in support from women (Saywell, *Canadian Annual Review*, 65).

Another analysis of this issue concluded that there was scant evidence for any "Trudeau effect" on women, but that women were more likely to shift their support to the Liberals if they were single, well educated, or in a household headed by a professional or an executive. The shift was even more pronounced among university-educated women, while women who were less educated, part of a farm family, or part of a household in which an unskilled labourer was the sole breadwinner tended not to support Trudeau. In other words, the same modern versus traditional tension was in play, with the exception of single women, who were more likely to vote for Trudeau regardless of the other factors (E.M. Schreiber, "Trudeaumania and the Women's Vote in the 1968 Federal Election," paper prepared for the 46th Annual Meeting of the Canadian Political Science Association, University of Toronto, June 3, 1974).

20 Other demographic factors provide little additional insight. Trudeau got a lower proportion of support from Protestants than did his rivals, but only slightly. Despite his Criminal Code amendments, he was supported by 65 percent of Catholic voters. Those who objected to the loosening of restrictions on divorce, abortion, and homosexuality strongly opposed Trudeau, but evidently they were a minority of Catholic voters. The Liberals did better among recent immigrants, especially non-English-speaking ethnic groups, while the Conservatives did better among the older settlers. These preferences, however, were in line with traditional party allegiances. None of these fine distinctions had sufficient influence, either alone or in combination with others, to qualify significantly the conclusion that it was among "modern" nationalist Canadians that Trudeau extended Liberal support, both in numbers and in depth of commitment.

21 Meisel, *Working Papers*, 25.

22 John Meisel's post-election survey found that the desire for a majority government was a prime consideration for 70 percent of those surveyed (ibid., 18). The Liberals' pollster reported that 87 percent of those he surveyed agreed with the statement that "the present government can't function well without a majority in Parliament." "They are fed up with division and the slow pace that comes of minority rule," the analyst concluded. It is interesting to note that the greatest growth in Liberal support came from the suburbs. (LAC, R5727-2-5-E, Liberal Party of Canada fonds, vol. 1120, file: A Survey of Voter Opinion in Canada – Research Services Ltd., June 1968).

23 "The Implicit Promise," editorial, *Peterborough Examiner*, June 28, 1968, repr. in Butler and Carrier, *Trudeau Decade*, 47.

24 Larry Zolf, *Dance of the Dialectic* (Toronto: James Lewis and Samuel, 1973), 27.

25 *Spectator*, June 1968, quoted in Douglas Stuebing, John R. Marshall, and Gary Oakes, *Trudeau: A Man for Tomorrow* (Toronto: Clarke Irwin, 1968), 187.

26 Winham and Cunningham, "Party Leader Images," 40.

27 An editorial in *Le Soleil* the day after the election commented that two Quebecs were evident in the election results, the urban and the rural (Butler and Carrier, *Trudeau Decade*, 43).

28 Allan J. Ryan, "PM Pierre."

29 Douglas Owram, *Born at the Right Time: A History of the Baby Boom Generation* (Toronto: University of Toronto Press, 1996), 96, 187.

30 As discussed earlier, Canadian federal politics already had a tendency to be leadership-oriented. Political scientist Peter Regenstreif thought the electorate was particularly volatile in 1968, and saw the personification of party through the leader as part of the explanation (Peter Regenstreif, "How They Voted: It Was Haves against Have-nots," *Toronto Daily Star*, June 26, 1968). Modern Canadians in particular were more likely than their compatriots to vote for the leader instead of along traditional partisan lines or in response to parish-pump issues (Meisel, *Working Papers*, 39).

31 David Steigerwald, *The Sixties and the End of Modern America* (New York: St. Martin's Press, 1995), 160.

32 Christian Borch suggests that crowd behaviour can be learned, performative behaviour: people develop a preconceived, socially conditioned idea of what crowds supposedly do, and when they find themselves in a crowd, act accordingly (Borch, *The Politics of Crowds: An Alternative History of Sociology* [Cambridge: Cambridge University Press, 2012], 13).

33 In a similar manner, it had seemed natural to one admirer in 1968 to ask Trudeau why he didn't marry Jacqueline Kennedy (Stuebing, Marshall, and Oakes, *Trudeau: A Man for Tomorrow*, 166). Richard Stanbury reports that this happened in Kitchener on May 21 (LAC, MG 32 C 5, Richard Stanbury fonds, vol. 13-1, file 1: Diary pp. 1-99 [+6 pp. unnumbered diary notes for May 1968], May 21, 1968).

34 Roy Shields, "Awesome Power of TV in Politics," *Toronto Daily Star*, June 26, 1968.

CONCLUSION: AFTER THE LOVE-IN

1 Library and Archives Canada, Canadian Broadcasting Corporation, Television: Kines from Parc, Toronto, *The Way It Is*, November 3, 1968, consultation copy VI 8402-0052.

2 Larry Zolf, *Just Watch Me: Remembering Pierre Trudeau* (Toronto: Lorimer, 1984), 20.

3 P.A. Dutil, "Trudeau 20 Years On: Time to Reconsider the Legends," *Globe and Mail*, June 24, 1988; John Duffy, *The Fights of Our Lives* (Toronto: HarperCollins, 2002), 244.

4 For a counterargument, see Bryan Palmer, *Canada's 1960s: The Ironies of Identity in a Rebellious Era* (Toronto: University of Toronto Press, 2009), especially "Prologue: Canada in the 1960s: Looking Backward," 3-24, and "Conclusion: Ironic Canadianism: National Identity and the 1960s," 415-30. In this interpretation, Canada lost its old British-derived identity in the 1960s and has yet to find another to replace it. A new identity never gelled due to continual challenges from disaffected groups challenging authority, including, most devastatingly, the violence and repression of the October Crisis in 1970. In his study of English Canadian identity in the same period, José Igartua agrees that the British identity was discarded. However, he traces a process in which a British ethnic nationalism gave way to a Canadian civic nationalism as the logic of British liberty, a core value of the former, led inexorably to the latter (Igartua, *The Other Quiet Revolution* [Vancouver: UBC Press, 2006], 12-15, 223).

5 Richard Gwyn remembered Trudeaumania as "our last joyous collective experience together" (Gwyn, *The Northern Magus: Pierre Trudeau and Canadians* [Toronto: McClelland and Stewart, 1980], 71). "For the generation of voters who lived through that heady, hopeful

time," observed another commentator, "the 1968 campaign retains the luminous quality of a treasured memory (Duffy, *Fights of Our Lives*, 244).

6 For a comprehensive critique of Trudeau's record as prime minister, see Bob Plamondum, *The Truth about Trudeau* (Ottawa: Great River Media, 2013).

7 Richard Gwyn, *The Northern Magus: Pierre Trudeau and Canadians* (Toronto: McClelland and Stewart, 1980), 71. Later Gwyn would credit Trudeau for inspiring a "Canadianism [which] means membership in a collective enterprise that, however diverse, pluralist, regionalized, or postmodern, inspires genuine pride, commands a real sense of belonging, and participates in a remarkable and virtually unparalleled human enterprise." He went on to argue that "today's concept of Canadianism is Trudeau's concept" (Gwyn, "Trudeau and Canadianism," in *Trudeau's Shadow: The Life and Legacy of Pierre Elliott Trudeau*, ed. J.L. Granatstein and Andrew Cohen [Toronto: Random House, 1999], 24-25). Pierre Berton saw 1967 as "a watershed year" in which "we had created a world-class, forward-looking nation," cited Judy LaMarsh's concurrence, and interpreted Trudeaumania as evidence that "Canadians didn't want the year to end, hoping the hoopla would go on forever" (Berton, 1967: *The Last Good Year* [Toronto: Doubleday, 1967], 359, 367).

8 Simon Enoch, "Changing the Ideological Fabric? A Brief History of (Canadian) Neoliberalism," *State of Nature* 5 (Autumn 2007), http://www.stateofnature.org; David Harvey, *A Brief History of Neoliberalism* (Oxford: Oxford University Press, 2005), 22, 39-63.

9 Critic Ronald Sutherland coined this phrase to describe the parallels between English and French Canadian cultural nationalism in the nineteenth and twentieth centuries (Sutherland, *Second Image: Comparative Studies in Québec/Canadian Literature* [Toronto: New Press, 1971], 23).

10 Christian Boucher, "Canada-US Values Distinct, Inevitably Carbon Copy, or Narcissism of Small Differences?" *Policy Horizons Canada*, Government of Canada, July 23, 2013. http://www.horizons.gc.ca/eng/content/feature-article-canada-us-values-distinct-inevitably-carbon-copy-or-narcissism-small. The debate over whether Canadians have values distinct from those of Americans is long-running, with pro and con positions finding plentiful evidence in different sources. As discussed above in Chapter 2, the similarities between the two countries dwarf their differences. Indeed, certain regions of North America exhibit greater consistency of values across the border than with other regions of their own country. As Paul Krugman has written, "Canada is essentially closer to the United States than it is to itself" (Paul Krugman, *Geography and Trade* [Cambridge, MA: MIT Press, 1991], 2). Nevertheless, the doctrine of nationalism requires an independent state to have a distinct identity, and Canada has had no shortage of cultural producers willing to imagine and publicize one.

Although Canadians used to take pride in being quietly patriotic in contrast to what they depicted as a comparatively chauvinistic American nationalism, there is evidence that Canadians' nationalism is becoming more like Americans' nationalism in becoming more bellicose and exclusionary (see Tracey Raney, "Quintessentially un-American? Comparing Public Opinion on National Identity in English Speaking Canada and the United States," *International Journal of Canadian Studies* 42 [2010]: 105-23; G. Millard, S. Riegel, and J. Wright, "Here's Where We Get Canadian: English-Canadian Nationalism and Popular Culture," *American Review of Canadian Studies* 321 [2002]: 11-34). The centennial–Expo–Trudeaumania complex of experiences was arguably a formative episode in this form of spectacular and celebratory nationalism. In insisting on their uniqueness Canadians became less unique, yet simultaneously needed to exhibit a distinctive identity more than ever.

CREDITS

A reasonable attempt has been made to secure permission to reproduce all material used. If there are errors or omissions they are wholly unintentional and the publisher would be grateful to hear of them.

PAGE 1: Photograph by Bob Chambers. Reproduced with permission of Bob Chambers. Private collection of Bob Chambers.

PAGE 7: Cartoon by John Yardley-Jones. Reproduced with permission of John Yardley-Jones. Library and Archives Canada (LAC), e011168474.

PAGE 12: Photograph by Doug Griffin. Toronto Star Collection, Getty Images, 505004148.

PAGE 18: Cartoon by Sid Barron, *Toronto Daily Star*, June 22, 1968. Reproduced with permission of the estate of Sid Barron. LAC, e011168470.

PAGE 30: Photograph by Jeff Goode. Toronto Star Collection, Getty Images, 502521851. Originally published in the *Toronto Daily Star*, June 19, 1968.

PAGE 44: Photography by Graetz Bros. Ltd. Reproduced with permission of Clara Thomas Archives and Special Collections, York University (CTASP). CTASP, Toronto Telegraph (TT) fonds, 1974-001, box 228, file 1657, Fashions, Dressed, 1967 (3 of 3), Graetz Bros. Ltd Print No. 313. Caption: "Cosmo Kismet of Montreal used vinyl in this dress from the National Collection. It was photographed at the Australian Pavilion at Expo," February 10, 1967.

PAGE 50: Page 50: (top) Photograph by Frank Grant. CTASP, TT fonds, 1974-001, box 168, file 1147, Oct. 12, 1963, Neg. 1505, ASC08192. (bottom) Photograph by Ethel Proulx. CTASP, TT fonds, 1974-001, box 168, file 1147,

Proulx, April 23, 1962, Neg. 1503. Caption: "A LITTLE GIRL WITH A BIG MESSAGE, The young Easter peace marcher is Suzy Irving."

PAGE 55: Cartoon by Warren Miller. Reproduced with permission of Condé Nast. The *New Yorker* Collection, The Cartoon Bank, TCB-83402.

PAGE 61: Photograph by Ken Oakes. Reproduced with permission of the *Vancouver Sun*. Originally published in the *Vancouver Sun*, March 26, 1967.

PAGE 72: Photograph by Duncan Cameron. © Government of Canada. Reproduced with the permission of LAC (2016). LAC, Duncan Cameron fonds, PA-142624.

PAGE 73: Song lyrics from "Atlantis" by Donovan Leitch. Copyright © 1968 by Donovan (Music) Limited/peermusic Canada Inc. Copyright © Renewed. International Rights Secured. Used by Permission. All Rights Reserved.

PAGE 80: Cartoon by Duncan Macpherson, *Toronto Daily Star*, n.d. Reproduced with permission of Torstar Syndication Services.

PAGE 93: Cartoon by Leonard Norris. Reproduced with permission of the estate of Leonard Norris. LAC, cr0016273.

PAGE 99: Cartoon by Duncan Macpherson, *Toronto Daily Star*, October 21, 1964. Reproduced with permission of Torstar Syndication Services. LAC, C-112829.

PAGE 102: Photograph by Peter Ward. CTASP, TT fonds, 1974-001, box 108, file 710. Caption: "[indecipherable handwritten word] ch kids Scarboro hold own parade, front Wendy Hook, 10. Ward," July 5, 1967, 108-710, ASC Image 1293.

PAGE 107: Photograph by John Franke. CTASP, TT fonds, 1974-001, box 108, file 710, Franke, Canada Centennial File. Caption: "Judy Raham (left) and Marilyn Kearn with Ralfe Ewing's Le Saisons de Confederation (left) and Jack Friend's Confederation mobile," April 19, 1967.

PAGE 110: (*top*) Photographer unknown. © Government of Canada. Reproduced with the permission of LAC (2016). LAC, Centennial Commission fonds, PA-183654. (*bottom*) Photographer unknown. LAC, PA-183650.

PAGE 112: (*top*) Photograph by Frank Grant. © Government of Canada. Reproduced with the permission of LAC (2016). LAC, Centennial

Commission fonds, PA-185522. (*bottom*) Map by Geoffrey Frazer. LAC, Centennial Commission fonds, PA-185467.

PAGE 115: Cartoon by Duncan Macpherson, *Toronto Daily Star*, 1967. Reproduced with permission of Torstar Syndication Services.

PAGE 123: Photographer unknown. © Government of Canada. Reproduced with the permission of LAC (2016). LAC, Canadian Corporation for the 1967 World Exhibition fonds, e000990869.

PAGE 126: Photograph by Graham Bezant. Toronto Star Collection, Getty Images, 502523921. Originally appeared in *Toronto Daily Star*, March 2, 1968.

PAGE 127: Song lyrics from *Jesus Christ Superstar*. Artists: Tim Rice and Andrew Lloyd Webber. Reproduced with permission of Hal Leonard Corporation.

PAGE 141: Reproduced with permission of *Maclean's* magazine.

PAGE 150: Photograph by Harold Whyte. CBC Still Photo Collection. Reproduced with permission of CBC. Richard Gwyn's quote in the caption is from *The Northern Magus: Pierre Trudeau and Canadians* (Toronto: McClelland and Stewart, 1980), 68.

PAGE 160: Photograph by Duncan Cameron. © Government of Canada. Reproduced with the permission of LAC (2016). LAC, Duncan Cameron fonds, e011172035.

PAGE 165: Cartoon by Berthio. Reproduced with permission of Roland Berthiaume. LAC, Collection Roland Berthiaume, e011179456.

PAGE 174: Photograph by Reg Innell. Toronto Star Collection, Getty Images, 502523947. Originally appeared in the *Toronto Daily Star*, May 9, 1968.

PAGE 188: Photograph by Dick Loek. CTASP, TT fonds, 1974-002, box 156, file Liberal Leadership convention, Apr. 8/68. Caption: "Trudeau gives Buddhist salutation," frame 19A.

PAGE 191: Photographer unknown. *Montreal Star*, n.d., Postmedia/STRCANWEST 1672650. Canadian Press.

PAGE 201: Cartoon by Duncan Macpherson, *Toronto Daily Star*, June 18, 1968. Reproduced with permission of Torstar Syndication Services. LAC, e011168472.

PAGE 206: Photograph by Duncan Cameron. © Government of Canada. Reproduced with the permission of LAC (2016). LAC, Duncan Cameron fonds, e011172039.

PAGE 221: Photographer unknown. Bettmann Collection, Getty Images, 515538718. Originally appeared in the *Toronto Daily Star*, n.d.

PAGE 225: Photograph by Dick Loek. CTASP, TT fonds, 1974-002, file 124, Liberal leadership convention, Apr. 4/68, Loek Negs not used, Frame 13.

PAGE 228: Photograph by Dick Loek. CTASP, TT fonds, 1974-002, box 156, file 141, Liberal leadership convention, Apr. 4/68, Loek Negs not used, Frame 13A.

PAGE 230: Photograph by Dick Loek. CTASP, TT fonds, 1974-002, box 156, file 124, Liberal leadership convention Apr. 4/68, Loek Negs not used, Frame 12-12A.

PAGE 232: Photograph by Duncan Cameron. © Government of Canada. Reproduced with the permission of LAC (2016). LAC, Duncan Cameron fonds, e011172043.

PAGE 236: Photograph by Duncan Cameron. © Government of Canada. Reproduced with the permission of LAC (2016). LAC, Centennial Commission fonds, PA-180806.

PAGE 244: Photograph by Boris Spremo. Toronto Star Collection, Getty Images, 499323157. Originally appeared in *Toronto Daily Star*, April 27, 1968.

PAGE 252: Photograph by Peter Bregg. Canadian Press, 79087.

PAGE 255: Cartoon by Sid Barron. Reproduced with permission of the estate of Sid Barron. LAC, cr0014574.

PAGE 257: Photograph by Duncan Cameron. © Government of Canada. Reproduced with the permission of LAC (2016). LAC, Duncan Cameron fonds, e011169450.

PAGE 260: Photograph by Norm Betts. CTASP, TT fonds, 1974-001, box 228, file 1658, Fashions, Dresses Only, 1968, (1 of 2), Betts. Caption: "Fashions of Trudeau fabric are the latest thing to hit Bloor st. The two cotton outfits above are from the Union Jack boutique."

PAGE 263: Photograph by Yousuf Karsh. Reproduced with the permission of the Estate of Yousuf Karsh. LAC, PA-163886.

PAGE 267: Photograph by Frank Lennon. Reproduced with the permission of the Estate of Frank Lennon. LAC, e008440331.

PAGE 270: Photograph by Dick Darrell. Toronto Star Collection, Getty Images, 502521877. Originally appeared in the *Toronto Daily Star*, June 20, 1968.

PAGE 274: Photograph by Duncan Cameron. © Government of Canada. Reproduced with the permission of LAC (2016). LAC, Duncan Cameron fonds, PA-180801.

PAGE 279: Photographer unknown. From Flickr photo album.

PAGE 281: Photographer unknown. Canadian Press, 791053.

PAGE 290: Cartoon by James Reidford. Canadian Press, STRGNMC 10527513. Originally appeared in the *Globe and Mail*, April 19, 1968.

PAGE 296: Photographer unknown. LAC, e011172049.

PAGE 298: Photograph by Joe Hourigan. Canadian Press, 1779853.

PAGE 302: Photograph by Blaise Edwards. Canadian Press, 790674.

PAGE 304: Photograph by Jeff Goode. Toronto Star Collection, Getty Images, 502521853. Originally appeared in *Toronto Daily Star*, June 24, 1968.

PAGE 306: Photograph by Duncan Cameron. © Government of Canada. Reproduced with the permission of LAC (2016). LAC, Duncan Cameron fonds, e011172050.

PAGE 317: Cartoon by Duncan Macpherson, *Toronto Daily Star*, June 26, 1968. Reproduced with permission of Torstar Syndication Services.

PAGE 326: Photograph by Duncan Cameron. © Government of Canada. Reproduced with the permission of LAC (2016). LAC, Duncan Cameron fonds, PA-180804.

PAGE 328: Poster by John Yardley-Jones. Reproduced with permission of John Yardley-Jones. Author's collection.

PAGE 339: Song lyrics from "Here Comes the Sun" by George Harrison. Reproduced with permission of Hal Leonard Corporation.

INDEX

Note: "(i)" after a page number indicates an illustration.